# Vocational Mathematics for Business

## 2d Edition

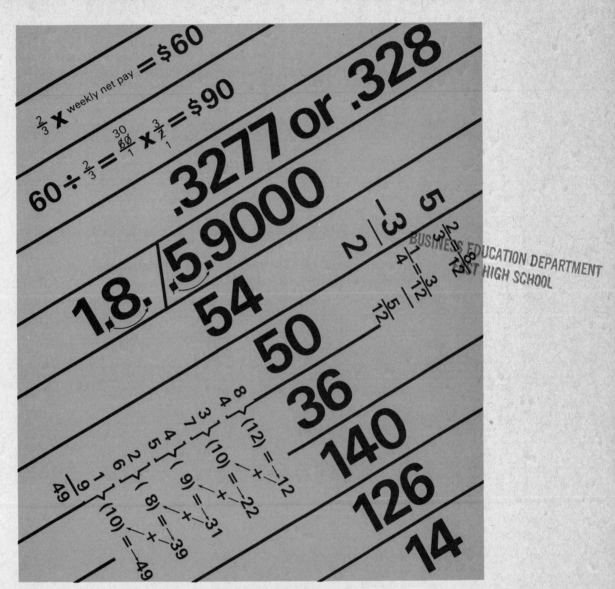

Marie Martinka

Teacher Emerita
Adult-Vocational Division
Milwaukee Area Technical College
Milwaukee, Wisconsin

Published by

MO6  **SOUTH-WESTERN PUBLISHING CO.**

CINCINNATI   WEST CHICAGO, ILL.   DALLAS   PELHAM MANOR, N.Y.   PALO ALTO, CALIF.

ISBN: 0-538-13060-1

Library of Congress Catalog Card Number: 76-11253

5 6 7 8 9 0 **H** 7 6 5 4 3 2 1

Printed in the United States of America

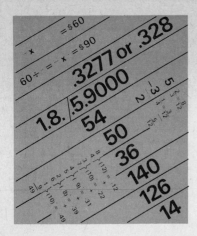

# PREFACE

This 2d Edition of *Vocational Mathematics for Business* is a text-workbook in basic business mathematics. The only requirement for this course is that the student know how to add, subtract, multiply, and divide with whole numbers.

Like the 1st Edition, the first six chapters of this 2d Edition cover work in the essentials of decimals, fractions, percents, and weights and measures. Recognizing the growing number of businesses in this country that are going metric, Chapter 5, Working with Weights and Measures, has been extensively revised to provide more coverage on the Système International d'Unités (SI). While the remaining chapters consist of business applications of the essentials, this 2d Edition contains a new Chapter 13 on Inventory Valuation, Cost of Goods Sold, and Depreciation. Further, Chapter 14 has been revised to cover only two number systems that are used in computer programming: the binary number system and the hexadecimal number system. An attempt has also been made to provide step-by-step explanations and more examples throughout this 2d Edition.

## TO THE STUDENT

To get the most from this course, follow the suggestions and procedures explained below.

**Text.** Each chapter is divided into Sections which cover one particular topic. Each Section, in turn, is subdivided into smaller Parts. Study the explanations and examples in each Part. In some cases, it is advisable to rework the examples on scratch paper to make sure you understand how to do the operation. Ask your instructor for help when necessary. After you have studied the Section, work the Assignment which immediately follows it. If your instructor approves, you may study a Part at a time and then do the Assignment for that Part before going on to study the next Part.

**Assignments.** Each Assignment is subdivided into the same Parts as the corresponding Section in the Text. When you have completed a Part, check your answers to the odd-numbered problems against those provided on pages 291 through 306 in this text-workbook. Make any corrections before continuing. Refer to the corresponding Part in the text if you have any trouble with a specific Part in the Assignment.

Do all your work in the space provided for the solution. You should have enough room if you make small, businesslike figures. Show all the steps in your solution so that your instructor can follow your work and help you in case of difficulty. It is important that you do your own work since mathematics can be learned only by doing. Follow your instructor's policy on the use of hand calculators in working the Assignments.

**Tests.** Upon satisfactory completion of an Assignment in the first six chapters, you are ready for a short Check Test on the work covered in the Section. If you score below 80 on the Check Test, review the work for more understanding. Your instructor may wish to retest you on the Section. Achievement tests (one test for each chapter and a final examination) are also available. You will be given these achievement tests when it has been determined that you are ready to be tested.

**Progress Record.** A Progress Record on the inside front cover of this text-workbook will enable you to keep a record of your Assignment and various test scores. Also printed on the inside front cover is a multiplication table for your review.

**Marie Martinka**

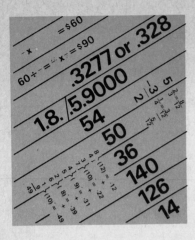

# CONTENTS

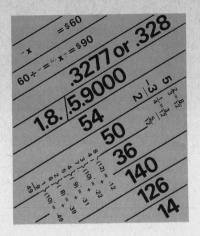

# *Working with Decimals*

The tools of business are the basic operations of arithmetic—addition, subtraction, multiplication, and division. The materials used are decimal numbers since this is a "dollars and cents" world. An employer will not take the excuse often given by students, "I have the right answer, but my decimal point is in the wrong place."

Computers and calculators do most of their work in decimals. When you work in an office, it is very likely that you will be concerned with the input or output of these machines. Therefore, you must be sure of yourself in working with decimals.

## Section 1-1 *The Decimal Number System*

The word **decimal** usually refers to a number which contains a decimal point. It may have digits only to the right of the point, or it may have digits on both sides of the point. A **digit** is a single figure: 0, 1, 2, 3, 4, 5, 6, 7, 8, or 9.

Actually the word decimal can have a much broader meaning since it comes from the Latin word for ten, **decem**. The numbers we use make up what is called the **decimal number system** because each digit has a value that is ten times the one to its right.

You should understand how to read or write both whole numbers and decimals and be able to compare them with one another for size.

### Part A Reading and Writing Whole Numbers

Digits are put together to form a number, but the value of the number depends on the order of the digits. For example, take the number 456. It is read or written as "four hundred fifty-six." It consists of:

$$4 \times 100 = 400$$
$$5 \times 10 = 50$$
$$6 \times 1 = \underline{\phantom{00}6}$$
$$456$$

Now take the same three digits and form another number, 645. It is read or written as "six hundred forty-five." Next put the 645 after the 456. The new number formed is 456,645. It is read or written as "four hundred fifty-six thousand six hundred forty-five." Note that the word "thousand" is used after the "four hundred fifty-six" to show the value of the new number, but 456 and 645 are read the same as if they were separate numbers.

If you can read a number in the hundreds correctly, then you can read any whole number by learning the names of the groups of three into which any whole number can be separated. Study the chart on the next page in which the blank spaces stand for digits. Each group is read or written as if it were a number by itself and then is followed by the group name. The last group of three has no name.

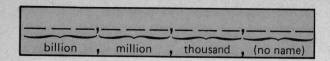

billion , million , thousand , (no name)

For the student's interest, the group names going to the left of billion are, respectively, trillion, quadrillion, quintillion, etc.

To read and write a large whole number, follow these steps:

1. Starting at the right, separate the number with commas into groups of three, if this has not been done. The last group marked off at the extreme left may have less than three digits.

*Example:* 22694735

Separate as follows: 22,694,735

2. Starting at the left, read the first group as if it were alone and then say the group name. Continue in the same manner to the end, reading each group of three and attaching the group name.

*Example:* 22,694,735

Read and write it as twenty-two million six hundred ninety-four thousand seven hundred thirty-five.

3. If a group of three digits starts with one or two zeros, read only the number which follows the zeros and give the group name, unless it is the last group.

*Example:* 90,001,052,006

Read and write it as ninety billion one million fifty-two thousand six.

4. If a group of three digits consists of three zeros, omit the group name entirely.

*Example:* 7,000,040,000

Read and write it as seven billion forty thousand.

In the examples given above, note the following points. Numbers in the hundreds group, such as 735 in the whole number 22,694,735, are read aloud without an *and* after the word hundred. Hundred is pronounced exactly as it is spelled— not "hunderd." In writing a number in words, a hyphen is used in combining two words to form numbers from twenty-one through ninety-nine. Also, note that the correct spelling for the number 40 is *forty,* not "fourty."

## Part B Writing Numbers from Words

In order to form a number from words, you must know the position of each group from its name and then be able to write correctly the number you hear or read. Follow these steps:

1. Write the first number you hear or read as if it were by itself. If no group name is given, it means that the number is in the hundreds or less.

*Examples:* "two hundred one" is 201
"twenty-nine" is 29

2. If group names are given, put a comma after the number before each group name and locate the number's position from the group name. When the group name is *thousand,* there must be one group of three digits after the comma.

*Example:* "seven hundred fifty thousand two hundred six" is written

7 5 0, 2 0 6

When the first group name is *million,* there must be two groups of three digits each after the first comma.

*Example:* "three million seven hundred fifty thousand two hundred six" is written

_ _ 3, 7 5 0, 2 0 6

When the first group name is *billion,* there must be three groups of three digits each after the first comma.

*Example:* "sixty-eight billion four hundred three million seven hundred fifty thousand two hundred six" is written

$$\underline{\ \ 6\ \ 8}, \underline{4\ \ 0\ \ 3}, \underline{7\ \ 5\ \ 0}, \underline{2\ \ 0\ \ 6}$$

3. After the first group number has been written, for any group after it which has only *two* digits, put a *zero* before the number to make a group of three digits.

*Example:* "four hundred three million fifty thousand two hundred six" is written

$$\underline{4\ \ 0\ \ 3}, \underline{0\ \ 5\ \ 0}, \underline{2\ \ 0\ \ 6}$$

After the first group number has been written, for any group after it which has only *one* digit, put *two zeros* before the number to make a group of three digits.

*Example:* "four hundred three million fifty thousand six" is written

$$\underline{4\ \ 0\ \ 3}, \underline{0\ \ 5\ \ 0}, \underline{0\ \ 0\ \ 6}$$

After the first group number has been written and a *following group name is omitted entirely and is not the last group,* write *three zeros* for that group.

*Example:* "four hundred three million two hundred six" is written

$$\underline{4\ \ 0\ \ 3}, \underline{0\ \ 0\ \ 0}, \underline{2\ \ 0\ \ 6}$$

4. If the *last* word you hear or read is a group name (billion, million, or thousand), the groups after it must have three zeros each.

*Example:* "fifteen billion" is written

$$\underline{\ \ 1\ \ 5}, \underline{0\ \ 0\ \ 0}, \underline{0\ \ 0\ \ 0}, \underline{0\ \ 0\ \ 0}$$

*Example:* "fifteen billion five million" is written

$$\underline{\ \ 1\ \ 5}, \underline{0\ \ 0\ \ 5}, \underline{0\ \ 0\ \ 0}, \underline{0\ \ 0\ \ 0}$$

*Example:* "fifteen billion five million five thousand" is written

$$\underline{\ \ 1\ \ 5}, \underline{0\ \ 0\ \ 5}, \underline{0\ \ 0\ \ 5}, \underline{0\ \ 0\ \ 0}$$

It is important to make clear businesslike figures to prevent errors when someone else reads them. Follow this sample for both size and shape:

The 0, 6, 8, and 9 are closed; the 2 and 3 have no loops or curlicues. Most business forms allow only small spaces in which to write numbers.

## Part C  Reading and Writing Decimals

If a decimal has a whole number to the left of the point, the whole number is read and written as described in Part A of this section; the decimal point itself is read and written as *and.*

The decimal part of the number must always end with its decimal place name. This name depends on the number of digits after the decimal point. Study the chart on page 4 in which each blank space stands for a digit.

To read and write the decimal part of a given number, follow these steps:

1. Read and write the number after the decimal point as if it were a whole number, as described in Part A.
2. Count the number of digits after the decimal point. Include all zeros after the point as digits in order to get the correct decimal place name. Add the decimal place name as given in the chart.

*Examples:*

a. .8 is read and written as eight-tenths

b. .07 is read and written as seven hundredths

c. .125 is read and written as one hundred twenty-five thousandths

d. .6408 is read and written as six thousand four hundred eight ten-thousandths

e. .01934 is read and written as one thousand nine hundred thirty-four hundred-thousandths

f. .000067 is read and written as sixty-seven millionths

. — tenths ............................................... 1 digit after the point
. — — hundredths ................................... 2 digits after the point
. — — — thousandths ............................ 3 digits after the point
. — — — — ten-thousandths .................... 4 digits after the point
. — — — — — hundred-thousandths ............ 5 digits after the point
. — — — — — — millionths .................... 6 digits after the point
. — — — — — — — ten-millionths ................ 7 digits after the point

g. 50,040.00075 is read and written as fifty thousand forty *and* seventy-five hundred-thousandths

Another way to get the right decimal place name is to count out the places digit by digit, starting with the first one after the decimal point: tenths, hundredths, thousandths, ten-thousandths, etc. Be sure to include all zeros as digits.

3. If the given number has a common fraction after the decimal part, read or write the fraction before giving the decimal place name. The fraction is not a digit and is not counted when finding the decimal place name. The place name is that of the last digit.

*Example:* 2.83⅓

Read and write it as two and eighty-three and one-third hundredths.

In the above examples, note that a hyphen is used in writing two-word place values, such as hundred-thousandths and ten-millionths. A hyphen is also used to write a fraction whose denominator is ten or under, such as two-thirds and three-fourths. A common fraction at the end of a decimal does not take a decimal place value since it is only a fractional part added to the last digit.

In business, shortcuts are taken when numbers are read aloud for checking purposes. For example, group names may be omitted and the word "comma" used instead; there may be a short pause between groups; the number may be read as a series of single digits; or the word "point" may be used instead of "and."

*Example:* The number 286,375.40285 may be read for checking purposes as:

two eighty-six (pause) three seventy-five point four zero two eight five

or

two eight six comma three seven five point four oh two eight five.

## Part D   Writing Decimals from Words

In writing a decimal from words, the key word is "and." There are two ways in which this key word can be used: (a) It can stand for the decimal point with a whole number before it and the decimal part of the number after it.

*Example:* "forty seven and three hundredths" is written as 47.03

(b) It can mean that a common fraction follows the number.

*Example:* "three and two-thirds thousandths" is written as .003⅔

Thus, there can be two "ands" in a given number, with the first one standing for the decimal point and the second one meaning that a common fraction follows the number.

*Example:* "one hundred twenty and six and three-fourths hundredths" is written as 120.06¾

To write a decimal number from words, follow these steps:

1. Write the whole number part of the decimal number as described in Part A.

2. For the decimal part of the number, write the number as if it were a whole number and then place the decimal point according to the

decimal place name. If the number just written has fewer digits than the decimal place name calls for, then put enough zeros before the number so the two match.

*Example:* "four thousand three and nine thousand seventy-six millionths" is written as 4,003.009076

There is another way of placing the decimal point correctly. Start with the last digit of the number just written and say its decimal place name. Going to the left, say each decimal place name through the tenths, and then put the decimal point before the number. It may be necessary to put zeros in front of the number.

*Example:* "six hundred thirty-nine hundred-thousandths"

The number you have just written is 639. Start with the 9 and say "hundred-thousandths." Then go to the 3 and say "ten-thousandths"; then to the 6 and say "thousandths." Since there are no more digits in 639, place a zero in front of the 6 (0639) and say "hundredths"; then put a zero in front of the 0639 (00639) and say "tenths." The decimal point is placed before the two zeros. Thus, the example is written correctly as follows:

.00639

3. If the word "and" is followed by a common fraction and a decimal place name, write the number and the fraction. To place the decimal point correctly, take the number part only and follow the rule in Step 2 above. The fraction is not a digit.

*Example:* "eighty-three and one-third thousandths"

First write 83⅓. Since the given decimal place name is thousandths, put a zero in front of the 8 and then the decimal point in front of the zero, as follows:

.083⅓

4. If the given number has two "ands," combine Steps 2 and 3.

*Example:* "twenty-seven and sixteen and two-thirds hundredths" is written 27.16⅔

## Decimal Fractions and Decimal Mixed Numbers

Ordinarily, when the word "fraction" is used, it refers to a **common fraction,** which is written as one number over another. The top number, called the **numerator,** gives the number of parts being taken. The bottom number, called the **denominator,** gives the total number of parts into which something is divided. For example, $\frac{3}{10}$ refers to three parts of something that was divided into ten parts.

Since $\frac{3}{10}$ and .3 sound exactly the same when read aloud, .3 is also a fraction. Usually it is called a **decimal fraction.** Thus, any common fraction whose denominator is 10, 100, 1,000, etc., can be changed into its corresponding decimal fraction form.

To change a common fraction with a denominator of 10, 100, 1,000, etc., to a decimal fraction, write the number of parts (the numerator) as a whole number. Then starting at the extreme right of this number and going to the left, point off the number of places indicated in the denominator. This is the same as the number of zeros in the denominator.

*Examples:*
$$\frac{359}{1,000} = .359$$

$$\frac{6,245}{10,000} = .6245$$

If necessary, prefix (i.e., add at the left of the number) enough zeros to make the correct number of places. The denominator has been replaced by the decimal point indicating the proper number of places.

*Examples:*
$$\frac{7}{100,000} = .00007$$

(Prefix 4 zeros to make the required 5 decimal places.)

$$\frac{1,001}{1,000,000} = .001001$$

(Prefix 2 zeros to make the required 6 decimal places.)

The word "decimal" is often used to refer to a number which contains a decimal point. Strictly speaking, however, it is either a decimal fraction, as described above, or a **decimal mixed number,** with the fractional parts being tenths, hundredths, thousandths, etc., according to the number of decimal places. Note that a decimal fraction has no whole number to the left of the decimal point, as shown in the examples above. A decimal mixed number, sometimes called a **mixed decimal,** consists of a whole number followed by a decimal fraction, such as 58.309.

A decimal mixed number may have a common fraction after the last decimal place. The word "and" is used to separate the whole number from the decimal fraction part and is used again to separate the decimal fraction from the ending common fraction.

**Example:** 8.43¾

Read it as "eight and forty-three and three-fourths hundredths."

The common fraction ending is a part of the last decimal place. In the example just given, the last decimal place is 3¾. It is in the hundredths position.

When the decimal fraction has only zeros followed by a common fraction, the decimal place name should be read as "a tenth," "a thousandth," etc.

**Example:** .00½

Read it as "one-half of a hundredth."

Care must be taken in pronouncing the endings of the decimal place names. For example, "sixteen and two-thirds of a hundredth" (16.00⅔) and "sixteen and two-thirds hundredths" (.16⅔) sound alike except for the place names. The "of a hundredth" shows that there must be two zeros after the point, while the "hundredths" shows that at least one of the two digits after the point is not a zero.

A common error in reading a decimal aloud or writing it out in words is to omit the "th" in the decimal place name. Note the difference between "five thousand" (5,000) and "five thousandths" (.005). Most decimal place names end in "ths"; only the fractional parts of a decimal place name end in "th."

**Examples:**

a. .06 is a decimal fraction. Its common fraction form is $\frac{6}{100}$. In both forms it is read as "six hundredths."

b. .83⅓ is a decimal fraction with a fractional ending. Its common fraction form is $\frac{83\frac{1}{3}}{100}$. In both forms it is read as "eighty-three and one-third hundredths."

c. 7.459 is a decimal mixed number. Its mixed number form is $7\frac{459}{1,000}$. In both forms it is read as "seven and four hundred fifty-nine thousandths."

d. 83.33⅓ is a decimal mixed number with a fractional ending. It can also be written as $83\frac{33\frac{1}{3}}{100}$. In both forms it is read as "eighty-three and thirty-three and one-third hundredths."

e. .00¾ is a decimal fraction with a fractional ending. It can also be written as $\frac{\frac{3}{4}}{100}$. In both forms it is read as "three-fourths of a hundredth."

Part

## F  Comparing Decimals

In most cases it is easy to see when one whole number is larger than another by comparing them place by place. For example, 67,529 is larger than 67,259 since the 5 in 67,529 is larger than the 2 in 67,259. More care must be taken, however, when the numbers being compared are decimals.

To find which of two decimals is the larger, follow these steps:

1. If the numbers are decimal mixed numbers, look at *only* the whole number part in each one. The number that has the larger whole number part is the larger, no matter what its decimal part is.

**Example:** 759.6 is larger than 758.99325

even though 758.99325 has more digits than 759.6.

2. If the whole number parts are exactly the same or if the numbers are decimal fractions without any whole number parts, then look at *only* the first digit after the decimal point (the tenths place) in each. The number that has the larger digit in this position is the larger, no matter what the rest of the decimal part is.

*Example:*   759.7 is larger than
                759.698

since 759.7 has a 7 in the tenths position while 759.698 has only a 6 in the same position. The fact that 698 without the point is larger than 7 does not make 759.698 the larger number. Only the digits in the tenths position, 7 and 6, are used to find which is the larger number.

3. If the numbers are exactly the same through the first decimal place, then look at *only* the second decimal place (the hundredths place) in each. The number that has the larger digit in the hundredths position is the larger.

*Example:*   759.72 is larger than
                759.71985

even though the second number has more digits.

Continue doing this until one place is found to be larger than another in the same position. If two numbers are exactly the same through the last decimal place of one of them but the other still has at least one more non-zero decimal place, then the second number is larger than the first.

*Example:*   759.72981 is larger than
                759.7298

4. Zeros can be added at the end of any decimal without changing the value of the number.

*Example:*   .6 = .60 = .600

They are all equal in value even though they are read or written differently and have different numbers of decimal places. Similarly, any zeros at the end of a decimal can be crossed out without changing the value of the number.

*Example:*   .6 = .6Ø = .6ØØ

Remember that this applies only to zeros at the end of a decimal, never to zeros at the end of a whole number.

In business, it is often necessary to arrange a series of numbers according to their size. Most of the time the numbers are arranged in a column with the largest number first and the smallest number last. Much the same rules are used for doing this as are used for finding the larger of two numbers. First look at the whole number parts and arrange them according to size. If two or more whole numbers are the same, then compare the decimal parts, place by place.

When decimals are written in a column, they are written so that the decimal points are under each other. The digits in the same positions are also placed under each other; that is, the tenths digits are put under each other and the hundredths digits are put under each other, etc. When this is done, the numbers are said to be **aligned** or in **alignment**.

When there are many numbers to be arranged according to size, as you put a number in a column it is a good idea to put a check mark after it or to draw a light line through it in the original list.

*Examples:*

a. Arrange these numbers in a column according to size. Start with the largest and end with the smallest: 971.56, 975.9, 95.1589, 971.84, 975.93, 95.518, 979.3, 95.54, 975.8994, 917.68.

Looking at only the whole number parts, we see that 979 is the largest, so 979.3 will be the first number in the column.

979.3 (first)

The next largest number is 975, but there are three numbers which have 975 as the whole number parts. These are: 975.9, 975.93, and 975.8994. Looking at the first decimal place, we see that there are two numbers which have .9 in the tenths position. Since 975.93 has a digit in the hundredths place, it becomes the second number and 975.9 is third. The fourth number is 975.8994. Our partial column now shows the following listing:

979.3
975.93    (second)
975.9    (third)
975.8994    (fourth)

The next largest whole number is 971. There are two 971's: 971.56 and 971.84. Since the .8 in 971.84 is larger than the .5 in 971.56, 971.84 becomes the fifth number and 971.56 is the sixth. The whole number next in size is 917, so 917.68 becomes the seventh number. Our partial listing now shows the following:

979.3
975.93
975.9
975.8994
971.84    (fifth)
971.56    (sixth)
917.68    (seventh)

Finally, there are three numbers with 95 as the whole number part. These are: 95.1589, 95.518, and 95.54. Comparing them, 95.54 becomes the eighth number and 95.518 is ninth. The number 95.1589 has only .1 in the

tenths place and is the smallest and last. The completed column shows the following:

979.3
975.93
975.9
975.8994
971.84
971.56
917.68
95.54    (eighth)
95.518    (ninth)
95.1589    (tenth)

b. Check the column below to see if the numbers are in the correct order.

890.00587
890.05
890.1

The numbers are in the wrong order. From largest to smallest, they are: 890.1, 890.05, and 890.00587.

Complete Assignment 1

NAME_____

DATE_____

# Assignment 1
# Section 1-1

## The Decimal Number System

|  | Perfect Score | Student's Score |
|---|---|---|
| Part A | 10 |  |
| Part B | 10 |  |
| Part C | 10 |  |
| Part D | 10 |  |
| Part E | 20 |  |
| Part F | 40 |  |
| TOTAL | 100 |  |

# Part A
### Reading and Writing Whole Numbers

*Directions:* In the spaces provided, write the following numbers in words. (2 points for each correct answer)

1. 641_____

2. 4932_____

3. 90058_____

4. 820006_____

5. 6000035_____

*Student's Score* _____

# Part B
### Writing Numbers from Words

*Directions:* In the spaces provided, write the following words in numbers. (2 points for each correct answer)

6. Four thousand one hundred twenty-three . . . . . . . . . . . . . . . . . . . . . . . . .    _____

7. Eighty-nine thousand one hundred . . . . . . . . . . . . . . . . . . . . . . . . . . . . .    _____

8. Five hundred thousand seventy . . . . . . . . . . . . . . . . . . . . . . . . . . . . . . .    _____

9. Two million two . . . . . . . . . . . . . . . . . . . . . . . . . . . . . . . . . . . . . . . . . .    _____

10. Six hundred million four thousand three . . . . . . . . . . . . . . . . . . . . . . . .    _____

*Student's Score* _____

# Part C
### Reading and Writing Decimals

*Directions:* In the spaces provided, write the following decimals in words. (2 points for each correct answer)

11. 240.793_____

12. 608.045_____

13. 4000.0004 _____

14. 10035.00056 _____

15. 6.043$\frac{3}{4}$ _____

# Part D

## *Writing Decimals from Words*

*Directions:* In the spaces provided, write the following words as decimals. (2 points for each correct answer)

16. Three thousand six and twenty-five thousandths .................... _____

17. Four hundred thousand forty-five and four hundred four ten-thousandths . _____

18. Eighty-nine and fifty millionths .................................. _____

19. Six and sixteen and two-thirds thousandths ........................ _____

20. Thirty and eight and one-third hundredths ......................... _____

*Student's Score* _____

# Part E

## *Decimal Fractions and Decimal Mixed Numbers*

*Directions:* In the spaces provided, write the following as decimals. (1 point for each correct answer)

21. Twenty-two and one-half thousandths ................................ _____

22. Sixteen and two-thirds hundredths ................................. _____

23. Sixteen and two-thirds of a hundredth ............................. _____

24. Nine hundred seventy-six and six and one-fourth hundredths ......... _____

25. Six hundred eighty-seven and one-fourth of a thousandth ............ _____

26. Six hundred thirty and eight and one-half thousandths .............. _____

27. One-fourth of a tenth .............................................. _____

28. Two-fifths of a hundredth ......................................... _____

29. Two-thirds of a thousandth ........................................ _____

30. Five and three-fourths ten-thousandths ............................ _____

31. $79\frac{34}{100}$ ............. _____  36. $190\frac{190}{100,000}$ ........... _____

32. $8\frac{3}{100}$ ............. _____  37. $\frac{23}{10,000}$ ............. _____

33. $\frac{1,495}{1,000}$ ............. _____  38. $\frac{12\frac{1}{2}}{100}$ ............. _____

34. $\frac{57}{100}$ ............. _____  39. $8\frac{8}{1,000,000}$ ............. _____

35. $\frac{41\frac{3}{4}}{1,000}$ ............. _____  40. $\frac{1}{100,000}$ ............. _____

*Student's Score* _____

# Part F

## Comparing Decimals

*Directions:* Underline the number which is larger in value. If they are equal, underline both. (1 point for each correct answer)

| | | | | |
|---|---|---|---|---|
| 41. .078 | .0078 | 56. 370.90 | 370.900 |
| 42. 839.06 | 839.060 | 57. .675 | .675001 |
| 43. .35 | .355 | 58. 28.214 | 28.124 |
| 44. 596.67 | 596.67 | 59. 300.125 | 301.025 |
| 45. .01 | .0092 | 60. 19.749 | 19.497 |
| 46. 57.58 | 55.78000 | 61. 80.06 | 80.60 |
| 47. .5 | .500 | 62. 10,718 | 10,871 |
| 48. 845,902 | 845,092 | 63. 6.177 | 61.77 |
| 49. .033 | .330 | 64. 442 | 442.00 |
| 50. .07388 | .070883 | 65. 43.67 | 43.76 |
| 51. .2 | .1875 | 66. 512.60 | 51.2600 |
| 52. 9,245.3 | 9,345.2 | 67. 712,590 | 712,509 |
| 53. .801 | .80100 | 68. .6333 | .63330 |
| 54. 160,094 | 106,094 | 69. 5.41825 | 5.4183 |
| 55. .6751 | .675001 | 70. 21.5 | 21.50 |

*Directions:* In the spaces provided, arrange the following groups of numbers in order of value. Place the largest first and align the remaining numbers with the decimal points under each other. (2 points for each correct answer)

| | | | |
|---|---|---|---|
| 71. 44.4 | _____ | 72. 63.7 | _____ |
| 3.44 | _____ | 6.37 | _____ |
| 444 | _____ | 637 | _____ |
| 4.440 | _____ | 6.307 | _____ |
| 400.40 | _____ | 60.37 | _____ |
| .44 | _____ | 673 | _____ |
| 4.4 | _____ | 6.0370 | _____ |
| 344 | _____ | 63.7370 | _____ |

**73.** 827.94     _____

    872.94     _____

    870.49     _____

    827.49     _____

    782.54     _____

    784.29     _____

    728.54     _____

    782.49     _____

**74.** 483.801     _____

    72.77     _____

    504.712     _____

    772     _____

    .9255     _____

    771.99     _____

    483.81     _____

    .92505     _____

    504.721     _____

    483.000     _____

**75.** 520     _____

    .4146     _____

    173.08     _____

    980.3     _____

    520.5     _____

    .4164     _____

    520.05     _____

    980.29     _____

    520.15     _____

    173.008     _____

*Student's Score* _____

# Section 1-2  Addition of Decimals

Over half of the calculations necessary in business consist of addition in some form. In order for a company to know how much profit it is making, it must have totals for such things as salaries, expenses, sales, cash paid out, cash owed to the company—to name only a few.

The numbers being added are called **addends**. The result of the addition is the **sum** or **total**.

## Part A  Adding Decimals Vertically

To add two or more decimal numbers in a column (vertical addition), follow these steps:

1. Place the numbers in a column with the decimal points under each other.
2. Start at the top and add down; then check by starting at the bottom and adding up.
3. Put the decimal point in the sum directly under the decimal points in the column.

If all the addends do not have the same number of decimal places, you may add zeros as necessary to give all addends the same number of places.

*Examples:*

a. Add these numbers vertically and check: .97, 45.2, 3.001, 64, .0008, 3.1875.

Place in a column with the decimal points under each other. Put a point after any whole number.

```
    .97                    .9700  ⎫
  45.2                   45.2000  ⎪
   3.001                  3.0010  ⎪
  64.         or         64.0000  ⎬  addends
    .0008                  .0008  ⎪
   3.1875                 3.1875  ⎭
 116.3593                116.3593    total
```

b. Add these numbers and check:

```
   .487                      .4870
   .395                      .3950
   .0023        or           .0023
   .5                        .5000
  1.3843                    1.3843
       Carry the 1 to the
       left of the decimal
       point.
```

Speed in adding can be gained by finding combinations of 10. For example, 1 + 9; 2 + 8; 3 + 7; 4 + 6; and 5 + 5. For more speed, try adding the sum of two numbers as you go along instead of adding only one at a time.

*Example:*  Find the sum of 8, 4, 3, 7, 4, 5, 2, 6, 1, 9.

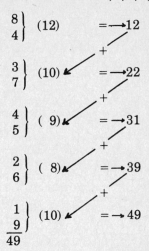

In review, note these points when adding a column of decimal numbers:

1. A decimal point is placed at the end of a whole number so that it is in the correct position in the column. Thus, in *Example a,* 64 is written as 64. or 64.0000.

2. The numbers are written in the columns so that the same places are under each other for easier adding.

3. The sum of a column is checked by adding in the opposite direction. There are other checking methods, but they are not given here.

4. If the sum of the tenths column, which is to the right of the decimal point, is 10 or more, the carryover is added to the units column, which is to the left of the decimal point.

5. The total must have as many decimal places as the greatest number of places in any one of the addends. Thus, in *Example b,* the number .0023 has the most places. In the same example, the sum of the tenths column is 13. If the 1 is not carried over to the left of the decimal point, then the answer would have five places instead of four, which would be wrong.

## Part B Adding Long Columns of Decimals

A long column of numbers may be broken down and added in separate parts to find **subtotals**. The subtotals are then added to find the total of the entire column.

When amounts of money are added, the *first* number and the *total* should have dollar signs.

*Example:* Add by using subtotals.

| | | |
|---|---|---|
| $934.96 | | |
| 829.17 | | |
| 100.84 | | |
| 873.12 | | |
| 257.90 | 2,995.99 | *subtotal* |
| 698.75 | | |
| 210.59 | | |
| 542.20 | | |
| 214.08 | | |
| 764.95 | 2,430.57 | *subtotal* |
| 1,347.62 | | |
| 764.00 | | |
| 2,089.37 | | |
| 481.63 | 4,682.62 | *subtotal* |
| | $10,109.18 | *total* |

## Part C Adding Decimals Horizontally

When numbers are written in a report so that they can be added both *horizontally* (across the page) and *vertically* (in a column), they are said to be **recapitulated** or **recapped**. The horizontal addition is called **crossfooting**. The numbers are not recopied in a column but are added across the page place by place.

The same numbers are added across and down. Therefore, the sum of the totals going across should equal the sum of the totals going down. This sum is called the **grand total**. It also serves as a check on the line totals and the column totals.

In the sales "recap" example shown below, the total for Clerk 1 is found by adding across. Mentally add: 4 (of 56.24) + 6 (of 43.76) + 3 (of 34.13) + 5 (of 88.25) + 0 (of 75.40) + 4 (of 58.94) = 22. Write the second 2 and carry the first 2 to the tenths figures, and add: 2 + 2 (of 56.24) + 7 (of 43.76) + 1 (of 34.13) + 2 (of 88.25) + 4 (of 75.40) + 9 (of 58.94) = 27. Write the 7 to make .72, and carry the 2 to the units figures. In the same way, add the units figures and then the tens figures to find the first line total, 356.72. Then find the rest of the line totals in the same way. The grand total is found by adding these line totals.

The column totals are found by adding down in the usual way. The grand total of these sums is found by adding horizontally. It should be the same as the grand total found by adding the line totals. If it is not, it shows that there are one or more errors in the line totals or column totals, or in the grand total. All totals must be checked.

Note that a dollar sign is placed before the first amount in each column and before each column total.

## Part D Checking Adding Machine Tapes

Adding machines are used a great deal in business. The paper tape output provides a record of the amounts added and their total.

When using an adding machine, the first step is to press the "Total" key to make sure there are no numbers entered in the machine for which the total was *not* found but the tape was torn off. An asterisk (*) shows that the machine is clear.

After the total has been found, the figures on the tape are checked against the original figures

*Example:* Find the total for each clerk and each department.

| Clerk | Dept. A | Dept. B | Dept. C | Dept. D | Dept. E | Dept. F | Totals |
|---|---|---|---|---|---|---|---|
| 1 | $ 56.24 | $ 43.76 | $ 34.13 | $ 88.25 | $ 75.40 | $ 58.94 | $ 356.72 |
| 2 | 29.98 | 70.31 | 88.27 | 31.72 | 30.24 | 75.25 | 325.77 |
| 3 | 80.55 | 69.42 | 75.20 | 56.47 | 46.32 | 80.20 | 408.16 |
| 4 | 75.97 | 48.09 | 83.10 | 76.38 | 74.24 | 61.22 | 419.00 |
| | $242.74 | $231.58 | $280.70 | $252.82 | $226.20 | $275.61 | $1,509.65 |

to make sure that the numbers have been entered into the machine correctly. One person may do this, or the original figures may be read aloud so that someone else checks the tape.

To check tape figures and make corrections if errors were made, follow these steps which are illustrated in the example below.

*Example:* Check and correct the tape.

| Original Figures | Tape | Corrections To Be Made |
|---|---|---|
| 467. 75 | 4 6 7.75.* | |
| 555 . 50 | (5.5 5 5.5 0) 555.50 | -5,000.00 |
| 3,020. 41 | 3. 0 2 0.41. | |
| 678. 82 | 6 7 8.82. | |
| 607. 10 | 6 0 7.10. | |
| 40. 00 | (4. 0 0) 40.00 | + 36.00 |
| 270. 33 | 2 7 0.33. | |
| 3,476. 98 | 3.4 7 6.98. | |
| 561. 55 | 5 6 1.55. | |
| 5,768. 89 | 5.7 6 8.(9 8).89 | -.09 |
| 12. 53 | 1 2.53. | |
| 300. 00 | 2 0,4 2 3.95* | 300.00 +300.00 |

+ 336. 00
20,759. 95
— 5,000. 09
15,759. 86 (CORRECT TOTAL)

1. If the tape number is right, a small dot or checkmark is put after it. (Note the dots beside the numbers which are the same in the "Original Figures" column and the "Tape" column.)

2. If the tape number is wrong, the incorrect figure is circled to show that it is wrong, and the correct figure is written to the right. The correction that must be made to the adding machine total is found and jotted down next to the corrected number. This is done by finding the difference between the original figure and the wrong figure entered into the machine.

If the wrong figure is larger than the original figure, it means that the tape total is too large by the amount of the difference. Since this must be subtracted from the tape total, a

minus sign is placed before the jotted-down correction. (Note that the second number was entered incorrectly. The 5,555.50 is circled and 555.50 is written at the right. The tape total is too large by 5,000.00 (5,555.50 − 555.50); so, −5,000 is written to the right of 555.50 to show that it must be subtracted from the tape total later.)

If the wrong figure is smaller than the original figure, it means that the tape total is too small by the amount of the difference. Since this must be added to the tape total, a plus sign is placed before the jotted-down correction. (Note that the sixth number was entered as 4.00 instead of 40.00. The 4.00 is circled and 40.00 is written at the right. The tape total is short by 36.00 (40.00 − 4.00); so, +36 is written to the right of 40.00 to show that it must be added to the tape total later.)

When only the last two digits are wrong, the entire number does not have to be circled. (Note that the tenth number was entered incorrectly with only the last two digits wrong. The correct .89 is written at the right. The machine added .98 instead of .89; so, the tape total is too large by .09 (.98 − .89). Thus, −.09 is written to the right of .89 to show that it must be subtracted from the tape total when the corrections are made at the end.

3. If a number in the original figures has not been entered in the machine, that number must be inserted in the tape and an arrow put in to show where it belongs. (Note that the last number in the column of original figures was omitted. Therefore, 300.00 is written between the 12.53 and the total; and an arrow is put in to show where 300.00 belongs. The number +300.00 is also written at the right (under the "Corrections To Be Made" column) to show that it must be added when the corrections are made.

4. After the last number has been checked, all the numbers with a plus sign in the "Corrections To Be Made" column are added. Their sum is then added to the tape total, as follows:

+ 36.00
+300.00
+336.00
20,423.95   (tape total)
20,759.95

**5.** The last step is to find the sum of all the numbers with a minus sign. Their sum is then subtracted from the new tape total found in Step 4, as follows:

$$
\begin{array}{r}
-.09 \\
-5,000.00 \\
\hline
-5,000.09
\end{array}
$$

$$
\begin{array}{r}
20,759.95 \\
-\ 5,000.09 \\
\hline
15,759.86
\end{array} \quad \text{(correct total)}
$$

The corrections in the tape total are made after *all* the numbers have been checked. Most companies will allow one or two errors if the corrections are made clearly; otherwise, a new tape must be run.

The example on the previous page shows more errors than are usually allowed. It was given as an example to show how corrections are made. Other than careless entering of a number, three types of errors are common: (1) reversing (or transposing) two digits, such as entering 98 instead of 89; (2) entering too many or too few digits when the same digit occurs several times in a row, such as entering 5,555.50 or 55.50 instead of 555.50; and (3) omitting a number entirely.

In the next example, there are six errors in the First Tape. See if you can find the errors and make the corrections in the same way as shown in the previous example. The Second Tape was run correctly to give you the correct total of the original figures.

*Example:* Check and correct the First Tape.

| Original Figures | First Tape |
|---|---|
| | * |
| 354.35 | 3 5 4. 3 5 |
| 855.89 | 8 5 5. 8 9 |
| 766.90 | 7 6 6. 0 9 |
| 7,844.99 | 7. 8 9 4. 9 9 |
| 90.76 | 9 0. 7 6 |
| 130.45 | 1 3 0. 5 4 |
| 8,604.29 | 8. 6 0 4. 2 9 |
| 200.25 | 2 0 0. 2 5 |
| 222.20 | 2 2. 2 0 |
| 998.60 | 9 9 8. 6 0 |
| 60.00 | 1 3 8. 1 5 |
| 138.15 | 6 4 3. 8 8 |
| 643.88 | 6 2 0. 0 0 |
| 620.00 | 8 8. 8 9 |
| 88.89 | 9 6 2. 7 5 |
| 926.75 | 2 2. 3 7 1. 6 3 * |

| Second Tape |
|---|
| * |
| 3 5 4. 3 5 |
| 8 5 5. 8 9 |
| 7 6 6. 9 0 |
| 7. 8 4 4. 9 9 |
| 9 0. 7 6 |
| 1 3 0. 4 5 |
| 8. 6 0 4. 2 9 |
| 2 0 0. 2 5 |
| 2 2 2. 2 0 |
| 9 9 8. 6 0 |
| 6 0. 0 0 |
| 1 3 8. 1 5 |
| 6 4 3. 8 8 |
| 6 2 0. 0 0 |
| 8 8. 8 9 |
| 9 2 6. 7 5 |
| 2 2 5 4 6. 3 5 * |

Complete Assignment 2

## Assignment 2
## Section 1-2

| | Perfect Score | Student's Score |
|---|---|---|
| Part A | 16 | |
| Part B | 8 | |
| Part C | 30 | |
| Part D | 46 | |
| TOTAL | 100 | |

### Addition of Decimals

# Part A

### Adding Decimals Vertically

*Directions:* Write each set of numbers in a column. Find the sum and write your answer in the spaces provided. Check by adding in the opposite direction. (2 points for each correct answer)

1. .93, .41, .46, .21, .29  = _____

2. .73, .87, .51, .59, .24  = _____

3. .756, .3, .85, .0951, = _____
   .00475, .14

4. .107, .56, .00833, = _____
   .84, .3125, .7

5. 238.08, 71, 9.72,   = _____
   67.449, 5.83, 54.0016

6. 6.08, 2, 381.85, 7.654, = _____
   8.31, .652, .0437

7. 375.98, 2.002, 300,   = _____
   .6875, .8, 91.27432

8. .5625, .4, 200, .39   = _____
   498.61461, 65.003

*Student's Score* _____

# Part B

## Adding Long Columns of Decimals

**Directions:** Add by using subtotals as indicated. Write the totals in the double-ruled spaces. (2 points for each correct answer)

9.  $667.54
    353.56
    76.12
    65.48  _____
    341.23
    689.74
    901.43
    54.17  _____  ==========

10. $  326.50
    875.46
    2,645.64
    16.67
    230.15  _____
    66.55
    543.30
    11.22
    5,873.38
    767.41  _____
    9.99
    7,450.30
    631.36
    275.24  _____  ==========

11. $580.46
    366.09
    110.57
    601.89
    85.58  _____
    401.11
    630.47
    275.46
    511.52
    730.84  _____  ==========

12. $   92.90
    261.25
    79.80
    359.87
    7,405.43  _____
    10.10
    876.54
    2,426.46
    1,780.27
    73.73  _____
    437.02
    260.35
    456.23
    14.87  _____  ==========

*Student's Score* _____

# Part C

## Adding Decimals Horizontally

**Directions:** Add horizontally and vertically. The grand total of the lines must equal the grand total of the columns. (3 points for each correct answer)

| | | | | | | |
|---|---|---|---|---|---|---|
| 251.76 | 160.43 | 205.94 | 149.69 | 187.32 | _____ | **13.** |
| 679.87 | 157.44 | 473.86 | 863.32 | 500.37 | _____ | **14.** |
| 894.77 | 494.73 | 548.76 | 677.74 | 294.93 | _____ | **15.** |
| 48.03 | 168.25 | 550.79 | 97.95 | 180.57 | _____ | **16.** |
| **17.** | **18.** | **19.** | **20.** | **21.** | **22.** | |

*Student's Score* _____

# Part D

## Checking Adding Machine Tapes

*Directions:* Check the adding machine tape against the original figures, making the corrections on the tape, and find the correct total. (4 points for each correct answer)

23.

| | |
|---|---|
| 574.99 | 5 7 4.9 9 * |
| 142.15 | 1 4 2.1 5 |
| 6.87 | 6.8 7 |
| 3.00 | 3 0.0 0 |
| 356.57 | 3 5 6.5 7 |
| 987.48 | 9 8 7.4 8 |
| 1,246.88 | 1.2 4 6.8 8 |
| 1,456.10 | 1.4 5 6.1 0 |
| 524.58 | 5 2 4.5 0 |
| 12.08 | 8 |
| 67.52 | 6 7.5 2 |
| 3,005.50 | 3.0 0 5.5 0 |
| 62.10 | 6 2.1 0 |
| 450.60 | 4 5 0.6 0 |
| 6,080.06 | 6.0 8 0.6 0 |
| | 1 4.9 9 1.9 4 * |

_____Correct Total

25.

| | |
|---|---|
| 19.15 | 1 9.1 5 * |
| 42.06 | 4 2.0 6 |
| 433.98 | 4 3 3.9 8 |
| 31.42 | 3 1.4 2 |
| 55.18 | 5 5.1 8 |
| 26.72 | 2 6.2 7 |
| 676.33 | 6 7 6.3 3 |
| 28.47 | 2 8.4 7 |
| 579.19 | 5.7 7 9.1 9 |
| 8.00 | 8 0 0.0 0 |
| 349.86 | 3 4 9.8 6 |
| 254.97 | 2 5 4.9 7 |
| 316.54 | 3 1 6.5 4 |
| 260.78 | 1 9 8.7 5 |
| 198.75 | 9.0 1 2.1 7 * |

_____Correct Total

24.

| | |
|---|---|
| 815.90 | 8 1 5.9 0 * |
| 742.15 | 7 4 2.1 5 |
| 6.33 | 6.3 3 |
| 424.68 | 4 2 4.8 6 |
| 525.36 | 5 2 5.3 6 |
| 417.84 | 4 1 7.8 4 |
| 7.95 | 2 6 8.0 5 |
| 268.05 | 9 8 7.1 9 |
| 987.19 | 1.3 0 0.2 7 |
| 1,030.27 | 3 1 9.0 4 |
| 319.04 | 2 2.8 5 |
| 22.85 | 3 3 1.4 2 |
| 331.42 | 9 4 4.1 6 |
| 944.16 | 5 5.5 0 |
| 555.50 | 7.1 6 0.9 2 * |

_____Correct Total

26.

| | |
|---|---|
| 676.04 | 6 7 6.0 4 * |
| 778.13 | 7 7 8.1 3 |
| 388.96 | 3 8 8.9 6 |
| 270.86 | 2 7 0.8 6 |
| 79.90 | 7 9 9.9 0 |
| 435.68 | 4 3 5.6 8 |
| 124.02 | 1 2 4.0 2 |
| 1,389.15 | 1.3 8 9.1 5 |
| 450.00 | 4.5 0 |
| 426.25 | 4 2 6.2 5 |
| 6,045.78 | 4 5.7 8 |
| 12.63 | 1 2.6 3 |
| 455.87 | 4 5 5.8 7 |
| 153.13 | 1 5 3.1 3 |
| 445.56 | 4 4 5.6 6 |
| | 6.4 0 6.5 6 * |

_____Correct Total

**Directions:** If the numbers in the two columns are the same, put a checkmark (√) in the space after the second number. If the numbers are different, put an (×) in the space after the second number. (1 point for each correct answer)

| | | | | | | | |
|---|---|---|---|---|---|---|---|
| 27. | 3,556.55 | 3,565.55 | _____ | 42. | 1,750.75 | 1,750.75 | _____ |
| 28. | 4,053.65 | 4,053.65 | _____ | 43. | 36,892.46 | 36,892.46 | _____ |
| 29. | 391.74 | 319.74 | _____ | 44. | 200.88 | 200.88 | _____ |
| 30. | 3,148.12 | 3,148.12 | _____ | 45. | 234.67 | 243.67 | _____ |
| 31. | 19,693.39 | 19,683.39 | _____ | 46. | 500.01 | 500.10 | _____ |
| 32. | 10,797.13 | 10,979.31 | _____ | 47. | 5,409.10 | 5,409.01 | _____ |
| 33. | 4,151.63 | 4,151.93 | _____ | 48. | 71,001.01 | 71,001.01 | _____ |
| 34. | 97.75 | 97.75 | _____ | 49. | 70,100.10 | 70,100.01 | _____ |
| 35. | 683.93 | 638.93 | _____ | 50. | 23,303.09 | 23,303.09 | _____ |
| 36. | 3,889.68 | 3,389.68 | _____ | 51. | 56,930.14 | 56,930.14 | _____ |
| 37. | 75,358.00 | 7,358.00 | _____ | 52. | 18,880.05 | 1,880.05 | _____ |
| 38. | 1,241.76 | 1,241.76 | _____ | 53. | 7,777.50 | 77,777.50 | _____ |
| 39. | 4,688.40 | 6,486.40 | _____ | 54. | 900.09 | 910.09 | _____ |
| 40. | 5,962.50 | 55,962.50 | _____ | 55. | 9,091.00 | 9,091.00 | _____ |
| 41. | 13,810.45 | 13,810.45 | _____ | 56. | 4,520.82 | 4,520.82 | _____ |

*Student's Score* _____

# Section 1-3   Subtraction of Decimals

Most business reports and records require some subtraction before they are completed. Subtraction is used in finding such things as the amount of increase or decrease, the net amount after a discount, and the net pay.

**Subtraction** is the operation of taking one number from another. It can be expressed in several ways. For example, $57.50 − $2.75 may also be indicated as:

1. Take $2.75 from $57.50.

2. Find the difference between $57.50 and $2.75.

3. Deduct $2.75 from $57.50.

4. How much more than $2.75 is $57.50?

The **minuend** is the number from which another number is taken. The **subtrahend** is the number being taken away or subtracted. The **difference** or **remainder** is the result of a subtraction.

Subtraction is checked by adding upward the difference and the subtrahend. The total of the difference and the subtrahend should equal the minuend. It is not necessary to recopy the numbers in order to add them for the check.

## Part A   Subtracting One Decimal from Another

To find the difference between two decimals which have the same number of places, write the larger number (the minuend) on top. Write the smaller number (the subtrahend) under it with the decimal points under each other. Subtract in the usual way. The decimal point in the answer (the difference) is placed directly under the others. Check by adding upward only.

*Example:*

```
 125.48 minuend ←— =
− 14.03 subtrahend │ ↑
 111.45 difference │ +
```

When a digit in the subtrahend is larger than the digit above it in the minuend, borrowing is necessary. If it helps you, draw a line through the minuend digit from which the 1 is borrowed and change it to one less.

*Example:*

```
              5 1 6 .
  567.18    5 6 7 .¹1 8
 −258.23   −2 5 8 . 2 3
            3 0 8 . 9 5
```

Sometimes it is necessary to go two or more places to the left for the first borrowing.

*Example:*

```
              9 9  9
  100.04    ¹1 0 1 0 ¹1 0 ¹1 4
 −  6.05   −        6 . 0 5
            9 3 . 9 9
```

One of the terms may have fewer decimal places than the other. In this case, add as many zeros to it as are needed to match the decimal places in the other term. Then subtract and check.

*Example:* How much more than 2.3125 is 5.2? (5.2 − 2.3125)

```
   5.2        5.2000  (add three zeros)
 −2.3125    −2.3125
              2.8875
```

## Part B   Subtracting a Decimal from a Whole Number

Errors in subtraction may be caused by not lining up the minuend and subtrahend correctly. This often occurs when one of them is a whole number written without a decimal point after it.

When the minuend is a whole number and the subtrahend is a decimal, place a decimal point after the whole number and add as many zeros as are needed to match the number of places in the subtrahend. Write the subtrahend directly under the minuend with the decimal points in line with each other. Since the minuend always has one or more zeros after the point, borrowing from the units digit is necessary in order to subtract the decimal part of the subtrahend.

*Example:* Deduct 69.72 from 124. (124 − 69.72)

```
   124        124.00  (add two zeros)
 − 69.72      69.72
               54.28
```

When the difference between two numbers is required, the smaller number may be given first. However, the minuend is always the larger number.

*Example:* Find the difference between .0583 and 27. (27 − .0583)

In this case, 27 must be the minuend since it is larger than .0583.

```
  27              27.0000   (add four zeros)
− .0583        −   .0583
                  26.9417
```

There are two common types of errors in subtraction which you must avoid: (1) lining up the first digits of both numbers instead of putting a decimal point and zeros after the minuend; and (2) bringing down the decimal part of the subtrahend into the answer without subtracting it. Both types of errors result in wrong answers.

## Part C  Subtracting a Whole Number from a Decimal

When the minuend is a decimal and the subtrahend is a whole number, put a point after the whole number and add as many zeros as are needed to match the places in the minuend. Subtract and check as usual.

*Example:* Find the difference between 45 and 50.86. (50.86 − 45)

```
  50.86          50.86
−45            −45.00   (add two zeros)
                 5.86
```

## Part D  Business Applications

In business, it is often necessary to find the increase or decrease of an amount from an earlier period to a later one. This is done by subtracting the smaller amount from the larger one. When the later-period amount is larger than the earlier-period amount, there is an **increase**. When the later-period amount is smaller than the earlier-period amount, there is a **decrease**.

In business reports, generally there are columns called "Increase" and "Decrease." The amount of increase or decrease is put in the correct column.

*Examples:* Find the amount of increase or decrease. Place the amount in the correct column.

|    | Last Month | This Month | Increase | Decrease |
|----|------------|------------|----------|----------|
| a. | 610.91 | 862.74 | _____ | _____ |
| b. | 677.41 | 529.48 | _____ | |

```
   862.74   (later period is larger)
−  610.91   (earlier period is smaller)
   251.83   Increase
```

```
   677.41   (earlier period is larger)
−  529.48   (later period is smaller)
   147.93   Decrease
```

Place the increase or decrease in the correct column, as follows:

| | | | |
|---|---|---|---|
| 610.91 | 862.74 | 251.83 | |
| 677.41 | 529.48 | | 147.93 |

In some reports, only the amount of change needs to be shown. When the change is an increase, a plus sign is put before the amount; when the change is a decrease, a minus sign is placed before the amount. The same figures as in the examples above are used in the examples below.

|    | Last Month | This Month | Change |
|----|------------|------------|--------|
| a. | 610.91 | 862.74 | +251.83 |
| b. | 677.41 | 529.48 | −147.93 |

Complete Assignment 3

# Assignment 3
# Section 1-3

## Subtraction of Decimals

|  | Perfect Score | Student's Score |
|---|---|---|
| Part A | 50 |  |
| Part B | 10 |  |
| Part C | 10 |  |
| Part D | 30 |  |
| TOTAL | 100 |  |

# Part A
### Subtracting One Decimal from Another

**Directions:** Subtract and check by adding back the subtrahend. (2 points for each correct answer)

| 1. | 6.38 − 4.55 | 2. | 85.68 − 48.83 | 3. | 78.19 − 38.24 | 4. | 81.07 − 14.50 |
|---|---|---|---|---|---|---|---|

| 5. | 246.03 − 25.99 | 6. | 675.01 − 396.87 | 7. | 5,665.04 − 1,486.75 | 8. | 4,703.90 − 1,263.43 |
|---|---|---|---|---|---|---|---|

| 9. | 8,099.86 − 6,254.87 | 10. | 15,000.25 − 1,637.02 | 11. | 12,002.12 − 3,218.02 | 12. | 15,733.96 − 10,727.05 |
|---|---|---|---|---|---|---|---|

| 13. | 78,852.34 − 51,205.69 | 14. | 91,086.94 − 69,876.07 | 15. | 38,568.13 − 19,603.42 | 16. | 7.57 − 1.741 |
|---|---|---|---|---|---|---|---|

| 17. | 95.35 − 89.147 | 18. | 124.9 − 99.965 | 19. | 132.3 − 46.5783 | 20. | 831.4 − 60.8129 |
|---|---|---|---|---|---|---|---|

**Directions:** Find the difference between the two numbers. Check by adding back the subtrahend. (2 points for each correct answer)

21. 41.75 and 3.47

22. 19.82 and 110.85

23. 526.74 and 622.80

24. 6,480.31 and 10,235.90

25. 25,610.54 and 24,928.50

*Student's Score* _____

# Part B

## Subtracting a Decimal from a Whole Number

*Directions:* Find the difference and check. (2 points for each correct answer)

26. 2 − .25

27. 4 − .3

28. 10 − 4.68

29. 753 − 25.816

30. 984 − 2.6729

*Student's Score* _____

# Part C

## Subtracting a Whole Number from a Decimal

*Directions:* Find the difference and check. (2 points for each correct answer)

31. 73.59 − 47

32. 56.27 − 40

33. 438.03 − 400

34. 7,697.99 − 7,000

35. 10,047.25 − 9,998

*Student's Score* _____

# Part D

## Business Applications

*Directions:* Find the amount of increase or decrease and write it in the correct column. (2 points for each correct answer)

| | Department | Last Month | This Month | Increase | Decrease |
|---|---|---|---|---|---|
| 36. | A | $ 2,200.47 | $ 2,044.64 | _____ | _____ |
| 37. | B | 1,899.11 | 1,953.16 | _____ | _____ |
| 38. | C | 2,647.83 | 3,705.29 | _____ | _____ |
| 39. | D | 4,562.78 | 3,941.29 | _____ | _____ |
| 40. | E | 844.52 | 865.49 | _____ | _____ |
| 41. | F | 7,358.90 | 5,499.85 | _____ | _____ |
| 42. | G | 25,895.06 | 26,348.28 | _____ | _____ |
| 43. | H | 42,009.11 | 34,762.07 | _____ | _____ |

*Directions:* Find the amount of change and write it in the "Change" column. Use a plus sign to show an increase and a minus sign to show a decrease. (2 points for each correct answer)

| | Department | Last Month | This Month | Change |
|---|---|---|---|---|
| 44. | A | $ 7,000.75 | $ 7,200.73 | _____ |
| 45. | B | 2,416.00 | 3,249.25 | _____ |
| 46. | C | 600.18 | 567.37 | _____ |
| 47. | D | 12,175.23 | 9,240.65 | _____ |
| 48. | E | 9,000.55 | 10,670.78 | _____ |
| 49. | F | 64,319.47 | 65,842.08 | _____ |
| 50. | G | 37,005.21 | 35,892.66 | _____ |

*Student's Score* _____

# Section 1-4  Multiplication of Decimals

In business, addition is the operation most widely used. Second to it in use is multiplication. Payroll, inventories, discounts, and interest are only a few of the many cases in which multiplication is necessary.

The first number in a multiplication problem is called the **multiplicand**. The number by which it is multiplied is called the **multiplier**. The result of the multiplication is called the **product**. When two or more numbers are multiplied to find their product, they are sometimes called **factors**. For example, since $6 \times 4 = 24$, the 6 and 4 are factors of 24. Other factors of 24 are 8 and 3, 12 and 2, and 24 and 1 since the product of each set is 24. **To factor** a given number means to find those numbers which, when multiplied together, result in the given number as the product.

In multiplication, one method is to write down the partial products by indenting them. For example, in finding the product of $3,687 \times 463$, one would work it as shown below.

*Example of First Method:*  $3,687 \times 463$

```
    3687   (multiplicand)
  × 463    (multiplier)
   11061
   22122   (partial products)
   14748
 1707081   (final product)
```

Another method of multiplication that is generally taught today is to take the digits of the multiplier at their full place value. In this second method, the following shortcuts are used: (1) to multiply by a number ending in one zero, multiply without the zero and then add one zero to the product; (2) to multiply by a number ending in two zeros, multiply without the zeros and then add two zeros to the product, etc. For example, taking the same multiplication problem illustrated in the first method above, the 6 of 463 is in the tens position and stands for 60. Thus, the 3687 is multiplied by 6 and one zero is added to the partial product. The 4 of 463 is in the hundreds position and stands for 400. Thus, the 3687 is multiplied by 4 and two zeros are added to the partial product. In this way, all the partial products are lined up at the right and are in their correct positions, as shown in the following example:

*Example of Second Method:*

```
    3687
  × 463
   11061
  221220
 1474800
 1707081
```

The steps used in the second method, as shown above, are:

1. Find the first partial product as you would in the first method: $3687 \times 3 = 11061$.

2. Find the second partial product by multiplying 3687 by 6 and adding one zero to get 221220. (The shortcut is used in multiplying 3687 by 60.)

3. Find the third partial product by multiplying 3687 by 4 and adding two zeros to get 1474800. (The shortcut is used in multiplying 3687 by 400).

Note that when the multiplier has one or more zeros and the first method is used, errors may arise because the partial products are not indented correctly. This cannot happen when the second method is used since there is no indenting and the partial products are all correctly lined up. Compare the two methods in the example below.

*Example:*  $9,036 \times 3,704$

| First Method | Second Method | |
|---|---|---|
| 9036 | 9036 | |
| × 3704 | × 3704 | |
| 36144 | 36144 | $(9036 \times 4)$ |
| 632520 | 6325200 | $(9036 \times 700)$ |
| 27108 | 27108000 | $(9036 \times 3000)$ |
| 33469344 | 33469344 | |

A common error in the first method is to indent the 27108 with respect to 632520 with the 8 under the 2 instead of the 5.

## Part A — Multiplying a Decimal by a Decimal or a Whole Number

Multiplication as it occurs in business usually deals with decimals. It is important that the decimal point is in the right place. To find the product of two numbers, one or both of which are decimals, follow these steps:

1. Find the product as if both were whole numbers. Do *not* line up the decimal points; do *not* add zeros to one number to match the decimal places of the other.

2. Count the decimal places (the digits after the point) in the multiplicand and in the multiplier; then add them together. This sum gives the total decimal places to be pointed off in the product.

3. Starting with the last digit of the product and going to the left, count off the total decimal places found in Step 2. Put the decimal point in front.

   After the point has been fixed in the product, check the decimal places that show after the point. Remember that even if the multiplication itself is correct but the decimal point is in the wrong place, the answer is wrong.

4. Zeros at the end of a product are used in counting the decimal places to be pointed off. The zeros may be dropped *after* the decimal point has been fixed. Zeros to the left of the point are never dropped since they belong to the whole number part of the product.

The second method of multiplication illustrated on the previous page is used in all of the following examples.

*Examples:* Find the products.

a. 502 × 3.65

```
      502   (no decimal places)
  ×  3.65   (2 decimal places)
     2510   total = 2 decimal places
    30120
   150600
  1832.30   (2 decimal places)
```

If the answer is not money, the end zero may be crossed out to give 1832.3.

b. 148.92 × .26005

```
    148.92   (2 decimal places)
  ×  .26005   (5 decimal places)
     74460   total = 7 decimal places
   89352000
  297840000
  38.7266460   (7 decimal places)
```

The end zero may be crossed out to give 38.726646.

c. 312.5 × .64

```
    312.5   (1 decimal place)
  ×   .64   (2 decimal places)
    12500   total = 3 decimal places
   187500
  200.000   (3 decimal places)
```

The three zeros after the decimal point may be dropped to give 200.

## Part B — Prefixing Zeros in the Product

The decimal point in a product is always fixed by starting with the last digit and counting to the left. When the product does not have enough decimal places to match the sum of the decimal places in the numbers being multiplied, prefix (put before) as many zeros as are needed to point off the correct number of places. Remember that the end zeros in the product must be counted.

*Examples:* Find the products.

a.
```
       .785   (3 decimal places)
  ×   .1004   (4 decimal places)
       3140   total = 7 decimal places
     785000
   .0788140   (Prefix one zero to obtain
              7 decimal places.)
```

b.
```
      .1632   (4 decimal places)
  ×   .0078   (4 decimal places)
      13056   total = 8 decimal places
     114240
  .00127296   (Prefix two zeros to obtain
              8 decimal places.)
```

## Part C    Rounding Off to a Given Number of Places

Often a calculation results in more decimal places than are needed. For example, an answer may be 56.3875, but only two decimal places are required. The 56.3875 is **rounded off** to 56.39; that is, it is expressed correctly to two decimal places.

Generally in rounding off a decimal to a given number of places, the whole number part to the left of the decimal point remains the same (see Step 5 below for an exception). In the decimal part, the last digit of the required place may stay the same or it may be increased by one.

To round off a decimal to a given number of places, follow these steps:

1. The whole number part (if there is one) of the decimal number must be used in the rounded answer.

2. In the decimal part, look only at the digit *after* the required place. You may wish to draw a line after the required place and underline the digit after it.

*Example:* Round off 56.12463 to two decimal places.

$$56.12|\underline{4}63$$

3. If the digit after the required place is less than 5, make no change in the required place and drop all places after it. In the example in Step 2 above:

$$56.12|\underline{4}63 = 56.12$$

4. If the digit after the required place is 5 or more, add 1 to the required place and drop all places after it.

*Example:* Round off 56.12663 to two decimal places.

$$\begin{array}{r} 56.12|\underline{6}63 \\ +\ 1\ \\ \hline 56.13|663 \end{array} = 56.13$$

5. If the decimal part is a series of nines through the required place and the place after it is 5 or

more, add one to the required place and carry it over to the whole number part.

*Example:* Round off 294.99963 to three decimal places.

$$\begin{array}{r} 294.999|\underline{6}3 \\ +\ 1\ \\ \hline 295.00063 \end{array} = 295.000$$

To summarize, in rounding off a number, look only at the digit after the required decimal place. The rest of the decimal places are always dropped.

*Examples:* Round off as indicated.

a. 32.6499 to one decimal place

$$32.6|\underline{4}99 = 32.6|\underline{4}99 = 32.6$$

The 99 does not change the 4 to a 5 since these two digits are dropped.

b. 32.6599 to one decimal place

$$\begin{array}{r} 32.6|\underline{5}99 = 32.6|599 \\ +\ 1\ \\ \hline = 32.7 \end{array}$$

c. 32.6549 to two decimal places

$$32.65|\underline{4}9 = 32.65|49 = 32.65$$

d. 32.6559 to two decimal places

$$\begin{array}{r} 32.65|\underline{5}9 = 32.65|59 \\ +\ 1\ \\ \hline = 32.66 \end{array}$$

e. 32.6492 to three decimal places

$$32.649|\underline{2} = 32.649|2 = 32.649$$

f. 32.64992 to three decimal places

$$\begin{array}{r} 32.649|\underline{9}2 = 32.649|92 \\ +\ 1\ \\ \hline = 32.650 \end{array}$$

g. 10.995064 to one, two, three, and four places respectively

$$\begin{array}{r} \text{One: } 10.9|\underline{9}5064 = 10.9|95064 \\ +\ 1\ \\ \hline = 11.0 \end{array}$$

Two: $10.99|\underline{5}064 = 10.99|\cancel{5}06\cancel{4}$
$$\underline{\quad + \quad 1 \quad}$$
$$= \overline{11.00}$$

Three: $10.995|\underline{0}64 = 10.995|\cancel{0}6\cancel{4} = 10.995$

Four: $10.9950|\underline{6}4 = 10.9950|\cancel{6}\cancel{4}$
$$\underline{\quad + \quad 1 \quad}$$
$$= \overline{10.9951}$$

## Part D
### Multiplying by a Decimal with a Fractional Ending

When the multiplicand or the multiplier or both are decimals which have a common fraction at the end, they are generally changed to complete decimals before they are multiplied. In order to change the number to a complete decimal, first learn these common fractions and their decimal forms:

$$\tfrac{1}{2} = .5$$
$$\tfrac{1}{3} = .333333 \text{ (or } .33\tfrac{1}{3})$$
$$\tfrac{2}{3} = .666667 \text{ (or } .66\tfrac{2}{3})$$
$$\tfrac{1}{4} = .25$$
$$\tfrac{3}{4} = .75$$
$$\tfrac{1}{6} = .166667 \text{ (or } .16\tfrac{2}{3})$$
$$\tfrac{5}{6} = .833333 \text{ (or } .83\tfrac{1}{3})$$

To change a decimal with a fractional ending to a complete decimal, follow this rule: Replace the common fraction with its decimal form but drop the point. A number can have only one decimal point, and there already is one in the decimal part before the common fraction.

*Examples:* Change to complete decimals.

a. $.93\tfrac{3}{4} = .9375$ ($\tfrac{3}{4} = .75$)
b. $.37\tfrac{1}{2} = .375$ ($\tfrac{1}{2} = .5$)
c. $.08\tfrac{1}{3} = .083333$ (see note below)
d. $.41\tfrac{2}{3} = .416667$ (see note below)

In *Examples c* and *d* the common fractions are repeating decimals: $\tfrac{1}{3} = .333333 \ldots$ and $\tfrac{2}{3} = .666666 \ldots$ If fewer decimal places are required, the number of 3's or 6's is decreased. If more places are required, the number of 3's or 6's is increased. In both cases, however, the last decimal place must be 3 for those decimals ending in repeating 3's and 7 for those ending in repeating

6's. At least six places should be used to get an accurate answer.

In *Example c* only four 3's are used for the $\tfrac{1}{3}$ since the number has two decimal places before the $\tfrac{1}{3}$. Therefore, only four 3's are needed to make the six places. Similarly, in *Example d* the $\tfrac{2}{3}$ is replaced with 6667 since the number has two places before the $\tfrac{2}{3}$. Note that the last 6 in the repeating decimal is rounded to a 7.

In summary, to multiply by a decimal with a common fraction ending, first change it to a complete decimal and then multiply as usual.

*Examples:* Find the products.

a. $20.37\tfrac{1}{2} \times .47$
   $20.37\tfrac{1}{2} = 20.375$
   $20.375 \times .47 = 9.57625$

b. $78.5 \times .68\tfrac{3}{4}$
   $.68\tfrac{3}{4} = .6875$
   $78.5 \times .6875 = 53.96875$

c. $10.31\tfrac{1}{4} \times 7.83\tfrac{1}{3}$
   $10.31\tfrac{1}{4} = 10.3125$
   $7.83\tfrac{1}{3} = 7.833333$
   $10.3125 \times 7.833333 = 80.7812465625$

For the student's interest, the exact answer to *Example c* is 80.78125 when it is worked as a decimal mixed number times a mixed number as explained in Chapter 3. Note that the above ten-place answer rounded off to five places gives the exact answer. In most cases, a result expressed correctly to two or three decimal places is all that is needed and therefore the completely accurate answer is unnecessary.

## Part E
### Multiplying by Ten and Its Multiples

Since any number multiplied by 0 is always 0, there are some shortcuts for multiplying by 10, 100, 1,000, and other numbers ending in one or more zeros.

To multiply any whole number by 10, add one zero to the number to get the product. To multiply any whole number by 100, add two zeros to the number to get the product. To multiply any whole number by 1,000, add three zeros to the number to get the product, etc. The number of zeros added to the multiplicand is always the same as the number of zeros in the multiplier. Thus, the long method of multiplication is not needed.

*Examples:* Use shortcuts to multiply.

a. $34 \times 10 = 340$ (add 1 zero to 34)

b. $68 \times 100 = 6,800$ (add 2 zeros to 68)

c. $70 \times 1,000 = 70,000$ (add 3 zeros to 70)

d. $351 \times 10,000 = 3,510,000$ (add 4 zeros to 351)

To multiply a decimal by 10, 100, 1,000, etc., somewhat the same rule is followed; but instead of adding zeros, the decimal point is moved to the right as many places as there are zeros in the multiplier.

*Examples:* Multiply by moving the decimal point to the right.

a. $1.935 \times 10 = 19.35$ (move the decimal point 1 place)

b. $.0367 \times 1,000 = 36.7$ (move the decimal point 3 places)

If the decimal has fewer places than the multiplier has zeros, add zeros to it in order to move the correct number of places to the right. As with shortcuts in multiplying whole numbers, do the multiplication only by moving the decimal point. Do not multiply the long way.

*Examples:*

a. $205.7 \times 100 = 20570. = 20,570$
(add a zero and move the decimal point 2 places)

b. $7.39 \times 10,000 = 73900. = 73,900$
(add two zeros and move the decimal point 4 places)

A multiple of a number contains that number *exactly*, without a remainder. Some multiples of 10 are: 20, 30, 110, 350, 900, 4,600, etc. All multiples of 10 end in one or more zeros.

When multiplying any number by a multiple of 10 other than 100, 1,000, etc., write the multiplier so that the end zeros are to the right of the

last digit of the top number. Multiply without the zeros and then add the zeros to the product when the multiplication is done.

*Example:* $106 \times 400$

$$
\begin{array}{r}
106 \\
\times\ 400 \\
\hline
42400 = 42,400
\end{array}
$$

Note that the 4 is written under the 6 with the two zeros to its right. Then 106 is multiplied by 4, and two zeros are added to the 424.

If the multiplicand is a decimal, fix the decimal point after the zeros have been added.

*Example:* $46,000 \times 32.47$ (same as $32.47 \times 46,000$)

$$
\begin{array}{r}
32.47 \\
\times\ 46000 \\
\hline
19482 \\
129880 \\
\hline
1493620.00 = 1,493,620.00
\end{array}
$$

Note that the 6 of the 46 is written under the 7 with the three zeros to its right. Then 3247 is multiplied by 46, and three zeros are added to the product, 149362, to give 149362000. As the last step, two decimal places are pointed off to give 1493620.00. Then the two end zeros are dropped to give the answer: 1,493,620.

*Example:* $.897 \times 5,900$

$$
\begin{array}{r}
.897 \\
\times\ 5900 \\
\hline
8073 \\
44850 \\
\hline
5292.300 = 5,292.300
\end{array}
$$

Note that the 9 of the 59 is written under the 7 with the two zeros to its right. Then 897 is multiplied by 59 and two zeros are added to the product, 52923, to give 5292300. As the last step, three decimal places are pointed off to give the answer: 5292.300 or 5,292.3.

There is another shortcut that can be used. Instead of adding the zeros at the end as in the examples given above, the zeros are taken care of before the multiplication is done. In this shortcut, move the decimal point of the top number (the multiplicand) as many places to the right as there are zeros in the multiplier, cross out the zeros in the multiplier, and then multiply and point off the decimal places as usual.

What happens in this second shortcut is that the multiplier is broken down into two factors, one of which is 10, 100, 1,000, etc. Since the order of multiplication does not matter, the multiplicand is multiplied first by the 10, 100, 1,000, etc., and then by the other factor.

*Example:*  3.65 × 2,500

Change the 2,500 to 100 × 25. Next, multiply 3.65 × 100 by moving the decimal point in 3.65 two places to the right, as follows: 3ᵪ65. Then multiply 365 × 25. In this case, there are no decimal places to be pointed off.

| 3ᵪ65. × 2500 | **First Shortcut** |
|---|---|
| 365 | 3.65 |
| × 25 | × 2500 |
| 1825 | 1825 |
| 7300 | 7300 |
| 9125 | 9125.00 |

*Example:*  4.892 × 6,700

Change this to 4ᵪ89.2 × 6700, then proceed as follows:

| | **First Shortcut** |
|---|---|
| 489.2 | 4.892 |
| × 67 | × 6700 |
| 34244 | 34244 |
| 293520 | 293520 |
| 32776.4 | 32776.400 |

# Part F Business Applications

Once or twice a year, many companies take a **physical inventory** in which all items on hand are counted and recorded. Usually this is done by departments. The inventory sheets generally show the stock number of each item carried and have columns for the quantity, the unit price, and the extension. While the multiplication may be done by a computer, often it is done on a calculating machine.

Most large retail stores now have cash registers linked to a computer so that a running inventory can be kept. By the end of a half-year or a year, this inventory may not be accurate. The physical inventory provides a check on the computer's inventory.

When the unit price is given in cents, the price in cents must be changed to a decimal before multiplying. This is done by dropping the cent sign and moving the decimal point two places to the left. Since most prices do not show a decimal point, put one after the last digit and then move the point. If there is a fractional ending, change the price to a complete decimal after the point has been moved. (See Part D of this section.)

*Examples:*  Change the cents to decimals.

a.  15¢ = .15¢ = .15

b.  5¼¢ = .05¼¢ = .0525

c.  ½¢ = .00½¢ = .005

After the quantities and the unit prices have been recorded, each quantity is multiplied by its unit price. This is called **extending** the inventory. (An **extension** is a multiplication.) When all the extensions have been completed, they are added to get the entire inventory for the department. As a last step, all the department inventories are added to get the complete inventory for the business.

Because even a department inventory is very long, the examples below show only a few typical extensions.

| Item | Quantity | Unit Price | Extension |
|---|---|---|---|
| Y-264 | 324 | 14½¢ (.145) | $ 46.98 |
| 4603 | 856 | 3½¢ (.035) | 29.96 |
| M-4802 | 19 | 7.61 | 144.59 |
| C-510 | 4,792 | ¼¢ (.0025) | 11.98 |

Complete Assignment 4

## Assignment 4
## Section 1-4

*Multiplication of Decimals*

|  | Perfect Score | Student's Score |
|---|---|---|
| Part A | 20 | |
| Part B | 10 | |
| Part C | 20 | |
| Part D | 10 | |
| Part E | 30 | |
| Part F | 10 | |
| TOTAL | 100 | |

# Part A

### *Multiplying a Decimal by a Decimal or a Whole Number*

*Directions:* Multiply and check. (1 point for each correct answer)

1.  $\begin{array}{r} 6 \\ \times\ .7 \\ \hline \end{array}$

2.  $\begin{array}{r} 9.36 \\ \times\ .4 \\ \hline \end{array}$

3.  $\begin{array}{r} 250 \\ \times\ .8 \\ \hline \end{array}$

4.  $\begin{array}{r} 4.006 \\ \times\ .5 \\ \hline \end{array}$

5.  $\begin{array}{r} .871 \\ \times\ .3 \\ \hline \end{array}$

6.  $\begin{array}{r} 4.2 \\ \times\ .16 \\ \hline \end{array}$

7.  $\begin{array}{r} 2.7 \\ \times\ 3.6 \\ \hline \end{array}$

8.  $\begin{array}{r} 8.02 \\ \times\ .17 \\ \hline \end{array}$

9.  $\begin{array}{r} 9.614 \\ \times\ .49 \\ \hline \end{array}$

10.  $\begin{array}{r} 18 \\ \times\ 2.187 \\ \hline \end{array}$

11.  $\begin{array}{r} 5.2 \\ \times\ 8.642 \\ \hline \end{array}$

12.  $\begin{array}{r} .071 \\ \times\ 3.09 \\ \hline \end{array}$

13.  $\begin{array}{r} 29.6 \\ \times\ 7.12 \\ \hline \end{array}$

14.  $\begin{array}{r} 23.8 \\ \times\ 925 \\ \hline \end{array}$

15.  $\begin{array}{r} 5.23 \\ \times\ 8.14 \\ \hline \end{array}$

16.  $\begin{array}{r} 3,560 \\ \times\ 4.03 \\ \hline \end{array}$

17.  $\begin{array}{r} 89.76 \\ \times\ .486 \\ \hline \end{array}$

18.  $\begin{array}{r} 1,009.8 \\ \times\ 30.05 \\ \hline \end{array}$

19.  $\begin{array}{r} 7.4019 \\ \times\ 8.007 \\ \hline \end{array}$

20.  $\begin{array}{r} 65.7314 \\ \times\ 500.08 \\ \hline \end{array}$

*Student's Score* _____

# Part B

## Prefixing Zeros in the Product

*Directions:* Multiply and check. (1 point for each correct answer)

| | | | |
|---|---|---|---|
| 21.    8<br>× .006 | 22.    28.7<br>× .003 | 23.    .89<br>× .04 | 24.    .007<br>× .098 |
| 25.    .105<br>× .054 | 26.    .198<br>× .075 | 27.    .1074<br>× .093 | 28.    4.06<br>× .0038 |
| 29.    1.009<br>× .00687 | 30.    .0562<br>× .00875 | | |

*Student's Score* _____

# Part C

## Rounding Off to a Given Number of Places

*Directions:* Round off to the number of places indicated by the columnar headings. (1 point for each correct answer)

| | One Place | Two Places | | | Three Places | Four Places |
|---|---|---|---|---|---|---|
| 31. 3.4375 | _____ | | 41. 36.63705 | | _____ | |
| 32. 16.8249 | _____ | | 42. 54.6135 | | _____ | |
| 33. .05098 | _____ | | 43. .00117 | | _____ | |
| 34. 99.995 | _____ | | 44. .1486 | | _____ | |
| 35. 10.9949 | _____ | | 45. 10.999549 | | _____ | |
| 36. 8.66666 | | _____ | 46. 10.999549 | | | _____ |
| 37. .0171 | | _____ | 47. .30002 | | | _____ |
| 38. .00171 | | _____ | 48. 99.999995 | | | _____ |
| 39. 1.65082 | | _____ | 49. 99.9999499 | | | _____ |
| 40. .0094949 | | _____ | 50. 49.494949 | | | _____ |

*Student's Score* _____

# Part D

## Multiplying by a Decimal with a Fractional Ending

**Directions:** Multiply and check. Change the decimal with a fractional ending to a complete decimal. (1 point for each correct answer)

51.  5.12½
   ×  .4

52.  8.37½
   ×  .5

53.  2.9
   × .62½

54.  2.75
   × .06¼

55.  5.836
   × .43¾

56.  .93¾
   × 28.4

57.  9.054
   × .33⅓

58.  7.66⅔
   × 83.1

59.  4,500.3
   ×  .16⅔

60.  3,222.5
   × .833⅓

*Student's Score* _____

# Part E

## Multiplying by Ten and Its Multiples

**Directions:** Multiply by moving the decimal point only. (1 point for each correct answer)

61. 78.6 × 10

62. 10 × 100.011

63. .0235 × 100

64. 96 × 100

65. .005 × 1,000

66. 85.5 × 1,000

67. .009 × 10,000

68. 10,000 × .0001

69. 100 × 1.35

70. 1,200 × 100

71. 2.3 × 1,000

72. 9.6351 × 1,000

73. 10 × .029

74. 11.0083 × 10

75. 7.3 × 1,000

76. 1,000 × 48.9

77. 10,000 × .6

78. 37.04 × 10,000

79. 21.5 × 100,000

80. 100,000 × .035

*Student's Score* _____

**Directions:** Multiply by using shortcuts. (1 point for each correct answer)

81. 2.5 × 320

82. 78.5 × 200

83. .064 × 1,200

84. 1.34 × 6,800

85. .0027 × 7,100

86. 325,000 × .409

87. .139 × 65,000

88. 7,200 × .058

89. 1.906 × 250,000

90. 68.75 × 4,900

*Student's Score* _____

# Part F

## Business Applications

**Directions:** Extend the inventory and find the total. (1 point for each correct answer) Abbreviations: cs. = case; # or lb = pound; bbl. = barrel; a unit price followed by one of the abbreviations means the cost of one unit per item.

| Quantity | Unit Price | Extension | | WORK SPACE |
|---|---|---|---|---|
| 91. 82 cs. | $3.75 cs. | $_____ | | |
| 92. 409# | 3¾¢ lb | _____ | | |
| 93. 675 lb | 7½¢ lb | _____ | | |
| 94. 55 cs. | 2.37½ cs. | _____ | | |
| 95. 2,400# | 6½¢ lb | _____ | | |
| 96. 3,550# | 5¼¢ lb | _____ | | |
| 97. 30 cs. | 11.98 cs. | _____ | | |
| 98. 17 bbl. | 6.95 bbl. | _____ | | |
| 99. 250 lb | 8½¢ lb | _____ | | |
| **100.** | TOTAL | _____ | | |

*Student's Score* _____

# Section 1-5   Division of Decimals

Of the four arithmetic operations, division occurs the least often. It is used to find averages, to figure percents, to distribute expenses, etc.

**Division** is the operation of finding how many times one number is contained in another. The **dividend** is the number being divided. The **divisor** is the number by which the dividend is divided; in other words, it is the number which "goes into" the dividend. The divisor is the number after the division sign, and it is written on the outside of the division form. The divisor may be smaller than, equal to, or larger than the dividend. The **quotient** is the answer to the division. If the division does not come out exactly, there is a **remainder**.

*Example:*  $4,064 \div 32 = 127$

$$\text{(divisor) } 32\overline{)4064} \text{ (dividend)} \quad 127 \text{ (quotient)}$$

Division is checked by multiplying the quotient by the divisor and adding the remainder if there is one. If the check is done with a rounded-off quotient, the product will be a little more or a little less than the original dividend.

Here are some division facts you should know:

1. Any number divided by itself is always 1.

2. Any number divided by 1 is always the same number.

3. Zero divided by any number is always 0. You cannot divide any number by 0; it is impossible.

## Part A   Review of Division with Whole Numbers

When dividing with the division form, it is important to place the quotient figures in their correct positions. The first quotient figure must be put directly above the last digit in the first partial dividend. Each of the remaining quotient figures must be placed directly above the dividend digit which was brought down. Many errors are caused by writing the quotient figures carelessly.

*Example:*  $407,872 \div 32$

| Method #1 | Method #2 | Check |
|---|---|---|
| | | 12746 |
| | | $\times \quad 32$ |
| 12746 | 12746 | 25492 |
| $32\overline{)407872}$ | $32\overline{)407872}$ | 382380 |
| 32 | 320000 | 407872 |
| 87 | 87872 | |
| 64 | 64000 | |
| 238 | 23872 | |
| 224 | 22400 | |
| 147 | 1472 | |
| 128 | 1280 | |
| 192 | 192 | |
| 192 | 192 | |
| — | — | |

Most of you perform division as shown in Method #1 above. Some of you, however, have learned to divide as shown in Method #2. In Method #2, the full positional value of the quotient digit is used to multiply by the divisor. In this case, the first digit in the quotient, 1, is taken as 10,000; so, $32 \times 10,000 = 320,000$. The next quotient digit, 2, is taken as 2,000; so, $32 \times 2,000 = 64,000$, etc. Only Method #1 is used in the rest of the examples that follow.

When the divisor has two or more digits, the use of a **trial divisor** helps in finding how many times the divisor goes into the dividend. The trial divisor is the first digit in the actual divisor if the second digit is less than 5.

*Example:*  $629\overline{)18982}$  with quotient digit 3

Note that 6 is used as the trial divisor since the second digit in 629 is 2. 6 goes into 18 three times; but since the actual divisor is 629, the division is 629 into 1898. The quotient digit 3 is written above the second 8.

If the second digit in the actual divisor is 5 or more, the trial divisor is one more than the first digit.

*Example:*  $692\overline{)18982}$  with quotient digit 2

Note that 7 is used as the trial divisor since the second digit in 692 is 9, which is 5 or more. 7

goes into 18 twice; so, the 2 is written above the second 8 of 1898, as shown.

There is one step in division that is often omitted and may cause errors. After subtracting and before bringing down the next dividend figure, always check the remainder of the subtraction just performed. If it is equal to or larger than the actual divisor, it means that the quotient figure used is not large enough and must be changed to at least one more.

*Example:*
$$\begin{array}{r} 2 \\ 62\overline{)18982} \\ \underline{124} \\ 65 \end{array}$$

Note that 65 is larger than 62. This means that the quotient digit 2 is too small. Change the 2 to a 3 before continuing the division, as follows:

$$\begin{array}{r} 3 \\ 62\overline{)18982} \\ \underline{186} \\ 3 \end{array}$$

If you had divided the 62 into the 65, there would be no place to put the 1. You cannot put it over the second 8 of 1898 since this 8 was not brought down.

After a dividend digit has been brought down to make the next partial dividend but the divisor is larger than this partial dividend, a zero must be put in the quotient above the digit brought down.

*Example:*
$$\begin{array}{r} 4009 \ \text{R} \ 123 \\ 246\overline{)986337} \\ \underline{984} \\ 2337 \\ \underline{2214} \\ 123 \end{array}$$

Check
$$\begin{array}{r} 4009 \\ \times \ 246 \\ \hline 24054 \\ 160360 \\ \underline{801800} \\ 986214 \\ + \quad 123 \\ \hline 986337 \end{array}$$

Note that in the second step of the last example, when the first 3 is brought down, the partial dividend is 23, which does not contain 246. A zero is written in the quotient above the 3. When the next 3 is brought down, the partial dividend is 233, which still does not contain 246. Therefore, another zero is written over the second 3. Care must be taken to place the zeros over the digits that were brought down. Otherwise, one or both of the zeros may be omitted carelessly.

When the divisor is a single digit, **short division** may be used. In this process, the subtraction and multiplication are done mentally. Only the quotient figures are written.

*Example:* $142,536 \div 6 = 23,756$

$$\begin{array}{r} 2\ 3\ 7\ 5\ 6 \\ 6\overline{)1\ 4\ {}^2 2\ {}^4 5\ {}^3 3\ {}^3 6} \end{array}$$

The five steps in their order are:

1. $14 \div 6 = 2$. $2 \times 6 = 12$. $14 - 12 = 2$.

2. Carry the 2 to the next dividend digit to make it 22. $22 \div 6 = 3$. $3 \times 6 = 18$. $22 - 18 = 4$.

3. Carry the 4 to the next dividend digit to make it 45. $45 \div 6 = 7$. $7 \times 6 = 42$. $45 - 42 = 3$.

4. Carry the 3 to the next dividend digit to make it 33. $33 \div 6 = 5$. $5 \times 6 = 30$. $33 - 30 = 3$.

5. Carry the 3 to the next dividend digit to make it 36. $36 \div 6 = 6$.

## Part B  Dividing a Decimal by a Decimal

The decimal point of the quotient must be fixed before starting the division. Since division can be done with only a whole number divisor, the decimal point in the divisor must be moved to the end. Then the decimal point in the dividend must be moved the same number of places to the right. The decimal point for the quotient is then placed directly above the new decimal point of the dividend. It may be necessary to add zeros to the dividend to have enough places.

*Example:* Divide to four places and round off the quotient to three decimal places: $.59 \div 1.8$

```
        .3277 = .328        Check
 1x8. /x5.9000
        5 4                .3277              .328
        50          × 1.8    or      × 1.8
        36          26216            2624
       140          32770            3280
       126          58986            .5904
       140        +    14
       126          .59000
        14
```

Note that three zeros were added to the dividend to extend the division. The quotient was rounded to .328, a little more than the actual answer. Therefore, when .328 is used for the check, the product is a little more than the actual dividend.

When the quotient must be carried out to a certain number of places, it may be necessary to extend the division by adding zeros to the dividend.

*Example:*  63.9 ÷ 2.457

```
              26.0073 = 26.007
    2x457. / 63x900.0000
             49 14
             14 760
             14 742
                18000
                17199
                 8010
                 7371
                  639
```

**Check**

```
   26.0073                        26.007
 ×   2.457        or            ×  2.457
  1820511                        182049
 13003650                       1300350
104029200                     10402800
520146000                     52014000
638999361                     63.899199
+      639
63.9000000
```

Note that, first, two zeros were added to fix the decimal point; then four more zeros were added to extend the division. The rounded quotient is a little less than the actual answer. Therefore, when 26.007 is used for the check, the product is a little less than the actual dividend.

For the student's interest, when the divisor decimal point is moved to the end, it is the same as multiplying the divisor by 10, 100, 1,000, etc., depending on the number of places moved to the right. In order not to change the problem, the dividend must also be multiplied by the same number by moving its decimal point the same number of places to the right. In the first example, both the divisor and the dividend are multiplied by 10. The quotient of the original .59 ÷ 1.8 is the same as 5.9 ÷ 18.

*Part*
**C**  *Dividing a Decimal by a Whole Number*

When the dividend is a decimal and the divisor is a whole number, the decimal point of the dividend is *not* moved since the divisor already is a whole number. The dividend decimal point stays in the same place, and the quotient point is put directly above it.

*Examples:*  Divide and check.

a.  87.5 ÷ 25

```
            3.5              Check
     25 / 87.5
         75                   3.5
        125                  ×25
        125                  175
                             700
                             87.5
```

b.  3.3463 ÷ 307

```
           .0109             Check
    307 / 3.3463
         3 07                .0109
         2763               ×  307
         2763                 763
                            32700
                            3.3463
```

c. .095 ÷ 32

```
      .002968          Check
32 / .095000
     64                .002968
     310             ×      32
     288                 5936
     220                89040
     192                94976
     280             +      24
     256               .095000
      24
```

A common error is to move the dividend decimal point to the right as many places as there are digits in the divisor. This is wrong; the only time the dividend decimal point is moved is when the divisor has a decimal point.

## Part D  Dividing a Whole Number by a Decimal

When the dividend is a whole number and the divisor is a decimal, place a decimal point at the end of the whole number. Add as many zeros after that point as there are decimal places in the divisor. After that, move the decimal point in the divisor to the end; and then move the dividend decimal point the same number of places to the right. Note that the new decimal point in the dividend is always *after* the last zero added. Put the quotient decimal point directly above the new dividend decimal point.

*Example:* Divide and check: 750 ÷ .125

```
.125. / 750.000.
```

Put a decimal point after the 750 and add three zeros: 750.000. Then move the divisor point three places to the right, the dividend decimal point also three places to the right, and lastly, put a point in the quotient directly above the new dividend point as shown above. Then proceed as follows:

```
      6 000.                 Check
.125. / 750.000.  = 6,000      .125
                             ×   6000
                             750.000
```

---

a. Divide and check: 9 ÷ 42.78

```
42.78. / 9.00.
```

```
         .2103              Check
42.78. / 9.00.0000
         8 55 6              42.78
           44 40           ×  .2103
           42 78            12834
            1 6200          427800
            1 2834          8556000
              3366          8996634
                          +    3366
                           9.000000
```

b. How many quarters are there in five dollars? (One quarter = 25¢ = .25)

To find how many quarters there are, divide the five dollars by .25.

```
         20.              Check
.25. / 5.00.               .25
       5 0               ×  20
                          5.00
```

A common error is to put a decimal point before the whole number instead of after it and then move this point to the right. This is wrong. Putting a decimal point in front of a whole number changes it to a decimal; but putting a point after the whole number does not change its value. Think of $10 (ten dollars). Putting a point before the 10 changes it to .10 or 10¢. Putting a point after it, $10., does not change its value.

## Part E  Dividing One Whole Number by Another to Several Places

When both the divisor and the dividend are whole numbers, there is no decimal point to move. Place a point after the dividend and put the quotient decimal point directly above it. Add as many zeros after the dividend decimal point as are necessary for the required number of places.

*Example:* 527 ÷ 6. Round the quotient to four decimal places.

Using short division:

$$\begin{array}{r} 87.8333 \\ 6\overline{)527.0000} \end{array}$$

**Check**

$$\begin{array}{r} 87.8333 \\ \times \quad 6 \\ \hline 526.9998 \\ = 527 \end{array}$$

This is also the method used to find the decimal form of a common fraction. The numerator is divided by the denominator to as many places as are required.

*Example:* $13 \div 32$

$$\begin{array}{r} .40625 = .4063 \\ 32\overline{)13.00000} \\ \underline{12\ 8} \\ 200 \\ \underline{192} \\ 80 \\ \underline{64} \\ 160 \\ \underline{160} \end{array}$$

**Check**

$$\begin{array}{r} .40625 \\ \times \quad 32 \\ \hline 81250 \\ 1218750 \\ \hline 13.00000 \end{array}$$

Note that the above division is the same as would be done to find the decimal form of 13/32. The numerator, 13, is divided by the denominator, 32. The decimal form of a common fraction is often called its **decimal equivalent**.

*Example:* Find the decimal equivalent of $\frac{7}{125}$.

$$\begin{array}{r} .056 \\ 125\overline{)7.000} \\ \underline{6\ 25} \\ 750 \\ \underline{750} \end{array}$$

**Check**

$$\begin{array}{r} 125 \\ \times\ .056 \\ \hline 750 \\ 6250 \\ \hline 7.000 \end{array}$$

## Part F Dividing with Numbers in Different Forms

When either the dividend or the divisor is a decimal and the other is a common fraction or a mixed number, generally it is better to do the division entirely in decimals. If the numbers are small, the division may be done entirely in fractions, as shown in Chapter 2.

Before starting the division, change the common fraction or mixed number to its decimal form. Then divide in the usual way.

*Examples:* (The details of the division and check are left to the student.)

a. $18.4 \div 7\frac{1}{8}$

$$\begin{array}{r} .125 \\ 8\overline{)1.000} \end{array}$$

$7\frac{1}{8} = 7.125$

$$\begin{array}{r} 2.58245 = 2.5825 \\ 7.125.\overline{)18,400.00000} \end{array}$$

b. $8\frac{39}{40} \div 5.6$

$$\begin{array}{r} .975 \\ 40\overline{)39.000} \end{array}$$

$8\frac{39}{40} = 8.975$

$$\begin{array}{r} 1.60267 = 1.6027 \\ 5.6.\overline{)8.9.75000} \end{array}$$

## Part G Dividing by Ten and Its Multiples

When the divisor is 10, 100, 1,000, etc., the division can be done by only moving the decimal point. The point is moved to the left as many places as there are zeros in the divisor.

When the dividend is a whole number, put a decimal point at the end of the number. To divide any whole number by 10, move its decimal point one place to the left. To divide any whole number by 100, move its decimal point two places to the left. To divide any whole number by 1,000, move the point three places to the left, etc. Prefix zeros as necessary.

*Examples:* Divide by moving the dividend decimal point only.

a. $234 \div 10 = 234. \div 10 = 23.4 = 23.4$

b. $31 \div 100 = 31. \div 100 = .31 = .31$

c. $5 \div 1,000 = 5. \div 1,000 = .005 = .005$

d. $48,562 \div 10,000 = 48,562. \div 10,000 = 4.8562 = 4.8562$

To divide any decimal by 10, 100, 1,000, etc., move its decimal point to the left as many places as there are zeros in the divisor. This is the same as with whole numbers. Prefix zeros as necessary to move the correct number of places. Never divide the long way.

*Examples:* Divide by moving the dividend decimal point only.

a. $16.76 \div 10 = 1.6\,76 = 1.676$

b. $5.946 \div 100 = .05\,946 = .05946$

c. $7,003.5 \div 1,000 = 7.003\,5 = 7.0035$

d. $60.75 \div 10,000 = .0060\,75 = .006075$

e. $42.914 \div 100,000 = .00042\,914$
$= .00042914$

When the divisor is a multiple of 10, other than 100, 1,000, etc., it can be expressed as some number times 10, 100, 1,000, etc. (For example, the divisor 5700 can be expressed as $57 \times 100$.) The division then is performed in two steps as shown in the example below.

*Example:* $4,653 \div 5,700$

5,700 is the same as $57 \times 100$

1. Divide by the 10, 100, 1,000, etc., by moving the decimal point of the dividend to the left. In this example,

$$4,653 \div 100 = 46.53$$

2. Divide by the other factor of the original divisor. In this example,

$$
\begin{array}{r}
.8163 \\
57\,\overline{\smash{)}\,46.5300} \\
45\ 6 \\ \hline
93 \\
57 \\ \hline
360 \\
342 \\ \hline
180 \\
171 \\ \hline
9 \ \text{(remainder)}
\end{array}
$$

The advantage of using the above method is that the end zeros in the original divisor are eliminated, thus simplifying the division.

Here is another example:

$2,798.05 \div 45,000$

45,000 is the same as $45 \times 1,000$

$2,798.05 \div 1,000 = 2.79805$

$$
\begin{array}{r}
.06217 \\
45\,\overline{\smash{)}\,2.79805} \\
2\ 70 \\ \hline
98 \\
90 \\ \hline
80 \\
45 \\ \hline
355 \\
315 \\ \hline
40 \ \text{(remainder)}
\end{array}
$$

Part
# H  Business Applications

In analyzing sales, costs, etc., an average often is desired. An **average** shows "about" what each number is in a group of figures. It is found by adding all the figures in the group and dividing this sum by the number of figures added.

*Examples:*

a. Find the average of the following grades: 83, 94, 88, 100, 96, 80, 79, 86.

The sum of the eight grades is 706. Then,

$$
\begin{array}{r}
88.25 \\
8\,\overline{\smash{)}\,706.00}
\end{array} = \text{average grade}
$$

b. The Jones Variety Store had sales of $23,590.78 for a period of 25 days. Find the average daily sales.

The sum of the daily sales is given. Then,

$$
\begin{array}{r}
943.631 \\
25\,\overline{\smash{)}\,23590.780}
\end{array} = \begin{array}{l} \$943.63 \text{ is} \\ \text{the average} \\ \text{daily sales} \end{array}
$$

**Complete Assignment 5**

## Assignment 5
## Section 1-5

### Division of Decimals

|  | Perfect Score | Student's Score |
|---|---|---|
| Part A | 8 | |
| Part B | 32 | |
| Part C | 8 | |
| Part D | 16 | |
| Part E | 8 | |
| Part F | 8 | |
| Part G | 16 | |
| Part H | 4 | |
| TOTAL | 100 | |

## Part A

### Review of Division with Whole Numbers

*Directions:* Find the quotient by short division and check. (1 point for each correct answer)

1. $2\overline{)348}$

2. $4\overline{)596}$

3. $3\overline{)3066}$

4. $2\overline{)69534}$

5. $5\overline{)2160}$

6. $8\overline{)2456}$

7. $9\overline{)60372}$

8. $7\overline{)21063}$

Student's Score _____

## Part B

### Dividing a Decimal by a Decimal

*Directions:* Divide and check. Round off the answer to three decimal places where necessary. (2 points for each correct answer)

9. $.4\overline{)7.2}$

10. $.5\overline{)2.8}$

11. $.06\overline{)2.807}$

12. $.09\overline{).33}$

13. $.0035\overline{).7}$

14. $.018\overline{)5.4}$

15. $.48\overline{).03883}$

16. $.086\overline{).00488}$

17. $.25\overline{)89.1}$

18. $2.5\overline{)43.675}$

19. $.0079\overline{).553}$

20. $.0038\overline{).0532}$

21. $4.836 \div 32.9$

22. $10.6 \div 2.36$

23. $1.414 \div 7.28$

24. $1.5 \div 1.135$

Student's Score _____

# Part C

## *Dividing a Decimal by a Whole Number*

*Directions:* Divide and check. Round off the answer to three decimal places where necessary. (2 points for each correct answer)

25. 23.2 ÷ 56

26. 45.815 ÷ 49

27. 5.428 ÷ 236

28. 3.59 ÷ 506

*Student's Score* _____

# Part D

## *Dividing a Whole Number by a Decimal*

*Directions:* Divide and check. Round off the answer to three decimal places where necessary. (2 points for each correct answer)

29. 14 ÷ 4.2

30. 329 ÷ .47

31. 646 ÷ .095

32. 504 ÷ .056

33. 112 ÷ .875

34. 38,927 ÷ 4.69

35. 6,642 ÷ 7.38

36. 567 ÷ 24.3

*Student's Score* _____

42

# Part E

## *Dividing One Whole Number by Another to Several Places*

*Directions:* Divide and check. Round off the answer to four decimal places where necessary. (1 point for each correct answer)

37. 2 ÷ 25          38. 6 ÷ 125          39. 125 ÷ 24          40. 463 ÷ 37

*Directions:* Find the decimal equivalents. Round off the answer to four decimal places. (1 point for each correct answer)

41. $\frac{7}{18}$          42. $\frac{9}{16}$          43. $\frac{8}{15}$          44. $\frac{5}{33}$

*Student's Score* _____

# Part F

## *Dividing with Numbers in Different Forms*

*Directions:* Divide in decimals and check. Round off the answer to three decimal places where necessary. (2 points for each correct answer)

45. $2\frac{1}{2}$ ÷ .05          46. $9\frac{1}{4}$ ÷ .4          47. 2.09375 ÷ $\frac{9}{16}$          48. 34.65 ÷ $5\frac{31}{40}$

*Student's Score* _____

# Part G

## Dividing by Ten and Its Multiples

*Directions:* Divide by moving the decimal point only. (1 point for each correct answer)

49. 473 ÷ 10

50. 56.7 ÷ 10

51. 63.9 ÷ 100

52. 3,840 ÷ 100

53. 8.44 ÷ 1,000

54. 75 ÷ 1,000

55. 57.6 ÷ 10,000

56. 80 ÷ 10,000

57. .005 ÷ 10

58. .0963 ÷ 100

59. 67,540 ÷ 1,000

60. 36.4 ÷ 10,000

*Directions:* Divide by using a shortcut and check. (1 point for each correct answer)

61. 28.35 ÷ 3,000

62. 22.4 ÷ 700

63. 28.4 ÷ 7,100

64. 539.4 ÷ 62,000

*Student's Score* _____

# Part H

## Business Applications

*Directions:* Solve the problem as indicated and write your answers in the spaces provided. (2 points for each correct answer)

65. Find the average of these grades: 95, 93, 85, 89, 91, 78, 88, 92, 75.

66. Jane's Custard Stand is open every day during the summer. The total sales for July were $78,472.25. What was the average daily sales?

Ans. _____

Ans. _____

*Student's Score* _____

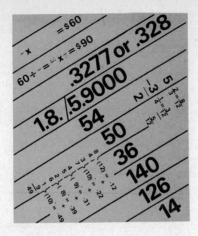

CHAPTER
2

# Working with Fractions

Fractions, as such, are not used as much as decimals in the modern business world. They are used enough, however, for you to understand how to work with them.

A **fraction** can be defined as one or more of the equal parts into which a unit (one whole thing) has been divided. This leads to another definition which is useful. A fraction also can mean that one number is to be divided by another number, with the fraction line taking the place of the division sign.

Fractions are numbers just as whole numbers and decimals are numbers. There are rules for adding, subtracting, multiplying, and dividing with fractions, just as there are rules for working with whole numbers and decimals.

## Section 2-1  Types of Fractions

A **common fraction** has a whole number above the line and a whole number below the line, such as $\frac{3}{4}$. The number above the line is called the **numerator,** and the number below the line is called the **denominator.** Together they are called the **terms** of the fraction. The form of the common fraction, $\frac{3}{4}$, is different from the form of the **decimal fraction**, .75, which is equal to it.

From the second definition given above, the fraction line also may show division; that is,

$\frac{3}{4}$ can also mean $4\overline{)3}$.

A common fraction may be proper or improper. In a **proper fraction,** the numerator is smaller than the denominator. For example:

$$\frac{3}{4}, \frac{9}{10}, \frac{11}{115}$$

In an **improper fraction,** the numerator is larger than the denominator. For example:

$$\frac{32}{30}, \frac{7}{4}, \frac{19}{12}$$

A **mixed number** is a whole number followed by a proper fraction. For example:

$$1\frac{3}{4}, \ 15\frac{2}{3}, \ 54\frac{7}{9}$$

Generally when the word "fraction" is used, it refers to a proper fraction.

### Part A  Changing a Common Fraction to Higher Terms

If both the numerator and the denominator of a common fraction are multiplied by the same number, the value of the fraction is not changed. In effect, this is the same as multiplying the fraction by one. When both the numerator and the denominator are multiplied by the same number, the fraction is said to be changed to **higher terms** or to an **equivalent fraction.**

*Examples:* Change to higher terms.

a. $\frac{3}{4} \times \frac{2}{2} = \frac{3 \times 2}{4 \times 2} = \frac{6}{8}$

b. $\frac{5}{6} \times \frac{7}{7} = \frac{5 \times 7}{6 \times 7} = \frac{35}{42}$

c. $\frac{7}{8} \times \frac{10}{10} = \frac{7 \times 10}{8 \times 10} = \frac{70}{80}$

To change a common fraction to higher terms with a given denominator, divide the denominator of the fraction into the new given denominator; then multiply both the old numerator and denominator by this quotient.

*Examples:* Change to higher terms with the new denominators.

a. Change $\frac{2}{3}$ to 24ths.

$$24 \div 3 = 8$$

$$\frac{2}{3} = \frac{2 \times 8}{3 \times 8} = \frac{16}{24}$$

b. Change $\frac{5}{8}$ to 32nds.

$$32 \div 8 = 4$$

$$\frac{5}{8} = \frac{5 \times 4}{8 \times 4} = \frac{20}{32}$$

c. Change $\frac{4}{3}$ to 27ths.

$$27 \div 3 = 9$$

$$\frac{4}{3} = \frac{4 \times 9}{3 \times 9} = \frac{99}{27}$$

## Part B — Reducing a Common Fraction to Lower Terms

Reducing a common fraction to lower terms is the opposite of changing a fraction to higher terms. In reducing, both the numerator and the denominator are divided by a number which goes exactly into each. In effect, this is the same as dividing the fraction by one, which does not change its value. A fraction is in **lowest terms** when no number except one will divide exactly into both the numerator and the denominator. When the number used in the division is the largest one possible, it is called the **greatest common divisor**. This is often abbreviated to G.C.D.

*Examples:* Reduce by using the G.C.D.

a. $\frac{30}{45} = \frac{30 \div 15}{45 \div 15} = \frac{2}{3}$

b. $\frac{36}{48} = \frac{36 \div 12}{48 \div 12} = \frac{3}{4}$

It is not absolutely necessary to use the G.C.D. in reducing fractions to their lowest terms. Another method of reducing fractions is **cancellation**, where both the numerator and the denominator are divided by a common divisor without showing what the common divisor is. If the greatest common divisor is not used the first time, the process is repeated until there is no further common divisor.

*Examples:* Reduce to lowest terms by cancellation.

a. $\frac{70}{84} = \frac{70}{84} = \frac{5}{6}$   The common divisors canceled in turn are 2 and 7.

b. $\frac{36}{90} = \frac{36}{90} = \frac{2}{5}$   The common divisors canceled in turn are 2, 3, and 3.

The cancellation in *Example b* could be shortened. After the first cancellation by 2, the result is $\frac{18}{45}$. The next divisor could be 9 to get the same result.

$$\frac{36}{90} = \frac{36}{90} = \frac{2}{5}$$

Even simpler, if the G.C.D. of 18 is seen easily, only one cancellation is needed.

$$\frac{36}{90} = \frac{36}{90} = \frac{2}{5}$$

c.

$$\frac{105}{420} = \frac{\cancel{105}}{\cancel{420}} = \frac{1}{4}$$

The common divisors canceled in turn are 3, 5, and 7.

(shown cancellation column: 1, 7, 35, 105, 420, 140, 28, 4)

In *Example c,* note that the numerator is canceled down to a 1. It is important to write the "1" in order to get the correct answer. If it is not written, the answer might be read carelessly as 4 instead of the correct $\frac{1}{4}$.

d. $\dfrac{800}{1,200}$

In *Example d,* the two end zeros in each term show that each contains 100. The cancellation by 100 can be done by crossing out the two zeros in both the top and bottom terms. The $\frac{8}{12}$ that is left is then reduced.

$$\frac{800}{1,200} = \frac{8\cancel{00}}{12\cancel{00}} = \frac{\cancel{8}}{\cancel{12}} = \frac{2}{3}$$

(cancellation: 2 above 8, 3 below 12)

The following steps will help you to find common divisors for use in cancellation. (The first 3 steps are called **divisibility rules.**)

1. If a number is even, it is divisible by at least 2.

*Example:* Reduce $\frac{14}{24}$ to lowest terms.

$$\frac{14}{24} = \frac{\cancel{14}}{\cancel{24}} = \frac{7}{12}$$

(cancellation: 7 above 14, 12 below 24)

2. If the digits in a number are added together and their sum is a number which contains 3 exactly, then the entire number is also divisible by 3.

*Example:* Reduce $\frac{12}{57}$ to lowest terms.

The sum of the digits in 12: $1 + 2 = 3$.
The sum of the digits in 57: $5 + 7 = 12$.

Since both sums are exactly divisible by 3, then 3 can be canceled into both 12 and 57.

$$\frac{12}{57} = \frac{\cancel{12}}{\cancel{57}} = \frac{4}{19}$$

(cancellation: 4 above 12, 19 below 57)

3. If the last digit of a number is a 0 or a 5, the number is divisible by 5.

*Example:* Reduce $\frac{60}{115}$ to lowest terms.

$$\frac{60}{115} = \frac{\cancel{60}}{\cancel{115}} = \frac{12}{23}$$

(cancellation: 12 above 60, 23 below 115)

4. If a common divisor cannot be found by any of the divisibility rules, a trial-and-error method of trying the prime numbers can be used. A **prime number** is any number greater than 1 that can be divided by only itself and one. The prime numbers are: 2, 3, 5, 7, 11, 13, 17, 19, 23, 29, 31, 37, etc. If the divisibility rules show that both the numerator and the denominator do not contain a 2, 3, or 5, the prime numbers are tried in turn to see if there is one that can be divided exactly into both. If a prime number is found, it becomes a common divisor that can be canceled into both the numerator and the denominator.

*Examples:* Reduce to lowest terms.

a. $\frac{33}{110}$

By trying the divisibility rules in order, you find that:

(1) 33 is odd, so 2 cannot be canceled into both terms.
(2) 33 contains a 3, but 110 does not $(1 + 1 + 0 = 2$, which is not divisible by 3).
(3) 33 does not end in either 0 or 5; so 5 cannot be canceled.
(4) Trying the prime numbers, you find that 7 does not go exactly into either 33 or 110. By trying 11, you find that $33 \div 11 = 3$ and $110 \div 11 = 10$. Therefore, 11 can be canceled into both terms.

$$\frac{33}{110} = \frac{\cancel{33}}{\cancel{110}} = \frac{3}{10}$$

(cancellation: 3 above 33, 10 below 110)

**b.** $\frac{57}{133}$

By trying the divisibility rules on 57 and 133 together, you can see that 2, 3, or 5 cannot be canceled. Further, the prime numbers 7, 11, 13, or 17 cannot be canceled. But $57 = 3 \times 19$ and $133 = 7 \times 19$; therefore, 19 is a common divisor and can be canceled.

$$\frac{57}{133} = \frac{\overset{3}{\cancel{57}}}{\underset{7}{\cancel{133}}} = \frac{3}{7}$$

Sometimes a fraction looks as if it cannot be reduced any further. In this case, factoring the numerator and denominator separately may show a common prime number.

**Examples:** Reduce to lowest terms.

**a.** $\frac{69}{184}$

$$69 = 3 \times 23$$
$$184 = \underbrace{2 \times 2 \times 2}_{8} \times 23$$

$$\frac{69}{184} = \frac{\overset{3}{\cancel{69}}}{\underset{8}{\cancel{184}}} = \frac{3}{8}$$

**b.** $\frac{26}{133}$

$$26 = 2 \times 13$$
$$133 = 7 \times 19$$

In *Example b* there are no common factors to cancel. This means that the fraction is in its lowest terms.

## Part C — Changing Mixed Numbers into Improper Fractions and Improper Fractions into Mixed Numbers

To change a mixed number to an improper fraction, multiply the whole number by the denominator of the fraction. Then add the numerator to this product, putting the sum over the denominator to form the improper fraction.

**Example:** Change $7\frac{3}{8}$ to an improper fraction.

$$7 \times 8 + 3 = 59; \quad 7\frac{3}{8} = \frac{59}{8}$$

To change an improper fraction to a mixed number, divide the numerator by the denominator only as far as the whole number part. The remainder is put over the denominator to form the fractional part of the mixed number. (The fractional part may have to be reduced to lowest terms.) If there is no remainder, the answer is a whole number.

**Examples:** Change to a mixed number or to a whole number.

**a.** $\frac{250}{8}$ $\quad 8\overline{)250}^{\,31\ R2}$ $\quad \frac{250}{8} = 31\frac{2}{8} = 31\frac{1}{4}$

**b.** $\frac{135}{15}$ $\quad 15\overline{)135}^{\,9} = 9$

## Part D — Changing a Decimal Fraction to a Common Fraction in Its Lowest Terms

To change a decimal fraction to a common fraction in lowest terms, first write the decimal fraction as a common fraction. The number after the decimal point is the numerator; the denominator is the place value which depends on the number of places after the point. (See the chart in Chapter 1, page 4.) Then, if necessary, reduce the common fraction to its lowest terms.

**Examples:** Change to common fractions in their lowest terms.

**a.** $.135 = \frac{135}{1,000} = \frac{\overset{27}{\cancel{135}}}{\underset{200}{\cancel{1,000}}} = \frac{27}{200}$

**b.** $.005 = \frac{\overset{1}{\cancel{5}}}{\underset{200}{\cancel{1,000}}} = \frac{1}{200}$

**c.** $.479 = \frac{479}{1,000}$ (Cannot be reduced.)

Complete Assignment 6

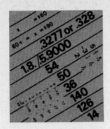

## Assignment 6
## Section 2-1

|  | Perfect Score | Student's Score |
|---|---|---|
| Part A | 20 | |
| Part B | 40 | |
| Part C | 20 | |
| Part D | 20 | |
| TOTAL | 100 | |

### Types of Fractions

# Part A

### Changing a Common Fraction to Higher Terms

*Directions:* Change the fractions to the higher terms indicated. (1 point for each correct answer)

1. $\dfrac{1}{2} = \dfrac{}{16}$

2. $\dfrac{2}{3} = \dfrac{}{12}$

3. $\dfrac{2}{3} = \dfrac{}{54}$

4. $\dfrac{1}{4} = \dfrac{}{56}$

5. $\dfrac{4}{5} = \dfrac{}{120}$

6. $\dfrac{5}{6} = \dfrac{}{96}$

7. $\dfrac{3}{7} = \dfrac{}{49}$

8. $\dfrac{3}{8} = \dfrac{}{112}$

9. $\dfrac{8}{9} = \dfrac{}{135}$

10. $\dfrac{7}{10} = \dfrac{}{140}$

11. $\dfrac{9}{11} = \dfrac{}{121}$

12. $\dfrac{11}{12} = \dfrac{}{156}$

13. $\dfrac{12}{13} = \dfrac{}{91}$

14. $\dfrac{11}{14} = \dfrac{}{98}$

15. $\dfrac{13}{15} = \dfrac{}{165}$

16. $\dfrac{15}{24} = \dfrac{}{144}$

17. $\dfrac{7}{20} = \dfrac{}{160}$

18. $\dfrac{21}{25} = \dfrac{}{150}$

19. $\dfrac{16}{27} = \dfrac{}{216}$

20. $\dfrac{23}{36} = \dfrac{}{288}$

Student's Score_____

# Part B

### Reducing a Common Fraction to Lower Terms

*Directions:* Reduce the fractions to lowest terms. (2 points for each correct answer)

21. $\dfrac{6}{8}$

22. $\dfrac{8}{10}$

23. $\dfrac{8}{12}$

24. $\dfrac{12}{25}$

25. $\dfrac{20}{32}$

26. $\dfrac{22}{33}$

27. $\dfrac{15}{35}$

28. $\dfrac{25}{40}$

29. $\dfrac{28}{42}$

30. $\dfrac{14}{91}$

31. $\dfrac{85}{255}$

32. $\dfrac{207}{299}$

33. $\frac{65}{114}$     34. $\frac{203}{319}$     35. $\frac{98}{161}$     36. $\frac{56}{197}$

37. $\frac{116}{1,000}$     38. $\frac{624}{1,000}$     39. $\frac{48}{2,000}$     40. $\frac{75}{2,000}$

*Student's Score* _____

# Part C

## *Changing Mixed Numbers into Improper Fractions and Improper Fractions into Mixed Numbers*

*Directions:* Change the mixed numbers to improper fractions. (1 point for each correct answer)

41. $3\frac{2}{3}$     42. $4\frac{3}{4}$     43. $19\frac{2}{5}$     44. $12\frac{5}{6}$

45. $18\frac{3}{7}$     46. $15\frac{1}{8}$     47. $3\frac{5}{9}$     48. $7\frac{9}{10}$

49. $10\frac{13}{16}$     50. $12\frac{16}{25}$

*Directions:* Change the improper fractions to mixed numbers or whole numbers. Reduce the fractions to lowest terms where necessary. (1 point for each correct answer)

51. $\frac{17}{2}$     52. $\frac{48}{5}$     53. $\frac{96}{16}$     54. $\frac{120}{24}$

55. $\frac{190}{114}$     56. $\frac{300}{48}$     57. $\frac{1,000}{36}$     58. $\frac{2,000}{58}$

59. $\frac{3,900}{114}$     60. $\frac{3,321}{72}$

*Student's Score* _____

# Part D

## *Changing a Decimal Fraction to a Common Fraction in Its Lowest Terms*

*Directions:* Change the decimal fractions to common fractions reduced to lowest terms. (2 points for each correct answer)

61. .05     62. .12     63. .125     64. .432

65. .0625     66. .0975     67. .568     68. .8126

69. .4399     70. .6278

*Student's Score* _____

# Section 2-2  Addition of Fractions

Fractions which have the same denominator or a **common denominator** are called **like terms**. When the denominators are different, they are called **unlike terms**. Before two or more fractions with different denominators can be added, they must be changed to higher terms all with the same denominator. In other words, only like terms can be added.

Most of the fractions used in business are halves, thirds, fourths, fifths, sixths, eighths, tenths, twelfths, and sixteenths. When addition involves some of these, it is easy to change them to like terms.

## Part A — Adding a Proper Fraction or a Mixed Number to a Whole Number

The sum of a whole number and a proper fraction is very easy to find. All that needs to be done is to put the fraction after the whole number. The sum is a mixed number.

*Examples:* Find the sum.

a. $5 + \frac{3}{8} = 5\frac{3}{8}$

b. $\frac{2}{3} + 12 = 12\frac{2}{3}$

The sum of a whole number and a mixed number is also easy to find. The two whole numbers are added and the fraction is put after their sum. The answer is a mixed number.

*Examples:* Find the sum.

a. $25 + 4\frac{7}{12} = 29\frac{7}{12}$

b. $30\frac{3}{10} + 21 = 51\frac{3}{10}$

## Part B — Adding Proper Fractions That Have a Common Denominator

To add proper fractions which have the same denominator (like terms), add their numerators and put this sum over the common denominator.

When the sum is an improper fraction, change it to a whole or a mixed number. Reduce the proper fraction to lowest terms where necessary.

*Examples:* Add the fractions.

a. $\frac{3}{8} + \frac{5}{8} = \frac{8}{8} = 1$

b. $\frac{11}{12} + \frac{7}{12} = \frac{18}{12} = 1\frac{6}{12} = 1\frac{1}{2}$

To add mixed numbers whose fractional parts have the same denominator, add the proper fractions first. Then add this sum to the total of the whole number parts.

*Examples:* Add the mixed numbers.

a. $4\frac{11}{12} + 5\frac{5}{12} + 11\frac{1}{12}$

$\frac{11}{12} + \frac{5}{12} + \frac{1}{12} = \frac{11+5+1}{12} = \frac{17}{12} = 1\frac{5}{12}$

$4 + 5 + 11 = 20$

$20 + 1\frac{5}{12} = 21\frac{5}{12}$

b. $8\frac{4}{15} + 6\frac{1}{15} + \frac{13}{15}$

$$\begin{array}{c|c} 8 & \frac{4}{15} \\ 6 & \frac{1}{15} \\ & \frac{13}{15} \\ \hline 14 & \frac{18}{15} = 1\frac{3}{15} = 1\frac{1}{5} \end{array}$$

$14 + 1\frac{1}{5} = 15\frac{1}{5}$

The form in *Example b* is preferred for finding the sum of three or more mixed numbers.

## Part C — Adding Proper Fractions That Have Unlike Denominators

Fractions with different denominators cannot be added directly. They must be changed to higher terms with the same denominator. When the common denominator is the smallest number possible, it is called the **least common denominator**. This is often abbreviated to L.C.D.

With most fractions used in business, such as halves, thirds, fourths, etc., the number which contains all the denominators usually can be seen easily. The common denominator is said to be found by inspection.

*Examples:* Find the least common denominator by inspection.

a. $\frac{1}{2} + \frac{2}{3} + \frac{5}{6}$

By inspecting the denominators, you can see that 2, 3, and 6 all go exactly into 6. So, 6 is the L.C.D.

b. $\frac{1}{2} + \frac{3}{4} + \frac{1}{6}$

By inspecting the denominators, the smallest number that contains 2, 4, and 6 is 12. So, 12 is the L.C.D.

c. $\frac{2}{3} + \frac{3}{8} + \frac{5}{12}$

In *Example c,* 24 is the only number that contains both 3 and 8 exactly. It also contains 12. So, 24 is the L.C.D.

When inspection does not show the L.C.D., a common denominator can be found by multiplying all the denominators. The product found is often not the least common denominator, but it can be used and is easy to find.

*Examples:* Find a common denominator by multiplication.

a. $\frac{2}{5} + \frac{7}{8} + \frac{5}{12}$    $5 \times 8 \times 12 = 480$

The actual L.C.D. is 120, but 480 can be used as a common denominator.

b. $\frac{2}{3} + \frac{3}{4} + \frac{7}{15}$    $3 \times 4 \times 15 = 180$

The actual L.C.D. is 60, but 180 can be used as a common denominator.

When multiplication is used to find a common denominator, the product may be much larger than it needs to be. If one or more of the denominators are contained exactly in other larger denominators, they can be omitted in the multiplication.

*Examples:* Find a common denominator by multiplication.

a. $\frac{3}{4} + \frac{5}{12} + \frac{3}{5}$    $12 \times 5 = 60$

Since 4 is contained in 12, it is omitted in the multiplication. In this case, 60 is also the L.C.D.

b. $\frac{1}{2} + \frac{5}{8} + \frac{3}{5} + \frac{3}{10}$    $8 \times 10 = 80$

Since 2 is contained in 8 and 5 is contained in 10, they are omitted in the multiplication. In this case, the actual L.C.D. is 40; but 80 can be used as a common denominator.

There are several methods of finding the least common denominator other than by inspection. Only the **repeated division method** is given here. It requires a little more work than some methods you may know, but it is easy to do. The repeated division method is explained in detailed steps by means of *Example a* below.

*Examples:* Find the L.C.D. by repeated division.

a. $\frac{3}{8} + \frac{5}{12} + \frac{3}{5} + \frac{9}{20} + \frac{7}{15}$

**Step 1.** Write only the denominators in line.

$$8 \quad 12 \quad 5 \quad 20 \quad 15$$

**Step 2.** If there is at least one number which is divisible by 2, divide 2 into it and into all other even numbers. Put the quotient below the number. Bring down any number that is not divisible by 2.

$$\frac{2\underline{\smash{)}8 \quad 12 \quad 5 \quad 20 \quad 15}}{4 \quad\; 6 \quad\; 5 \quad 10 \quad 15}$$

**Step 3.** Keep dividing by 2 until there are only odd numbers left.

$$\frac{2\underline{\smash{)}4 \quad 6 \quad 5 \quad 10 \quad 15}}{2\underline{\smash{)}2 \quad 3 \quad 5 \quad\; 5 \quad 15}}$$
$$1 \quad 3 \quad 5 \quad\; 5 \quad 15$$

**Step 4.** If there is at least one number that contains a 3, repeat the process with 3's until it can no longer be divided into any of the numbers brought down.

$$\frac{3\underline{\smash{)}1 \quad 3 \quad 5 \quad 5 \quad 15}}{1 \quad 1 \quad 5 \quad 5 \quad\; 5}$$

**Step 5.** Repeat the division operation with the prime numbers in turn until all the numbers brought down are 1's. In this example, only the prime number 5 is needed.

$$\begin{array}{c|ccccc}5 & 1 & 1 & 5 & 5 & 5\\\hline & 1 & 1 & 1 & 1 & 1\end{array}$$

**Step 6.** Multiply all the divisors at the left. The product you obtain is the L.C.D.

$$\begin{array}{c|ccccc}2 & 8 & 12 & 5 & 20 & 15\\2 & 4 & 6 & 5 & 10 & 15\\2 & 2 & 3 & 5 & 5 & 15\\3 & 1 & 3 & 5 & 5 & 15\\5 & 1 & 1 & 5 & 5 & 5\\\hline & 1 & 1 & 1 & 1 & 1\end{array}$$

L.C.D. $= 2 \times 2 \times 2 \times 3 \times 5 = 120$

b. $\frac{2}{3} + \frac{7}{12} + \frac{9}{32} + \frac{5}{48} + \frac{3}{56}$

$$\begin{array}{c|ccccc}2 & 3 & 12 & 32 & 48 & 56\\2 & 3 & 6 & 16 & 24 & 28\\2 & 3 & 3 & 8 & 12 & 14\\2 & 3 & 3 & 4 & 6 & 7\\2 & 3 & 3 & 2 & 3 & 7\\3 & 3 & 3 & 1 & 3 & 7\\7 & 1 & 1 & 1 & 1 & 7\\\hline & 1 & 1 & 1 & 1 & 1\end{array}$$

L.C.D. $= 2 \times 2 \times 2 \times 2 \times 2 \times 3 \times 7 = 672$

After either the least common denominator or a common denominator is found, each fraction is changed to higher terms in that denominator. This makes all the fractions like terms, and they can be added as explained in Part B.

*Examples:* Add the proper fractions.

a. $\frac{2}{3} + \frac{3}{8} + \frac{5}{12}$

By inspection, the least common denominator is 24.

$$\frac{2}{3} = \frac{16}{24}$$

$$\frac{3}{8} = \frac{9}{24}$$

$$\frac{5}{12} = \frac{10}{24}$$

$$\frac{35}{24} = 1\frac{11}{24}$$

b. $\frac{2}{5} + \frac{7}{8} + \frac{5}{12}$

Using multiplication to find a common denominator: $5 \times 8 \times 12 = 480$.

$$\frac{2}{5} = \frac{192}{480}$$

$$\frac{7}{8} = \frac{420}{480}$$

$$\frac{5}{12} = \frac{200}{480}$$

$$\frac{812}{480} = 1\frac{332}{480} = 1\frac{83}{120}$$

c. $\frac{3}{8} + \frac{5}{12} + \frac{23}{56}$

Using repeated division to find the L.C.D.:

$$\begin{array}{c|ccc}2 & 8 & 12 & 56\\2 & 4 & 6 & 28\\2 & 2 & 3 & 14\\3 & 1 & 3 & 7\\7 & 1 & 1 & 7\\\hline & 1 & 1 & 1\end{array}$$

$\frac{3}{8} = \frac{63}{168}$

$\frac{5}{12} = \frac{70}{168}$

$\frac{23}{56} = \frac{69}{168}$

$$\frac{202}{168} = 1\frac{34}{168} = 1\frac{17}{84}$$

## Part D
## Adding Mixed Numbers That Have Unlike Denominators

To add two or more mixed numbers whose fractional parts have different denominators, first add the fractions as shown in Part C. Then add this sum to the total of the whole numbers.

*Examples:* Add the mixed numbers.

a. $3\frac{1}{3} + 6\frac{11}{12} + 5\frac{1}{6}$

$$\frac{1}{3} + \frac{11}{12} + \frac{1}{6} = \frac{4}{12} + \frac{11}{12} + \frac{2}{12} = \frac{17}{12} = 1\frac{5}{12}$$

$$3 + 6 + 5 + 1\frac{5}{12} = 15\frac{5}{12}$$

b. $5\frac{1}{4} + 2\frac{2}{5} + 8\frac{7}{8}$

$$\begin{array}{r|l}5 & \frac{1}{4} = \frac{10}{40}\\2 & \frac{2}{5} = \frac{16}{40}\\8 & \frac{7}{8} = \frac{35}{40}\\\hline 15 & \frac{61}{40} = 1\frac{21}{40}\\+\,1 & \frac{21}{40}\\\hline 16 & \frac{21}{40}\end{array}$$

## Part E — Adding Decimals That Have Common Fraction Endings

Decimals with common fraction endings can be added only if they have the same number of decimal places. The common fractions are added first. If this sum is a proper fraction, it is placed after the total of the decimal part. If the sum is an improper fraction, it is changed to a mixed number and then added to the decimals in the last decimal place. It is done this way because each common fraction ending is a fractional part more than the last decimal place in the number.

*Example:* Add $32.66\frac{2}{3}$, $22.37\frac{1}{2}$, and $34.43\frac{3}{4}$.

$$
\begin{array}{r|l}
32.66 & \frac{2}{3} = \frac{8}{12} \\
22.37 & \frac{1}{2} = \frac{6}{12} \\
34.43 & \frac{3}{4} = \frac{9}{12} \\
\hline
89.46 & \quad \frac{23}{12} = 1\frac{11}{12} \\
\phantom{89.4}1 & \frac{11}{12} \ldots \ldots \text{This is really } .01\frac{11}{12}. \\
\hline
89.47 & \frac{11}{12}
\end{array}
$$

For the student's information, this type of addition does not occur very often in business. When it does, it is more likely that the decimals with fractional endings are converted to complete decimals first and then added.

## Part F — Adding Decimals and Common Fractions

Sometimes numbers to be added are in different forms. Some are decimals and others are common fractions or mixed numbers. Before they can be added, all numbers must be in the same form; that is, all must be decimals or all must be common fractions or mixed numbers. The decimals can be changed to common fractions as shown in Part D of Section 2-1 in this chapter, or the common fractions can be changed to decimals as shown in Part E of Section 1-5 in Chapter 1. The method used depends on the form in which the answer is required.

*Example:* Find the sum of $\frac{3}{4}$ and .55.

**Adding in fractions:**

$$.55 = \frac{55}{100} = \frac{11}{20}$$

$$
\begin{array}{l}
\frac{3}{4} = \frac{15}{20} \\
+\frac{11}{20} = \frac{11}{20} \\
\hline
\quad \frac{26}{20} = \frac{13}{10} = 1\frac{3}{10}
\end{array}
$$

**Adding in decimals:**

$$
\begin{array}{r}
\frac{3}{4} = .75 \\
+.55 = \underline{.55} \\
1.30 = 1.3
\end{array}
$$

## Part G — Business Applications

Although most of the work in business now is done in decimals because of computers and electronic calculators, fractions are used in connection with yard goods. Fabrics, drapery materials, carpeting, etc., are bought and sold by the yard and fractional parts of a yard. Often the fractional parts are given in quarters: $\frac{1}{4}$, $\frac{2}{4}$ ($\frac{1}{2}$), and $\frac{3}{4}$, but the quarters are written as small raised numbers. For example, $50^2$ stands for $50\frac{2}{4}$ or $50\frac{1}{2}$ yards.

*Example:* Find the total yardage in five bolts of dress material given as: $40^3$, $43^2$, $35^3$, $39^2$, $50^1$.

Add the small raised numbers:

$$3 + 2 + 3 + 2 + 1 = 11$$

The 11 stands for $\frac{11}{4}$ or $2\frac{3}{4}$ yards. This is added to the whole numbers:

$$40 + 43 + 35 + 39 + 50 + 2\frac{3}{4} = 209\frac{3}{4} \text{ yds.}$$

**Complete Assignment 7**

## Assignment 7
## Section 2-2

### Addition of Fractions

| | Perfect Score | Student's Score |
|---|---|---|
| Part A | 10 | |
| Part B | 10 | |
| Part C | 25 | |
| Part D | 25 | |
| Part E | 10 | |
| Part F | 10 | |
| Part G | 10 | |
| TOTAL | 100 | |

# Part A

### Adding a Proper Fraction or a Mixed Number to a Whole Number

*Directions:* Add as indicated. (2 points for each correct answer)

1. $6 + \frac{2}{3}$

2. $\frac{3}{4} + 5$

3. $\frac{1}{100} + 16$

4. $2 + 4\frac{1}{4}$

5. $7\frac{3}{8} + 9$

Student's Score_____

# Part B

### Adding Proper Fractions That Have a Common Denominator

*Directions:* Add as indicated. (2 points for each correct answer)

6. $\frac{1}{8} + \frac{3}{8}$

7. $\frac{7}{12} + \frac{11}{12}$

8. $\frac{7}{15} + \frac{8}{15}$

9. $7\frac{2}{5} + \frac{1}{5} + 8\frac{4}{5} + 9\frac{3}{5}$

10. $7\frac{2}{9} + 1\frac{8}{9} + \frac{5}{9} + 6\frac{7}{9}$

Student's Score_____

# Part C

### Adding Proper Fractions That Have Unlike Denominators

*Directions:* Add as indicated. (5 points for each correct answer)

11. $\frac{1}{5}$
 $\frac{3}{10}$

12. $\frac{1}{6}$
 $\frac{11}{12}$

13. $\frac{2}{3}$
 $\frac{3}{4}$
 $\frac{5}{12}$

14. $\frac{5}{6}$
 $\frac{3}{8}$
 $\frac{7}{12}$
 $\frac{5}{16}$

15. $\frac{1}{5}$
 $\frac{17}{24}$
 $\frac{5}{6}$
 $\frac{7}{8}$

Student's Score_____

# Part D
## Adding Mixed Numbers That Have Unlike Denominators

*Directions:* Add as indicated. (5 points for each correct answer)

| 16. $5\frac{5}{8}$ | 17. $6\frac{3}{20}$ | 18. $14\frac{1}{6}$ | 19. $46\frac{2}{9}$ | 20. $39\frac{3}{25}$ |
|---|---|---|---|---|
| $4\frac{7}{16}$ | $15\frac{2}{3}$ | $29\frac{2}{5}$ | $23\frac{1}{2}$ | $42\frac{1}{6}$ |
| | | $27\frac{5}{12}$ | $19\frac{7}{15}$ | $10\frac{9}{10}$ |

*Student's Score* _____

# Part E
## Adding Decimals That Have Common Fraction Endings

*Directions:* Add as indicated. (2 points for each correct answer)

| 21. $.62\frac{1}{2}$ | 22. $6.91\frac{2}{3}$ | 23. $85.68\frac{3}{4}$ | 24. $26.43\frac{3}{4}$ | 25. $98.93\frac{3}{4}$ |
|---|---|---|---|---|
| $.87\frac{1}{2}$ | $5.66\frac{2}{3}$ | $73.37\frac{1}{2}$ | $13.16\frac{2}{3}$ | $43.33\frac{1}{3}$ |
| | | $30.66\frac{2}{3}$ | $45.41\frac{2}{3}$ | $85.06\frac{1}{4}$ |

*Student's Score* _____

# Part F
## Adding Decimals and Common Fractions

*Directions:* Change the decimals to common fractions and add. (2 points for each correct answer)

26. $3\frac{1}{2} + 8.25$    27. $53.5 + 26\frac{1}{4}$    28. $.375 + 7\frac{1}{2}$

29. $7\frac{1}{8} + 45.05$    30. $8.875 + 3\frac{7}{20}$

*Student's Score* _____

# Part G
## Business Applications

*Directions:* Find the total yardage of the dress materials in the following problems. (5 points for each correct answer)

31. 5 bolts: $52^3 + 58^2 + 65^3 + 45^1 + 55^2$    32. 5 bolts: $56^1 + 43^2 + 58^1 + 47^3 + 55^3$

*Student's Score* _____

# Section 2-3  Subtraction of Fractions

The same general rules used in the addition of fractions apply in subtracting fractions. In order to take one common fraction from another, both must have the same denominator.

Remember that subtraction is also indicated by such phrases as: find the difference between _____ and _____; deduct _____ from _____; how much larger than _____ is _____; take _____ from _____, etc.

## Part A  Subtracting Fractions Without Borrowing

To find the difference between two fractions with the same denominator, take the smaller numerator from the larger one and place this difference over the common denominator. Reduce the answer to lowest terms where necessary.

*Examples:* Subtract as indicated.

a. $\frac{11}{12} - \frac{5}{12}$

$$\frac{11}{12} - \frac{5}{12} = \frac{11-5}{12} = \frac{6}{12} = \frac{1}{2}$$

b. Find the difference between $\frac{2}{15}$ and $\frac{13}{15}$.

$$\frac{13}{15} - \frac{2}{15} = \frac{13-2}{15} = \frac{11}{15}$$

To find the difference between two mixed numbers whose fractional parts have the same denominator, borrowing is not necessary if the numerator of the minuend fraction is larger than the numerator of the subtrahend fraction. First, find the difference between the fractions; and then the difference between the whole numbers.

*Example:* $7\frac{5}{8} - 2\frac{1}{8}$

$$\begin{array}{r} 7\frac{5}{8} \\ -2\frac{1}{8} \\ \hline 5\frac{4}{8} = 5\frac{1}{2} \end{array}$$

To subtract a whole number from a mixed number, first find the difference between the whole numbers and then put the fraction after this difference.

*Example:* Find the difference between 12 and $21\frac{2}{3}$.

$$\begin{array}{r} 21\frac{2}{3} \\ -12 \\ \hline 9\frac{2}{3} \end{array}$$

To subtract fractions with different denominators, first change them to like terms (fractions with the same denominator). Then find the difference between the numerators and place this over the common denominator. Reduce the answer to lowest terms where necessary.

*Examples:* Subtract as indicated.

a. How much smaller than $\frac{5}{6}$ is $\frac{1}{3}$?

$$\begin{array}{r} \frac{5}{6} = \frac{5}{6} \\ -\frac{1}{3} = \frac{2}{6} \\ \hline \frac{3}{6} = \frac{1}{2} \end{array}$$

b. Deduct $\frac{3}{20}$ from $\frac{1}{3}$.

$$\begin{array}{r} \frac{1}{3} = \frac{20}{60} \\ -\frac{3}{20} = \frac{9}{60} \\ \hline \frac{11}{60} \end{array}$$

To find the difference between two mixed numbers (or between a mixed number and a proper fraction) when the fractions have different denominators, first change the fractions to like terms. If the new numerator in the minuend fraction is larger than the numerator in the subtrahend fraction, borrowing is not necessary. Find the difference between the fractions and then the difference between the whole numbers.

*Examples:* Subtract as indicated.

a. $5\frac{2}{3} - 3\frac{1}{4}$

$$\begin{array}{r|l} 5 & \frac{2}{3} = \frac{8}{12} \\ -3 & \frac{1}{4} = \frac{3}{12} \\ \hline 2 & \frac{5}{12} = 2\frac{5}{12} \end{array}$$

b. Take $\frac{2}{15}$ from $4\frac{3}{8}$.

$$\begin{array}{r|l} 4 & \frac{3}{8} = \frac{45}{120} \\ - & \frac{2}{15} = \frac{16}{120} \\ \hline 4 & \frac{29}{120} = 4\frac{29}{120} \end{array}$$

# Subtracting Fractions by Borrowing

Borrowing as it is done in subtracting fractions is very different from borrowing in subtracting whole numbers or decimals. The one that is borrowed from the whole number in the minuend must be changed to a fraction whose numerator and denominator are both the same as the common denominator of the fractions being subtracted. For example, if the common denominator is 12, the borrowed one is changed to 12/12; if the common denominator is 60, the borrowed one is changed to 60/60.

To find the difference between two mixed numbers whose fractional parts have the same denominator but the numerator of the minuend fraction is smaller than the numerator of the subtrahend fraction, it is necessary to borrow one from the whole number in the minuend. The one is changed to a fraction whose numerator and denominator are the same as the common denominator and it is then added to the minuend fraction. The minuend fraction becomes larger than the subtrahend fraction and the subtraction can be performed. After that, the whole numbers are subtracted.

*Examples:* Subtract as indicated.

**a.** $14\frac{7}{12} - 9\frac{11}{12}$

Borrow 1 from the 14 and change it to $\frac{12}{12}$. Then proceed as follows:

$$
\begin{array}{c|c}
3 & \\
1\!\!\!/4 & \frac{7}{12} + \frac{12}{12} = \frac{19}{12} \\
-\ 9 & \qquad\qquad \frac{11}{12} \\
\hline
4 & \qquad\qquad \frac{8}{12} = \frac{2}{3}
\end{array}
$$

The answer is $4\frac{2}{3}$.

**b.** Find the difference between $25\frac{13}{16}$ and $43\frac{5}{16}$.

Borrow 1 from the 43 and change it to $\frac{16}{16}$. Then proceed as follows:

$$
\begin{array}{c|c}
2 & \\
4\!\!\!/3 & \frac{5}{16} + \frac{16}{16} = \frac{21}{16} \\
-25 & \qquad\qquad \frac{13}{16} \\
\hline
17 & \qquad\qquad \frac{8}{16} = \frac{1}{2}
\end{array}
$$

The answer is $17\frac{1}{2}$.

Except for the last step, the same procedure is used for finding the difference between a mixed number and a proper fraction when the fractions have the same denominator but the proper fraction is larger than the fraction in the mixed number.

*Example:* $3\frac{1}{8} - \frac{5}{8}$

$$
\begin{array}{c|c}
2 & \\
3\!\!\!/ & \frac{1}{8} + \frac{8}{8} = \frac{9}{8} \\
- & \qquad\qquad \frac{5}{8} \\
\hline
2 & \qquad\qquad \frac{4}{8} = \frac{1}{2}
\end{array}
$$

The answer is $2\frac{1}{2}$.

Instead of a mixed number, the minuend may be a whole number without any fractional part. It can be thought of as a mixed number whose fraction has a numerator of 0 and a denominator that is the same as the denominator of the fraction in the subtrahend. Borrowing in this case is always necessary.

*Examples:* Subtract as indicated.

**a.** Find the difference between $16\frac{2}{9}$ and 25.

In the subtraction, write 25 as $25\frac{0}{9}$; then borrow 1 from 25, change it to $\frac{9}{9}$, and add it to $\frac{0}{9}$.

$$
\begin{array}{c|c}
4 & \\
2\!\!\!/5 & \frac{0}{9} + \frac{9}{9} = \frac{9}{9} \\
-16 & \qquad\qquad \frac{2}{9} \\
\hline
8 & \qquad\qquad \frac{7}{9}
\end{array}
$$

**b.** Take $9\frac{5}{8}$ from 17.

In the subtraction, write only 17, *not* $17\frac{0}{8}$. Borrow 1 from 17, change it to $\frac{8}{8}$, and write it directly above the $\frac{5}{8}$.

$$
\begin{array}{c|c}
6 & \\
1\!\!\!/7 & \frac{8}{8} \\
-\ 9 & \frac{5}{8} \\
\hline
7 & \frac{3}{8}
\end{array}
$$

To find the difference between two mixed numbers (or a mixed number and a proper fraction) with different denominators, the first step is always to change the fractions to like terms. When the new numerator of the minuend fraction is smaller than the new numerator of the subtrahend fraction, borrowing is necessary. The same procedure for borrowing as shown above is used.

**Examples:** Subtract as indicated.

a. How much larger than $3\frac{11}{16}$ is $10\frac{3}{5}$?

The least common denominator is found by multiplication: $16 \times 5 = 80$. Change the fractions to like terms with the same denominator of 80:

$$
\begin{array}{r|l}
10 & \frac{3}{5} = \frac{48}{80} \\
-\ 3 & \frac{11}{16} = \frac{55}{80} \\
\hline
\end{array}
$$

Borrow 1 from 10 and change it to $\frac{80}{80}$:

$$
\begin{array}{r|l}
9 & \\
\cancel{10} & \frac{3}{5} = \frac{48}{80} + \frac{80}{80} = \frac{128}{80} \\
-\ 3 & \frac{11}{16} = \frac{55}{80} \\
\hline
6 & \frac{73}{80}
\end{array}
$$

The answer is $6\frac{73}{80}$.

b. Deduct $\frac{5}{12}$ from $4\frac{3}{10}$.

Change the fractions to like terms with the least common denominator of 60:

$$
\begin{array}{r|l}
4 & \frac{3}{10} = \frac{18}{60} \\
- & \frac{5}{12} = \frac{25}{60} \\
\hline
\end{array}
$$

Borrow 1 from 4 and change it to $\frac{60}{60}$:

$$
\begin{array}{r|l}
3 & \\
\cancel{4} & \frac{3}{10} = \frac{18}{60} + \frac{60}{60} = \frac{78}{60} \\
- & \frac{5}{12} = \frac{25}{60} \\
\hline
3 & \frac{53}{60}
\end{array}
$$

The answer is $3\frac{53}{60}$.

## Part C  Business Applications

A stock record is a card or sheet on which a record is kept of all the goods that are placed in a stockroom or warehouse after an order has been delivered. When some of the goods are taken out, this is also recorded. A separate stock record is kept for each item handled in the business. The quantity that comes in is recorded in a column labeled **Received**; the quantity that is taken out is recorded in a column labeled **Issued**.

The stock record is kept up-to-date by the stock clerk in charge. Starting with the balance on hand, any quantity that is issued is subtracted and any quantity that is received is added to the previous balance. The information on the stock record is used for ordering purposes.

To keep from running out of stock on an item, most companies try to keep a minimum amount of stock on hand. When the balance falls below a desired amount, an order for more stock is placed. All orders are numbered for checking when the stock is received.

A request for stock to be taken out or issued is called a **requisition**. All requisitions are numbered for reference.

Nowadays a computer is often used to keep a running record of the stock on hand. The printout may look different, but the information on it is very similar to that on a stock record.

In the example below, stock record amounts are recorded in gross. One gross equals 12 dozen. For example, if the requisition is for 185 dozen, the 185 dozen are changed to $15\frac{5}{12}$ gross ($185 \div 12$) on the stock record.

**Example:** Complete the following stock record.

1. May 8—Balance on hand is 26 gross.

2. May 12—Received $45\frac{1}{4}$ gross on Order No. 3796.

3. May 14—Issued $15\frac{5}{12}$ gross on Requisition No. 540.

4. May 16—Issued $17\frac{1}{3}$ gross on Requisition No. 593.

5. May 17—Received $48\frac{3}{4}$ gross on Order No. 4231.

6. May 18—Issued $16\frac{5}{6}$ gross on Requisition No. 612.

| | Date | Received | | Issued | | Balance |
|---|---|---|---|---|---|---|
| | | Order No. | Quantity | Req. No. | Quantity | |
| (1) | May 8 | | | | (on hand) | 26 gross |
| (2) | 12 | 3796 | $45\frac{1}{4}$ | | | $71\frac{1}{4}$ |
| (3) | 14 | | | 540 | $15\frac{5}{12}$ | $55\frac{5}{6}$ |
| (4) | 16 | | | 593 | $17\frac{1}{3}$ | $38\frac{1}{2}$ |
| (5) | 17 | 4231 | $48\frac{3}{4}$ | | | $87\frac{1}{4}$ |
| (6) | 18 | | | 612 | $16\frac{5}{6}$ | $70\frac{5}{12}$ |

Stock No. _____ B-64 _____

Minimum Amount
50 gross

## Explanation

(1) Balance on hand on May 8 is 26 gross.

(2) On May 12, $45\frac{1}{4}$ gross are received. This is added to the 26 gross. The new balance is $71\frac{1}{4}$ gross. It is written in the Balance column under the 26 gross.

(3) and (4) The issues of May 14 and May 16 are subtracted in that order to leave a current balance of $38\frac{1}{2}$ gross. Since this is below the desired minimum amount, an order is placed. It is not recorded until it is received.

(5) On May 17, the order is received. $48\frac{3}{4}$ gross are added to the balance of $38\frac{1}{2}$ gross to give a new balance of $87\frac{1}{4}$ gross.

(6) On May 18, the issue of $16\frac{5}{6}$ gross is subtracted from $87\frac{1}{4}$ gross to give a balance on hand of $70\frac{5}{12}$ gross.

Complete Assignment 8

# Assignment 8
# Section 2-3

| | Perfect Score | Student's Score |
|---|---|---|
| Part A | 40 | |
| Part B | 40 | |
| Part C | 20 | |
| TOTAL | 100 | |

## Subtraction of Fractions

# Part A

### Subtracting Fractions Without Borrowing

*Directions:* Subtract as indicated. (4 points for each correct answer)

1. $\frac{5}{6} - \frac{1}{6}$

2. $\frac{2}{5} - \frac{2}{5}$

3. $7\frac{3}{4} - 2\frac{1}{4}$

4. $9\frac{11}{12} - 6\frac{5}{12}$

5. Take 3 from $18\frac{7}{16}$.

6. Deduct 13 from $23\frac{5}{9}$.

7. Find the difference between $\frac{2}{3}$ and $\frac{5}{6}$.

8. How much larger than $\frac{2}{5}$ is $\frac{7}{10}$?

9. $\quad 6\frac{11}{12}$
   $-4\frac{3}{8}$

10. $\quad 54\frac{7}{8}$
    $-47\frac{5}{8}$

Student's Score _____

# Part B

### Subtracting Fractions by Borrowing

*Directions:* Subtract as indicated. (4 points for each correct answer)

11. $\quad 4\frac{1}{8}$
    $-1\frac{5}{8}$

12. $\quad 12\frac{1}{5}$
    $- 9\frac{3}{5}$

13. $\quad 16$
    $- 3\frac{4}{7}$

14. $\quad 27$
    $- 9\frac{3}{4}$

Student's Score _____

15. $37\frac{3}{10}$
    $- 5\frac{2}{3}$

16. $23\frac{5}{12}$
    $-12\frac{4}{5}$

17. $85\frac{1}{6}$
    $-49\frac{7}{8}$

18. $63\frac{9}{16}$
    $-58\frac{5}{6}$

19. $93\frac{2}{15}$
    $-64\frac{7}{9}$

20. $106\frac{4}{25}$
    $- 99\frac{7}{15}$

# Part C

## *Business Applications*

*Directions:* Complete the stock record below. (4 points for each correct answer)

Stock No. ___B-65___                    Minimum Amount
                                         50 gross

| Date | Received | | Issued | | Balance |
|---|---|---|---|---|---|
| | Order No. | Quantity | Req. No. | Quantity | |
| May 20 | | | | | $95\frac{1}{3}$ |
| 21 | | | 645 | $34\frac{3}{4}$ | |
| 23 | | | 657 | $35\frac{11}{12}$ | |
| 25 | 4258 | $62\frac{1}{2}$ | | | |
| 27 | | | 669 | $28\frac{1}{6}$ | |
| 28 | | | 680 | $41\frac{5}{8}$ | |

21.
22.
23.
24.
25.

# Section 2-4  Multiplication of Fractions

Multiplication with common fractions and mixed numbers occurs occasionally in actual business practice. It is used most often when a calculator is not available. As mentioned earlier, decimals are much more widely used in business computations.

There are two ways to find the product of two common fractions, either proper or improper.

1. Cancel any common divisors in the numerator of one and the denominator of the other. If a number is canceled in a numerator, it must also be canceled only in a denominator. In other words, cancelling is done only from "top to bottom." If the cancellation results in 1, the 1 must be written to prevent a possible error in reading or writing the answer.

*Example:* $\dfrac{2}{3} \times \dfrac{3}{4}$    $\dfrac{\cancel{2}^{1}}{\cancel{3}_{1}} \times \dfrac{\cancel{3}^{1}}{\cancel{4}_{2}} = \dfrac{1}{2}$

2. Find the product of the two numerators and place it over the product of the two denominators. Reduce the new fraction to lowest terms.

*Example:* $\dfrac{2}{3} \times \dfrac{3}{4}$    $\dfrac{2 \times 3}{3 \times 4} = \dfrac{6}{12} = \dfrac{1}{2}$

## Part A  Multiplying Two or More Proper Fractions

Either method of multiplying fractions may be used to multiply two proper fractions. When the numbers are large, the cancellation method is easier to use.

*Example:*  $\dfrac{3}{16} \times \dfrac{14}{15}$    $\dfrac{\cancel{3}^{1}}{\cancel{16}_{8}} \times \dfrac{\cancel{14}^{7}}{\cancel{15}_{5}} = \dfrac{7}{40}$

or  $\dfrac{3 \times 14}{16 \times 15} = \dfrac{\cancel{42}^{7}}{\cancel{240}_{40}} = \dfrac{7}{40}$

To find the product of three or more proper fractions, generally the cancellation method is pre-ferable. The cancellation must be only into one numerator and one denominator at a time. The numbers canceled need not be *adjoining* (next to each other).

*Example:*  $\dfrac{9}{14} \times \dfrac{2}{5} \times \dfrac{8}{9} \times \dfrac{35}{72}$

Follow these steps in canceling:

(1) 9 into numerator 9 and denominator 9.
(2) 2 into numerator 2 and denominator 14.
(3) 7 into numerator 35 and denominator 7 of the canceled 14.
(4) 5 into numerator 5 of the canceled 35 and denominator 5.
(5) 8 into numerator 8 and denominator 72.

$$\dfrac{\cancel{9}^{1}}{\cancel{14}_{7}^{\,}} \times \dfrac{\cancel{2}^{1}}{\cancel{5}_{1}} \times \dfrac{\cancel{8}^{1}}{\cancel{9}_{1}} \times \dfrac{\cancel{35}^{\cancel{5}^{1}}}{\cancel{72}_{9}} = \dfrac{1}{9}$$

Note that all the numerators cancel down to 1 to make the answer $\frac{1}{9}$.

## Part B  Multiplying a Proper Fraction by a Whole Number

Either method of multiplying fractions can be used to multiply a proper fraction by a whole number. The whole number is placed over 1 so that it will have a numerator and a denominator.

*Examples:*

a. $\dfrac{5}{8}$ of 44

$\dfrac{5}{\cancel{8}_{2}} \times \dfrac{\cancel{44}^{11}}{1} = \dfrac{55}{2} = 27\dfrac{1}{2}$ or $\dfrac{5 \times 44}{8 \times 1} = \dfrac{\cancel{220}^{55}}{\cancel{8}_{2}} = 27\dfrac{1}{2}$

b. $5 \times \dfrac{1}{5}$

$$\frac{1}{\cancel{5}} \times \frac{1}{\cancel{5}} = 1 \qquad or \qquad \frac{5 \times 1}{1 \times 5} = \frac{5}{5} = 1$$

Note in *Example b* that when only 1's are left in the numerators and denominators, the answer is 1, and not 0.

<table>
<tr><td rowspan="2">Part</td><td rowspan="5"></td></tr>
</table>

## Part C — Multiplying a Mixed Number by a Proper Fraction or by a Whole or a Mixed Number

To find the product of a mixed number times a proper fraction, first change the mixed number to an improper fraction before multiplying. (As explained in Part C on page 48 in this chapter, a mixed number is changed to an improper fraction by multiplying the whole number part by the denominator, adding the numerator, and placing the sum over the denominator.)

**Example:** $5\frac{1}{6} \times \frac{3}{4}$

$$5\frac{1}{6} = 5 \times 6 + 1 \text{ all over } 6 = \frac{31}{6}$$

$$\frac{31}{\cancel{6}^{}} \times \frac{\cancel{3}^{1}}{4} = \frac{31}{8} = 3\frac{7}{8}$$

To find the product of a mixed number times a whole number, again change the mixed number to an improper fraction before multiplying. Then place the whole number over 1.

**Example:** $7\frac{1}{4} \times 16$

$$\frac{29}{\cancel{4}} \times \frac{\cancel{16}^{4}}{1} = 116$$

To find the product of a mixed number times another mixed number, change the mixed numbers to improper fractions before multiplying. The multiplication is done the same as in Part A on page 63. The same procedure is followed for three or more factors.

**Examples:**

a. $6\frac{3}{10} \times 8\frac{1}{3}$

$$\frac{\cancel{63}^{21}}{\cancel{10}_{2}} \times \frac{\cancel{25}^{5}}{\cancel{3}_{1}} = \frac{105}{2} = 52\frac{1}{2}$$

b. $2\frac{2}{3} \times \frac{7}{10} \times \frac{3}{4} \times 1\frac{7}{8}$

$$\frac{\cancel{8}^{1}}{\cancel{3}_{1}} \times \frac{7}{\cancel{10}_{2}} \times \frac{\cancel{3}^{1}}{4} \times \frac{\cancel{15}^{3}}{\cancel{8}_{1}} = \frac{21}{8} = 2\frac{5}{8}$$

## Part D — Multiplying a Decimal by a Proper Fraction or by a Mixed Number

In multiplying a decimal by a proper fraction or a mixed number, it is often simpler to do the multiplication in fractions rather than in complete decimals.

To multiply a decimal by a proper fraction, first put the decimal over 1 so that it has a numerator and a denominator. Then multiply the numerator of the proper fraction by the decimal numerator. As the last step, divide this product by the denominator of the proper fraction.

**Examples:**

a. $\frac{2}{3} \times 15.6$

$$\frac{2}{3} \times \frac{15.6}{1} = \frac{2 \times 15.6}{3 \times 1} = \frac{31.2}{3} = 10.4$$
$$= 10\frac{2}{5}$$

$$3\overline{)31.2}^{\,10.4}$$

b. $\frac{7}{15} \times 478.95$

$$\frac{7}{15} \times \frac{478.95}{1} = \frac{7 \times 478.95}{15 \times 1} = \frac{3352.65}{15}$$
$$= 223.51$$

$$15\overline{)3352.65}^{\,223.51}$$

**c.** $\frac{13}{24} \times .0834$

$$\frac{13}{24} \times \frac{.0834}{1} = \frac{13 \times .0834}{24 \times 1} = \frac{1.0842}{24}$$

$$= .045175$$

$$\begin{array}{r} .045175 \\ 24\,\overline{)1.084200} \end{array}$$

Note that, while either method of multiplying with fractions may be used, the second method is easier to use. In the cancellation method, care must be taken to retain the decimal point when canceling. For this reason, only the second method is shown here.

To multiply a decimal by a mixed number, first change the mixed number to an improper fraction. Then multiply the improper fraction by the decimal in the same way as with a proper fraction.

*Examples:*

**a.** $3\frac{3}{4} \times 76.8$

$$3\frac{3}{4} = \frac{15}{4}$$

$$\frac{15}{4} \times \frac{76.8}{1} = \frac{15 \times 76.8}{4} = \frac{1152.0}{4} = 288$$

$$\begin{array}{r} 288 \\ 4\,\overline{)1152} \end{array}$$

**b.** $5\frac{7}{8} \times 904.25$

$$5\frac{7}{8} = \frac{47}{8}$$

$$\frac{47}{8} \times \frac{904.25}{1} = \frac{47 \times 904.25}{8} = \frac{42499.75}{8}$$

$$\begin{array}{r} 5312.46875 \\ 8\,\overline{)42499.75000} \end{array} = 5312.46875$$

## Part E
### Multiplying a Mixed Number by a Whole Number, by a Decimal, or by Another Mixed Number

A mixed number can be multiplied by a whole number, a decimal, or another mixed number

without changing it to an improper fraction. Usually this method is used when dealing with numbers over ten.

The multiplication of a mixed number by a whole number can be done in three separate steps, which are combined at the end. These steps are:

1. Multiply the fractional part of the mixed number by the whole number.
2. Multiply the whole number part of the mixed number by the whole number.
3. Add the two products found in Steps 1 and 2.

*Examples:*

**a.** $132 \times 57\frac{3}{8}$

Step 1: $\dfrac{3}{8} \times 132 = \dfrac{3}{8} \times \dfrac{\overset{33}{\cancel{132}}}{1} = \dfrac{99}{2} = 49\frac{1}{2}$

Step 2: 
$$\begin{array}{r} 132 \\ \times\ \ 57 \\ \hline 924 \\ 6600 \\ \hline 7524 \end{array}$$

Step 3: 
$$\begin{array}{r} + \ \ 49\frac{1}{2} \\ \hline 7573\frac{1}{2} \end{array}$$

**b.** $468\frac{2}{3} \times 91$

Step 1: $\dfrac{2}{3} \times \dfrac{91}{1} = \dfrac{182}{3} = 60\frac{2}{3}$

Step 2: 
$$\begin{array}{r} 468 \\ \times\ \ 91 \\ \hline 468 \\ 42120 \\ \hline 42588 \end{array}$$

Step 3: 
$$\begin{array}{r} + \ \ 60\frac{2}{3} \\ \hline 42648\frac{2}{3} \end{array}$$

It is possible to change the form of the addition in Step 3. The product found in Step 1 can be added directly to the partial products of the multiplication in Step 2. Care must be taken not to indent the first partial product. *Example a* would have this form:

$$\begin{array}{r} 132 \\ \times\ 57\frac{3}{8} \\ \hline 49\frac{1}{2} \\ 924 \\ 6600 \\ \hline 7573\frac{1}{2} \end{array}$$

The first method is preferred, however, since an error cannot be made because of wrong indenting.

When either the multiplicand or the multiplier, or both, are decimals, the numbers are multiplied first as if there were no decimals. After the multiplication is completed, the correct number of decimal places is pointed off. Remember that a fractional ending does not take a decimal place.

*Examples:*

a. $32.78 \times 29\frac{1}{4}$

**Step 1:** $\frac{1}{4} \times \frac{3278}{1} = \frac{1}{\cancel{4}_2} \times \frac{\cancel{3278}^{1639}}{1} = 819\frac{1}{2}$

**Step 2:**
$$\begin{array}{r} 3278 \\ \times\ \ \ 29 \\ \hline 29502 \\ 65560 \\ \hline 95062 \end{array}$$

**Step 3:**
$$\begin{array}{r} +\ \ 819\frac{1}{2} \\ \hline 95881\frac{1}{2} \end{array}$$

Pointing off two places, the answer is 958.81$\frac{1}{2}$.

b. $163.45\frac{1}{3} \times 8.6$

**Step 1:** $\frac{1}{3} \times \frac{86}{1} = \frac{86}{3} = 28\frac{2}{3}$

**Step 2:**
$$\begin{array}{r} 16345 \\ \times\ \ \ \ \ 86 \\ \hline 98070 \\ 1307600 \\ \hline 1405670 \end{array}$$

**Step 3:**
$$\begin{array}{r} +\ \ \ \ \ 28\frac{2}{3} \\ \hline 1405698\frac{2}{3} \end{array}$$

Pointing off three places, the answer is 1405.698$\frac{2}{3}$.

Finding the product of two large mixed numbers is a difficult operation when it is done in fractions. In business, this is almost always done in decimals. The operation is explained here only for the student's interest and is not included in the assignment or in the tests. It is explained by means of an example, with each step given separately and then pointed out in the calculation.

*Example:* $157\frac{1}{2} \times 79\frac{3}{4}$

**Steps**

1. Multiply the fractions.
2. Multiply the fraction in the multiplicand by the whole number part of the multiplier.
3. Multiply the fraction in the multiplier by the whole number part of the multiplicand.
4. Multiply the whole number parts.
5. Add the products found in the first four steps. Care must be taken to put the fractions under each other.

$$\begin{array}{r} 157\ \frac{1}{2} \\ \times\ 79\ \frac{3}{4} \end{array}$$

**Step 1:** $\frac{1}{2} \times \frac{3}{4}$ .............. $\frac{3}{8}$
**Step 2:** $\frac{1}{2} \times 79$ ............. $39\frac{1}{2}$
**Step 3:** $\frac{3}{4} \times 157$ ........... $117\frac{3}{4}$
**Step 4:** $157 \times 79$ .......... $12403$
**Step 5:** Total .............. $12559\frac{13}{8} = 1\frac{5}{8}$
$$\begin{array}{r} +\ \ \ 1\ \frac{5}{8} \\ \hline 12560\ \frac{5}{8} \end{array}$$

## Part F Business Applications

When fractions or mixed numbers occur in a business calculation, it is often simpler to work in fractions than in decimals, especially when a calculator is not available. The symbol @ stands for *at*.

*Example:* Find the cost of $92\frac{5}{12}$ dozen @ 96¢ per dozen.

$\frac{5}{12} \times \frac{96}{1} = \frac{5}{\cancel{12}_1} \times \frac{\cancel{96}^{8}}{1} = 40$

$$\begin{array}{r} 92 \\ \times\ \ \ 96 \\ \hline 552 \\ 8280 \\ \hline 8832 \\ +\ \ \ \ 40 \\ \hline 8872 \end{array}$$

Pointing off two places = \$88.72

**Complete Assignment 9**

## Assignment 9
## Section 2-4

*Multiplication of Fractions*

|  | Perfect Score | Student's Score |
|---|---|---|
| Part A | 20 |  |
| Part B | 10 |  |
| Part C | 20 |  |
| Part D | 20 |  |
| Part E | 20 |  |
| Part F | 10 |  |
| TOTAL | 100 |  |

# Part A

### Multiplying Two or More Proper Fractions

*Directions:* Find the products. (2 points for each correct answer)

1. $\frac{1}{3} \times \frac{3}{8}$     2. $\frac{1}{4} \times \frac{4}{5}$     3. $\frac{1}{10} \times \frac{3}{8}$     4. $\frac{9}{20} \times \frac{7}{8}$     5. $\frac{5}{6} \times \frac{9}{16}$

6. $\frac{5}{8} \times \frac{4}{9}$     7. $\frac{7}{10} \times \frac{5}{8}$     8. $\frac{4}{15} \times \frac{5}{12}$     9. $\frac{5}{6} \times \frac{6}{7} \times \frac{3}{10}$     10. $\frac{8}{9} \times \frac{3}{16} \times \frac{5}{8} \times \frac{4}{15}$

*Student's Score* _____

# Part B

### Multiplying a Proper Fraction by a Whole Number

*Directions:* Find the products. (2 points for each correct answer)

11. $\frac{1}{6} \times 6$     12. $7 \times \frac{1}{7}$     13. $36 \times \frac{2}{15}$     14. $\frac{3}{4} \times 18$     15. $12 \times \frac{3}{5}$

*Student's Score* _____

# Part C

### Multiplying a Mixed Number by a Proper Fraction or by a Whole or Mixed Number

*Directions:* Find the products. (2 points for each correct answer)

16. $\frac{1}{6} \times 2\frac{2}{3}$     17. $1\frac{2}{5} \times \frac{5}{8}$     18. $3 \times 6\frac{2}{3}$     19. $6\frac{3}{4} \times 4$

20. $12\frac{2}{8} \times 4\frac{1}{2}$     21. $13\frac{1}{3} \times 3\frac{3}{5}$     22. $\frac{7}{10} \times 1\frac{1}{8} \times 6\frac{2}{3}$     23. $4\frac{1}{2} \times 2\frac{2}{15} \times 3\frac{1}{3}$

24. $2\frac{5}{8} \times \frac{3}{20} \times 5\frac{1}{3} \times 3\frac{3}{4}$     25. $1\frac{1}{5} \times 2\frac{3}{8} \times \frac{16}{27} \times 6\frac{2}{3}$

*Student's Score* _____

# Part D

### Multiplying a Decimal by a Proper Fraction or by a Mixed Number

*Directions:* Find the products. (4 points for each correct answer)

26. $\frac{3}{4} \times 28.8$

27. $87.5 \times \frac{2}{3}$

28. $2\frac{3}{5} \times .12$

29. $4.82 \times 1\frac{2}{3}$

30. $3\frac{1}{2} \times .75$

*Student's Score* _____

# Part E

### Multiplying a Mixed Number by a Whole Number, by a Decimal, or by Another Number

*Directions:* Find the products. (4 points for each correct answer)

31.
$$\begin{array}{r} 76 \\ \times\ 4\frac{1}{2} \\ \hline \end{array}$$

32.
$$\begin{array}{r} 85\frac{2}{15} \\ \times\ 30 \\ \hline \end{array}$$

33.
$$\begin{array}{r} 1.08\frac{2}{3} \\ \times\ 90 \\ \hline \end{array}$$

34.
$$\begin{array}{r} .496 \\ \times\ 25\frac{5}{8} \\ \hline \end{array}$$

35.
$$\begin{array}{r} 2.33\frac{1}{3} \\ \times\ .68 \\ \hline \end{array}$$

*Student's Score* _____

# Part F

### Business Applications

*Directions:* Find the cost of each item and the total. Show your work at the right. (2 points for each correct answer)

**WORK SPACE**

36. $43\frac{1}{2}$ yd. @ 87¢ a yard    = $ _____

37. $65\frac{3}{8}$ yd. @ $2.40 a yard    = _____

38. $26\frac{2}{3}$ doz. @ 57¢ per doz.    = _____

39. $18\frac{7}{12}$ doz. @ $3.60 per doz.    = _____

40.            Total = $ _____

*Student's Score* _____

# Section 2-5  Division of Fractions

Division of fractions, as such, does not have much business usage, but it is used to solve some problems.

Division is the reverse, or **inverse**, of multiplication. The rule for dividing by a fraction is to invert the divisor and multiply it by the dividend. To invert a fraction, turn it upside down. The inverted fraction is called the **reciprocal** of the original fraction.

*Example:* $\dfrac{5}{12} \div \dfrac{3}{4}$

$$\frac{5}{12} \div \frac{3}{4} = \frac{5}{\cancel{12}_{3}} \times \frac{\cancel{4}^{1}}{3} = \frac{5}{9}$$

Another way of stating the rule is: multiply the dividend (the number *before* the division sign) by the reciprocal of the divisor (the number *after* the division sign). Note that since the dividend is the number that is to be divided, it remains the same; only the divisor is inverted.

## Part A  Dividing by a Proper Fraction

To divide by a proper fraction, follow the rule of inverting the divisor and multiplying it by the dividend. The examples given below are divided into three groups according to the form of the dividend: proper fraction, whole number, or mixed number.

*Examples:*

**When the dividend is a proper fraction.**

a. $\dfrac{3}{10} \div \dfrac{5}{8}$

$$\frac{3}{10} \div \frac{5}{8} = \frac{3}{\cancel{10}_{5}} \times \frac{\cancel{8}^{4}}{5} = \frac{12}{25}$$

b. $\dfrac{2}{3} \div \dfrac{2}{3}$

$$\frac{2}{3} \div \frac{2}{3} = \frac{2}{3} \times \frac{3}{2} = \frac{6}{6} = 1$$

Note that, just as with whole numbers, any fraction divided by itself is always equal to 1, as shown in *Example b* above.

**When the dividend is a whole number.**

a. $18 \div \dfrac{3}{5}$

$$18 \div \frac{3}{5} = \frac{\cancel{18}^{6}}{1} \times \frac{5}{\cancel{3}_{1}} = 30$$

b. $25 \div \dfrac{2}{15}$

$$25 \div \frac{2}{15} = \frac{25}{1} \times \frac{15}{2} = \frac{375}{2} = 187\frac{1}{2}$$

Note that when a whole number is divided by a proper fraction, the answer is always larger than the whole number.

**When the dividend is a mixed number.**

Before dividing, the mixed number must be changed to an improper fraction.

a. $5\dfrac{3}{5} \div \dfrac{7}{8}$

$$5\frac{3}{5} \div \frac{7}{8} = \frac{28}{5} \div \frac{7}{8} = \frac{\cancel{28}^{4}}{5} \times \frac{8}{\cancel{7}_{1}} = \frac{32}{5} = 6\frac{2}{5}$$

b. $15\dfrac{3}{4} \div \dfrac{3}{10}$

$$15\frac{3}{4} \div \frac{3}{10} = \frac{63}{4} \div \frac{3}{10} = \frac{\cancel{63}^{21}}{\cancel{4}_{2}} \times \frac{\cancel{10}^{5}}{\cancel{3}_{1}} = \frac{105}{2} = 52\frac{1}{2}$$

## Part B  Dividing by a Whole Number

Before dividing a fraction by a whole number, put the whole number over 1. Then follow the general rule of inverting the divisor and multiplying it by the dividend. Again, the examples given here are divided into three groups according to the form of the dividend.

## Examples:

### When the dividend is a proper fraction.

a. $\frac{4}{5} \div 8$

$$\frac{4}{5} \div 8 = \frac{4}{5} \div \frac{8}{1} = \frac{4}{5} \times \frac{1}{\cancel{8}_2} = \frac{1}{10}$$

b. $\frac{9}{16} \div 15$

$$\frac{9}{16} \div 15 = \frac{9}{16} \div \frac{15}{1} = \frac{9}{16} \times \frac{1}{\cancel{15}_5} = \frac{3}{80}$$

### When the dividend is a whole number.

a. $8 \div 36$

$$8 \div 36 = \frac{8}{1} \div \frac{36}{1} = \frac{8}{1} \times \frac{1}{\cancel{36}_9} = \frac{2}{9}$$

Rather than following the general rule for dividing fractions as shown in *Example a* above, the dividend can be put over the divisor since the fraction line also indicates division, as in *Example b* below. The result is then reduced to lowest terms.

b. $56 \div 80$

$$56 \div 80 = \frac{56}{80} = \frac{\cancel{56}^7}{\cancel{80}_{10}}$$

### When the dividend is a mixed number.

Again, before dividing, the mixed number must be changed to an improper fraction.

a. $4\frac{2}{3} \div 2$

$$4\frac{2}{3} \div 2 = \frac{14}{3} \div \frac{2}{1} = \frac{\cancel{14}^7}{3} \times \frac{1}{\cancel{2}_1} = \frac{7}{3} = 2\frac{1}{3}$$

b. $5\frac{1}{4} \div 12$

$$5\frac{1}{4} \div 12 = \frac{21}{4} \div \frac{12}{1} = \frac{\cancel{21}^7}{4} \times \frac{1}{\cancel{12}_4} = \frac{7}{16}$$

## Part C — Dividing by a Mixed Number

Before dividing a fraction by a mixed number, change the mixed number to an improper fraction and then follow the general rule for division of fractions. The examples given here are again divided into three groups according to the form of the dividend.

## Examples:

### When the dividend is a proper fraction.

a. $\frac{7}{8} \div 2\frac{1}{3}$

$$\frac{7}{8} \div 2\frac{1}{3} = \frac{7}{8} \div \frac{7}{3} = \frac{\cancel{7}^1}{8} \times \frac{3}{\cancel{7}_1} = \frac{3}{8}$$

b. $\frac{7}{25} \div 1\frac{2}{3}$

$$\frac{7}{25} \div 1\frac{2}{3} = \frac{7}{25} \div \frac{5}{3} = \frac{7}{25} \times \frac{3}{5} = \frac{21}{125}$$

### When the dividend is a whole number.

a. $15 \div 6\frac{2}{3}$

$$15 \div 6\frac{2}{3} = \frac{15}{1} \div \frac{20}{3} = \frac{\cancel{15}^3}{1} \times \frac{3}{\cancel{20}_4} = \frac{9}{4} = 2\frac{1}{4}$$

b. $24 \div 3\frac{3}{4}$

$$24 \div 3\frac{3}{4} = \frac{24}{1} \div \frac{15}{4} = \frac{\cancel{24}^8}{1} \times \frac{4}{\cancel{15}_5} = \frac{32}{5} = 6\frac{2}{5}$$

### When the dividend is a mixed number.

a. $8\frac{2}{3} \div 4\frac{4}{5}$

$$8\frac{2}{3} \div 4\frac{4}{5} = \frac{26}{3} \div \frac{24}{5} = \frac{\cancel{26}^{13}}{3} \times \frac{5}{\cancel{24}_{12}} = \frac{65}{36} = 1\frac{29}{36}$$

**b.** $234\frac{7}{8} \div 155\frac{1}{2}$

$$234\frac{7}{8} \div 155\frac{1}{2} = \frac{1879}{8} \div \frac{311}{2} = \frac{1879}{\cancel{8}} \times \frac{\overset{1}{\cancel{2}}}{311}$$
$$\underset{4}{}$$

$$= \frac{1879}{1244} = 1\frac{635}{1244}$$

When the mixed numbers to be divided are large, as in *Example b* above, the division is performed more easily in decimals, as follows:

$$234.875 \div 155.5 = 1.51045$$

Another method of dividing fractions, called the **common multiple method**, is useful when the dividend and the divisor are mixed numbers. This method is longer than the method of inverting the divisor and multiplying by the dividend. For this reason, it is not recommended when proper fractions or whole numbers are involved.

To divide by the common multiple method, follow these steps:

1. Write the dividend as the numerator of a fraction whose denominator is the divisor.

2. Multiply both terms by the product of the denominators. The result is a fraction whose numerator and denominator are both whole numbers.

3. Reduce this new fraction to lowest terms.

*Example a* below uses the same problem given in *Example a* at the bottom of the right-hand column on the previous page so that the two methods can be compared.

## Examples:

**a.** $8\frac{2}{3} \div 4\frac{1}{5}$

**Step 1:** $\dfrac{8\frac{2}{3}}{4\frac{1}{5}}$

**Step 2:** $\dfrac{8\frac{2}{3} \times 15}{4\frac{1}{5} \times 15} = \dfrac{\dfrac{26}{\cancel{3}} \times \dfrac{\cancel{15}}{1} = 130}{\dfrac{24}{\cancel{5}} \times \dfrac{\cancel{15}}{1} = 72}$

**Step 3:** $\dfrac{130}{72} = \dfrac{65}{36} = 1\dfrac{29}{36}$

**b.** $2\frac{1}{4} \div 4\frac{1}{2}$

**Step 1:** $\dfrac{2\frac{1}{4}}{4\frac{1}{2}}$

**Step 2:** $\dfrac{2\frac{1}{4} \times 8}{4\frac{1}{2} \times 8} = \dfrac{\dfrac{9}{\cancel{4}} \times \dfrac{\overset{2}{\cancel{8}}}{1} = 18}{\dfrac{9}{\cancel{2}} \times \dfrac{\cancel{8}}{1} = 36}$

**Step 3:** $\frac{18}{36} = \frac{1}{2}$

## Part D — Reducing Complex Fractions and Decimal Fractions

A **complex fraction** is a fraction whose numerator or denominator, or both, contains a proper fraction or a mixed number. As in any fraction, the main fraction line can indicate division.

To reduce a complex fraction to a proper fraction or a mixed number, follow the general rule for dividing by fractions or use the common multiple method.

*Examples:* Reduce the complex fractions.

**a.** $\dfrac{3\frac{3}{4}}{7\frac{1}{2}}$

$$\frac{3\frac{3}{4}}{7\frac{1}{2}} = 3\frac{3}{4} \div 7\frac{1}{2} = \frac{15}{4} \div \frac{15}{2} = \frac{\overset{1}{\cancel{15}}}{\underset{2}{\cancel{4}}} \times \frac{\overset{1}{\cancel{2}}}{\underset{1}{\cancel{15}}} = \frac{1}{2}$$

*or*

$$\frac{3\frac{3}{4}}{7\frac{1}{2}} = \frac{3\frac{3}{4} \times 8}{7\frac{1}{2} \times 8} = \frac{\frac{15}{4} \times \frac{8}{1}}{\frac{15}{2} \times \frac{8}{1}} = \frac{30}{60} = \frac{1}{2}$$

**b.** $\dfrac{8\frac{5}{6}}{9}$

$$\frac{8\frac{5}{6}}{9} = 8\frac{5}{6} \div 9 = \frac{53}{6} \div \frac{9}{1} = \frac{53}{6} \times \frac{1}{9} = \frac{53}{54}$$

A decimal fraction with a fractional ending can be reduced to a common fraction by changing it to a complex fraction with a numerator and denominator, and then reducing it. The numerator becomes the mixed number after the decimal point; and the denominator becomes 10, 100, 1,000, etc., depending on the number of decimal places. This method is used when the fractional ending cannot be changed to an exact decimal. (Converting decimals with fractional endings is discussed in greater detail in the next chapter.)

**Examples:** Reduce to common fractions.

**a.** $.58\frac{1}{3}$

$$.58\tfrac{1}{3} = \frac{58\tfrac{1}{3}}{100} = 58\tfrac{1}{3} \div 100 = \frac{175}{3} \div \frac{100}{1}$$

$$= \frac{\overset{7}{\cancel{175}}}{3} \times \frac{1}{\underset{4}{\cancel{100}}} = \frac{7}{12}$$

**b.** $.444\frac{4}{9}$

$$.444\tfrac{4}{9} = \frac{444\tfrac{4}{9}}{1,000} = 444\tfrac{4}{9} \div 1,000$$

$$= \frac{4000}{9} \div \frac{1000}{1} = \frac{\overset{4}{\cancel{4000}}}{9} \times \frac{1}{\underset{1}{\cancel{1000}}} = \frac{4}{9}$$

## Part E — Business Applications

Civil service examinations often have word problems to solve. In some problems the whole amount must be found when only a fractional part of it is given. For example, when you change the words of a problem into the following form:

Fraction of Whole amount = Number
(given)      (to be found)      (given)

the word *of* stands for multiplication. The equation now becomes:

Fraction × Whole amount = Number
(given)      (to be found)      (given)

The problem can then by solved by dividing the given Number by the given Fraction, as follows:

$$\frac{\text{Number (given)}}{\text{Fraction (given)}} = \text{Whole amount}$$

Note that multiplication cannot be used since there is only one number (the fraction) connected to the multiplication sign. There must be numbers on both sides of the multiplication sign.

If you are puzzled as to why you should divide, think of a very simple problem like the following: 4 × what number = 36. You know the answer is 9 since 4 × 9 = 36. Since division is the inverse of multiplication, to find the unknown number in an indicated multiplication, divide the known product (36) by the one known number (4) to find the other number in the multiplication. Thus, 36 ÷ 4 = 9.

The procedure in solving a problem in which a fraction is the only known number in an indicated multiplication is exactly the same. That is, divide the given number (the product) by the fraction to find the other number in the indicated multiplication.

**Examples:** Solve the problems.

**a.** Mary Ann Forbes spends $60 a week for living expenses. This is $\frac{2}{3}$ of her net pay for a week. What is her weekly pay?

$$\tfrac{2}{3} \times \text{weekly net pay} = \$60$$

$$60 \div \tfrac{2}{3} = \frac{\overset{30}{\cancel{60}}}{1} \times \frac{3}{\underset{1}{\cancel{2}}} = \$90$$

**b.** A company spent $4,200 for advertising in one month. This was $\frac{3}{16}$ of the amount allowed for advertising for the entire year. What was the annual amount allowed?

$$\tfrac{3}{16} \times \text{annual amount} = \$4,200$$

$$4200 \div \tfrac{3}{16} = \frac{\overset{1400}{\cancel{4200}}}{1} \times \frac{16}{\underset{1}{\cancel{3}}} = \$22,400$$

**Complete Assignment 10**

NAME_____

DATE_____

# Assignment 10
# Section 2-5

## Division of Fractions

|  | Perfect Score | Student's Score |
|---|---|---|
| Part A | 30 | |
| Part B | 10 | |
| Part C | 40 | |
| Part D | 10 | |
| Part E | 10 | |
| TOTAL | 100 | |

## Part A

### Dividing by a Proper Fraction

*Directions:* Divide as indicated. (2 points for each correct answer)

1. $\frac{1}{3} \div \frac{1}{2}$

2. $\frac{1}{8} \div \frac{1}{4}$

3. $\frac{3}{8} \div \frac{5}{16}$

4. $\frac{3}{4} \div \frac{3}{4}$

5. $\frac{14}{15} \div \frac{2}{5}$

6. $7 \div \frac{1}{5}$

7. $15 \div \frac{6}{7}$

8. $14 \div \frac{2}{3}$

9. $3 \div \frac{5}{6}$

10. $5 \div \frac{2}{9}$

11. $2\frac{5}{8} \div \frac{7}{24}$

12. $1\frac{7}{8} \div \frac{3}{5}$

13. $6\frac{2}{3} \div \frac{1}{12}$

14. $9\frac{3}{4} \div \frac{7}{18}$

15. $8\frac{4}{9} \div \frac{2}{9}$

Student's Score _____

## Part B

### Dividing by a Whole Number

*Directions:* Divide as indicated. (2 points for each correct answer)

16. $\frac{2}{5} \div 6$

17. $\frac{5}{8} \div 10$

18. $5 \div 6$

19. $10 \div 35$

20. $9\frac{1}{3} \div 4$

Student's Score _____

## Part C

### Dividing by a Mixed Number

*Directions:* Divide as indicated. (2 points for each correct answer)

21. $\frac{1}{6} \div 1\frac{1}{5}$

22. $\frac{3}{5} \div 3\frac{1}{3}$

23. $\frac{7}{8} \div 2\frac{1}{3}$

24. $\frac{3}{4} \div 1\frac{5}{16}$

25. $\frac{11}{15} \div 1\frac{3}{8}$

26. $4 \div 13\frac{1}{2}$

27. $2 \div 1\frac{2}{3}$

28. $240 \div 4\frac{1}{2}$

29. $15 \div 2\frac{2}{3}$

30. $180 \div 5\frac{5}{8}$

**31.** $2\frac{3}{4} \div 2\frac{3}{8}$      **32.** $7\frac{1}{5} \div 4\frac{1}{2}$      **33.** $2\frac{5}{8} \div 1\frac{5}{12}$      **34.** $1\frac{2}{3} \div 2\frac{1}{2}$      **35.** $1\frac{1}{6} \div 2\frac{2}{3}$

**36.** $1\frac{5}{6} \div 1\frac{5}{6}$      **37.** $4\frac{4}{5} \div 2\frac{2}{5}$      **38.** $15\frac{1}{2} \div 7\frac{3}{4}$      **39.** $175\frac{1}{2} \div 2\frac{1}{4}$      **40.** $429\frac{3}{8} \div 12\frac{3}{5}$

*Student's Score* _____

# Part D

## *Reducing Complex Fractions and Decimal Fractions*

**Directions:** Reduce the complex and decimal fractions to proper fractions or mixed numbers. (2 points for each correct answer)

**41.** $\dfrac{\frac{9}{20}}{\frac{3}{5}}$      **42.** $\dfrac{6\frac{1}{3}}{7\frac{11}{12}}$      **43.** $\dfrac{6\frac{1}{2}}{4}$      **44.** $\dfrac{3}{9\frac{3}{4}}$      **45.** $.20\frac{5}{6}$

*Student's Score* _____

# Part E

## *Business Applications*

**Directions:** Solve the problems and write your answers in the spaces provided. (5 points for each correct answer)

**46.** A firm allowed $\frac{7}{12}$ of its operations budget for selling expenses. If the selling expenses amounted to $84,000, what is the total amount in the operations budget?

**47.** The cost of a pair of mittens is $\frac{9}{16}$ of the selling price. If the mittens cost $1.50, what is the selling price?

Ans._____

Ans._____

*Student's Score* _____

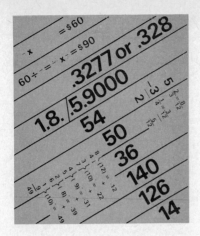

# CHAPTER 3

# Working with Equivalents

Decimal equivalents and fractional equivalents have many applications in business. Fractions and mixed numbers are used to express quantities, prices, and discounts. When operations with these numbers are done on a calculator, they must be changed to their decimal forms and rounded off to the number of decimal places required for an accurate answer.

On the other hand, certain widely used decimals can be reduced to simple common fractions. When these decimals occur in a computation, the fractional forms provide shortcuts that are easy to apply. Actually by using a shortcut, you can "beat" a calculator by getting the answer mentally or with some simple paper-and-pencil work.

## Section 3-1 Decimal Equivalents and Fractional Equivalents

The **decimal equivalent** of a common fraction or mixed number is its decimal form. The **fractional equivalent** of a decimal fraction is its common fraction form.

### Part A  Finding the Decimal Equivalent of a Common Fraction

To find the decimal equivalent of a common fraction, divide the numerator by the denominator. Follow these steps:

1. In a long division form, put the numerator on the inside as the dividend; put the denominator on the outside as the divisor. Then place a decimal point after the dividend and another one directly above it in the answer position. Now add zeros after the dividend. Usually five zeros are enough, although you may not have to use all of them or you may have to add more.

**Example:** Find the decimal equivalent of $\frac{7}{18}$.

**Step 1.** $18\overline{)7.00000}$

2. Carry the division out to *one more place than required* when the division does not produce an exact answer.

**Step 2.**
$$
\begin{array}{r}
.38888 \\
18\overline{)7.00000} \\
\underline{5\,4\phantom{0000}} \\
160\phantom{000} \\
\underline{144\phantom{000}} \\
160\phantom{00} \\
\underline{144\phantom{00}} \\
160\phantom{0} \\
\underline{144\phantom{0}} \\
160 \\
\underline{144} \\
16 \\
\end{array}
$$

3. Round off the quotient to the required number of places. Usually four places are enough for most calculations.

**Step 3.**    .38888 = .3889

The example on page 75 also illustrates a repeating decimal with 8 as the repeating digit or **repetend**. When the same number appears twice in a row as a remainder (16 in this case), a repeating decimal is indicated and the actual division can be stopped. The rest of the quotient will consist of the same repeating digits.

When the decimal form of a common fraction is used in a calculation, it is sometimes necessary to round off the equivalent to more than four decimal places to get more accurate results. This is done under two conditions which are given and illustrated below.

1. When the rounded-off equivalent has one or more zeros after the decimal point, more places should be used. The division should be carried out far enough so that the rounded-off equivalent will have at least four non-zero digits after the zeros. The zeros are only place-holders and do not affect the numerical value of the answer.

**Example:** $\frac{1}{144} \times \$2,000$

$$144 \overline{\smash{)}\, \begin{matrix} .0069444 \\ 1.0000000 \end{matrix}}$$

**Using Four Places**       **Using Six Places**

$$\begin{matrix} .0069 \\ \times \quad 2000 \\ \hline 13.8000 \end{matrix} = \$13.80 \qquad \begin{matrix} .006944 \\ \times \quad 2000 \\ \hline 13.888000 \end{matrix} = \$13.89$$

Note that the answer is nine cents more when six decimal places are used.

2. When the repeating decimals end in 3's or 6's, the decimal equivalent used should have at least six places for accurate results. For very large numbers, seven or eight places may be necessary. Compare the results in the following examples.

**a.** $\frac{1}{3}$ of 69,000

Using the fraction $\frac{1}{3}$ in this multiplication problem would give the exact answer: $\frac{1}{3} \times 69,000 = 23,000$.

Using the decimal equivalent of $\frac{1}{3}$ to four, five, six, and seven places would give the following:

$$\begin{matrix}
.3333 & \times & 69,000 & = & 22,997.70 \\
.33333 & \times & 69,000 & = & 22,999.77 \\
.333333 & \times & 69,000 & = & 22,999.98 \\
.3333333 & \times & 69,000 & = & 22,999.997 \\
& & & = & 23,000
\end{matrix}$$

**b.** $\frac{1}{6} \times 69,000$

Using the fraction $\frac{1}{6}$ in this multiplication problem would give the exact answer: $\frac{1}{6} \times 69,000 = 11,500$.

Using the decimal equivalent of $\frac{1}{6}$ to four, five, six, and seven places would give the following:

$$\begin{matrix}
.1667 & \times & 69,000 & = & 11,502.30 \\
.16667 & \times & 69,000 & = & 11,500.23 \\
.166667 & \times & 69,000 & = & 11,500.02 \\
.1666667 & \times & 69,000 & = & 11,500.002 \\
& & & = & 11,500
\end{matrix}$$

In *Examples a* and *b* above, note that the last decimal place for those ending in 3's is rounded to 3, but the last decimal place for those ending in 6's is rounded to 7.

In finding the decimal equivalent of a fraction whose denominator contains only 2's and 5's, the division always comes out exactly.

**Examples:**  Find the decimal equivalents.

**a.** $\frac{3}{32}$

$$32 \overline{\smash{)}\, \begin{matrix} .09375 \\ 3.00000 \end{matrix}} \qquad (32 = 2 \times 2 \times 2 \times 2 \times 2)$$

**b.** $\frac{6}{625}$

$$625 \overline{\smash{)}\, \begin{matrix} .0096 \\ 6.00000 \end{matrix}} \qquad (625 = 5 \times 5 \times 5 \times 5)$$

When the denominator of the fraction contains any other prime numbers (except one), the division does not come out exactly. The equivalent always must be rounded off.

**Examples:**  Find the decimal equivalents.

**a.** $\frac{1}{30}$

$$30 \overline{\smash{)}\, \begin{matrix} .03333 \\ 1.00000 \end{matrix}} = .0333$$

b. $\frac{2}{19}$

$$19 \overline{)\begin{array}{c} .10526 \\ 2.00000 \end{array}} = .1053$$

When the quotient ends in a repeating decimal, or repetend, the repetend may be written in two ways shown below. The first way, however, is more often used.

1. A repetend may be written with dots following the repeating part.

*Examples:* $\frac{5}{6}$ (.8333) = .833. . .
$\frac{1}{12}$ (.0833) = .0833. . .

2. A repetend may be written with one or more dots or a bar over the repeating part.

*Examples:* $\frac{4}{11}$ (.3636) = $.\overset{..}{3}\overset{}{6}$ or $.\overline{36}$

$\frac{6}{7}$ (.8571428) = $.\overset{.}{8}5714\overset{.}{2}$

or $.\overline{857142}$

To find the decimal equivalent of a mixed number, replace the fractional part of the mixed number with its decimal equivalent.

*Example:* Find the decimal equivalent of $4\frac{3}{8}$.

$$\frac{3}{8} = .375; \quad 4\frac{3}{8} = 4.375$$

## Part B Finding the Fractional Equivalent of a Decimal Fraction

To change a decimal fraction to its fractional equivalent, write it with a numerator and denominator, and then reduce to lowest terms. (See Section 2-1, Part D, on page 48 in Chapter 2.)

*Examples:* Change to fractional equivalents.

a. .264

$$.264 = \frac{\overset{33}{\cancel{264}}}{\underset{125}{\cancel{1000}}} = \frac{33}{125}$$

b. .0084

$$.0084 = \frac{\overset{21}{\cancel{84}}}{\underset{2500}{\cancel{10000}}} = \frac{21}{2500}$$

When the decimal fractions end in a series of 3's or a series of 6's rounded off to 7 in the last place, it is very likely that these are rounded-off repetends. For example, .8333 can be $.83\frac{1}{3}$ rounded off. Such decimal fractions can be changed to their fractional equivalents as shown in Part C below.

To change a mixed decimal to its mixed number form, find the fractional equivalent of the decimal part first; then replace the decimal with its fractional equivalent.

*Example:* Change 4.0625 to its mixed number form.

$$.0625 = \frac{625}{10,000} = \frac{1}{16}$$

$$4.0625 = 4\frac{1}{16}$$

## Part C Finding the Fractional Equivalent of a Decimal with a Fractional Ending

There are two ways to change a decimal with a fractional ending to its fractional equivalent. These are:

1. Change the number to a complete decimal (see Section 1-4, Part D, page 28 in Chapter 1) and then reduce to a fraction.

*Examples:* Change to fractional equivalents.

a. $.93\frac{3}{4} = .9375 = \frac{\overset{15}{\overset{375}{\cancel{9375}}}}{\underset{\underset{16}{100}}{\cancel{10,000}}} = \frac{15}{16}$

$$
\begin{array}{r}
371 \\
\cancel{1855} \\
\cancel{46375} \\
\cancel{100,000} \\
\cancel{4,000} \\
800
\end{array}
$$

b. $.46\frac{3}{8} = .46375 = \dfrac{\cancel{46375}}{\cancel{100,000}} = \dfrac{371}{800}$

2. The second method must be used when the fractional ending cannot be changed exactly to a complete decimal, such as $.55\frac{5}{9}$ or $.41\frac{2}{3}$. In this method, the mixed decimal is first changed to a complex fraction. That is, the mixed number after the decimal point becomes the numerator; and the denominator is 10, 100, 1,000, etc., depending upon the number of decimal places. Then the complex fraction is reduced by dividing the numerator by the denominator, working in fractions. (See Section 2-5, Part D, pages 71-72 in Chapter 2.)

*Examples:* Change to fractional equivalents.

a. $.16\frac{2}{3}$

$$.16\frac{2}{3} = \frac{16\frac{2}{3}}{100} = \frac{50}{3} \div \frac{100}{1} = \frac{\cancel{50}}{3} \times \frac{1}{\cancel{100}_2} = \frac{1}{6}$$

Note that $.16\frac{2}{3} = .166667$ when rounded off to six decimal places. Therefore, in reverse, it is safe to assume that $.166667 = .16\frac{2}{3} = \frac{1}{6}$.

b. $.285\frac{5}{7}$

$$.285\frac{5}{7} = \frac{285\frac{5}{7}}{1,000} = 285\frac{5}{7} \div \frac{1000}{1}$$

$$= \frac{2000}{7} \div \frac{1000}{1} = \frac{\cancel{2000}^2}{7} \times \frac{1}{\cancel{1000}_1} = \frac{2}{7}$$

## Part D  Changing Cents to Decimals

An amount of money less than one dollar can be written either with a cents sign (¢) after the amount or with a decimal point before the amount and no cents sign. Prices under one dollar are often given as amounts with the cents sign, such as 29¢, 5¢, 2½¢, etc. Before these amounts can be used in multiplication or division, they must be changed to their decimal forms.

Since 100¢ = $1.00, 1¢ is $1.00 divided by 100, or .01. Therefore, to change an amount written with a cents sign to a decimal, put a decimal point after the last digit, drop the ¢ sign, and move the decimal point two places to the left.

*Example:* 12¢ = 12.¢ = .12.¢ = .12 = $0.12

If the amount written has a fractional ending, generally it is changed to a complete decimal after the decimal point has been moved. Sometimes, however, one-third and two-thirds endings are kept.

*Examples:*

a. $2\frac{1}{2}¢ = 2.\frac{1}{2}¢ = .02.\frac{1}{2}¢ = .025 = \$0.025$

b. $16\frac{2}{3}¢ = 16\frac{2}{3}¢ = .16.\frac{2}{3}¢ = .16\frac{2}{3} = \$0.16\frac{2}{3}$

Note in all the above examples that when an amount of money less than one dollar is written as a decimal, often a dollar sign followed by a zero is put *before* the decimal point to show no whole dollars.

## Part E  Business Applications

When fractions or mixed numbers occur in a computation that is to be done on a calculator, generally they are changed to their decimal equivalents. Usually four decimal places are enough, but when the ending is $\frac{1}{3}$ or $\frac{2}{3}$, six or more places should be used for accurate results.

*Examples:* Change to complete decimals for work on a calculator.

a. $15\frac{7}{8} + 2\frac{2}{5} = 15.875 + 2.4$

b. $79.12\frac{1}{2} - 43\frac{3}{4} = 79.125 - 43.75$

c. $2{,}675 @ 41\frac{2}{3}¢ = 2675 \times .416667$

d. $4{,}950 @ 3\frac{1}{3}¢ = 4950 \times .033333$

e. $3\frac{2}{25} \div 76\frac{5}{8} = 3.08 \div 76.625$

**Complete Assignment 11**

## Assignment 11
## Section 3-1

### Decimal Equivalents and Fractional Equivalents

|  | Perfect Score | Student's Score |
|---|---|---|
| Part A | 20 | |
| Part B | 20 | |
| Part C | 20 | |
| Part D | 20 | |
| Part E | 20 | |
| TOTAL | 100 | |

## Part A

### Finding the Decimal Equivalent of a Common Fraction

*Directions:* Find the decimal equivalents rounded off to four decimal places. (2 points for each correct answer)

1. $\frac{1}{12}$   2. $\frac{5}{12}$   3. $\frac{11}{24}$   4. $\frac{5}{24}$   5. $\frac{9}{32}$

6. $\frac{59}{64}$   7. $\frac{177}{25}$   8. $\frac{239}{25}$   9. $\frac{51}{1,256}$   10. $\frac{14}{3,265}$

*Student's Score* _____

## Part B

### Finding the Fractional Equivalent of a Decimal Fraction

*Directions:* Change to fractional equivalents and reduce to lowest terms. (2 points for each correct answer)

11. .05   12. .02   13. .346   14. .785   15. .005

16. .008   17. .0025   18. .0082   19. .1875   20. .9375

*Student's Score* _____

# Part C

## *Finding the Fractional Equivalent of a Decimal with a Fractional Ending*

***Directions:*** Change to fractional equivalents and reduce to lowest terms. (2 points for each correct answer)

**21.** $.26\frac{2}{3}$ **22.** $.56\frac{2}{3}$ **23.** $.02\frac{1}{2}$ **24.** $.06\frac{1}{4}$ **25.** $.208\frac{1}{3}$

**26.** $.458\frac{1}{3}$ **27.** $.133\frac{1}{3}$ **28.** $.466\frac{2}{3}$ **29.** $.571\frac{3}{7}$ **30.** $.222\frac{2}{9}$

*Student's Score* ________

# Part D

## *Changing Cents to Decimals*

***Directions:*** Change the cents to their decimal forms. (2 points for each correct answer)

**31.** 60¢ **32.** 99¢ **33.** 8¢ **34.** 1¢ **35.** $6\frac{1}{2}$¢

**36.** $1\frac{3}{4}$¢ **37.** $3\frac{1}{3}$¢ **38.** $\frac{1}{2}$¢ **39.** $\frac{1}{4}$¢ **40.** 250¢

*Student's Score* ________

# Part E

## *Business Applications*

***Directions:*** Change to complete decimals for work on a calculator. Do not work the problems. (2 points for each correct answer)

**41.** $2\frac{3}{4} + 59\frac{5}{8}$ **42.** $5\frac{1}{2} + 2.93\frac{3}{4}$ **43.** $75\frac{1}{2} - 43.75$

**44.** $98.26 - 9\frac{2}{3}$ **45.** 4,860 @ $33\frac{1}{3}$¢ **46.** 2,675 @ $66\frac{2}{3}$¢

**47.** $8\frac{9}{16} \times 3.75$ **48.** $56.25 \times 7\frac{7}{12}$ **49.** $3\frac{1}{12} \div 11.625$

**50.** $46\frac{5}{6} \div 24.41\frac{2}{3}$

*Student's Score* ________

# Section 3-2  Aliquot Parts and Fractional Equivalents

Certain decimals that can be changed to fractional parts of 1, $1.00, or 100% often occur in business. These particular numbers are called **aliquot parts of 1, $1.00, or 100%**. Any number can be an aliquot part of some other number. The aliquot parts of 1, however, are used the most since they relate to unit prices which can be changed to fractional parts of $1.00 or to rates which can be changed to fractional parts of 100%. (This latter use is explained in the next chapter on percentage.) The aliquot parts of 100 also have some business use.

In the general definition of an aliquot part, when *part* of a number can be divided exactly into the number, without a remainder, then the part is called an **aliquot** part of the number. In other words, when a number (larger) can be divided by a part of itself (smaller) so that the quotient is a whole number, then the smaller number (the part) is an aliquot part of the larger number. The aliquot part also can be expressed as a *fractional part* of the larger number.

## Examples:

**a.** Is 9 an aliquot part of 27? Yes, since $27 \div 9 = 3$; and $9 = \frac{1}{3}$ of 27.

**b.** Is 10 an aliquot part of 27? No, since $27 \div 10 = 2$ with a remainder of 7.

**c.** Is 25¢ an aliquot part of $1.00? Yes, since $\$1.00 \div .25 = 4$; and $25¢ = \frac{1}{4}$ of $1.00.

**d.** Is $33\frac{1}{3}$ an aliquot part of 100? Yes, since $100 \div 33\frac{1}{3} = 3$; and $33\frac{1}{3} = \frac{1}{3}$ of 100.

In the examples above, only 25¢ and $33\frac{1}{3}$ would have any business usage since 25¢ can be changed to $\frac{1}{4}$ of $1.00 and $33\frac{1}{3}$ to $\frac{1}{3}$ of 100. In the remainder of this section, you will learn how to use an aliquot part in a calculation. Since only the aliquot parts of $1.00 or of 100 have any practical business use, others are not discussed here.

## Part A  Aliquot Parts of 1 or $1.00

Finding the fractional equivalent of an aliquot part of 1 or $1.00 (the fractional part) is the same as finding the fractional equivalent of a decimal or a decimal with a fractional ending, as explained in Parts B and C of Section 3-1. When an aliquot part is expressed in cents, the cents must be changed to a decimal.

**Example:** Find the fractional equivalent of $16\frac{2}{3}¢$ $(.16\frac{2}{3})$ as an aliquot part of $1.00.

$$.16\tfrac{2}{3} = \frac{16\frac{2}{3}}{100} = \frac{50}{3} \div \frac{100}{1} = \frac{\overset{1}{\cancel{50}}}{3} \times \frac{1}{\underset{2}{\cancel{100}}} = \frac{1}{6}$$

Below are other examples of aliquot parts of 1 or $1.00 and their fractional equivalents.

| Aliquot Part | Fractional Part of 1 or $1.00 |
|---|---|
| **a.** $.5 = .50 = 50¢$ | $\frac{1}{2}$ |
| **b.** $.33\frac{1}{3} = 33\frac{1}{3}¢$ | $\frac{1}{3}$ |
| **c.** $.06\frac{1}{4} = 6\frac{1}{4}¢$ | $\frac{1}{16}$ |

The fractional equivalent of a true aliquot part has a numerator of 1. A multiple of an aliquot part, such as .75, which equals $\frac{3}{4}$, has a numerator greater than 1 but the same denominator. Generally, however, the multiples are included with aliquot parts.

Below are some examples of multiples of aliquot parts.

| Multiples of Aliquot Parts | Fractional Part of 1 or $1.00 |
|---|---|
| **a.** $.66\frac{2}{3} = 66\frac{2}{3}¢$ $(.33\frac{1}{3} \times 2)$ | $\frac{2}{3}$ |
| **b.** $.75 = 75¢$ $(.25 \times 3)$ | $\frac{3}{4}$ |
| **c.** $83\frac{1}{3} = 83\frac{1}{3}¢$ $(.16\frac{2}{3} \times 5)$ | $\frac{5}{6}$ |

You should learn the aliquot parts and their fractional equivalents given in Table 3-1 on page 82 since they provide shortcuts. Percents are included in the table for later use.

# Table 3-1 Aliquot Parts of 1, $1.00, and 100% with Their Fractional Equivalents

|  | Decimal Form | Cents Form | Percent Form | Fractional Equivalent |
|---|---|---|---|---|
| Halves | .5 (.50) | 50¢ | 50% | $\frac{1}{2}$ |
| Thirds | .33$\frac{1}{3}$ or .333333 | 33$\frac{1}{3}$¢ | 33$\frac{1}{3}$% | $\frac{1}{3}$ |
|  | .66$\frac{2}{3}$ or .666667 | 66$\frac{2}{3}$¢ | 66$\frac{2}{3}$% | $\frac{2}{3}$ |
| Fourths | .25 | 25¢ | 25% | $\frac{1}{4}$ |
|  | .75 | 75¢ | 75% | $\frac{3}{4}$ |
| Fifths | .2 (.20) | 20¢ | 20% | $\frac{1}{5}$ |
|  | .4 (.40) | 40¢ | 40% | $\frac{2}{5}$ |
|  | .6 (.60) | 60¢ | 60% | $\frac{3}{5}$ |
|  | .8 (.80) | 80¢ | 80% | $\frac{4}{5}$ |
| Sixths | .16$\frac{2}{3}$ or .166667 | 16$\frac{2}{3}$¢ | 16$\frac{2}{3}$% | $\frac{1}{6}$ |
|  | .83$\frac{1}{3}$ or .833333 | 83$\frac{1}{3}$¢ | 83$\frac{1}{3}$% | $\frac{5}{6}$ |

|  | Decimal Form | Cents Form | Percent Form | Fractional Equivalent |
|---|---|---|---|---|
| Eighths | .12$\frac{1}{2}$ or .125 | 12$\frac{1}{2}$¢ | 12$\frac{1}{2}$% | $\frac{1}{8}$ |
|  | .37$\frac{1}{2}$ or .375 | 37$\frac{1}{2}$¢ | 37$\frac{1}{2}$% | $\frac{3}{8}$ |
|  | .62$\frac{1}{2}$ or .625 | 62$\frac{1}{2}$¢ | 62$\frac{1}{2}$% | $\frac{5}{8}$ |
|  | .87$\frac{1}{2}$ or .875 | 87$\frac{1}{2}$¢ | 87$\frac{1}{2}$% | $\frac{7}{8}$ |
| Twelfths | .08$\frac{1}{3}$ or .083333 | 8$\frac{1}{3}$¢ | 8$\frac{1}{3}$% | $\frac{1}{12}$ |
|  | .41$\frac{2}{3}$ or .416667 | 41$\frac{2}{3}$¢ | 41$\frac{2}{3}$% | $\frac{5}{12}$ |
|  | .58$\frac{1}{3}$ or .583333 | 58$\frac{1}{3}$¢ | 58$\frac{1}{3}$% | $\frac{7}{12}$ |
|  | .91$\frac{2}{3}$ or .916667 | 91$\frac{2}{3}$¢ | 91$\frac{2}{3}$% | $\frac{11}{12}$ |
| One Fifteenth | .06$\frac{2}{3}$ or .066667 | 6$\frac{2}{3}$¢ | 6$\frac{2}{3}$% | $\frac{1}{15}$ |
| One Sixteenth | .06$\frac{1}{4}$ or .0625 | 6$\frac{1}{4}$¢ | 6$\frac{1}{4}$% | $\frac{1}{16}$ |

Referring to Table 3-1, note that those thirds, sixths, twelfths, and one fifteenth which have a $\frac{1}{3}$ or $\frac{2}{3}$ ending in the two-place decimal are changed to six-place decimals. Remember that you can extend these decimals to as many places as needed but the $\frac{1}{3}$ ending must be rounded to 3 in the last place and the $\frac{2}{3}$ ending must be rounded to 7 in the last place.

## Part B Multiplying by an Aliquot Part of 1 or $1.00

When an aliquot part of 1 or $1.00 is to be multiplied by another number, use the shortcut instead of multiplying the long way. That is, replace the aliquot part (in decimals or cents) with its fractional form and then multiply in fractions. Remember that when the aliquot part is in cents, the answer should be expressed in dollars and cents.

In the examples that follow, the shortcut method of using fractions is given at the left. For purposes of comparison, the long way of using decimals is given at the right.

NOTE: The fractional equivalent of an aliquot part is given as a part of 1 or $1.00, such as 25¢ = $\frac{1}{4}$ of $1.00. Since multiplying any number by 1 gives the original number, the 1 or $1.00 can be omitted in the multiplication.

**Using Fractions** **Using Decimals**

**a.** 164 @ 25¢ each

25¢ = $\frac{1}{4}$ × \$1.00 25¢ = .25

$$\frac{\overset{41}{\cancel{164}}}{1} \times \frac{1}{\underset{1}{\cancel{4}}} = \$41 \qquad \begin{array}{r} 164 \\ \times\ .25 \\ \hline 820 \\ 3280 \\ \hline 41.00 \end{array}$$

**b.** 48 @ 87½¢ each

87½¢ = $\frac{7}{8}$ × \$1.00 87½¢ = .875

$$\frac{\overset{6}{\cancel{48}}}{1} \times \frac{7}{\underset{1}{\cancel{8}}} = \$42 \qquad \begin{array}{r} .875 \\ \times\ 48 \\ \hline 7000 \\ 35000 \\ \hline 42.000 \end{array}$$

**c.** 7,236 @ 41⅔¢

41⅔¢ = $\frac{5}{12}$ × \$1.00 42⅔¢ = .416667

$$\frac{\overset{603}{\cancel{7236}}}{1} \times \frac{5}{\underset{1}{\cancel{12}}} = \$3{,}015 \qquad \begin{array}{r} .416667 \\ \times\ 7236 \\ \hline 2500002 \\ 12500010 \\ 83333400 \\ 2916669000 \\ \hline 3015.002412 \end{array}$$

**d.** 330 × .06⅔

.06⅔ = $\frac{1}{15}$ × 1 .06⅔ = .066667

$$\frac{\overset{22}{\cancel{330}}}{1} \times \frac{1}{\underset{1}{\cancel{15}}} = 22 \qquad \begin{array}{r} .066667 \\ \times\ 330 \\ \hline 2000010 \\ 20000100 \\ \hline 22.000110 \end{array}$$

When the examples above are worked by using fractions, there are no decimal places to point off since the other numbers are all whole numbers. The decimal point in the aliquot part disappears when the fractional form is used. When the decimal form is used, as shown at the right-hand column, it is necessary to point off as many places as there are in the aliquot part.

To multiply a decimal by an aliquot part of 1 or \$1.00, put the decimal over 1 and change the aliquot part to its fractional form. Multiply the numerators and divide the product by the denominator. (See Section 2-4, Part D, pages 64-65 in Chapter 2.) Although this method involves both multiplication and division, in most cases the work is simpler than multiplying by the decimal form of the aliquot part. In the examples given below, the long way of using decimals is again given for purposes of comparison.

**Using Fractions** **Using Decimals**

**a.** 79.25 × 66⅔¢

66⅔¢ = $\frac{2}{3}$ × \$1.00 66⅔¢ = .666667

$$\frac{79.25}{1} \times \frac{2}{3} = \frac{158.5}{3} = \$52.83 \qquad \begin{array}{r} .666667 \\ \times\ 79.25 \\ \hline 3333335 \\ 13333340 \\ 600000300 \\ 4666669000 \\ \hline 52.83335975 \end{array}$$

**b.** 87.56 × .375

.375 = $\frac{3}{8}$ × 1

$$\frac{87.56}{1} \times \frac{3}{8} = \frac{262.68}{8} = 32.835 \qquad \begin{array}{r} 87.56 \\ \times\ .375 \\ \hline 43780 \\ 612920 \\ 2626800 \\ \hline 32.83500 \end{array}$$

## Part C Multiplying by a Decimal Mixed Number That Has a Decimal Aliquot Part

If a decimal mixed number has an aliquot part of 1 or \$1.00 as its decimal part, it is possible to use a shortcut when multiplying it by another number. First, change the decimal part to its fractional equivalent so that the decimal mixed number becomes a mixed number. Then multiply in three steps as shown in Section 2-4, Part E, pages 65-66 in Chapter 2.

*Examples:* Multiply as indicated.

a. $648 \times 3.625$

$.625 = \dfrac{5}{8} \times 1$

$3.625 = 3\dfrac{5}{8}$

**Step 1:** $\dfrac{5}{\cancel{8}} \times \dfrac{\cancel{648}^{81}}{1} = 405$

**Step 2.** $\begin{array}{r} 648 \\ \times\ 3\frac{5}{8} \\ \hline 1944 \end{array}$

**Step 3.** $\begin{array}{r} +\ 405 \\ \hline 2349 \end{array}$

b. $89.5 @ \$4.08\frac{1}{3}$

$.08\frac{1}{3} = \dfrac{1}{12} \times \$1.00$

$\$4.08\frac{1}{3} = \$4\frac{1}{12}$

**Step 1.** $\dfrac{1}{12} \times \dfrac{895}{1} = 74\frac{7}{12}$

**Step 2.** $\begin{array}{r} 895 \\ \times\ 4\frac{1}{12} \\ \hline 3580 \end{array}$

**Step 3.** $\begin{array}{r} +\ 74\frac{7}{12} \\ \hline 3654\frac{7}{12} \end{array}$

Pointing off one decimal place, the correct answer to *Example b* above is $365.4\frac{7}{12}$ or $365.45833 = \$365.46$. *Example b* is a case in which the long way of using decimals, $89.5 \times 4.0833$, is probably easier to work.

## Part D  Dividing by an Aliquot Part of 1 or $1.00

When a divisor is a decimal which is an aliquot part of 1 or $1.00, it is possible to use a shortcut. The aliquot part is changed to its fractional equivalent and the division is done in fractions.

*Examples:* Divide as indicated.

a. $863 \div .25$

$.25 = \dfrac{1}{4} \times 1$

$863 \div \dfrac{1}{4} = \dfrac{863}{1} \times \dfrac{4}{1} = 3{,}452$

b. $\$79.83 \div 66\frac{2}{3}¢$

$66\frac{2}{3}¢ = \dfrac{2}{3} \times \$1.00$

$\dfrac{79.83}{1} \div \dfrac{2}{3} = \dfrac{79.83}{1} \times \dfrac{3}{2} = \dfrac{239.49}{2}$

$= 119.745 = \$119.75$

## Part E  Multiplying by an Aliquot Part of 100

The aliquot parts of 100 have no particular business usage. When they occur as prices or quantities, their fractional equivalents provide a shortcut. Referring to Table 3-1 on page 82, if you were to take away the decimal points in the two-place decimals, you would have the aliquot parts of 100. Their fractional equivalents also would be of 100. For example, 25 equals $\frac{1}{4}$ of 100.

To multiply by an aliquot part of 100, replace the aliquot part with the fractional part times 100, and then multiply. You must multiply by 100 since the aliquot parts are fractional parts of 100, not 1.

*Example:* Multiply 30.72 by $58\frac{1}{3}$.

$58\frac{1}{3} = \dfrac{7}{12} \times 100$

$\dfrac{30.72}{1} \times \dfrac{7}{12} \times \dfrac{100}{1} = \dfrac{21{,}504}{12} = 1{,}792$

**Complete Assignment 12**

# Assignment 12
# Section 3-2

## Aliquot Parts and Fractional Equivalents

| | Perfect Score | Student's Score |
|---|---|---|
| Part A | 28 | |
| Part B | 36 | |
| Part C | 12 | |
| Part D | 12 | |
| Part E | 12 | |
| TOTAL | 100 | |

## Part A

### Aliquot Parts of 1 or $1.00

*Directions:* Write the fractional equivalents of 1 or $1.00 of the given aliquot parts. (2 points for each correct answer)

1. .375

2. .83⅓

3. 50¢

4. 8⅓¢

5. .8

6. .666667

7. 62½¢

8. 75¢

*Directions:* Write the aliquot parts which equal the given fractional parts of 1 or $1.00. (2 points for each correct answer)

9. $\frac{1}{3} \times \$1.00$

10. $\frac{3}{8} \times 1$

11. $\frac{7}{12} \times 1$

12. $\frac{2}{5} \times \$1.00$

13. $\frac{1}{4} \times \$1.00$

14. $\frac{5}{6} \times \$1.00$

Student's Score _____

## Part B

### Multiplying by an Aliquot Part of 1 or $1.00

*Directions:* Multiply by using the fractional parts of 1 or $1.00. Show the fractions used. (2 points for each correct answer)

15. $124 \times 25$¢

16. $118 \times 50$¢

17. $480 \times 66\frac{2}{3}$¢

18. $360 \times .33\frac{1}{3}$

19. $216 \times .41\frac{2}{3}$

20. $606 \times .83\frac{1}{3}$

21. $256 \times .62\frac{1}{2}$

22. $240 \times 12\frac{1}{2}$¢

23. $930 \times 30$¢

24. 790 × 70¢

25. 384 × .75

26. 376 × .375

27. 612 × 16⅔¢

28. 1,890 × 8⅓¢

29. 4,480 × 87½¢

30. 660 × 6⅔¢

31. 488 × 6¼¢

32. 876 × 91⅔¢

*Student's Score* _____

# Part C

## *Multiplying by a Decimal Mixed Number That Has a Decimal Aliquot Part*

**Directions:** Multiply by using fractional parts of 1 or $1.00. Show the mixed numbers used. (2 points for each correct answer)

33. 424 × $1.75

34. 720 × $1.12½

35. 564 × $2.83⅓

36. 984 × $2.16⅔

37. 420 × $3.41⅔

38. 360 × $3.87½

*Student's Score* _____

# Part D

## *Dividing by an Aliquot Part of 1 or $1.00*

**Directions:** Divide by using fractional parts of 1 or $1.00. Show the fractions used. (2 points for each correct answer)

39. 24 ÷ .75

40. 75 ÷ .25

41. $84 ÷ 37½¢

42. $25 ÷ 62½¢

43. 350 ÷ .58⅓

44. 870 ÷ .08⅓

*Student's Score* _____

# Part E

## *Multiplying by an Aliquot Part of 100*

**Directions:** Multiply by using fractional parts of 100. Show the fractions used. (2 points for each correct answer)

45. 16⅔ × 96

46. 144 × 33⅓

47. 7.62 × 83⅓

48. 62½ × 48¢

49. 87½ × 72¢

50. 496 × 6¼

*Student's Score* _____

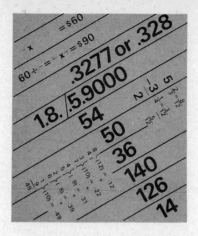

# Working with Percents

Percents are used in business to state rates such as interest and discount; to show parts to be taken; to present relationships and comparisons, such as percents of increase in sales from one month to the next; and to find a whole amount when only a percent of it is known. Generally it is easier to compare numbers in their percent forms than to compare these same numbers expressed as decimals or fractions.

The numbers that you have used so far have been whole numbers, decimals, common fractions, or mixed numbers. In some cases it was necessary to change from one of the forms to another, such as from the fraction $\frac{3}{8}$ to its decimal form, .375. **Percent** is another form in which numbers can be stated and to which decimals, fractions, and mixed numbers can be changed.

You should understand the meaning of percents and be able to convert them to other forms and to use them in business computations without a calculator. A percent key on a calculator can only simplify the mechanical operations with percents, but you must know how to use it correctly. On many calculators, the percent key is activated only if the percent is entered after depressing the multiplication or division key. Then it multiplies or divides immediately.

## Section 4-1 Percent Conversions

A number in percent form cannot be used directly in multiplication or division. It must be changed to one of the other number forms in order to multiply or divide with it. (Some calculators display the decimal form when the percent key is depressed; in others, the change is only internal.) But percents, by themselves, can be added or subtracted without being changed to other forms.

By the definition of percent, a number followed by a percent sign means that number "per hundred." Since "per hundred" is the same as "/100" or "$\frac{1}{100}$" when the slash line is changed to a straight line, the percent sign can be replaced by the word "hundredths." In numbers this means that the percent can be changed to either a "hun-

dredths" decimal or to a fraction with a denominator of 100. For example, $5\% = 5$ hundredths $= .05 = \frac{5}{100}$. The line in a fraction may indicate that the numerator is to be divided by the denominator. Therefore, a denominator of 100 means that whatever is in the numerator is to be divided by 100. This leads to a general rule: *To convert any number in percent form to another form, drop the percent sign and divide the number that remains by 100.* The result then can be put into the required form.

The rest of this section explains in detail how a percent is changed or *converted* to its decimal or fractional form, as well as how to change any number to its percent form.

## Part A — Converting a Percent to a Decimal or a Whole Number

To change a number in percent form to its decimal form, follow the general rule for conversion given on page 87, but use the shortcut for dividing by 100. The general rule can be restated as: To change any number in percent form to its decimal equivalent, *drop the percent sign and move the decimal point in the remaining number two places to the left.*

*Converting percents between 1% and 100% (inclusive) to decimals or whole numbers.* Before starting the conversion, if there is no decimal point in the number, put one in the correct place. In a whole number, put it after the last digit. In a mixed number, put it after the last digit in the whole number part and before the fraction. Then follow the shortcut conversion rule given above.

*Examples:* Convert the percents to their decimal equivalents.

a. $60\% = 60.\% = .60_x = .6$

b. $8\% = 8.\% = .08_x = .08$

c. $6.25\% = .06_x25 = .0625$

d. $16\tfrac{2}{3}\% = 16.\tfrac{2}{3}\% = .16.\tfrac{2}{3} = .1667$

e. $43\tfrac{3}{4}\% = 43.\tfrac{3}{4}\% = .43_x\tfrac{3}{4} = .43\tfrac{3}{4} = .4375$

Generally it is preferable to change a decimal with a fractional ending to a complete decimal, as shown in *Examples d* and *e* above. For most work, four decimal places are enough. There are some exceptions for those decimals that end in $\tfrac{1}{3}$ or $\tfrac{2}{3}$ (see Chapter 3, page 78).

Note that when converting percents between 1% and 100% inclusive, their decimal forms cannot be less than .01 or more than 1.00.

If you would replace the percent signs with cent signs in each of the examples just worked, you would be converting an amount of money expressed in cents to its decimal form. *Cents* and *percents* are very much alike. The rules are the same to convert cents and percents to their decimal forms. Note that 1¢ and 1% both equal .01; and 100¢ and 100% both equal 1.00. (Table 3-1 on page 82 also brings out this similarity.)

*Examples:* Change the cents and percents to their decimal forms.

| | Cents | Percents | Decimal Form for Both |
|---|---|---|---|
| a. | 60¢ | 60% | .60 or .6 |
| b. | 8¢ | 8% | .08 |
| c. | $16\tfrac{2}{3}$¢ | $16\tfrac{2}{3}$% | $.16\tfrac{2}{3}$ or .1667 |

*Converting percents less than 1% to decimals or whole numbers.* Percents that are less than 1% have either a common or a decimal fraction before the percent sign. For example: $\tfrac{1}{2}$% or .5%. Before starting the conversion, put two zeros in front of the number; if the number is a common fraction, put the decimal point after the two zeros or before the fraction. Then follow the shortcut conversion rule.

*Examples:* Convert the percents to their decimal equivalents.

a. $.5\% = 00.5\% = .00_x5 = .005$

$\tfrac{1}{2}\% = 00.\tfrac{1}{2}\% = .00_x\tfrac{1}{2} = .005$

b. $.75\% = 00.75\% = .00_x75 = .0075$

$\tfrac{3}{4}\% = 00.\tfrac{3}{4}\% = .00_x\tfrac{3}{4} = .0075$

c. $.33\tfrac{1}{3}\% = 00.33\tfrac{1}{3}\% = .00_x33\tfrac{1}{3} = .003333$

$\tfrac{1}{3}\% = 00.\tfrac{1}{3}\% = .00_x\tfrac{1}{3} = .003333$

d. $.025\% = 00.025\% = .00_x025 = .00025$

$\tfrac{1}{40}\% = 00.\tfrac{1}{40}\% = .00_x\tfrac{1}{40} = .00025$

In the examples above, note that common fraction endings are changed to their decimal forms (see Chapter 1, page 28). Also note that when converting percents less than 1%, their decimal forms must have at least two zeros after the decimal point.

*Converting percents greater than 100% to decimals or whole numbers.* Before starting the conversion, if the number before the percent sign is a whole or mixed number, put a decimal point after the last digit or before a fraction. Then follow the shortcut conversion rule.

*Examples:* Convert the percents to their decimal equivalents.

a. $102\% = 102.\% = 1.02\overset{\curvearrowleft}{x} = 1.02$

b. $250\% = 250.\% = 2.50\overset{\curvearrowleft}{x} = 2.50 \text{ or } 2.5$

c. $400\% = 400.\% = 4.00\overset{\curvearrowleft}{x} = 4.00 \text{ or } 4$

d. $106\tfrac{2}{3}\% = 106.\tfrac{2}{3}\% = 1.06\overset{\curvearrowleft}{x}\tfrac{2}{3} = 1.06\tfrac{2}{3} = 1.0667$

$106.66\tfrac{2}{3}\% = 1.06\overset{\curvearrowleft}{x}66\tfrac{2}{3} = 1.0667$

Be sure to move the decimal point *only two* places to the left. Again, after the point has been moved, change any common fraction endings to their decimal equivalents.

Note that when converting percents greater than 100%, the results must be either whole numbers or decimal mixed numbers.

## Part B  Converting a Percent to a Common Fraction or a Mixed Number

There are several ways to convert a percent to its common fraction or mixed number equivalent. However, only two of them are given here, with the first being recommended as the easier way. The second is given on page 90 for those who may prefer that method.

The first way is this: To convert a percent to its common fraction or mixed number form, first change it to its decimal form, as shown in Part A. Then change the decimal to its fractional or mixed number equivalent.

As in Part A, the details of conversion will be given in three groups: percents between 1% and 100% (this time *not* including 100%); percents less than 1%; and percents greater than 100%. In the examples for each group, the same percents illustrated in Part A are used since their decimal forms have already been found. Where the percent has a $\tfrac{1}{3}$ or a $\tfrac{2}{3}$ ending, the two-place decimal with the fractional ending is used rather than the rounded-off decimal.

***Converting percents between 1% and 100% (not including 100%) to common fractions.*** Since the decimal forms of these percents are at least .01

but less than 1.00, their common fraction forms must be at least $\tfrac{1}{100}$ but less than 1.

*Examples:* Convert the percents to their fractional equivalents.

a. $60\% = .6 = \dfrac{\overset{3}{\cancel{6}}}{\underset{5}{\cancel{10}}} = \dfrac{3}{5}$

b. $8\% = .08 = \dfrac{\overset{2}{\cancel{8}}}{\underset{25}{\cancel{100}}} = \dfrac{2}{25}$

c. $6.25\% = .0625 = \dfrac{\overset{1}{\cancel{625}}}{\underset{16}{\cancel{10,000}}} = \dfrac{1}{16}$

d. $16\tfrac{2}{3}\% = .16\tfrac{2}{3} = \dfrac{16\tfrac{2}{3}}{100} = 16\tfrac{2}{3} \div \dfrac{100}{1}$

$= \dfrac{\overset{1}{\cancel{50}}}{3} \times \dfrac{1}{\underset{2}{\cancel{100}}} = \dfrac{1}{6}$

e. $43\tfrac{3}{4}\% = .4375 = \dfrac{\overset{\overset{7}{\cancel{175}}}{\cancel{4375}}}{\underset{\underset{16}{\cancel{400}}}{\cancel{10,000}}} = \dfrac{7}{16}$

***Converting percents less than 1% to common fractions.*** The decimal forms of these percents have at least three decimal places and at least two zeros after the point. Therefore, when the decimal is first changed to a common fraction, *before reducing*, the denominator must have at least *three zeros*. A frequent error in converting these small percents is to drop the percent sign without doing anything further.

As in Part A, in the examples that follow, the decimal and common fraction forms of the same percent are used. Note that if the percent sign is dropped from the common fraction forms and two zeros are added to the denominator of the fraction, the result is the desired fractional equivalent of the percent.

*Examples:* Convert the percents to their fractional equivalents.

a. $\left.\begin{array}{l}.5\% \\ \tfrac{1}{2}\% \end{array}\right\}$ $= .005 = \dfrac{\overset{1}{\cancel{5}}}{\underset{200}{\cancel{1000}}} = \dfrac{1}{200}$

b. $\left.\begin{array}{l}.75\% \\ \tfrac{3}{4}\% \end{array}\right\}$ $= .0075 = \dfrac{\overset{3}{\cancel{75}}}{\underset{400}{\cancel{10,000}}} = \dfrac{3}{400}$

c. $\left.\begin{array}{l}.33\tfrac{1}{3}\% \\ \tfrac{1}{3}\% \end{array}\right\}$ $= .0033\tfrac{1}{3} = \dfrac{33\tfrac{1}{3}}{10,000}$

$= \dfrac{\overset{1}{\cancel{100}}}{\underset{100}{3}} \times \dfrac{1}{\cancel{10,000}} = \dfrac{1}{300}$

d. $\left.\begin{array}{l}.025\% \\ \tfrac{1}{40}\% \end{array}\right\}$ $= .00025 = \dfrac{\overset{1}{\cancel{25}}}{\underset{4,000}{\cancel{100,000}}} = \dfrac{1}{4,000}$

***Converting percents greater than 100% to mixed or whole numbers.*** Since 100% equals 1, a percent that is greater than 100% must be more than 1. Therefore, the conversion must result in a mixed or a whole number.

*Examples:* Convert the percents to mixed or whole numbers.

a. $102\% = 1.02 = 1\dfrac{\overset{1}{\cancel{2}}}{\underset{50}{\cancel{100}}} = 1\dfrac{1}{50}$

b. $250\% = 2.5 = 2\tfrac{1}{2}$

c. $400\% = 4.00 = 4$

d. $106\tfrac{2}{3}\% = 1.06\tfrac{2}{3} = 1\dfrac{6\tfrac{2}{3}}{100} = 1\dfrac{1}{15}$

Note in *Example d* that, when the fractional part of a mixed number is a complex fraction, generally it is reduced separately as follows:

$\dfrac{6\tfrac{2}{3}}{100} = 6\tfrac{2}{3} \div \dfrac{100}{1} = \dfrac{\overset{}{\cancel{20}}}{3} \times \dfrac{1}{\underset{5}{\cancel{100}}} = \dfrac{1}{15}$

The second method of converting a percent to its common fraction or mixed number form is based on the fact that dividing any number by 100 is the same as multiplying it by $\tfrac{1}{100}$. The conversion rule can be restated as: To convert a percent to its common fraction or mixed number form, drop the percent sign and multiply the remaining number by $\tfrac{1}{100}$. Any decimal fractions should be changed to their fractional forms before multiplying.

While the arithmetic is simpler in this method, it requires learning another conversion rule. To illustrate this method, the same examples under the first method are used for purposes of comparison.

*Examples:* Convert the percents (between 1% and 100%, not including 100%) to their fractional equivalents.

a. $60\% = 60 \times \dfrac{1}{100} = \dfrac{\overset{3}{\cancel{60}}}{1} \times \dfrac{1}{\underset{5}{\cancel{100}}} = \dfrac{3}{5}$

b. $8\% = 8 \times \dfrac{1}{100} = \dfrac{\overset{2}{\cancel{8}}}{1} \times \dfrac{1}{\underset{25}{\cancel{100}}} = \dfrac{2}{25}$

c. $6.25\% = 6\tfrac{1}{4} \times \dfrac{1}{100} = \dfrac{\overset{1}{\cancel{25}}}{4} \times \dfrac{1}{\underset{4}{\cancel{100}}} = \dfrac{1}{16}$

d. $16\tfrac{2}{3}\% = 16\tfrac{2}{3} \times \dfrac{1}{100} = \dfrac{\overset{1}{\cancel{50}}}{3} \times \dfrac{1}{\underset{2}{\cancel{100}}} = \dfrac{1}{6}$

e. $43\tfrac{3}{4}\% = 43\tfrac{3}{4} \times \dfrac{1}{100} = \dfrac{\overset{7}{\cancel{175}}}{4} \times \dfrac{1}{\underset{4}{\cancel{100}}} = \dfrac{7}{16}$

*Examples:* Convert the percents (less than 1%) to their fractional equivalents.

a. $.5\% = \tfrac{1}{2}\% = \dfrac{1}{2} \times \dfrac{1}{100} = \dfrac{1}{200}$

b. $.75\% = \tfrac{3}{4}\% = \dfrac{3}{4} \times \dfrac{1}{100} = \dfrac{3}{400}$

c. $.33\frac{1}{3}\% = \frac{1}{3}\% = \frac{1}{3} \times \frac{1}{100} = \frac{1}{300}$

d. $.025\% = \frac{1}{40}\% = \frac{1}{40} \times \frac{1}{100} = \frac{1}{4,000}$

*Examples:* Convert the percents (greater than 100%) to mixed or whole numbers.

a. $102\% = 102 \times \frac{1}{100} = \frac{\overset{51}{\cancel{102}}}{1} \times \frac{1}{\underset{50}{\cancel{100}}} = 1\frac{1}{50}$

b. $250\% = 250 \times \frac{1}{100} = \frac{\overset{5}{\cancel{250}}}{1} \times \frac{1}{\underset{2}{\cancel{100}}} = \frac{5}{2} = 2\frac{1}{2}$

c. $400\% = 400 \times \frac{1}{100} = \frac{\overset{4}{\cancel{400}}}{1} \times \frac{1}{\underset{1}{\cancel{100}}} = \frac{4}{1} = 4$

d. $106\frac{2}{3}\% = 106\frac{2}{3} \times \frac{1}{100} = \frac{\overset{16}{\cancel{320}}}{3} \times \frac{1}{\underset{5}{\cancel{100}}} = 1\frac{1}{15}$

## Part C — Converting a Decimal or a Whole Number to Its Percent Equivalent

The general rule to convert any number to its percent form is to multiply the number by 100 and add the percent sign. Note that this is the reverse of what was done in changing a percent to its decimal or fractional form. Since the percent sign stands for "$\frac{1}{100}$," multiplying the number by 100 and then adding the percent sign is the same as multiplying the number by 100 and then dividing it by 100. This is the same as multiplying the number by 1. The value of the number is not changed, only its form.

Since the shortcut to multiply a decimal number by 100 is to move the decimal point two places to the right, the rule can be restated as: To change a decimal or a whole number to a percent, move the decimal point in the number two places to the right and add a percent sign.

The decimal equivalents found in Part A are used as examples to illustrate this rule so that you can compare the operations.

*Converting decimals between .01 and 1.00 (inclusive) to percent equivalents.* If the number has only one decimal place, as in *Example a* below, before starting the conversion add a zero to it in order to move the decimal point two places to the right.

*Examples:* Convert the decimals to their percent equivalents.

a. $.6 = 60.\% = 60\%$

b. $.08 = 08.\% = 8\%$

c. $.0625 = 06.25\% = 6.25\%$

d. $.16\frac{2}{3} = 16.\frac{2}{3}\% = 16\frac{2}{3}\%$

e. $.43\frac{3}{4} = 43.\frac{3}{4}\% = 43\frac{3}{4}\%$

   $.4375 = 43.75\% = 43.75\%$

Note that when the numbers have been converted into their percent forms, the decimal point is dropped if the result is a whole or a mixed number as in *Examples a, b,* and *d,* and the first form of *Example e.*

*Converting decimals less than .01 to percent equivalents.* Decimals less than .01 always have at least three decimal places and at least two zeros after the decimal point. For example, .009 or .0009. Therefore, the number in the converted percent equivalent must always be a decimal or a common fraction.

*Examples:* Convert the decimals to their percent equivalents.

a. $.005 = 00.5\% = .5\% = \frac{1}{2}\%$

b. $.0075 = 00.75\% = .75\% = \frac{3}{4}\%$

c. $.0033\frac{1}{3}\% = 00.33\frac{1}{3}\% = .33\frac{1}{3}\% = \frac{1}{3}\%$

d. $.00025 = 00.025\% = .025\% = \frac{1}{40}\%$

*Converting decimal mixed numbers and whole numbers greater than 1 to percent equivalents.* If the decimal mixed number has only one decimal place, add a zero to it at the end, as in *Example b* at the top of page 92. Add two zeros to a whole number.

**Examples:** Convert the numbers to their percent equivalents.

a. $1.02 = 1.02.\% = 102\%$

b. $2.5 = 2.50 = 2.50.\% = 250\%$

c. $4 = 4.00 = 4.00.\% = 400\%$

d. $1.06\frac{2}{3} = 1.06.\frac{2}{3}\% = 106\frac{2}{3}\%$

## Part D  Converting a Common Fraction or a Mixed Number to Its Percent Equivalent

There are two ways to convert a common fraction or a mixed number to its percent equivalent. The first way is recommended as being the easier. The second is given for those who may prefer that method.

In the first method, the rule may be stated as: To convert a common fraction or a mixed number to its percent equivalent, first change it to its decimal form, then move the decimal point two places to the right, and add a percent sign.

**Examples:** Convert the numbers to their percent equivalents.

a. $\frac{2}{25} = .08 = .08.\% = 8\%$

b. $\frac{1}{6} = .16\frac{2}{3} = .16.\frac{2}{3}\% = 16\frac{2}{3}\%$

c. $\frac{1}{16} = .0625 = .06.25\% = 6.25\% = 6\frac{1}{4}\%$

d. $\frac{1}{300} = .0033\frac{1}{3} = .00.33\frac{1}{3}\% = .33\frac{1}{3}\% = \frac{1}{3}\%$

e. $1\frac{1}{15} = 1.06\frac{2}{3} = 1.06.\frac{2}{3}\% = 106\frac{2}{3}\%$

f. $2\frac{1}{2} = 2.50 = 2.50.\% = 250\%$

Note that after the number has been converted to its percent equivalent, any decimal fraction in the percent may be changed to its common fraction form, as in *Example c* above. Note

also that if the decimal form is a repeating decimal, as in *Example d* above, generally only two decimal places and the fractional ending are used in the percent equivalent.

The rule for the second conversion method can be stated as: To change a common fraction or a mixed number to its percent equivalent, multiply the number by 100 directly and add a percent sign to the result. The same examples in the first method are used to illustrate the second method so that you can compare the two ways.

**Examples:** Convert the numbers to their percent equivalents.

a. $\frac{2}{25} = \frac{2}{25} \times \frac{\overset{4}{100}}{1}\% = 8\%$

b. $\frac{1}{6} = \frac{1}{6} \times \frac{\overset{50}{100}}{1}\% = \frac{50}{3}\% = 16\frac{2}{3}\%$

c. $\frac{1}{16} = \frac{1}{16} \times \frac{\overset{25}{100}}{1}\% = \frac{25}{4}\% = 6\frac{1}{4}\%$

d. $\frac{1}{300} = \frac{1}{300} \times \frac{\overset{1}{100}}{1}\% = \frac{1}{3}\%$

e. $1\frac{1}{15} = \frac{16}{15} \times \frac{\overset{20}{100}}{1}\% = \frac{320}{3}\% = 106\frac{2}{3}\%$

f. $2\frac{1}{2} = \frac{5}{2} \times \frac{\overset{50}{100}}{1}\% = 250\%$

**Complete Assignment 13**

# Assignment 13
# Section 4-1

|  | Perfect Score | Student's Score |
|---|---|---|
| Part A | 25 | |
| Part B | 25 | |
| Part C | 25 | |
| Part D | 25 | |
| TOTAL | 100 | |

## Percent Conversions

# Part A

## Converting a Percent to a Decimal or a Whole Number

*Directions:* Convert the percents to their decimal or whole number equivalents. (1 point for each correct answer)

1. 25%    2. 50%    3. 1%    4. 7%    5. 18%

6. 79%    7. 47.5%    8. $41\frac{2}{3}\%$    9. $4\frac{1}{2}\%$    10. $8\frac{1}{3}\%$

11. 2.25%    12. $12\frac{1}{2}\%$    13. $87\frac{1}{2}\%$    14. $\frac{1}{2}\%$    15. $\frac{2}{3}\%$

16. .25%    17. .1%    18. .03%    19. .98%    20. 109%

21. 225%    22. 400%    23. 500%    24. $237\frac{1}{2}\%$    25. $113\frac{1}{3}\%$

Student's Score _____

# Part B

## Converting a Percent to a Common Fraction or a Mixed Number

*Directions:* Convert the percents to their common fraction or mixed number equivalents. (1 point for each correct answer)

26. 50%    27. 25%    28. 1%    29. 7%    30. 16%

31. 95%    32. $4\frac{1}{2}\%$    33. $6\frac{1}{4}\%$    34. $12\frac{1}{2}\%$    35. $9\frac{1}{2}\%$

36. $3\frac{1}{4}\%$    37. $62\frac{1}{2}\%$    38. $83\frac{1}{3}\%$    39. $\frac{1}{2}\%$    40. $\frac{1}{3}\%$

41. $\frac{2}{5}\%$    42. $\frac{5}{8}\%$    43. $\frac{7}{10}\%$    44. $\frac{9}{20}\%$    45. 240%

46. 660%    47. 275%    48. 530%    49. $112\frac{1}{2}\%$    50. $216\frac{2}{3}\%$

Student's Score _____

# Part C

## Converting a Decimal or a Whole Number to Its Percent Equivalent

*Directions:* Convert the numbers to their percent equivalents. (1 point for each correct answer)

| | | | | |
|---|---|---|---|---|
| 51. .25 | 52. .5 | 53. .01 | 54. .04 | 55. .4 |
| 56. .2 | 57. .165 | 58. .625 | 59. .01$\frac{2}{3}$ | 60. .58$\frac{1}{3}$ |
| 61. .02$\frac{1}{2}$ | 62. .01$\frac{1}{4}$ | 63. .07$\frac{1}{2}$ | 64. .001 | 65. .005 |
| 66. .0025 | 67. .0004 | 68. .0009 | 69. 1.25 | 70. 1.5 |
| 71. 2 | 72. 3 | 73. 3.8 | 74. 4.1 | 75. 2.66$\frac{2}{3}$ |

*Student's Score* _____

# Part D

## Converting a Common Fraction or a Mixed Number to Its Percent Equivalent

*Directions:* Convert the common fractions or mixed numbers to their percent equivalents. (1 point for each correct answer)

| | | | | |
|---|---|---|---|---|
| 76. $\frac{1}{4}$ | 77. $\frac{1}{2}$ | 78. $\frac{2}{3}$ | 79. $\frac{3}{4}$ | 80. $\frac{1}{5}$ |
| 81. $\frac{5}{6}$ | 82. $\frac{3}{8}$ | 83. $\frac{7}{9}$ | 84. $\frac{9}{10}$ | 85. $\frac{11}{12}$ |
| 86. $\frac{2}{15}$ | 87. $\frac{5}{16}$ | 88. $\frac{19}{20}$ | 89. $\frac{3}{100}$ | 90. $\frac{1}{125}$ |
| 91. $\frac{1}{150}$ | 92. $\frac{1}{200}$ | 93. $\frac{3}{400}$ | 94. $\frac{7}{800}$ | 95. 1$\frac{1}{4}$ |
| 96. 2$\frac{1}{3}$ | 97. 3$\frac{1}{2}$ | 98. 4$\frac{3}{4}$ | 99. 5$\frac{2}{3}$ | 100. 6$\frac{1}{5}$ |

*Student's Score* _____

# Section 4-2  Finding a Percentage

The word "percentage" has two meanings. It can refer to that area of arithmetic in which percents are used in some way. It also can refer specifically to the product found when a given percent is multiplied by a given number. For example, when you figure a sales tax, such as 5% of $4.50, you are finding a **percentage**. The word "of" indicates multiplication in this case.

The given percent is called the **rate**; the given number is called the **base**. The following formula is used to find percentages.

$$\text{Percentage} = \text{Base} \times \text{Rate}$$
$$P = B \times R$$

In the formula, the base (B) is given first because it must be entered first on many calculators.

It is a good idea, however, to identify the parts of the formula before applying it in a problem. This procedure will prove useful in later sections of this chapter. An example of a percentage problem is:

Find 4% of $25.  P = ? (percentage)
  B = $25 (base)
  R = 4% (rate)

In a percentage problem like the above, the rate and base can be identified easily since they are connected to each other by the word "of" or by a multiplication sign.

It was pointed out at the beginning of this chapter that a number in percent form cannot be used directly in multiplication or division. In order to multiply by a percent, the percent must be converted to its decimal or common fraction form. The decimal form is used when the fractional form is not easy to use. To solve the percentage problem given above, therefore, 4% (R) must first be converted to its decimal form, which is .04. Then the formula can be applied as follows:

$$P = B \times R$$
$$P = \$25 \times .04 = \$1.00$$

Note that the base in the above problem is an amount of money; in other problems the base may be some other quantity. The percentage (the product) found is always stated in the same terms as the base, whether it be money, a weight, or a measure. Sometimes errors are made by add-

ing the percent sign to the answer. Remember that the percent sign is dropped when the percent is converted to a decimal or a fraction.

The rest of this section explains in detail how to use the percentage formula with various percents.

## Part A  Multiplying by Percents Between 1% and 100%

Most of the percents (R) used in business lie between 1% and 100%. The rate is changed to a decimal or to a proper fraction, depending on which form is easier to use with the given base.

The first three examples given below are special cases which should always be worked by using shortcuts. Since 1% = .01, the percentage in *Example a* is found by moving the decimal point of the base (B) *two* places to the left. Since 10% = .10 = .1, the percentage in *Example b* is found by moving the decimal point of the base *one* place to the left. Since 100% = 1 and multiplying any number by 1 gives the same number, when the rate is 100% as in *Example c*, the percentage is always the same as the base.

### Examples:

a. 1% of $65.79
   $P = B \times R$
   $P = \$65.79 \times .01 = \$.65_{\curvearrowleft}79 = \$0.66$

b. 10% of $365
   $P = B \times R$
   $P = \$365 \times .1 = \$36.5_{\curvearrowleft} = \$36.50$

c. 100% of $1,698.53
   $P = B \times R$
   $P = \$1,698.53 \times 1 = \$1,698.53$

In the remaining examples that follow, the problems are worked both in decimals and fractions so that you can see which form is easier to use.

d. 5% of $320
   $P = B \times R$, where $R = 5\% = .05 = \frac{1}{20}$
   $P = \$320 \times .05$

   $$\begin{array}{r} 320 \\ \times\ .05 \\ \hline 16.00 \end{array} = \$16.00$$

$$P = \$320 \times \tfrac{1}{20}$$

$$= \frac{\overset{16}{\cancel{320}}}{1} \times \frac{1}{\underset{1}{\cancel{20}}} = \$16.00$$

e. 28% of 4,578 people
$P = B \times R$, where $R = 28\% = .28 = \tfrac{7}{25}$
$P = 4{,}578 \times .28$

$$
\begin{array}{r}
4578 \\
\times\ \ .28 \\
\hline
36624 \\
91560 \\
\hline
1281.84 \\
\end{array}
= 1{,}282 \text{ people}
$$

$$P = \frac{4578}{1} \times \frac{7}{25}$$

$$= \frac{32046}{25} = 1281.84 = 1{,}282 \text{ people}$$

f. $2\tfrac{1}{4}\%$ of \$1,500
$P = B \times R$, where $R = 2\tfrac{1}{4}\% = .0225 = \tfrac{9}{400}$
$P = \$1{,}500 \times .0225$

$$
\begin{array}{r}
.0225 \\
\times\ \ \ 1500 \\
\hline
1125 \\
2250 \\
\hline
33.7500 \\
\end{array}
= \$33.75
$$

Note in *Example f* above that the two zeros of the 1,500 are not used in the multiplication but are brought down to the answer before pointing off.

$$P = \$1{,}500 \times \tfrac{9}{400}$$

$$= \frac{\overset{15}{\cancel{1500}}}{1} \times \frac{9}{\underset{4}{\cancel{400}}} = \frac{135}{4} = \$33.75$$

## Part B  Using Aliquot Parts of 100%

Since 100% equals 1, the aliquot parts of 100% and 1 have the same fractional equivalents. Table 3-1 on page 82 gives the fractional equivalents of percents that frequently occur in business.

Multiplication with the fractional form of a percent often is shorter and simpler than with the decimal form. Therefore, the fractional form should be used as much as possible, especially when the denominator can be canceled into the base in a percentage problem. As mentioned in the previous chapter, usually you can beat a calculator if you multiply by the fraction mentally.

*Examples:*

a. 25% of \$240
$P = B \times R$, where $R = 25\% = \tfrac{1}{4}$

$$= \frac{\overset{60}{\cancel{240}}}{1} \times \frac{1}{\underset{1}{\cancel{4}}} = \$60.00$$

b. $58\tfrac{1}{3}\%$ of 492
$P = B \times R$, where $R = 58\tfrac{1}{3}\% = \tfrac{7}{12}$

$$= \frac{\overset{41}{\cancel{492}}}{1} \times \frac{7}{\underset{1}{\cancel{12}}} = 287$$

c. $66\tfrac{2}{3}\%$ of \$2,496
$P = B \times R$, where $R = 66\tfrac{2}{3}\% = \tfrac{2}{3}$

$$= \frac{\overset{832}{\cancel{2496}}}{1} \times \frac{2}{\underset{1}{\cancel{3}}} = 1664 = \$1{,}664.00$$

Note that if *Example c* above were done in decimals, it would have to be $\$2{,}496 \times .666667$ in order to get an accurate answer.

## Part C  Multiplying by Percents Less than 1%

When the rate is a percent less than 1%, care must be taken in converting the percent to its decimal or proper fraction form. The decimal form must have at least two zeros after the decimal point; the proper fraction form must have at least two zeros in the denominator before reducing.

*Examples:*

a. $\tfrac{1}{2}\%$ of \$124.50
$P = B \times R$, where $R = \tfrac{1}{2}\% = .005 = \tfrac{1}{200}$

$$P = 124.50 \times .005$$

$$124.5$$
$$\times \quad .005$$
$$\overline{.6225} = \$0.62$$

$$P = \frac{\overset{62.25}{\cancel{124.50}}}{1} \times \frac{1}{\underset{100}{\cancel{200}}} = .6225 = \$0.62$$

After the percentage has been found, mentally take 1% of the base by moving its decimal point two places to the left. The percentage found by multiplying by a percent less than 1% must be smaller than 1% of the base.

> **Check:** $124.50 \times 1\% = \$1.245$. The percentage found in *Example a* is smaller than $1.245.

b. $.375\% \times \$480$
   $P = B \times R$, where $R = .375\% = .00375 = \frac{3}{800}$

$$P = \$480 \times .00375$$

$$\begin{array}{r} .00375 \\ \times \quad 480 \\ \hline 3000 \\ 15000 \phantom{0}\\ \hline 1.80000 = \$1.80 \end{array}$$

$$P = \frac{\overset{3}{\cancel{480}}}{1} \times \frac{3}{\underset{5}{\cancel{800}}} = \frac{9}{5} = 1\frac{4}{5} = \$1.80$$

> **Check:** $480 \times 1\% = \$4.80$. The percentage found in *Example b* is smaller than $4.80.

Not only can 1% of the base be used as a check, but also it can be used to find the percentage when the rate is less than 1%. A fractional percent—whether it is a decimal fraction or a proper fraction—equals that same fractional part of 1%.

**Example:** $\frac{1}{2}\% = .5\% = .005 = \frac{1}{200}$

$$1\% \qquad = .01 \quad = \tfrac{1}{100}$$

$$\tfrac{1}{2} \times 1\% = \tfrac{1}{2} \times .01 \quad = \frac{.01}{2} = .005$$

*or* $\qquad = \frac{1}{2} \times \frac{1}{100} = \frac{1}{200}$

Thus, another method of multiplying the base by a fractional percent is to find 1% of the base first, and then multiply the result by the decimal or fraction before the percent sign.

*Examples:*

a. $\frac{1}{4}\%$ of $68.96

$$P = B \times R$$

$$1\% \times 68.96 = .6896$$

$$P = .6896 \times \tfrac{1}{4} = .1724 = \$0.17$$

b. $\frac{2}{3}\%$ of $542.40

$$P = B \times R$$

$$1\% \times 542.40 = 5.4240$$

$$P = \frac{5.424}{1} \times \frac{2}{3} = \frac{10.848}{3} = 3.616 = \$3.62$$

## Part D  *Multiplying by Percents Larger than 100%*

When the percent is more than 100%, care must be taken in converting it correctly to its decimal, whole number, or mixed number form. Remember to move the decimal point only two places to the left to find the decimal equivalent.

*Examples:*

a. 400% of $395
   $P = B \times R$, where $R = 400\% = 4$
   $P = \$395 \times 4 = \$1,580$

b. 125% of 788
   $P = B \times R$, where $R = 125\% = 1.25 = 1\frac{1}{4}$
   $P = 788 \times 1.25$

$$\begin{array}{r} 788 \\ \times \quad 1.25 \\ \hline 3940 \\ 15760 \phantom{0}\\ 78800 \phantom{00}\\ \hline 985.00 \end{array}$$

$$P = \frac{\overset{197}{\cancel{788}}}{1} \times \frac{5}{\underset{1}{\cancel{4}}} = 985$$

c. 350% of $1,675
$$P = B \times R, \text{ where } R = 350\% = 3.5 = 3\frac{1}{2}$$
$$P = \$1,675 \times 3.5$$

$$\begin{array}{r} 1675 \\ \times\ \ 3.5 \\ \hline 8375 \\ 50250 \\ \hline 5862.5 \end{array} = \$5,862.50$$

$$P = \frac{1675}{1} \times \frac{7}{2} = \$5,862.50$$

Remember that when the base is multiplied by a rate that is more than 100%, the percentage must always be larger than the base. If the rate is 200%, the percentage is two times the base; if the rate is 300%, the percentage is 3 times the base, etc.

## Part E  Business Applications

A large part of the business usage of percents consists of taking a percent of a number to figure discounts, interest, commissions, etc. These applications are discussed separately in later chapters.

Another application consists of distributing overhead expenses to the various departments of a company. Overhead expenses are those overall expenses, such as heat, light, rent, janitorial service, insurance, etc., which are necessary to run a business. One of the ways by which distribution is made is to charge to each department the same percent of the overhead expenses as the percent of floor space occupied by the department.

*Example:* A company has a total overhead expense for the month of $18,400. Distribute this amount among the five departments according to the given percent of floor space occupied.

| Department | Percent of Floor Space |
|---|---|
| A | 14.3 |
| B | $33\frac{1}{3}$ |
| C | $16\frac{2}{3}$ |
| D | 28.6 |
| E | 7.1 |
| | 100.0 |

Note that the percents must add up to exactly 100% in order that the full amount can be distributed.

Department A:   $18,400 × 14.3%

$$\begin{array}{r} 18400 \\ \times\ \ .143 \\ \hline 552 \\ 7360 \\ 18400 \\ \hline 2631.200 \end{array} = \$2,631.20$$

Department B:   $18,400 × $33\frac{1}{3}$%

$$18400 \times \tfrac{1}{3} = \$6,133.33$$

Department C:   $18,400 × $16\frac{2}{3}$%

$$18400 \times \tfrac{1}{6} = \$3,066.67$$

Department D:   $18,400 × 28.6%

$$\begin{array}{r} 18400 \\ \times\ \ .286 \\ \hline 1104 \\ 14720 \\ 36800 \\ \hline 5262.400 \end{array} = \$5,262.40$$

Department E:   $18,400 × 7.1%

$$\begin{array}{r} 18400 \\ \times\ \ .071 \\ \hline 184 \\ 12880 \\ \hline 1306.400 \end{array} = \$1,306.40$$

The tabulated answer to the problem is presented below:

| Department | Percent of Floor Space | Amount |
|---|---|---|
| A | 14.3 | $ 2,631.20 |
| B | $33\frac{1}{3}$ | 6,133.33 |
| C | $16\frac{2}{3}$ | 3,066.67 |
| D | 28.6 | 5,262.40 |
| E | 7.1 | 1,306.40 |
| | 100.0 | $18,400.00 |

Complete Assignment 14

# Assignment 14
# Section 4-2

*Finding a Percentage*

| | Perfect Score | Student's Score |
|---|---|---|
| Part A | 20 | |
| Part B | 20 | |
| Part C | 30 | |
| Part D | 15 | |
| Part E | 15 | |
| TOTAL | 100 | |

## Part A

### Multiplying by Percents Between 1% and 100%

*Directions:* Find the percentage. Round off all answers to two decimal places. (1 point for each correct answer)

1. 20% of 17.65

2. 25% of 36.4

3. 11% of .827

4. 22% of $3.65

5. 3.4% of $250

6. 4.3% of $79

7. 68% of .932

8. 29% of .175

9. 6% of $0.98

10. 5% of $0.75

11. 45% of 8.60

12. 35% of 4.80

13. 9½% of $250

14. 5½% of $950

15. 7¾% of $10.80

16. 8⅔% of $14.50

17. 5.85% of $762

18. 6.25% of $8,500

19. 7.35% of $16,000

20. 9.65% of $7,400

*Student's Score* _____

Assignment 14

# Part B
## Using Aliquot Parts of 100%

**Directions:** Find the percentage by changing the percent to its proper fraction form. Round off all answers to two decimal places. (1 point for each correct answer)

21. 50% of 254

22. 25% of 180

23. 12½% of 9,600

24. 33⅓% of 7,200

25. 66⅔% of $480

26. 8⅓% of $240

27. 6⅔% of $75.75

28. 6¼% of $96.80

29. 20% of $69.85

30. 40% of $85.50

31. 87½% of 5,600

32. 83⅓% of 5,400

33. 60% of .25

34. 80% of .75

35. 16⅔% of $320.40

36. 91⅔% of $120

37. 41⅔% of $96

38. 62½% of .048

39. 37½% of .016

40. 75% of .144

*Student's Score* _____

# Part C
## Multiplying by Percents Less than 1%

**Directions:** Find the percentage. Round off all answers to two decimal places. (2 points for each correct answer)

41. ¾% of 260

42. ¼% of 412

43. ½% of 2,000

44. ⅓% of 2,400

45. .12½% of $6,000

46. .28% of $4.40

47. .85% of $3.20

48. .01% of 45,189

49. .02% of 6,350

50. ⅔% of $3,900

51. ⅔% of $2,400

52. ⅙% of $64.20

53. ⅛% of $8.24

54. .0375% of 4,800

55. .075% of 6,400

*Student's Score* _____

Assignment 14

# Part D

## Multiplying by Percents Larger than 100%

**Directions:** Find the percentage. Round off all answers to two decimal places. (1 point for each correct answer)

**56.** 110% of $8.32

**57.** 150% of $7.69

**58.** 137½% of $56

**59.** 225% of .32

**60.** 475% of .85

**61.** 360% of .98

**62.** 240% of 1.35

**63.** 325% of $90

**64.** 216⅔% of 4.28

**65.** 180% of $2,400

**66.** 175% of $2,888

**67.** 287½% of 800

**68.** 550% of 7,950

**69.** 236% of $4.56

**70.** 163% of $9.38

*Student's Score* _____

# Part E

## Business Applications

**Directions:** Find the percentage as indicated. (1 point for each correct answer)

**71.** The Mitchell Company had a total of $20,850 for overhead expenses for the month of June. Distribute this amount among the eight departments according to the floor space occupied. Write your answers in the spaces provided.

| Department | Percent of Floor Space | Amount |
|---|---|---|
| A | 15.6 | $_____ |
| B | 8⅓ | _____ |
| C | 14.3 | _____ |
| D | 17.8 | _____ |
| E | 3.4 | _____ |
| F | 16⅔ | _____ |
| G | 22.3 | _____ |
| H | 1.6 | _____ |
| | 100.0 | $_____ |

**72.** The cost of building a new home was estimated at $36,400. Of this amount, 15% was for electrical work; ½% for insurance; 32% for labor; 30% for materials and supplies; 12½% for plumbing; and 2% for miscellaneous expenses. The rest was the building contractor's profit. Find the amount estimated for each item. Write your answers in the spaces provided.

| | |
|---|---|
| Electrical work | $ _____ |
| Insurance | _____ |
| Labor | _____ |
| Materials and Supplies | _____ |
| Plumbing | _____ |
| Miscellaneous Expense | _____ |
| Profit | _____ |

*Student's Score* _____

# Section 4-3  Finding What Percent One Number Is of Another

Percents are used in business to compare and analyze various figures. The percent of increase or decrease in sales from one month to the next, the percent of cost to selling price, the percent of a particular expense to total expense, and the percent of net profit to net sales are a few examples.

When you are asked to find what percent one number is of another, the problem is usually expressed in one of two ways. For example:

1. 24 is what percent of 96?
2. What percent of 96 is 24?

Remember that the numbers given in the above problem are the percentage (P = 24) and the base (B = 96). The percent you are asked to find is the rate (R). The formula for finding the rate can be found easily from the basic formula, $P = B \times R$. Divide both sides of the equation by B so that R stands alone, as follows:

$$\frac{P}{B} = \frac{\overset{1}{\cancel{B}} \times R}{\underset{1}{\cancel{B}}} \ or \ \frac{P}{B} = R \ or \ R = \frac{P}{B}$$

Since the fraction line in $\frac{P}{B}$ can indicate division, the formula for finding R can be written as:

$$R = P \div B$$

Before using the formula for finding the rate, it is important to choose the right numbers for the percentage (P) and the base (B) from the given figures in the problem. The base (B) is always the given number after the word "of." The percentage is the other given number.

To find what percent one number is of another, follow these two steps:

1. Divide the percentage (P) by the base (B).
2. Change the quotient to a percent by multiplying it by 100 and then adding a percent sign.

*Example:*  48 is what percent of 192?

**Step 1:**  R = P ÷ B  *or*  R = 48 ÷ 192

$$R = \frac{.25}{192 \, \overline{\smash{)}\, 48.00}}$$

**Step 2:**  .25 = ₓ25.% = 25%

In Step 2, remember to use the shortcut: To multiply any number by 100, move the decimal point two places to the right.

The result is checked by multiplying the given base by the rate. The product should be the same as the given percentage.

$$\textbf{Check:}\ 192 \times 25\% = \frac{\overset{48}{\cancel{192}}}{1} \times \frac{1}{\underset{1}{\cancel{4}}} = 48$$

## Part A  Finding Percents Between 1% and 100%

Most of the percents that occur as rates in business are between 1% and 100%. When the base (B) is larger than the percentage (P) but not more than 100 times the percentage, the required rate is between 1% and 100%.

In business reports, generally the rate needs to be expressed correctly to one decimal place in the percent. Therefore, the division must be carried out to four places where necessary, so that the quotient can be rounded off to three decimal places.

In the following examples, the steps are numbered to show: (1) the division and, (2) the conversion to a percent.

*Examples:*

a. 32 is what percent of 144?

**Step 1:** R = P ÷ B *or* R = 32 ÷ 144

$$R = \frac{.2222 \ or \ .222}{144 \, \overline{\smash{)}\, 32.0000}}$$

**Step 2:** .222 = ₓ22.2% = 22.2%

**Check:**  144 × 22.2% = 144 × .222

$$
\begin{array}{r}
144 \\
\times \ .222 \\
\hline
288 \\
2880 \\
22800 \\
\hline
31.968 \ \text{(a little less than 32)}
\end{array}
$$

Note that when the quotient is rounded off, the check will not come out exactly to the given percentage. It will be a little *less* if the third decimal place in the quotient was not changed.

b. $25.96 is what percent of $685?

**Step 1:** R = P ÷ B *or* R = 25.96 ÷ 685

$$R = \frac{.0378 \text{ or } .038}{685\,\overline{)\,25.9600}}$$

**Step 2:** .038 = ͺ03.8% = 3.8%

**Check:** 685 × 3.8% = 685 × .038

```
      685
   ×  .038
   ─────────
     5480
    20550
   ─────────
   26.030  (a little more than 25.96)
```

Note that when the third decimal place in the quotient is changed in the rounding off, the check will come out a little *more* than the given percentage.

c. What percent of $337.20 is $285.71?

**Step 1:** R = P ÷ B *or* R = 285.71 ÷ 337.20

$$R = \frac{.8473 \text{ or } .847}{337{.}2\,\overline{)\,285{.}7{.}1000}}$$

**Step 2:** .847 = ͺ84.7% = 84.7%

**Check:** 337.20 × 84.7% = 337.2 × .847

```
      337.2
   ×   .847
   ─────────
     23604
    134880
   2697600
   ─────────
   285.6084  (a little less than 285.71)
```

As in Part A of Section 4-2 (pages 95-96), there are three special cases which should always be done mentally and for much the same reasons. The examples below are worked in detail to show you why you can find the rates mentally in these special cases.

*Examples:*

a. When P × 100 = B, then R = 1%.

R = ?          R = P ÷ B
P = 8.63          = 8.63 ÷ 863
B = 863           = .01 = 1%

b. When P × 10 = B, then R = 10%.

R = ?          R = P ÷ B
P = 86.3          = 86.3 ÷ 863
B = 863           = .1 = .10 = 10%

c. When P = B, then R = 100%.

R = ?          R = P ÷ B
P = 863           = 863 ÷ 863
B = 863           = 1 = 100%

Note that *Example c* above shows that any number is 100% of itself.

Occasionally a rate must be expressed correctly to two decimal places. In this case, in Step 1 the division must be carried out to five places so that the quotient can be rounded off to four places.

*Example:* What percent of 460 is 250?

**Step 1:** R = P ÷ B *or* R = 250 ÷ 460

$$R = \frac{.54347 \text{ or } .5435}{460\,\overline{)\,250.00000}}$$

**Step 2:** .5435 = ͺ54.35% = 54.35%

**Check:** 460 × 54.35% = 460 × .5435

```
      .5435
   ×   460
   ─────────
    32610
   217400
   ─────────
   250.0100  (a little more than 250)
```

<sup></sup>*Part* **Finding Percents**
**B** **Less than 1%**

When the base (B) is more than 100 times the percentage (P), the required percent (R) is less than 1%. Therefore, the number before the percent sign must be a decimal fraction or a proper fraction.

*Examples:*

a. 2 is what percent of 400?

Step 1: R = P ÷ B *or* R = 2 ÷ 400

$$R = 400\overline{)2.000}\;\;.005$$

Step 2: .005 = ͺ00.5% = .5% = ½%

Check: 400 × ½% = 400 × .005 = 2.000

b. What percent of $50.63 is 48¢?

Step 1: R = P ÷ B *or* R = .48 ÷ 50.63

$$R = 50ͺ63.\overline{)ͺ48.0000}\;\;.0094 \text{ or } .009$$

Step 3: .009 = ͺ00.9% = .9%

Check: $50.63 × .9% = $50.63 × .009

$$\begin{array}{r} 50.63 \\ \times\ \ .009 \\ \hline .45567 \text{ (a little less than .48)} \end{array}$$

c. What fractional percent of 2,400 is 3?

Step 1: R = P ÷ B *or* R = 3 ÷ 2,400

$$R = 2400\overline{)3.0000}\;\;.0012\tfrac{1}{2} \text{ or } .00125$$

Step 2: .00125 = ͺ00.125% = ⅛%

Check: $2,400 \times \tfrac{1}{8}\% = \dfrac{\cancel{2400}}{1} \times \dfrac{1}{\cancel{800}} = 3$

In the examples above, note that in Step 1 the quotient in its decimal form has at least two zeros after the decimal point.

## Part C  *Finding Percents Greater than 100%*

When the base (B) is less than the percentage (P), the required rate (R) is greater than 100%.

Therefore, the number before the percent sign must be a whole number, a mixed number, or a decimal mixed number.

*Examples:*

a. 484 is what percent of 121?

Step 1: R = P ÷ B *or* R = 484 ÷ 121

$$R = 121\overline{)484.}\;\;4.$$

Step 2: 4 = 400%

Check: 121 × 400% = 121 × 4 = 484

b. $23.58 is what percent of $17.50?

Step 1: R = P ÷ B *or* R = 23.58 ÷ 17.50

$$R = 17ͺ5.\overline{)23ͺ5.8000}\;\;1.3474 \text{ or } 1.347$$

Step 2: 1.347 = 1ͺ34.7% = 134.7%

Check: $17.50 × 134.7% = 17.5 × 1.347

$$\begin{array}{r} 1.347 \\ \times\ 17.5 \\ \hline 6735 \\ 94290 \\ 134700 \\ \hline 23.5725 \text{ (a little less than $23.58)} \end{array}$$

c. ¾ is what percent of $\tfrac{9}{16}$ ?

Step 1: R = P ÷ B *or* R = ¾ ÷ $\tfrac{9}{16}$

$$R = \dfrac{\cancel{3}^{1}}{\cancel{4}_{1}} \times \dfrac{\cancel{16}^{4}}{\cancel{9}_{3}} = \dfrac{4}{3} = 1\tfrac{1}{3}$$

Step 2: 1⅓ × 100 = 133⅓%

Check: $\dfrac{9}{16} \times 133\tfrac{1}{3}\% = \dfrac{9}{16} \times 1\tfrac{1}{3} = \dfrac{\cancel{9}^{3}}{\cancel{16}_{4}} \times \dfrac{\cancel{4}^{1}}{\cancel{3}_{1}} = \tfrac{3}{4}$

Remember that the base and the percentage must be identified correctly. The number after the word "of" is always the base, even if it is smaller than the percentage.

A frequent error in problems of finding what percent one number is of another lies in omitting Step 2; the quotient must be multiplied by 100 before affixing the percent sign.

## Part D Business Applications

In analyzing its business operations, a company often is interested in the percent of increase or decrease in its departmental sales for comparable periods. Generally this is expressed as a percent of change. (See Section 1-3, Part D, page 22.) This is the percent that the increase or decrease in the later period is of the earlier period. A plus sign is placed before a percent of increase, and a minus sign before a percent of decrease.

**Example:** Given the following data, what is the percent of change in the monthly sales of last year compared to this year?

| Month | Sales Last Year | Sales This Year |
|---|---|---|
| January | $20,000 | $23,000 |
| February | 16,000 | 18,000 |
| March | 15,000 | 14,000 |
| April | 22,000 | 18,000 |

The first step in solving this problem is to find the *amount* of change, not the rate. Finding the difference between the amount of sales this year and the amount of sales last year for each month results in the following:

Jan.: $23,000 - $20,000 = $3,000 (inc.)
Feb.: $18,000 - $16,000 = $2,000 (inc.)
Mar.: $15,000 - $14,000 = $1,000 (dec.)
Apr.: $22,000 - $18,000 = $4,000 (dec.)

The amount of change for each month is the increase or decrease, or P in the formula, R = P ÷ B. Thus, the increase or decrease becomes the dividend.

The second step is to identify which numbers in the given set of figures represent the base (B), or the divisor. Would the base be "Last Year" figures or "This Year" figures? In any comparison that involves periods of time, the earlier period always represents the base. This is true whether there is an increase or decrease in the later period. Thus, each number in the "Last Year" column becomes the base, or divisor.

The final step is to find the percent of change, or rate (R), for each month. Using the formula, R = P ÷ B:

January:   R = $3,000 ÷ $20,000 = .15 = 15.0%
February: R = $2,000 ÷ $16,000 = .125 = 12.5%
March:    R = $1,000 ÷ $15,000 = .067 = - 6.7%
April:    R = $4,000 ÷ $22,000 = .182 = -18.2%

As a check, the percent of change (R) should be multiplied by the amount in the earlier period (B); the product should be the increase or decrease (P).

The complete business report for the above problem is presented below. In most business reports that are arranged in columns and rows, the dollar sign and percent sign are used only with the numbers in the first row and the totals. (Note that the report below does not have a total.) Also, in most reports the percent is expressed correctly to one decimal place. Therefore, when the percent is an exact whole number, as for January in the report below, a zero is placed in the tenths position to indicate that the tenths digit was not omitted in error.

### MONTHLY SALES

| Month | Last Year | This Year | Amount of Change | Percent of Change |
|---|---|---|---|---|
| January | $20,000 | $23,000 | $3,000 | +15.0% |
| February | 16,000 | 18,000 | 2,000 | +12.5 |
| March | 15,000 | 14,000 | 1,000 | - 6.7 |
| April | 22,000 | 18,000 | 4,000 | -18.2 |

Complete Assignment 15

## Assignment 15
## Section 4-3

|            | Perfect Score | Student's Score |
|------------|---------------|-----------------|
| Part A     | 30            |                 |
| Part B     | 30            |                 |
| Part C     | 30            |                 |
| Part D     | 10            |                 |
| TOTAL      | 100           |                 |

*Finding What Percent
One Number Is of Another*

## Part A

### Finding Percents Between 1% and 100%

*Directions:*  Find the percent as indicated and check. (3 points for each correct answer)

1. What percent of 50 is 4?

2. What percent of 40 is 8?

3. $2.64 is what percent of $48?

4. $19.50 is what percent of $260?

5. What percent is $17\frac{1}{2}$ of $187\frac{1}{2}$?

6. What percent is 15.9 of $238\frac{1}{2}$?

7. What percent of .88 is .66?

8. What percent of $4.00 is $2.75?

9. $262.50 is what percent of $650.25?

10. $18.60 is what percent of $59.43?

*Student's Score* _____

# Part B

## Finding Percents Less Than 1%

**Directions:** Find the percent as indicated and check. Express the answer either as a decimal fraction or as a common fraction percent. (3 points for each correct answer)

11. What percent of 200 is 1?

12. What percent of 625 is 2.5?

13. $2.00 is what percent of $500?

14. What percent is $1.00 of $145?

15. What percent is .854 of 244?

16. 162.5 is what percent of 56,000?

17. $5.50 is what percent of $2,200?

18. $1.80 is what percent of $425?

19. What percent of 90 is $\frac{3}{4}$?

20. $\frac{3}{8}$ is what percent of $41\frac{2}{3}$?

*Student's Score* _____

# Part C

## *Finding Percents Greater Than 100%*

*Directions:*  Find the percent as indicated and check. (3 points for each correct answer)

**21.** What percent of 500 is 1,000?

**22.** What percent of $1.50 is $1.50?

**23.** $4\frac{1}{2}$ is what percent of $1\frac{1}{8}$?

**24.** $\frac{7}{8}$ is what percent of $\frac{2}{3}$?

**25.** What percent is 468.3 of 267.6?

**26.** What percent is $216.26 of $196.60?

**27.** What percent of 1.42 is 4.97?

**28.** What percent of $7.20 is $24.84?

**29.** 614.68 is what percent of 270.4?

**30.** $15 is what percent of $3.50?

*Student's Score* _____

# Part D

## Business Applications

*Directions:* Complete the following report. For each percent of change, place a plus sign before an increase and a minus sign before a decrease. (1 point for each correct answer)

### MONTHLY SALES

| | Month | Last Year | This Year | Amount of Change | Percent of Change |
|---|---|---|---|---|---|
| 31. | July | $20,000 | $18,000 | _____ | _____ |
| 32. | August | 23,000 | 22,000 | _____ | _____ |
| 33. | September | 25,000 | 28,000 | _____ | _____ |
| 34. | October | 27,000 | 36,000 | _____ | _____ |
| 35. | November | 26,000 | 24,000 | _____ | _____ |

*Student's Score* _____

# Section 4-4  Finding a Number When a Percent of It Is Given

The third application of percents occurs much less often in business than finding a percentage or finding what percent one number is of another. It deals with finding the entire number when only a given percentage is known.

When you are asked to find a number when only a given percent of it is known, the problem is usually expressed in one of two ways. For example:

1. 6% of what number is 24?
2. 24 is 6% of what number?

Remember that you have two known factors in the above problem: the percentage (P = 24) and the percent (R = 6%). The unknown number you are required to find is the base (B). The formula for the base can be found from the basic formula, P = B × R. Divide both sides of the equation by R so that B stands alone:

$$\frac{P}{R} = \frac{B \times \overset{1}{\cancel{R}}}{\underset{1}{\cancel{R}}} \quad or \quad \frac{P}{R} = B \quad or \quad B = \frac{P}{R}$$

Since the fraction line in $\frac{P}{R}$ may indicate division, the formula also can be stated as:

$$B = P \div R$$

Before using the formula, convert the percent (R) to either a decimal fraction or a common fraction.

*Example:*  6% of what number is 24?

$$B = P \div R \ or \ B = 24 \div 6\%$$

$$B = \underset{.06. \, \overline{\smash{)}24{,}00.}}{4\,00.}$$

*or* $\quad B = 24 \div \frac{6}{100} = \frac{\overset{4}{\cancel{24}}}{1} \times \frac{100}{\underset{1}{\cancel{6}}} = 400$

It is especially important to check this type of percent problem since it is the most difficult of

the three types. To check, multiply the base (the answer) by the given rate (R); the product should be the same as the given percentage (P).

**Check:** 6% of 400 = .06 × 400 = 24.00

## Part A  Finding a Number When the Given Percent Is Between 1% and 100%

Most business applications of this case deal with percents that are between 1% and 100%. The formula, B = P ÷ R, is applied. When the rate (R) is between 1% and 100%, the required base (B) is always larger than the percentage (P).

As stated earlier, the division can be done either in decimals or in fractions, depending on the form to which the percent is converted.

Generally it is easier to use the fractional form of the converted percent under two conditions: (1) when the numerator of the fraction is 1, or (2) when, after the fraction is inverted during the division process, the denominator can be canceled into the given percentage (P).

*Examples:*

a. 25% of what number is 90?

$$B = P \div R \ or \ B = 90 \div 25\%$$
$$B = 90 \div \tfrac{1}{4}$$

$$B = \frac{90}{1} \times \frac{4}{1} = 360$$

**Check:**  25% of 360 = .25 × 360 = 90

b. 76¢ is 5% of what number?

$$B = P \div R \ or \ B = 76¢ \div 5\%$$
$$B = .76 \div \tfrac{1}{20}$$

$$B = \frac{.76}{1} \times \frac{20}{1} = 15.20 \ or \ \$15.20$$

**Check:** 5% of \$15.20  = .05 × 15.20
$$= .76 = 76¢$$

c. 66⅔% of what number is 150?

B = P ÷ R *or* B = 150 ÷ 66⅔%
B = 150 ÷ ⅔

$$B = \frac{\overset{75}{\cancel{150}}}{1} \times \frac{3}{\cancel{2}} = 225$$
$$\phantom{B = }1$$

**Check:** 66⅔% of 225 = ⅔ × 225 = 150

In most other cases, the decimal form of the converted percent is easier to use. While converting the percent, remember to drop the percent sign and move the decimal point in the remaining number two places to the left.

*Examples:*

a. 560 is 28% of what number?

B = P ÷ R *or* B = 560 ÷ 28%
B = 560 ÷ .28

$$B = \quad 28. \overline{\smash{\big)}\,560\,00.} \quad 20\,00.$$

B = 2,000

**Check:** 28% of 2,000 = .28 × 2,000

$$
\begin{array}{r}
.28 \\
\times \ 2000 \\
\hline
560.00
\end{array}
$$

b. $120.23 is 65% of what number?

B = P ÷ R *or* B = $120.23 ÷ 65%
B = $120.23 ÷ .65

$$B = \quad 65. \overline{\smash{\big)}\,120\,23.000} \quad 1\,84.969$$

B = $184.97

**Check:** 65% of $184.97 = .65 × 184.97

$$
\begin{array}{r}
184.97 \\
\times \quad .65 \\
\hline
92485 \\
1109820 \\
\hline
120.2305
\end{array}
$$

When the division is done in decimals as in the above examples, remember to place the decimal point of the quotient correctly. When the dividend is a whole number, put a decimal point after it so that the point can be moved to the right. The quotient decimal point is fixed *after* the dividend decimal point has been moved.

As in the preceding two sections, there are three special cases which should always be done mentally. The examples below are worked in detail only to show you why you can find the base mentally in these special cases.

*Examples:*

a. When R = 1%, then B = P × 100.

B = ?            B = P ÷ R
P = 7.98             = 7.98 ÷ .01
R = 1% = .01
$$\quad .01 \overline{\smash{\big)}\,7.98.} \quad 7\,98.$$
= 7.98 × 100 = 798

b. When R = 10%, then B = P × 10.

B = ?            B = P ÷ R
P = 79.8             = 79.8 ÷ .1
R = 10% = .1        = 
$$\quad 1. \overline{\smash{\big)}\,79.8.} \quad 79\,8.$$
= 79.8 × 10 = 798

c. When R = 100%, then B = P.

B = ?            B = P ÷ R
P = 798              = 798 ÷ 1
R = 100% = 1        = 798

Again, note in *Example c* above that 100% of a number is the same number.

**Part B** ## Finding a Number When the Given Percent Is Less than 1%

To find a number when the given percent is less than 1%, the same formula is followed: B = P ÷ R. Before applying the formula, pay particular attention in converting the percent. When converting to a decimal equivalent, be sure that there are at least two zeros after the decimal point. When converting to a proper fraction equivalent, remember that there must be at least two ending zeros in the denominator before the fraction is reduced. (Use the shortcut to convert a percent in which the number is a proper fraction: Drop the percent sign and add two zeros to the denominator of the fraction.)

## Examples:

a. $\frac{1}{2}$% of what number is 70?

$$B = P \div R \ or \ B = 70 \div \tfrac{1}{2}\%$$

$$B = 70 \div \frac{1}{200} = \frac{70}{1} \times \frac{200}{1} = 14,000$$

Check: $\frac{1}{2}$% of 14,000 $= \frac{1}{\cancel{200}} \times \overset{70}{\cancel{14,000}} = 70$

b. .65% of what number is $22.68?

$$B = P \div R \ or \ B = \$22.68 \div .65\%$$
$$B = \$22.68 \div .0065$$

$$B = \underset{.0065.\overline{\smash)22.6800.000}}{\quad 3489.230}$$

$$B = \$3,489.23$$

Check: .65% of $3,489.23 = .0065 \times 3,489.23

$$
\begin{array}{r}
3489.23 \\
\times \quad .0065 \\
\hline
1744615 \\
20935380 \\
\hline
22.679995
\end{array}
$$

c. $7.50 is $\frac{2}{3}$% of what number?

$$B = P \div R \ or \ B = \$7.50 \div \tfrac{2}{3}\%$$
$$B = \$7.50 \div \frac{2}{300} = \$7.50 \div \frac{1}{150}$$

$$B = \frac{7.50}{1} \times \frac{150}{1} = 1125$$

Check: $\frac{2}{3}$% of 1,125 $= \frac{1}{\cancel{150}} \times \frac{\cancel{1125}}{1} = 7\frac{1}{2}$

## Finding a Number When the Given Percent Is More Than 100%

To find a number when the given percent is more than 100%, the same formula is followed: B = P ÷ R. Before applying the formula, take particular care in converting the percent. Remember that the converted percent must be either a mixed number or a decimal mixed number.

When the given percent (R) is more than 100%, the required base (B) must be less than the given percentage (P).

## Examples:

a. 137$\frac{1}{2}$% of what number is $8.80?

$$B = P \div R \ or \ B = \$8.80 \div 137\tfrac{1}{2}\%$$
$$B = 8.80 \div 1.375$$

$$B = \underset{1.375.\overline{\smash)8.8000.0}}{\qquad 6.4 \ or \ \$6.40}$$

or $B = 8.80 \div 1\frac{3}{8}$

$$B = \frac{8.8}{1} \times \frac{8}{11} = \frac{70.4}{11} = 6.4$$

Check: 137$\frac{1}{2}$% of $6.40 = 1.375 \times 6.4

$$
\begin{array}{r}
1.375 \\
\times \quad 6.4 \\
\hline
5500 \\
82500 \\
\hline
8.8000 \ = \ \$8.80
\end{array}
$$

b. $56.47 is 104% of what number?

$$B = P \div R \ or \ B = \$56.47 \div 104\%$$
$$B = 56.47 \div 1.04$$

$$B = \underset{1.04.\overline{\smash)56.47.000}}{\qquad 54.298 \ or \ \$54.30}$$

Check: 104% of $54.30 = 1.04 \times 54.3

$$
\begin{array}{r}
1.04 \\
\times \quad 54.3 \\
\hline
312 \\
4160 \\
52000 \\
\hline
56.472 \ = \ \$56.47
\end{array}
$$

**c.** 33.12 is 345% of what number?

$B = P \div R$ *or* $B = 33.12 \div 345\%$
$B = 33.12 \div 3.45$

$$B = \quad \underset{3.45. \overline{\smash{)}33.12.0}}{9.6}$$

**Check:** 345% of 9.6 = 3.45 × 9.6

$$
\begin{array}{r}
3.45 \\
\times\ 9.6 \\
\hline
2070 \\
31050 \\
\hline
33.120 \text{ or } 33.12
\end{array}
$$

## Part D  Business Applications

One of the business uses of finding the entire number when a percent of it is given relates to finding the selling price of an article when two factors are known: (1) the cost of the article, and (2) the percent that the cost is of the selling price. In terms of base, rate, and percentage:

Known cost of the article $\qquad = P$
Known percent that the cost is of
   the selling price $\qquad\qquad = R$
Unknown selling price $\qquad\quad = B$

Thus, the applicable formula is $B = P \div R$. This formula can be restated as:

Selling Price = Given Cost ÷ Given Percent

To find the selling price, then, divide the cost by the percent that it is of the selling price. As a check, multiply the given percent by the answer (selling price); the product should be the same as the cost.

*Examples:*

**a.** Find the selling price of a chair which costs $24 if the cost is 60% of the selling price.

$B = P \div R$
Selling Price = Cost ÷ Percent

Selling Price = $24 ÷ 60%
Selling Price = 24 ÷ .6

$$\text{Selling Price} = \underset{.6. \overline{\smash{)}24.0.}}{4\,0.} = \$40$$

**Check:** 60% of $40 = .6 × 40 = 24.0 = $24

**b.** Find the selling price of a radio which costs $39.86 if the cost is 57% of the selling price.

$B = P \div R$
Selling Price = Cost ÷ Percent

Selling Price = $39.86 ÷ 57%
Selling Price = 39.86 ÷ .57

$$\text{Selling Price} = \underset{.57. \overline{\smash{)}39.86.000}}{69.929} \text{ or } \$69.93$$

**Check:** 57% of $69.93 = .57 × 69.93

$$
\begin{array}{r}
69.93 \\
\times\ .57 \\
\hline
48951 \\
349650 \\
\hline
39.8601 \text{ or } \$39.86
\end{array}
$$

Complete Assignment 16

## Assignment 16
## Section 4-4

|  | Perfect Score | Student's Score |
|---|---|---|
| Part A | 45 | |
| Part B | 15 | |
| Part C | 30 | |
| Part D | 10 | |
| TOTAL | 100 | |

*Finding a Number*
*When a Percent of It Is Given*

# Part A
### Finding a Number When the Given Percent Is Between 1% and 100%

*Directions:* Find the number as indicated and check. (3 points for each correct answer)

1. 288 is 12% of what number?

2. 558 is 18% of what number?

3. 84 is 66⅔% of what number?

4. 900 is 75% of what number?

5. 64% of what number is $56.95?

6. 35% of what number is $16.98?

7. $16.25 is 81¼% of what number?

8. $2.56 is 68¾% of what number?

9. 95% of what number is $31.35?

10. 85% of what number is $12.60?

11. 25% of what number is $\frac{1}{2}$?

14. .875 is $2\frac{1}{2}$% of what number?

12. 75% of what number is $\frac{3}{5}$?

15. 96% of what number is .32?

13. .37$\frac{1}{2}$ is 62$\frac{1}{2}$% of what number?

*Student's Score* _____

# Part B

### *Finding a Number When the Given Percent Is Less Than 1%*

*Directions:* Find the number as indicated and check. (3 points for each correct answer)

16. $5.00 is $\frac{1}{4}$% of what number?

19. .375% of what number is $2.25?

17. $1.50 is $\frac{1}{2}$% of what number?

20. $8.83 is .04% of what number?

18. .75% of what number is $1.35?

*Student's Score* _____

# Part C

### Finding a Number When the Given Percent Is More Than 100%

**Directions:** Find the number as indicated and check. (3 points for each correct answer)

**21.** $1\frac{1}{2}$ is 150% of what number?

**22.** $6\frac{1}{4}$ is 125% of what number?

**23.** $112\frac{1}{2}$% of what number is 2,700?

**24.** 140% of what number is 4,800?

**25.** 65¢ is 72% of what number?

**26.** 96¢ is 116% of what number?

**27.** $137\frac{1}{2}$% of what number is $67.54?

**28.** 375% of what number is $7.53?

**29.** $2,000 is 225% of what number?

**30.** $900 is 135% of what number?

*Student's Score* _____

# Part D

## Business Applications

Directions: Find the selling price. (2 points for each correct answer)

| | Cost | Percent of Selling Price | Selling Price |
|---|---|---|---|
| 31. | $469 | 62½% | _____ |
| 32. | $6.45 | 70% | _____ |
| 33. | $3.30 | 60% | _____ |
| 34. | $99.20 | 40% | _____ |
| 35. | $910 | 35% | _____ |

*Student's Score* _____

# Working with Weights and Measures

CHAPTER 5

A system of weights and measures is vital to business and industry. Standardized units of measurement are needed in the manufacture and sale of goods so that sizes and weights have the same meaning for all concerned.

Most of the world uses the International Metric System of measurement units, often called only **SI** (for Le Système International d'Unités). It is a modernized metric system adopted in 1960. The United States is in the process of converting to this system from the **U.S. Customary**, or **English system**. Most of the conversion should be completed within the next few years, but total conversion will take longer. Until this changeover is accomplished, however, you must know both systems.

Since many metric measurements are in decimal mixed number form, the student should be aware that most European countries use a comma in place of a decimal point. Thus, 4.836 is written as 4,836. Then, instead of using commas to separate number groups, they leave spaces between them. For example, 4,236,078 is written as: 4 236 078. This method of writing large numbers is used here with SI system numbers. Most decimal fractions are preceded by a 0. Thus, .75 is usually written as 0,75.

In this chapter you will learn how to work in each system and how to use the measures in business problems.

## Section 5-1  Working with the U.S. Customary and the SI Systems

A particular weight or measure, whether it is U.S. Customary or SI, consists of a number followed by the name of the measurement unit (sometimes called the **denomination**), such as 5 feet, 2 meters, 3 pounds, 4 kilograms, etc. To save time and space, **symbols** standing for the various units are used. No period is placed after the symbol, and no "s" is used for plurals. Thus, the measures cited above would appear as:

　　5 ft　　　2 m　　　3 lb　　　4 kg

The symbols for both systems that are commonly

used in business are shown in all the tables in this chapter.

While the U.S. Customary system has been in existence for a long time, it is difficult to learn. Originally, an inch was equal to three barleycorns laid end to end; a yard was the distance from the tip of a king's nose to the end of his thumb when his arm was stretched out. Eventually, of course, all units were defined more precisely. But when you examine the various measures in Table 5-1 on page 120, you can see that in order to change from one unit to another, you must know how many smaller units there are

# Table *5-1*  *U.S. Customary System of Weights and Measures*

|  | Unit | Symbol | Equivalents in Other Units |
|---|---|---|---|
| **Linear** (Length or Distance) | * inch | in. | 0.083 feet or 0.028 yards |
|  | foot | ft | 12 inches or 0.333 yards |
|  | yard | yd | 3 feet or 36 inches |
|  | rod | rd | 5½ yards or 16½ feet |
|  | mile | mi | 320 rods or 5,280 feet |
| **Area** | square inch | sq in. | 0.007 square feet |
|  | square foot | sq ft | 144 square inches |
|  | square yard | sq yd | 9 square feet |
|  | square rod | sq rd | 30¼ square yards |
|  | ** acre | A | 160 square rods |
|  | square mile | sq mi | 640 acres or 1 section (sec) |
|  | township | twp | 36 square miles |
| **Volume** | cubic inch | cu in. | 0.00058 cubic feet |
|  | cubic foot | cu ft | 1,728 cubic inches |
|  | cubic yard | cu yd | 27 cubic feet |
| **Weight** (Avoirdupois) | grain | gr | 0.037 drams |
|  | dram | dr | 27 11/32 grains |
|  | ounce | oz | 16 drams |
|  | pound | lb | 16 ounces |
|  | hundredweight | cwt | 100 pounds |
|  | ton | T | 2,000 pounds or 20 hundredweight |
| **Capacity** (Dry Measure) | pint | pt | ½ quart |
|  | quart | qt | 2 pints |
|  | peck | pk | 8 quarts |
|  | bushel | bu | 4 pecks |
| **Capacity** (Liquid Measure) | pint | pt | 16 ounces |
|  | quart | qt | 2 pints |
|  | gallon | gal | 4 quarts |
|  | barrel | bbl | 31½ gallon |
|  | cubic foot | cu ft | 7½ gallons |
| **Household Measure** | teaspoon | tsp or t |  |
|  | tablespoon | tbsp or T | 3 teaspoons |
|  | cup | c | 16 tablespoons |
|  | pint | pt | 2 cups |
| **Time** | second | s |  |
|  | minute | min | 60 seconds |
|  | hour | h | 60 minutes |
|  | day | da | 24 hours |
|  | week | wk | 7 days |
|  | month | mo | 4⅓ weeks (generally) |
|  | year | yr | 365 days or 366 in a leap year |

---

* The symbol for "inch" has a period to prevent confusion between the word "in" and this symbol.

** A city lot of 60 feet by 120 feet is about ⅙ of an acre.

# Table 5-2  SI System of Weights and Measures

| | Unit | Symbol | Equivalent to | Equivalent in Meters | Number of Units in One Meter |
|---|---|---|---|---|---|
| **Linear** | millimeter | mm | | .001 m | 1 m = 1000 mm |
| | centimeter | cm | 10 millimeters | .01 m | 1 m = 100 cm |
| | decimeter | dm | 10 centimeters | .1 m | 1 m = 10 dm |
| | meter | m | 10 decimeters | base unit | base unit |
| | dekameter | dam | 10 meters | 10 m | 1 m = .1 dam |
| | hectometer | hm | 10 dekameters | 100 m | 1 m = .01 hm |
| | kilometer | km | 10 hectometers | 1000 m | 1 m = .001 km |
| **Area** | square millimeter | $mm^2$ | | | |
| | square centimeter | $cm^2$ | 100 square millimeters | | |
| | square decimeter | $dm^2$ | 100 square centimeters | | |
| | square meter | $m^2$ | 100 square decimeters | | |
| **Area (Dry land)** | centare | ca | 1 square meter | | |
| | hectare | ha | 10 000 square meters | | |
| **Volume** | cubic millimeter | $mm^3$ | | | |
| | *cubic centimeter | $cm^3$ | 1000 cubic millimeters | | |
| | **cubic decimeter | $dm^3$ | 1000 cubic centimeters | | |
| | cubic meter | $m^3$ | 1000 cubic decimeters | | |

| | Unit | Symbol | Equivalent to | Equivalent in Grams | Number of Units in One Gram |
|---|---|---|---|---|---|
| **Weight** | milligram | mg | | .001 g | 1 g = 1000 mg |
| | centigram | cg | 10 milligrams | .01 g | 1 g = 100 cg |
| | decigram | dg | 10 centigrams | .1 g | 1 g = 10 dg |
| | gram | g | 10 decigrams | original base unit | |
| | dekagram | dag | 10 grams | 10 g | 1 g = .1 dag |
| | hectogram | hg | 10 dekagrams | 100 g | 1 g = .01 hg |
| | ***kilogram | kg | 10 hectograms | 1000 g | 1 g = .001 kg |
| | metric ton | t | 1000 kilograms | | |

| | Unit | Symbol | Equivalent to | Equivalent in Liters | Number of Units in One Liter |
|---|---|---|---|---|---|
| **Capacity (Liquid and Dry Measure)** | milliliter | mL | | .001 L | 1 L = 1000 mL |
| | centiliter | cL | 10 milliliters | .01 L | 1 L = 100 cL |
| | deciliter | dL | 10 centiliters | .1 L | 1 L = 10 dL |
| | liter | L | 10 deciliters | base unit | base unit |
| | dekaliter | daL | 10 liters | 10 L | 1 L = .1 daL |
| | hectoliter | hL | 10 dekaliters | 100 L | 1 L = .01 hL |
| | kiloliter | kL | 10 hectoliters | 1000 L | 1 L = .001 kL |

---

*Used for measuring very small quantities of liquid such as medicine: 1 cubic centimeter (cc) = 1 milliliter.
**Used for measuring most quantities of liquid such as gasoline and milk: 1 cubic decimeter $(dm^3)$ = 1 liter.
***The kilogram is the base unit which is in common everyday use: 1kg = weight of 1 liter of water.

in the next larger unit. There is no set pattern. For example, 12 inches equal one foot; three feet equal one yard; 5½ yards equal one rod, etc. To add to the difficulty, there are two measures for capacity: a dry measure and a liquid measure.

Table 5-2 on page 121 gives those International Metric System weights and measures most commonly used in business and daily life. Note that the measures in the SI system are based on 10, 100, or 1,000. In order to understand the makeup of the SI system, you must learn the meaning of the prefixes and their order in the system. A **prefix** is one or more letters placed before a word to change its meaning. For example, the prefix **kilo** before **gram** makes **kilogram**. There are two types of prefixes: (1) those used for measures *larger* than the base unit, such as kilo, hecto, deka—all of which are Greek in origin; and (2) those used for measures *smaller* than the base unit, such as deci, centi, milli—which are of Latin origin. The meanings of these prefixes are illustrated below.

### Larger than Base Prefixes

| Prefix | Base Unit | Meaning |
|--------|-----------|---------|
| kilo | gram | 1,000 × base unit |
| hecto | gram | 100 × base unit |
| deka | gram | 10 × base unit |

### Smaller than Base Prefixes

| | | |
|--------|-----------|---------|
| deci | meter | .1 × base unit |
| centi | meter | .01 × base unit |
| milli | meter | .001 × base unit |

Note that when the prefixes are written horizontally, they correspond to the place values of our decimal number system:

| | | | **base** | | | |
|------|-------|------|------|------|-------|-------|
| kilo | hecto | deka | **unit** | deci | centi | milli |
| ↑ | ↑ | ↑ | ↑ | ↑ | ↑ | ↑ |
| 1,000 | 100 | 10 | 1 | .1 | .01 | .001 |

According to the above illustrations, some SI measurements can be defined as follows:

1. A milliliter is a thousandth of a liter or .001 liters.
2. A centigram is a hundredth of a gram or .01 grams.
3. A kilometer is one thousand times a meter or 1,000 meters.

There are other larger-than-base and smaller-than-base prefixes, but they are used mostly for scientific work. Of those given above, hecto, deka, and deci are not used very much in daily life. For example, the 400 meter dash is never called the 4 hectometer dash; nor are 40 liters of gasoline called 4 decaliters. (One exception is the dekagram—equivalent to about 3 ounces—which currently is being used for small quantities of expensive candy, cold meat, etc.) Nevertheless, Table 5-2 includes these prefixes to show how all the measures in the system are formed.

Note also that the kilogram (1,000 g) is explained in Table 5-2 as the base unit in common everyday use. The original base unit was the gram (equivalent to the weight of a small paper clip), which has been found to be too small for ordinary use. The kilogram, therefore, is the only base unit with a prefix.

## Part A  Changing to the Next Smaller or the Next Larger Unit

In the U.S. Customary system a measure can consist of two or more parts, such as 9 feet 3 inches. In the SI system it is rare for a measure to be expressed in more than one unit. Decimal parts of a unit are used instead, such as 4.5 centimeters rather than 4 centimeters and 5 millimeters.

***Changing to the next smaller or the next larger unit in the Customary system.*** To change a measure from a given unit, or denomination, to the next smaller one, multiply the quantity by the number of smaller units that are contained in one unit of the larger denomination. Continue this process if even smaller denominations are desired.

*Examples:*

a. Change 2½ feet to inches.

$$1 \text{ ft} = 12 \text{ in.}$$
$$2\tfrac{1}{2} \text{ ft} = 2\tfrac{1}{2} \times 12 \text{ in.} = 30 \text{ in.}$$

b. Change ¾ ton to pounds.

$$1 \text{ T} = 2,000 \text{ lb}$$
$$\tfrac{3}{4} \text{ T} = \tfrac{3}{4} \times 2,000 \text{ lb} = 1,500 \text{ lb}$$

c. Change 2 square yards to square inches.

1 sq yd = 9 sq ft
2 sq yd = 2 × 9 sq ft = 18 sq ft
1 sq ft = 144 sq in.
18 sq ft = 18 × 144 sq in. = 2,592 sq in.

If the given measure has two or more parts, such as 5 yards 3 feet or 6 yards 4 feet 2 inches, follow these steps:

1. Start with the *largest* unit (the first one) and change it to the next smaller unit.
2. Add the converted units to similar units in the given measure.
3. Continue this process until the desired unit, or denomination, is reached.

*Examples:*

a. Change 3 pounds 5 ounces to ounces.

1 lb = 16 oz
3 lb = 3 × 16 oz = 48 oz
48 oz + 5 oz = 53 oz

b. Change 3 gallons 2 quarts 1 pint to pints.

1 gal = 4 qt
3 gal = 3 × 4 qt = 12 qt
12 qt + 2 qt = 14 qt
1 qt = 2 pt
14 qt = 14 × 2 = 28 pt
28 pt + 1 pt = 29 pt

To change a measure from a given unit to the next larger one, divide the quantity in the given measure by the number of the smaller units that are contained in one unit of the larger denomination. Continue this process if even larger denominations are desired.

*Examples:*

a. Change 32 inches to feet and inches.

$$1 \text{ ft} = 12 \text{ in.}$$
$$32 \div 12 = 2 \text{ ft } 8 \text{ in.}$$

$$\begin{array}{r} 2 \text{ ft} \\ 12\overline{)32} \\ \underline{24} \\ 8 \text{ in.} \end{array}$$

Note that if the answer required only feet, it would be $2\frac{8}{12}$ or $2\frac{2}{3}$.

b. Change 45 cubic feet to cubic yards.

$$1 \text{ cu yd} = 27 \text{ cu ft}$$
$$45 \div 27 = 1\frac{18}{27} \text{ cu yd}$$
$$= 1\frac{2}{3} \text{ cu yd}$$

$$\begin{array}{r} 1 \text{ cu yd} \\ 27\overline{)45} \\ \underline{27} \\ 18 \text{ cu ft} \end{array}$$

c. Change 60 ounces to pounds and ounces.

$$1 \text{ lb} = 16 \text{ oz}$$
$$60 \div 16 = 3 \text{ lb } 12 \text{ oz}$$

$$\begin{array}{r} 3 \text{ lb} \\ 16\overline{)60} \\ \underline{48} \\ 12 \text{ oz} \end{array}$$

If the given measure has two or more parts, follow these steps:

1. Start with the *smallest* unit (the last one) and change it to the next larger unit.
2. Add the converted units to similar units in the given measure.
3. Continue this process until the desired unit, or denomination, is reached.

*Examples:*

a. Change 3 hours 48 minutes 15 seconds to hours.

1 min = 60 s
15 s = 15 ÷ 60 = $\frac{1}{4}$ min
48 min + $\frac{1}{4}$ min = $48\frac{1}{4}$ min
1 h = 60 min
$48\frac{1}{4}$ min = $48\frac{1}{4} \div 60 = 0.804$ h
3 h + 0.804 h = 3.804 h

b. Change 3 quarts 1 pint to part of a gallon.

1 qt = 2 pt
1 pt = 1 ÷ 2 = $\frac{1}{2}$ qt
3 qt + $\frac{1}{2}$ qt = $3\frac{1}{2}$ qt
1 gal = 4 qt
$3\frac{1}{2}$ qt = $3\frac{1}{2} \div 4 = \frac{7}{2} \times \frac{1}{4} = \frac{7}{8}$ gal

***Changing to the next smaller or the next larger unit in the SI system.*** Changing a measure from a given unit to another unit, either smaller or larger, is very easy to do in the SI system. Each denomination is 10 times the next smaller unit in linear, weight, and capacity measurements; 100 times the next smaller unit in area measurements; and 1,000 times the next smaller unit in volume measurements.

To change the unit in a given measure to the next smaller one, multiply the quantity in the measure by the number of smaller units contained in one unit of the given measure. Depending on the kind of measure, the number of smaller units contained in one unit of the given measure is always 10, 100, or 1,000. Therefore, use the shortcut for multiplying. If the quantity is a whole number, add as many zeros to it as there are zeros in the multiplier. If the quantity is a decimal mixed number, move the decimal point one place to the right for each zero in the multiplier.

## Examples:

a. Change 3 centiliters to milliliters.

$$1 \text{ cL} = 10 \text{ mL}$$
$$3 \text{ cL} = 3 \times 10 \text{ mL} = 30 \text{ mL}$$

b. Change 4.5 square decimeters to square centimeters.

$$1 \text{ dm}^2 = 100 \text{ cm}^2$$
$$4.5 \text{ dm}^2 = 4.5 \times 100 \text{ cm}^2 = 450 \text{ cm}^2$$

c. Change 30.375 cubic meters to cubic decimeters.

$$1 \text{ m}^3 = 1\ 000 \text{ dm}^3$$
$$30.375 \text{ m}^3 = 30.375 \times 1\ 000 \text{ dm}^3$$
$$= 30\ 375 \text{ dm}^3$$

If still a smaller unit is wanted, keep multiplying by 10, 100, or 1,000 until the required unit is reached. The work can be shortened if a base unit is reached in the process. Multiply the quantity found up to this point by the number of required smaller units contained in one base unit, as given in Table 5-2 on page 121.

## Examples:

a. Change 4 dekagrams to centigrams.

$$1 \text{ dag} = 10 \text{ g}$$
$$4 \text{ dag} = 4 \times 10 \text{ g} = 40 \text{ g}$$
$$1 \text{ g} = 100 \text{ cg}$$
$$40 \text{ g} = 40 \times 100 \text{ cg} = 400 \text{ cg}$$

b. Change 2.4 square meters to square centimeters.

$$1 \text{ m}^2 = 100 \text{ dm}^2$$
$$2.4 \text{ m}^2 = 2.4 \times 100 \text{ dm}^2 = 240 \text{ dm}^2$$
$$1 \text{ dm}^2 = 100 \text{ cm}^2$$
$$240 \text{ dm}^2 = 240 \times 100 \text{ cm}^2 = 24\ 000 \text{ cm}^2$$

Note that the above calculation can be done in one step:

$$2.4 \text{ m}^2 = 2.4 \times 100 \times 100 \text{ cm}^2 = 24\ 000 \text{ cm}^2$$

c. Change 8.69 cubic decimeters to cubic millimeters.

$$1 \text{ dm}^3 = 1\ 000 \text{ cm}^3$$
$$8.69 \text{ dm}^3 = 8.69 \times 1\ 000 \text{ cm}^3 = 8\ 690 \text{ cm}^3$$
$$1 \text{ cm}^3 = 1\ 000 \text{ mm}^3$$
$$8\ 690 \text{ cm}^3 = 8\ 690 \times 1\ 000 \text{ mm}^3 = 8\ 690\ 000 \text{ mm}^3$$

*or*

$$8.69 \text{ dm}^3 = 8.69 \times 1\ 000 \times 1\ 000 \text{ mm}^3$$
$$= 8\ 690\ 000 \text{ mm}^3$$

To change a measure from a given unit to the next larger one, divide the quantity in the given measure by the number of smaller units in the next larger denomination. Use the shortcut for division: move the decimal point one place to the left for each zero in the divisor.

## Examples:

a. Change 4 600 milligrams to centigrams.

$$1 \text{ cg} = 10 \text{ mg}$$
$$4\ 600 \text{ mg} = 4\ 600 \text{ mg} \div 10 \text{ mg} = 460 \text{ cg}$$

b. Change 47.25 square decimeters to square meters.

$$1 \text{ m}^2 = 100 \text{ dm}^2$$
$$47.25 \text{ dm}^2 = 47.25 \text{ dm}^2 \div 100 \text{ dm}^2 = 0.4725 \text{ m}^2$$

c. Change 750 cubic millimeters to cubic centimeters.

$$1 \text{ cm}^3 = 1\ 000 \text{ mm}^3$$
$$750 \text{ mm}^3 = 750 \text{ mm}^3 \div 1\ 000 \text{ mm}^3 = 0.75 \text{ cm}^3$$

If a still larger unit is wanted, keep dividing by 10, 100, or 1,000 until the required unit is reached. The work can be shortened if a base unit is reached in the process. Divide the quantity found up to this point by the number of base units in one unit of the required larger denomination.

*Examples:*

a. Change 7 500 centigrams to kilograms.

1 g = 100 cg
7 500 cg = 7 500 cg ÷ 100 cg = 75 g
1 kg = 1 000 g
75 g = 75 g ÷ 1 000 g = 0.075 kg

b. Change 804.5 square centimeters to square meters.

1 dm² = 100 cm²
804.5 cm² = 804.5 cm² ÷ 100 cm² = 8.045 dm²
1 m² = 100 dm²
8.045 dm² = 8.045 dm² ÷ 100 dm² = 0.0845 m²

c. Change 9 360 cubic millimeters to cubic decimeters.

1 cm³ = 1 000 mm³
9 360 mm³ = 9 360 mm³ ÷ 1 000 mm³
        = 9.36 cm³
1 dm³ = 1 000 cm³
9.36 cm³ = 9.36 cm³ ÷ 1 000 cm³
        = 0.00936 dm³

After you have learned to change one SI unit to another by using the methods given above, you may wish to use another conversion method. This does not require a table, but you must know the order of the prefixes. Since it is easier to work with the prefixes listed horizontally, that arrangement is used here.

**base**
kilo hecto deka **unit** deci centi milli

Start with the prefix in the given measurement and count the number of places up to but not including the prefix to which the given measure is to be changed. Then follow these three rules:

1. For any measures that are neither square measures (area) nor cubic measures (volume),

when changing to a smaller unit, move the decimal point in the quantity the same number of places to the right, adding zeros as necessary. When changing to a larger unit, move the decimal point in the quantity the same number of places to the left.

*Examples:*

a. Change 8.5 kilograms to centigrams.

Starting with "kilo," count 5 places to the right, up to "centi."

8.5 kg = 8.50000. cg = 850 000 cg

b. Change 1 670 millimeters to meters.

Starting with "milli," count 3 places to the left, up to "base unit."

1 670 mm = 1.670 m = 1.67 m

2. For square measures, count the places to the right or left as above, move the decimal point to the right or left as required, but move it *twice* the number of places counted. Note in Table 5-2 that 100 smaller units equal one unit of the next larger denomination. Thus, to change from one unit to the next smaller or next larger, you must multiply or divide by 100. Or, in this method, move the decimal point two places to the right or to the left for each one-unit change.

*Examples:*

a. Change 4.75 square meters to square centimeters.

Starting with "base unit," count two places to the right, up to "centi." Move the decimal point 4 places to the right.

4.75 m² = 4.7500. cm² = 47 500 cm²

b. Change 4 666.9 square millimeters to square meters.

Starting with "milli," count 3 places to the left, up to "base unit." Move the decimal point 6 places to the left.

4 666.9 mm² = .004666.9 m² = 0.0046669 m²

3. For cubic measures, count the places to the right or left as above, move the decimal point to the right or left as required, but move it *three* times the number of places counted. Note in Table 5-2 that for each one-unit change to the next smaller or next larger denomination, you must multiply or divide by 1,000. In this method, move the decimal point three places to the right or left for each one-unit change.

*Examples:*

a. Change 1.8 cubic meters to cubic centimeters.

Starting with "base unit," count 2 places to the right, up to "centi." Move the decimal point 6 places to the right.

$$1.8 \text{ m}^3 = 1,800000. \text{ cm}^3 = 1\,800\,000 \text{ cm}^3$$

b. Change 243 750 000 cubic millimeters to cubic meters.

Starting with "milli," count 3 places to the left, up to "base unit." Move the decimal point 9 places to the left.

$$243\,750\,000 \text{ mm}^3 = .243750000, \text{ m}^3$$

$$= 0.24375 \text{ m}^3$$

The student should be aware that many of the examples on changing to other units do not occur in ordinary usage. They are given here only to illustrate conversions within the SI system.

## Part B Converting from One System to the Other

Until full conversion to the SI system (metrication) is completed, you must know how to convert a measure in one system to its equivalent in the other system. Table 5-3 on the next page shows some of the commonly used SI and U.S. Customary equivalents.

*Converting measures and weights.* To change a measure expressed in one system to its equivalent in the other system, multiply the quantity in the given measure by the number of equivalent units in the other system.

*Examples:*

a. Convert 6 inches to centimeters.

1 in. = 2.54 cm
6 in. = 6 × 2.54 cm = 15.24 cm

b. Convert 1 500 meters to feet.

1 m = 3.281 ft
1 500 m = 1 500 × 3.281 ft = 4 921.5 ft

c. Convert 60 miles to kilometers.

1 mi = 1.609 km
60 mi = 60 × 1.609 km = 96.54 km

d. Convert 100 kilometers to miles.

1 km = 0.621 mi
100 km = 100 × .621 mi = 62.1 mi

e. Convert 2 pounds to kilograms.

1 lb = 453.592 g = .454 kg
2 lb = 2 × .454 kg = .908 kg

f. Convert 75 kilograms to pounds.

1 kg = 2.205 lb
75 kg = 75 × 2.205 lb = 165.375 lb

g. Convert 15 gallons to liters.

1 gal = 3.785 L
15 gal = 15 × 3.785 L = 56.775 L

h. Convert 8 liters to quarts (liquid).

1 L = 1.057 qt
8 L = 8 × 1.057 qt = 8.456 qt

i. Convert 2 cups (liquid) to liters.

1 c = 237 mL = 0.24 L
2 c = 2 × 0.24 L = 0.48 L

j. Convert 80 acres to hectares.

1 A = 0.405 ha
80 A = 80 × 0.405 ha = 32.4 ha

k. Convert 50 hectares to acres.

# Table 5-3   Equivalents of SI and U.S. Customary Systems

|  | U.S. Customary to S.I. | S.I. to U.S. Customary |
|---|---|---|
| **Linear** | 1 in. = 2.54 cm or 25.4 mm<br>1 ft = 0.305 m or 30.5 cm<br>1 yd = 0.914 m or 9.14 dm<br>1 rd = 5.029 m<br>1 mi = 1.609 km | 1 mm = 0.0394 in.<br>1 cm = 0.394 in.<br>1 dm = 3.937 in.<br>1 m = 39.37 in. or 3.281 ft or 1.094 yd<br>1 km = .621 mi |
| **Area** | 1 sq in. = 6.452 cm²<br>1 sq ft = 0.093 m²<br>1 sq yd = 0.836 m²<br>1 A = 0.405 ha | 1 cm² = 0.155 sq in.<br>1 m² = 10.764 sq ft<br>1 km² = 0.386 sq mi<br>1 ha = 2.471 A |
| **Volume** | 1 cu in. = 16.387 cm³<br>1 cu ft = 0.0283 m³<br>1 cu yd = 0.765 m³ | 1 cm³ = 0.061 cu in.<br>1 dm³ = 0.0353 cu ft<br>1 m³ = 1.308 cu yd |
| **Weight** | 1 gr = 0.0648 g<br>1 dr = 1.772 g<br>1 oz = 28.350 g<br>1 lb = 453.592 g or .454 kg<br>1 T = .907 t | 1 mg = 0.0154 gr<br>1 cg = 0.154 gr<br>1 dag = 1.543 gr<br>1 g = 0.0353 oz<br>1 kg = 2.205 lb<br>1 t = 1.102 T |
| **Capacity (Dry Measure)** | 1 pt = 0.551 L<br>1 qt = 1.101 L | 1 L = 1.816 pt<br>1 L = 0.908 qt |
| **Capacity (Liquid Measure)** | 1 pt = 0.473 L<br>1 qt = 0.946 L<br>1 gal = 3.785 L | 1 L = 2.114 pt<br>1 L = 1.057 qt<br>1 daL = 2.642 gal |
| **Household Measure** | 1 t = 5 mL<br>1 T = 15 mL<br>*1 c (dry) = 275 mL<br>1 c (liquid) = 237 mL<br>1 pt = 0.473 L | 1 mL = .2 t<br>1 dL = 6.8 T<br>1 L = 3.6 c (dry)<br>1 L = 4.2 c (liquid) |

* Most dry ingredients are weighed: 1 c sugar = 190 g; 1 c flour = 140 g

1 ha = 2.471 A
50 ha = 50 × 2.471 A = 123.55 A

***Converting temperatures.*** While temperature is not a business measure, it is an important part of daily living. By now you probably know that temperature is also expressed in degree Celsius. Note the following examples of temperatures expressed in both degree Celsius and on the Fahrenheit scale.

| | degree Celsius | Fahrenheit |
|---|---|---|
| Water boils at | 100°C | 212°F |
| Water freezes at | 0°C | 32°F |
| Normal human body temp. | 37°C | 98.6°F |
| Pleasant summer day | 24°C | 75°F |

To change from Fahrenheit to degree Celsius, subtract 32° from the given Fahrenheit temperature and multiply the result by $\frac{5}{9}$.

*Examples:*

a. Change 212°F to degree Celsius.

$212° - 32° = 180°$
$180° \times \frac{5}{9} = 100°C$

b. Change 25°F to degree Celsius.

$25° - 32° = -7°$
$-7° \times \frac{5}{9} = -3.9°C$ or $-4°C$

To change from degree Celsius to degree Fahrenheit, multiply the given degree Celsius by $\frac{9}{5}$ and add 32° to the result.

*Examples:*

a. Change 100°C to degrees Fahrenheit.

$100° \times \frac{9}{5} = 180°$
$180° + 32° = 212°F$

b. Change −40°C to degrees Fahrenheit.

$-40° \times \frac{9}{5} = -72°$
$-72° + 32° = -40°F$

Note that −40° is the only temperature that is the same in both scales.

## Part C *Adding Measures*

Measures can be added when they are expressed in the same unit and even when they are expressed in two or more parts. Each operation is explained and illustrated first in the U.S. Customary system and then in the SI system so that you can make comparisons. As you will see, the work is simpler in the SI system.

**Adding measures expressed in the same unit.** To add measures expressed in the same unit, the procedure is the same in both systems. Add the quantities and attach the denomination to the sum.

*Example:* Add: 10 in.
9 in.
8 in.
27 in. = 2 ft 3 in.

Note that in the U.S. Customary system, the answer usually is changed to larger units where possible, unless the original unit is *specified* (named).

*Example:* Add: 15 mm
34 mm
34 mm
83 mm

Note that in the SI system, the answer is usually kept in the original unit, unless another unit is specified.

**Adding measures consisting of two or more parts.** In the U.S. Customary system, to add measures which consist of two or more parts, first arrange them so that like units are under each other (inches under inches, feet under feet, etc.). Then add each column separately. Starting with the sum at the extreme right, take out any units that can be changed to the next larger denomination, but keep the remainder in the smaller unit. Then add this result to any like units in the column immediately to the left. Change this new sum in the same way and continue with this process, one at a time, through the last column on the left.

*Examples:*

a. Add: 3 cups 8 tablespoons 2 teaspoons + 4 cups 1 teaspoon + 11 tablespoons 2 teaspoons.

$$
\begin{array}{rrr}
3c & 8\,T & 2\,t \\
4c & & 1\,t \\
& 11\,T & 2\,t \\
\hline
7c & 19\,T & 5\,t \\
\end{array}
$$

$$
\begin{array}{rrrl}
7\,c & 19\,T & 5\!\!\!/\,t & (5\,t = 1\,T\,2\,t) \\
+ & 1\,T & 2\,t & \\
\hline
7\,c & 20\,T & 2\,t & \\
\end{array}
$$

$$
\begin{array}{rrrl}
7\,c & 2\!\!\!0\,T & 2\,t & (20\,T = 1\,c\,4\,T) \\
+\;1\,c & 4\,T & & \\
\hline
8\,c & 4\,T & 2\,t & \\
\end{array}
$$

b. Add: 2 feet + 3 yards 11 inches + 6 yards 1
   foot 8 inches + 9 inches + 2 yards 2 feet

$$
\begin{array}{llll}
 & 2 \text{ ft} & & \\
3 \text{ yd} & & 11 \text{ in.} \\
6 \text{ yd} & 1 \text{ ft} & 8 \text{ in.} \\
 & & 9 \text{ in.} \\
2 \text{ yd} & 2 \text{ ft} & \\
\hline
11 \text{ yd} & 5 \text{ ft} & 28 \text{ in.}
\end{array}
$$

11 yd   5 ft   2̶8̶ ̶i̶n̶.   (28 in. = 2 ft 4 in.)
+ _____ 2 ft   4 in.
11 yd   7 ft   4 in.

11 yd   7̶ ̶f̶t̶   4 in.   (7 ft = 2 yd 1 ft)
+ ___ 2 yd   1 ft
13 yd   1 ft   4 in.

Note that with small measures like these, yards are not changed to rods.

In the SI system a measure generally is expressed in only one unit, but it may be necessary to add measures given in various different units. Before adding, change all the measures to a common unit—usually the one specified for the answer.

*Examples:* Add: 5.25 meters, 23 centimeters, 250 millimeters, 16 meters, 9.2 centimeters, and 74 millimeters. Express the answer in meters.

$$
\begin{array}{llll}
5.25 & \text{m} & = & 5.25 \text{ m} \\
23 & \text{cm} & = & 0.23 \text{ m} \\
250 & \text{mm} & = & 0.25 \text{ m} \\
16 & \text{m} & = & 16 \text{ m} \\
9.2 & \text{cm} & = & 0.092 \text{ m} \\
74 & \text{mm} & = & 0.074 \text{ m} \\
\hline
 & & & 21.896 \text{ m}
\end{array}
$$

<sub></sub>

## Part D

# Subtracting Measures

Measures expressed in the same unit or in different units may also be subtracted.

*Subtracting measures expressed in the same unit.* In either system, when both the minuend and the subtrahend are expressed in the same unit, the subtraction is done as usual and the denomination is attached to the difference.

*Examples:*

a. Take 32 lb from 75 lb.

$$
\begin{array}{r}
75 \text{ lb} \\
- \underline{32 \text{ lb}} \\
43 \text{ lb}
\end{array}
$$

b. Take 70.5 kg from 165.4 kg.

$$
\begin{array}{r}
165.4 \text{ kg} \\
- \underline{70.5 \text{ kg}} \\
94.9 \text{ kg}
\end{array}
$$

*Subtracting measures consisting of two or more parts.* In the U.S. Customary system, when the measures consist of two or more parts, arrange like units under each other. If the minuend does not have some of the units contained in the subtrahend, allow for them with 0 quantities. Then subtract. If it is necessary to borrow from the next larger unit, change the borrowed one to the number of smaller units contained in it and add this to the given number of smaller units.

*Example:* Take 5 yards 2 feet 8 inches from 8 yards 1 foot 3 inches.

$$
\begin{array}{lll}
8 \text{ yd} & 1 \text{ ft} & 3 \text{ in.} \\
-5 \text{ yd} & 2 \text{ ft} & 8 \text{ in.}
\end{array}
$$

Borrow 1 ft = 12 in., leaving 0 ft. 12 in. + 3 in. = 15 in.

$$
\begin{array}{lll}
 & 0 & 15 \\
8 \text{ yd} & \cancel{1} \text{ ft} & \cancel{3} \text{ in.} \\
-5 \text{ yd} & 2 \text{ ft} & 8 \text{ in.} \\
\hline
 & & 7 \text{ in.}
\end{array}
$$

Borrow 1 yd = 3 ft, leaving 7 yd. 0 ft + 3 ft = 3 ft:

$$
\begin{array}{lll}
7 & 3 & 15 \\
\cancel{8} \text{ yd} & \cancel{0} \text{ ft} & \cancel{3} \text{ in.} \\
-5 \text{ yd} & 2 \text{ ft} & 8 \text{ in.} \\
\hline
2 \text{ yd} & 1 \text{ ft} & 7 \text{ in.}
\end{array}
$$

Occasionally it is necessary to go two or more places to the left to borrow one from a larger unit. Change the borrowed one to the next smaller unit. Then keep borrowing and changing until the desired smaller unit is reached.

**Example:** Find the difference between 26 gallons and 17 gallons 2 quarts 1 pint.

$$
\begin{array}{lll}
26\,\text{gal} & 0\,\text{qt} & 0\,\text{pt} \\
-17\,\text{gal} & 2\,\text{qt} & 1\,\text{pt} \\
\end{array}
$$

Since the minuend has no quarts or pints, first borrow 1 gal = 4 qt, leaving 25 gal. Next borrow 1 qt = 2 pt, leaving 3 qt. Then subtract.

$$
\begin{array}{lll}
 & 3 & \\
25 & \cancel{4} & 2 \\
\cancel{26}\,\text{gal} & \cancel{0}\,\text{qt} & \cancel{0}\,\text{pt} \\
-17\,\text{gal} & 2\,\text{qt} & 1\,\text{pt} \\
\hline
8\,\text{gal} & 1\,\text{qt} & 1\,\text{pt} \\
\end{array}
$$

In the SI system, when the minuend and subtrahend are given in different units, first express both in a common unit—usually the one in which the answer is desired. Then subtract.

**Example:** Take 475 centimeters from 6.3 meters. Express the result in meters.

$$
\begin{array}{lll}
6.3\,\text{m} & = & 6.30\,\text{m} \\
-475\,\text{cm} & = & 4.75\,\text{m} \\
\hline
 & & 1.55\,\text{m} \\
\end{array}
$$

## Part E Multiplying Measures

A measure—whether expressed in the same unit or in two or more parts—may be multiplied by some number or by still another measure.

**Multiplying one denomination by some number.** In both systems, when a measure in only one unit is multiplied by some number, the product is in the same unit. It may be changed to other units if so specified.

**Examples:**

a. Multiply 9 ounces by 5 and express the product in pounds and ounces.

$$9\,\text{oz} \times 5 = 45\,\text{oz}$$
$$45\,\text{oz} \div 16\,\text{oz} = 2\,\text{lb}\ 13\,\text{oz}$$

b. Multiply 480 milligrams by 25 and express the product in grams.

$$480 \times 25 = 12\ 000\,\text{mg}$$
$$12\ 000\,\text{mg} \div 1\ 000\,\text{mg} = 12\,\text{g}$$

**Multiplying measures consisting of two or more parts by some number.** In the U.S. Customary system, to multiply a measure having two or more parts by some number, first multiply each part separately. Then, starting at the right, change to larger units as shown in Part C of this chapter.

**Example:** Multiply 3 yards 2 feet 10 inches by 8.

$$
\begin{array}{llll}
 & 3\,\text{yd} & 2\,\text{ft} & 10\,\text{in.} \\
\times & & & 8 \\
\hline
 & 24\,\text{yd} & 16\,\text{ft} & 80\,\text{in.} \\
 & 24\,\text{yd} & 16\,\text{ft} & \cancel{80\,\text{in.}} & (80\,\text{in.} = 6\,\text{ft}\ 8\,\text{in.}) \\
+ & & 6\,\text{ft} & 8\,\text{in.} \\
\hline
 & 24\,\text{yd} & \cancel{22\,\text{ft}} & 8\,\text{in.} & (22\,\text{ft} = 7\,\text{yd}\ 1\,\text{ft}) \\
+ & 7\,\text{yd} & 1\,\text{ft} & \\
\hline
 & 31\,\text{yd} & 1\,\text{ft} & 8\,\text{in.} \\
\end{array}
$$

In the SI system, when the multiplicand is given in different units, first express all units in a common unit—usually the one in which the answer is desired. Then multiply.

**Example:** Multiply 3 meters 60 centimeters 6 millimeters by 8. Express the answer in meters.

$$3\,\text{m}\ 60\,\text{cm}\ 6\,\text{mm} = 3.606\,\text{m}$$

$$
\begin{array}{r}
3.606\,\text{m} \\
\times\quad 8 \\
\hline
28.848\,\text{m} \\
\end{array}
$$

Note that this is the same problem as above but worked in the SI system.

**Multiplying measures expressed in different denominations.** Measures of length or distance are called **linear** (from line) measures. The product of two linear measures is a **square** measure. The product of three linear measures is a **cubic** measure. Generally the measures must be in the same unit for multiplication. For example, feet can be multiplied only by feet to get square feet; and meters by meters by meters to get cubic meters.

If the measures to be multiplied are in different units or if they consist of two or more parts (as they may in the U.S. Customary system), express them in the same unit before multiplying. Then express the answer as specified.

## Examples:

a. Multiply 4 feet 4 inches by 8 feet 7 inches. Express the answer in square yards, square feet, and square inches.

4 ft 4 in. = 52 in.
8 ft 7 in. = 103 in.
52 in. × 103 in. = 5,356 sq in.
5,356 sq in. ÷ 144 sq in. = 37 sq ft 28 sq in.
37 sq ft ÷ 9 sq ft = 4 sq yd 1 sq ft

Answer = 4 sq yd 1 sq ft 28 sq in.

b. Find the product and express it in cubic centimeters: 1.25 meters × .8 meter × 25 cm.

1.25 m = 125 cm
0.8 m = 80 cm
125 cm × 80 cm × 25 cm = 250 000 cm³

There are some exceptions to the rule that measures must be in the same unit for multiplication. Most of the exceptions are in the scientific fields, but a common one occurs with lumber in the U.S. Customary system.

A **board foot**, the unit by which lumber is sold in the United States, is 1 foot long, 1 foot wide, and 1 inch thick. The standard way of describing a piece of lumber, however, is in terms of thickness (in inches) and of width (in inches). Thus, a "2 by 4" refers to a board that is 2 inches thick and 4 inches wide. The length is expressed in feet. Therefore, when board feet are computed, the width must be converted to its equivalent fractional part of a foot.

The number of board feet in a piece of lumber is found by multiplying the thickness in inches by the width in feet by the length in feet.

*Example:* Find the number of board feet in a 2 by 4 by 12 piece of lumber.

4 in. = 4 in. ÷ 12 in. = $\frac{1}{3}$ ft
2 in. × $\frac{1}{3}$ ft × 12 ft = 8 board ft

The student should be aware that in an unfinished piece of lumber, the thickness and width may be a little more or a little less than the measurements specified. All finished lumber, however, is standardized at a smaller thickness and width than the stated measurements. Thus, a 2 by 4 is standardized at $1\frac{5}{8}$ inches by $3\frac{5}{8}$ inches,

but its cost is figured on 2 inches by 4 inches.

Since the computation of board feet is a highly specialized area, it is not included in the assignment. The lumber industry has made elaborate tables to find the total number of board feet when the number of pieces and their thickness, width, and length are given.

## Part F Dividing Measures

As in the multiplication of measures, a measure—whether expressed in the same unit or in two or more parts—may be divided by some number or by still another measure.

*Dividing one denomination by some number.* In both systems, when a measure in only one denomination is divided by some number, the quotient is in the same unit. It may be changed to other units if so specified.

## Examples:

a. Divide 35 yards by 6.

35 yd ÷ 6 = $5\frac{5}{6}$ yd or 5 yd 2 ft 6 in.
*Note:* $\frac{5}{6}$ yd = $\frac{5}{6}$ × 3 ft = $2\frac{1}{2}$ ft = 2 ft 6 in.

b. Divide 46 meters by 8.

46 m ÷ 8 = 5.75 m or 575 cm or 5 750 mm

*Dividing measures consisting of two or more parts by some number.* In the U.S. Customary system, to divide a measure consisting of two or more parts by some number, start with the largest unit at the left. If the division does not come out exactly, change the remainder to the next smaller denomination and add any like units in the measure. Continue the division in the same way for the remaining parts.

*Example:* Divide 20 gallons 3 quarts 1 pint by 12.

$$
\begin{array}{r|r|r}
 & \text{1 gal} & \text{2 qt} & 1\frac{11}{12}\text{ pt} \\
12\overline{)20\text{ gal}} & \text{3 qt} & \text{1 pt} \\
\underline{12} & +\ \underline{32\text{ qt}} & +\ \underline{22\text{ pt}} \\
8\text{ gal} & 35\text{ qt} & 23\text{ pt}
\end{array}
$$

$$
\begin{array}{r|r}
12\overline{)35\text{ qt}} & 12\overline{)23\text{ pt}} \\
\underline{24\text{ qt}} & \underline{12} \\
11\text{ qt} & 11
\end{array}
$$

In the SI system, when the dividend is given in different units, first express all units in a common unit—usually the one in which the answer is desired. Then divide.

*Example:* Divide 85 liters 80 centiliters by 12. Express the answer in liters.

$$85 \text{ L } 80 \text{ cL} = 85.8 \text{ L}$$
$$85.8 \text{ L} \div 12 = 7.15 \text{ L}$$

***Dividing measures expressed in different denominations.*** Generally one measure can be divided by another measure only when both are expressed in the same unit. This is true for both in the U.S. Customary and the SI systems. As in multiplication, there are some exceptions which are not discussed here. The quotient, or answer, in dividing measures is a number of pieces, packages, another unit, etc.

*Examples:*

a. A bolt of goods contains 48 yards. How many pieces, each 4 feet long, can be cut from it?

$$48 \text{ yd} = 48 \times 3 \text{ ft} = 144 \text{ ft}$$
$$144 \text{ ft} \div 4 \text{ ft} = 36 \text{ pieces}$$

b. Change 25 000 cubic millimeters to cubic centimeters.

$$1 \text{ cm}^3 = 1\ 000 \text{ mm}^3$$
$$25\ 000 \text{ mm}^3 \div 1\ 000 \text{ mm}^3 = 25 \text{ cm}^3$$

c. The liquid in a 6 liter container is to be poured into small bottles each containing 75 milliliters. How many bottles are needed?

$$6 \text{ L} = 6\ 000 \text{ mL}$$
$$6\ 000 \text{ mL} \div 75 \text{ mL} = 80 \text{ bottles}$$

Complete Assignment 17

## Assignment 17
## Section 5-1

*Working with the*
*U.S. Customary and the*
*SI Systems*

|  | Perfect Score | Student's Score |
|---|---|---|
| Part A | 40 | |
| Part B | 20 | |
| Part C | 10 | |
| Part D | 10 | |
| Part E | 10 | |
| Part F | 10 | |
| TOTAL | 100 | |

# Part A
### *Changing to the Next Smaller or the Next Larger Unit*

*Directions:* Change the measures and write your answers in the units indicated on the answer lines. (2 points for each correct answer)

1. 12 tablespoons
   to teaspoons

   _____t

2. ⅔ yard
   to inches

   _____in.

3. 5½ pounds
   to ounces

   _____oz

4. 3,500 pounds
   to hundredweights

   _____cwt

5. 0.15 hour
   to minutes

   _____min

6. 8.4 sq feet
   to sq inches

   _____sq in.

7. ¾ ton
   to pounds

   _____lb

8. 2 gallons
   to quarts

   _____qt

9. 27 inches
   to feet and inches

   ____ft____in.

10. 39 sq feet
    to sq yards

    _____sq yd

11. 12 ounces
    to pounds

    _____lb

12. 19 quarts
    to gallons

    _____gal

13. 38 minutes
    to hours

    _____h

14. 5¼ feet
    to yards

    _____yd

15. 87 cu feet
    to cu yards

    _____cu yd

16. 5.7 meters
    to centimeters

    _____cm

17. 8 632 milliliters
    to liters

    _____L

18. 1 200 grams
    to kilograms

    _____kg

19. 0.75 liter
    to milliliters

    _____mL

20. 4.5 cu meters
    to cu centimeters

    _____cm³

*Student's Score* _____

# Part B
## Converting from One System to the Other

**Directions:** Change the measures and write your answers in the units indicated on the answer lines. (2 points for each correct answer)

**21.** 15 feet
to meters

_____ m

**22.** 7 gallons
to liters

_____ L

**23.** 9 liters
to dry quarts

_____ qt

**24.** 250 meters
to yards and feet

___ yd ___ ft

**25.** 3 pounds
to kilograms

_____ kg

**26.** 4 kilograms
to pounds

_____ lb

**27.** 4 ounces
to dekagrams

_____ dag

**28.** 227 grams
to ounces

_____ oz

**29.** 270 cu inches
to cu centimeters

_____ cm³

**30.** 72 sq meters
to sq feet

_____ sq ft

*Student's Score _____*

# Part C
## Adding Measures

**Directions:** Add the measures and express the sums in the units indicated on the answer lines. (2 points for each correct answer)

**31.** 38 min
15 min
29 min

___ h ___ min

**32.** 2 ft  5 in.
2 ft 10 in.
1 ft 11 in.

___ yd ___ ft ___ in.

**33.** 2 sq yd  8 sq ft   95 sq in.
5 sq yd        118 sq in.
        5 sq ft  26 sq in.

___ sq yd ___ sq ft ___ sq in.

**34.** 93 cg + 105 mg + .75 kg

_____ kg

**35.** 78 cm + 3.5 m + 562 cm

_____ cm

*Student's Score _____*

# Part D
## Subtracting Measures

*Directions:* Subtract the measures and write your answers in the units indicated on the answer lines. (2 points for each correct answer)

**36.** 4 yd − 1 ft 8 in.

_____yd _____ft _____in.

**37.** 12 cu yd   8 cu ft
− 3 cu yd  16 cu ft  560 cu in.
‾‾‾‾‾‾‾‾‾‾‾‾‾‾‾‾‾‾‾‾‾‾‾‾‾‾‾

_____cu yd _____cu ft _____cu in.

**38.** 5 gal 1 qt − 2 gal 3 qt 1 pt

_____gal _____qt _____pt

**39.** 17.2 m − 495 cm

_____cm

**40.** 5 L − 145 mL

_____L

*Student's Score* _____

# Part E
## Multiplying Measures

*Directions:* Multiply the measures and express the products in the units indicated on the answer lines. (1 point for each correct answer)

**41.**   9 h   12 min
×        6
‾‾‾‾‾‾‾‾‾‾‾‾

_____da _____h _____min

**42.**   5 sq yd  7 sq ft  36 sq in.
×                              7
‾‾‾‾‾‾‾‾‾‾‾‾‾‾‾‾‾‾‾‾‾‾‾‾‾‾‾

_____sq yd _____sq ft _____sq in.

**43.** 7 ft 3 in. × 8 ft 10 in.

_____sq yd _____sq ft _____sq in.

**44.** 6 ft 8 in. × 9 ft 4 in.

_____sq yd _____sq ft _____sq in.

**45.** 35 in. × 10 in. × 24 in.

_____ cu ft _____ cu in.

**46.** 2 yd 2 ft × 5 yd 1 ft × 8 yd 2 ft

_____ cu yd _____ cu ft

**47.** 245 mL × 12

_____L

**48.** 425 g × 36

_____kg

**49.** 2.4 m × 120 cm

_____m²

**50.** 1.6 m × 364 mm × 10 cm

_____cm³

_Student's Score _____

# Part F
### _Dividing Measures_

_Directions:_ Divide the measures and write your answers in the units indicated on the answer lines. (2 points for each correct answer)

**51.** 12 lb 15 oz ÷ 3

_____lb _____oz

**52.** 34 gal 2 qt ÷ 12

_____gal _____qt _____pt

**53.** 26 yd 9 in. ÷ 15

_____yd _____ft _____in.

**54.** 32 400 cg ÷ 48

_____kg

**55.** 7 375 g ÷ 25

_____kg

_Student's Score _____

# Section 5-2 Using Weights and Measures in Business Problems

Measures have widespread use in business and industry. Linear, square, and cubic measures are used in finding distances, areas, and volumes in construction, manufacturing, engineering, etc.

In addition, many of the other measures are used in buying and selling goods. Prices often are quoted for a specific number of pieces such as a dozen, a hundred, or a thousand; for a specific weight such as a pound or a kilogram; or for a specific volume such as a gallon or a liter.

In both the SI and the U.S. Customary systems, the cost of an item may be quoted in terms of a basic unit; and orders for that item generally are stated in the same unit. That is, if the price is quoted per pound, the quantity ordered is given in pounds; if the price is quoted per kilogram, the quantity ordered is given in kilograms or a part of a kilogram (rarely less than one-fourth of a kilogram).

However, when the quantity ordered is expressed in a unit different from the unit used in the quoted price, the problems of conversion differ between the two systems. In the SI system it is very easy to change from one unit to another because the system is based on ten.

*Example:* Find the cost of 10 dekagrams of candy priced at $7.00 per kilogram.

$$10 \text{ dag} = .10 \text{ kg} = 0.1 \text{ kg}$$

$$\text{Cost} = 0.1 \text{ kg} \times \$7.00 = \$0.70$$

In the U.S. Customary system, when the quantity ordered is in a different unit, changing to the same unit expressed in the quoted price requires more work than in the SI system. For this reason, in Parts B through E of this section, only U.S. Customary system measures are discussed and illustrated.

## Part A  Perimeter, Area, and Volume

Perimeter, area, and volume are measurable properties that you may be asked to find in solving some business problems. To solve such problems—which involve linear, square, and cubic measures—often a simple sketch showing the measurements will aid in the solution.

*Finding the perimeter.* The **perimeter** of a surface is the distance around the surface. It is always expressed in linear units. For example, the perimeter of a **rectangle**, a surface with four right angles like a football field, is the *sum of twice the length plus twice the width.* Generally the same unit of measurement is used for the length and the width, but this is not absolutely necessary. The length could be expressed in yards and the width in feet, with the total expressed in yards and feet. In SI measurements, the length could be expressed in meters and the width in centimeters, with the total expressed in meters and centimeters; but this is rarely done. Generally the centimeters are changed to meters for the total.

*Examples:*

a. How many feet of link fence are needed to enclose a rectangular yard that is 50 feet long and 35 feet wide? (The number of feet needed is the perimeter.)

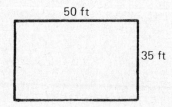

$$\text{Perimeter} = (2 \times 50 \text{ ft}) + (2 \times 35 \text{ ft})$$
$$= 100 \text{ ft} + 70 \text{ ft} = 170 \text{ ft}$$

b. Base molding is to be installed around a room that measures 7.5 meters long and 550 centimeters wide. There is one door which is one meter wide. How many meters of molding are needed?

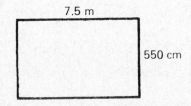

$$550 \text{ cm} = 5.5 \text{ m}$$
$$\text{Perimeter} = (2 \times 7.5 \text{ m}) + (2 \times 5.5 \text{ m})$$
$$= 15 \text{ m} + 11 \text{ m} = 26 \text{ m}$$

$$\text{Molding needed} = 26 \text{ m} - 1 \text{ m} = 25 \text{ m}$$

**Finding the area.** Area refers to a surface within a set of lines and is always expressed in square units. For example, the area of a rectangular surface, such as a wall, the side of a box, the land on which a building stands, etc., is found by *multiplying the length by the width*. Remember that the measurements of the length and the width must be expressed in the same unit before multiplying. That is, both length and width must be expressed in feet, in yards, in meters, etc.

Carpeting and linoleum generally are sold by the square yard or square meter. Some widths of carpeting are sold by the "running yard" or "running meter" but the width is taken into consideration in determining the price. With regard to paint, the area that can be covered by the contents of the can usually is stated in square feet or square meters.

## Examples:

**a.** A hallway rug is 3 meters long and 126 centimeters wide. If the cost of the rug is $20 per running meter, what is the cost per square meter?

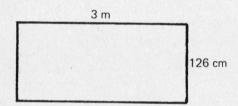

3 m

126 cm

Area = 3 m × 1.26 m = 3.78 m²
Cost of the rug = 3 m × $20 = $60
Cost per sq m = $60 ÷ 3.78 = $15.87

**b.** The label on a can of paint states that the coverage is up to 450 square feet of surface. Is one can enough to paint the walls and ceiling of a room that is 12 feet 6 inches long, 9 feet wide, and 7 feet 10 inches high?

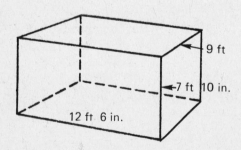

9 ft

7 ft 10 in.

12 ft 6 in.

Area of front
and back walls = $2 \times 12\frac{1}{2}$ ft $\times 7\frac{5}{6}$ ft
= $195\frac{5}{6}$ sq ft

Area of
side walls = $2 \times 9$ ft $\times 7\frac{5}{6}$ ft = 141 sq ft

Area of
ceiling = $12\frac{1}{2}$ ft $\times 9$ ft = $112\frac{1}{2}$ sq ft

Add all areas: $195\frac{5}{6}$ sq ft
$\phantom{Add all areas:}$ 141$\phantom{\frac{5}{6}}$ sq ft
$\phantom{Add all areas:}$ $112\frac{1}{2}$ sq ft
$\phantom{Add all areas:}$ $449\frac{1}{3}$ sq ft

Since no allowance was made for doors and windows that would not be painted, one can should be enough.

**Finding the volume.** Volume refers to the inside space or capacity of a container, a room, a hole, etc., and is always expressed in cubic units. The volume of something that is box-shaped or a **rectangular solid** is found by *multiplying the length by the width by the height (or depth)*. These three measures, or *dimensions*, must be expressed in the same unit to get a product in cubic units.

## Examples:

**a.** Find the cost of the concrete in a driveway that is 30 feet long, 12 feet wide, and 8 inches thick if the concrete costs $20 per cubic yard.

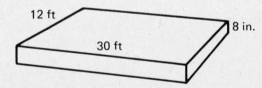

12 ft

8 in.

30 ft

8 in. = $\frac{8}{12}$ ft = $\frac{2}{3}$ ft
Volume = 30 ft × 12 ft × $\frac{2}{3}$ ft = 240 cu ft
240 cu ft ÷ 27 = $8\frac{8}{9}$ cu yd
Cost = $8\frac{8}{9}$ × $20 = $177.78

**b.** Find the number of cubic centimeters in a box that is 1.25 meters long, .8 meter wide, and 25 centimeters deep.

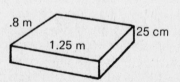

.8 m

25 cm

1.25 m

1.25 m = 125 cm
.8 m = 80 cm
Volume = 125 cm × 80 cm × 25 cm
= 250 000 cm³

## Part B C, Cwt, and M

Building materials, hardware, food, office supplies, etc., often are priced by the hundred (per C), by the hundredweight (per **cwt**), or by the thousand (per **M**). The unit "cwt" is usually stated on a 100-pound bag or box of something like flour or sugar.

*Finding the number of C's or cwt's.* When the quantity ordered is stated in pieces or pounds but the unit price is per C or per cwt, divide the quantity by 100 to find the number of C's or cwt's. (Use the shortcut: move the decimal point in the quantity two places to the left.) Then multiply the number of C's or cwt's by the unit price to find the total cost. If the quantity ordered is less than 100, express the number of C's or cwt's as a decimal.

*Examples:*

a. 1,500 pieces at $69.75 per C

Number of C's = 1,500 ÷ 100 = 15 C
Cost = 15 C × $69.75 per C = $1,046.25

b. 75 pieces at $124 per C

Number of C's = 75 ÷ 100 = 0.75C
Cost = 0.75 C × $124 per C = $93.00

Note that a quoted price in exact dollars is written $124 per C as in the above example. When the total cost is in exact dollars, it is written as $93.00.

c. 580 pounds at $4.25 per cwt.

Number of cwt's = 580 lb ÷ 100 lb = 5.8 cwt
Cost = 5.8 cwt × $4.25 per cwt = $24.65

*Finding the number of M's.* When the quantity ordered is stated in pieces or feet, but the unit price is per M, divide the quantity by 1,000 to find the number of M's. (Use the shortcut: move the decimal point in the quantity three places to the left.) Then multiply the number of M's by the unit price to find the cost. If the quantity is less

than 1,000, express the number of M's as a decimal.

*Examples:*

a. 7,500 pieces at $90 per M

Number of M's = 7,500 ÷ 1,000 = 7.5 M
Cost = 7.5 M × $90 per M = $675.00

b. 500 pieces at $79.50 per M

Number of M's = 500 ÷ 1,000 = 0.5 M
Cost = 0.5 M × $79.50 = $39.75

## Part C Pounds, Ounces, and Tons

There are times when the quantity ordered is stated either in pounds alone or in pounds and ounces but the unit price may be expressed as per ounce, per pound, or per ton.

*Finding the cost when the unit price is per ounce.* Multiply the given number of pounds by 16 and add any ounces that are given in the quantity to find the total number of ounces. (Remember that you are changing to a smaller unit and, therefore, the number of ounces must be greater than the number of pounds.) Then multiply the total number of ounces by the unit price to find the cost.

*Examples:*

a. 2 pounds at 25¢ per ounce.

Number of oz = 2 × 16 oz = 32 oz
Cost = 32 oz × $0.25 per oz = $8.00

b. 5 pounds 11 ounces at $1.10 per ounce

Number of oz = 5 × 16 oz + 11 oz = 91 oz
Cost = 91 oz × $1.10 per oz = $100.10

*Finding the cost when the unit price is per pound.* Change the given number of ounces in the quantity to a fractional part of a pound by dividing it by 16. Then add any pounds that are given in the quantity. Generally the fractional part of a pound is expressed as a decimal fraction or a decimal mixed number. Then multiply by the unit price to find the cost.

*Examples:*

a. 10 ounces at 85¢ per pound

Number of lb = 10 oz ÷ 16 oz = .625 lb
Cost = .625 lb × $0.85 per lb = $0.53

b. 3 pounds 5 ounces at 79¢ per pound

Number of lb = 5 oz ÷ 16 oz + 3 lb
= 0.3125 lb + 3 lb = 3.3125 lb
Cost = 3.3125 lb × $0.79 per lb = $2.62

***Finding the cost when the unit price is per ton.***
Materials such as coal, steel, iron, and fertilizer often are sold with the weight stated in pounds in order to figure the shipping charges. The unit price, however, is per ton. To find the number of tons, divide the quantity by 2,000. Then multiply the number of tons by the price per ton. (Use the shortcut for dividing by 2,000: first divide the number of pounds by 2 and then move the decimal point of the result three places to the left.)

*Examples:*

a. 8,400 pounds at $20.50 per ton

Number of T = 8,400 lb ÷ 2,000 lb
= 8,400 lb ÷ 2 ÷ 1,000 lb
= 4,200 lb ÷ 1,000 lb = 4.2 T
Cost = 4.2 T × $20.50 per T = $86.10

b. 620 pounds at $90 per ton

Number of T = 620 lb ÷ 2,000 lb = 0.31 T
Cost = 0.31 T × $90 per T = $27.90

# Part D  Pieces, Dozens, and Gross

There are 12 pieces in one **dozen** and 144 pieces in one **gross**. There are 12 dozen in one gross. Quantities ordered may be expressed in pieces, in dozens, or in gross but the unit price may be stated in non-identical units.

***Finding the cost when the unit price is per piece.***
When the quantity ordered is stated in dozens or gross but the price is per piece, find the total number of pieces by multiplying the dozens by 12 and the gross by 144.

*Examples:*

a. 75 dozen at 5½¢ per piece

Number of pieces = 75 × 12 = 900 pieces
Cost = 900 pieces × $0.055 per piece = $49.50

b. 4½ gross at 12¢ each

Number of pieces = 4½ × 144 = 648 pieces
Cost = 648 pieces × $0.12 per piece = $77.76

***Finding the cost when the unit price is per dozen.***
When the quantity ordered is stated in pieces but the price is per dozen, divide the number of pieces by 12 to find the number of dozens, or the fractional part of a dozen. Then multiply the result by the price per dozen.

*Example:* 9 pieces at 98¢ per dozen

Number of dozen = 9 ÷ 12 = 0.75 doz
Cost = 0.75 doz × $0.98 per doz
= $0.74

***Finding the cost when the unit price is per gross.***
When the quantity ordered is stated in pieces but the price is per gross, divide by 144 to find the number of gross or the fractional part of a gross. Then multiply the result by the price per gross.

*Example:* 225 pieces at $36 per gross

Number of gross = 225 ÷ 144
= 1.5625 gross

Cost = 1.5625 gross × $36 per gross
= $56.25

When the quantity ordered is stated in dozens but the price is per gross, divide by 12 to find the number of gross or the fractional part of a gross. Then multiply the result by the price per gross.

*Example:* 10 dozen at $65 per gross

Number of gross = 10 ÷ 12 = $\frac{5}{6}$ gross
Cost = .833333 gross × $65 per gross
= $54.17

**Complete Assignment 18**

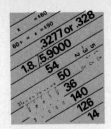

# Assignment 18
# Section 5-2

## Using Weights and Measures in Business Problems

|  | Perfect Score | Student's Score |
|---|---|---|
| Part A | 20 | |
| Part B | 20 | |
| Part C | 30 | |
| Part D | 30 | |
| TOTAL | 100 | |

## Part A
### Perimeter, Area, and Volume

**Directions:** Solve the problems, showing all work. Write your answers in the spaces provided. (2 points for each correct answer)

1. A city lot is 85 feet long and 120 feet wide. How many feet of fencing are needed to enclose it?

   Ans._____

2. A rectangular yard is 10.5 meters long and 8.75 meters wide. How many meters of fencing are needed to enclose it?

   Ans._____

3. How many square meters are there in the four walls and ceiling of a room which is 5.5 meters long, 4 meters wide, and 2.5 meters high?

   Ans._____

4. How many square feet are there in the four walls and ceiling of a room which is 15 feet long, 12 feet wide, and 8 feet high?

   Ans._____

5. A floor is 16 feet by 10 feet 6 inches. How much does it cost to cover it with linoleum at $6 per square yard?

   Ans._____

6. A floor is 7.5 meters by 4.5 meters. How much does it cost to cover it with carpeting at $15 per square meter?

   Ans._____

7. An excavation for a building is 15 meters long, 9 meters wide, and 4 meters deep. What is the cost of removing the ground at $3 per cubic meter?

   Ans._____

8. What is the cost of the concrete for a driveway that is 45 feet long, 10 feet wide and 8 inches thick if the concrete costs $18 per cubic yard?

   Ans._____

9. How many gallons of water are needed to fill a tank 3 feet long, 1 foot wide, and 10 inches deep? (Change the inches to feet.)

   Ans._____

10. How many liters of water are needed to fill a tank 1 meter long, 30 centimeters wide, and 25 centimeters deep? (Find cubic decimeters.)

    Ans._____

*Student's Score* _____

# Part B

## C, Cwt, and M

*Directions:* Find the cost. (1 point for each correct answer)

11. 700 pieces at $3.25 per C

12. 800 pieces at $16 per C

13. 76 pieces at $4.50 per C

14. 24 pieces at $9.50 per C

15. 32 pieces at $14.75 per C

16. 84 pieces at $38.50 per C

17. 2,900 lb at $4.60 per cwt

18. 474 lb at $5 per cwt

19. 50 lb at $21.25 per cwt

20. 98 lb at $11.50 per cwt

21. 15,400 lb at $2 per cwt

22. 20,600 lb at $4 per cwt

23. 1,800 ft at $37 per M

24. 1,490 ft at $42 per M

25. 1,820 pieces at $2.50 per M

26. 36,000 pieces at $51 per M

27. 4,500 ft at $90 per M

28. 15,750 ft at $10 per M

29. 300 pieces at $5.89 per M

30. 500 pieces at $16.40 per M

*Student's Score* _____

# Part C
## *Pounds, Ounces, and Tons*

*Directions:* Find the cost. (2 points for each correct answer)

**31.** 5 lb at 75¢ per oz

**32.** 8 lb at 49¢ per oz

**33.** 10 lb 15 oz at 60¢ per oz

**34.** 7 lb 8 oz at 37½¢ per oz

**35.** 3 lb 4 oz at $1.25 per oz

**36.** 19 lb 2 oz at 12½¢ per oz

**37.** 14 oz at $1.49 per lb

**38.** 5 oz at $15 per lb

**39.** 37 lb 13 oz at 80¢ per lb

**40.** 10 lb 7 oz at 50¢ per lb

*Directions:* Find the cost. (1 point for each correct answer)

**41.** 2,600 lb at $32 per T

**42.** 8,800 lb at $35 per T

**43.** 5,200 lb at $31.60 per T

**44.** 16,650 lb at $28 per T

**45.** 15,780 lb at $50 per T

**46.** 1,000 lb at $37.50 per T

**47.** 840 lb at $80 per T

**48.** 160 lb at $200 per T

**49.** 896 lb at $60 per T

**50.** 450 lb at $36 per T

*Student's Score* _____

# Part D
## *Pieces, Dozens, and Gross*

*Directions:*  Find the cost. (2 points for each correct answer)

**51.** 72 articles at $10.98 per doz

**52.** 96 pieces at 25¢ per doz

**53.** 16 pieces at $12.60 per doz

**54.** 150 pieces at $1.25 per doz

**55.** 10 pieces at $7.80 per doz

**56.** 8 pieces at $16 per doz

**57.** 520 pieces at $4.50 per gross

**58.** 200 articles at $1.80 per gross

**59.** 50 pieces at $36 per gross

**60.** 90 pieces at $160 per gross

**61.** 24 doz at $9.98 per gross

**62.** 18 doz at $15 per gross

**63.** $3\frac{1}{2}$ doz at $3.60 each

**64.** 14 gross at 95¢ each

**65.** $9\frac{3}{4}$ gross at $0.88 each

*Student's Score* _____

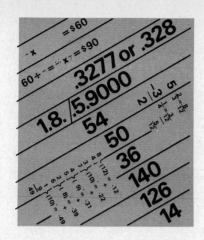

# Shortcuts and Estimating with Rounded-Off Numbers

CHAPTER
6

Most of the computation in business is done with the aid of calculators or computers, but there still is need for paper-and-pencil figuring. The use of shortcuts increases accuracy and speed by simplifying the operations.

Estimating with rounded-off numbers is used in business to get an approximate idea of sizes, costs, or values. In mathematics, you find out if the result of a calculation is "about right" by estimating the answer. Thus, a further check on your work, and particularly on the decimal point, is provided by the estimate. If you use a hand calculator, it is especially important that you have a good idea of what the answer should be. It is very easy to make errors by depressing the wrong keys or forgetting to depress the decimal point key.

## Section 6-1  Shortcuts in Calculating

There are many shortcuts available for addition, subtraction, multiplication, and division; but most of them require learning new rules. Some shortcuts, however, are so useful that they are worthwhile learning.

### Part A  Adding from Left to Right

Adding two numbers from left to right is much the same as adding them from right to left. The difference is that before you write the sum of the two digits being added, you look at the combination to the right. If their sum is 10 or more, there will be a carryover of one to the sum at the left. As you proceed in the adding from left to right, always check for possible carryovers.

The procedure is explained step by step in the examples given.

**Examples:**

a.   78
    +39

**Step 1:** Start with 7 + 3, but do not write the 10 yet. Look to the right at 8 + 9 = 17. There will be a carryover of 1 to the 7 + 3 to make it 11. Write the 11 under the 3.

```
  7 8
+ 3 9
-----
  1 1
```

**Step 2:** Go to 8 + 9 = 17. Since the 1 was carried over already, write only the 7 under the 9.

```
  7 8
+ 3 9
-----
1 1 7
```

b.   563.25
    +915.47

**Step 1:** Start with 5 + 9, but do not write the 14 yet. Look to the right at 6 + 1 = 7. Since there will be no carryover, write the 14 under the 9.

```
  563.25
+915.47
 14
```

**Step 2:** Go to the 6 + 1, but do not write the 7 yet. Look to the right at 3 + 5 = 8. Since there will be no carryover, write the 7 under the 1.

```
  563.25
+915.47
 147
```

**Step 3:** Go to the 3 + 5, but do not write the 8 yet. Look to the right at 2 + 4 = 6. Since there will be no carryover, write the 8 under the 5.

```
  563.25
+915.47
 1478.
```

**Step 4:** Go to the 2 + 4, but do not write the 6 yet. Look to the right at 5 + 7 = 12. There will be a carryover of 1 to the 2 + 4 to make it 7. Write the 7 under the 4.

```
  563.25
+915.47
 1478.7
```

**Step 5:** Go to the 5 + 7 = 12. Since the 1 already has been carried over, write only the 2 under the 7.

```
  563.25
+915.47
 1478.72
```

c.
```
  1257.34
+8463.90
```

**Step 1:** 1 + 8 = 9. No carryover.

```
  1257.34
+8463.90
 9
```

**Step 2:** 2 + 4 + 1 = (carryover from 5 + 6).

```
  1257.34
+8463.90
 97
```

**Step 3:** 5 + 6 + 1 = 12 (carryover from 7 + 3). Since the 1 already has been carried over, write only the 2.

```
  1257.34
+8463.90
 972
```

**Step 4:** 7 + 3 + 1 = 11 (carryover from 3 + 9). Since the first one already has been carried over, write only the second 1.

```
  1257.34
+8463.90
 9721.
```

**Step 5:** 3 + 9 = 12. No carryover. Write only the 2.

```
  1257.34
+8463.90
 9721.2
```

**Step 6:** 4 + 0 = 4.

```
  1257.34
+8463.90
 9721.24
```

When the sum to the right is 9, go to the next right for a possible carryover to the 9. The 9 becomes 10 and results in a double carryover. When necessary, go even further to the right.

*Example:*
```
  3852.69
+9847.32
```

**Step 1:** 3 + 9 + 1 = 13 (carryover from 8 + 8).

```
  3852.69
+9847.32
 13
```

**Step 2:** Since the three combinations to the right of 8 + 8 all equal 9, go to 9 + 2 = 11. There will be a carryover of 1. This carryover of 1 changes each of the 9's to the left to 10.

Thus: $8 + 8 + 1 = 17$ (carryover from $5 + 4 + 1$)

$5 + 4 + 1 = 10$ (carryover from $2 + 7 + 1$)

$2 + 7 + 1 = 10$ (carryover from $6 + 3 + 1$)

$6 + 3 + 1 = 10$ (carryover from $9 + 2$)

```
  3 8 5 2 . 6 9
+ 9 8 4 7 . 3 2
 1 3 7 0 0 . 0
```

**Step 3:** $9 + 2 = 11$

```
  3 8 5 2 . 6 9
+ 9 8 4 7 . 3 2
 1 3 7 0 0 . 0 1
```

## Part B Subtracting from Left to Right

Subtraction from left to right is somewhat like addition from left to right in that you always look at the combination to the right before subtracting. Instead of looking for a carryover, however, look to see if a 1 will need to be borrowed in order to subtract the combination to the right. If it will be necessary to do this, change the minuend digit to one less, and then subtract.

*Examples:*

a.
```
  5627
− 4281
```

**Step 1:** Start with $5 − 4$, but do not write the 1 yet. Look to the right at $6 − 2$. Since this can be subtracted without borrowing, write the 1 under the 4.

```
  5 6 2 7
− 4 2 8 1
  1
```

**Step 2:** Go to $6 − 2$, but do not write the 4 yet. Look to the right at $2 − 8$. In order to subtract this, 1 will have to be borrowed from the 6, changing it to 5. Thus, $5 − 2 = 3$. Write the 3 under the 2.

```
    5
  5 ₆¹2 7
− 4 2 8 1
  1 3
```

**Step 3:** Go to $2 − 8$. Since 1 already has been borrowed, this is $12 − 8$. Do not write the 4 yet. Look to the right at $7 − 1$. Since this can be subtracted without borrowing from the 12, write the 4 under the 8.

```
    5
  5 ₆¹2 7
− 4 2 8 1
  1 3 4
```

**Step 4:** $7 − 1 = 6$. Write the 6 under the 1.

```
    5
  5 ₆¹2 7
− 4 2 8 1
  1 3 4 6
```

b.
```
  6783.45
− 1875.32
```

**Step 1:** Start with $6 − 1$, but do not write the 5 yet. Look to the right at $7 − 8$. In order to subtract this, 1 will have to be borrowed from the 6, changing it to 5. Thus, $5 − 1 = 4$. Write the 4 under the 1.

```
  5
  ₆¹7 8 3 . 4 5
− 1 8 7 5 . 3 2
  4
```

**Step 2:** Go to $7 − 8$. Since 1 already has been borrowed, this is $17 − 8$. Do not write the 9 yet. Look to the right at $8 − 7$. Since this can be subtracted without borrowing from the 17, write the 9 under the 8.

```
  5
  ₆¹7 8 3 . 4 5
− 1 8 7 5 . 3 2
  4 9
```

**Step 3:** Go to $8 − 7$, but do not write the 1 yet. Look to the right at $3 − 5$. In order to subtract this, 1 will have to be borrowed from the 8, changing it to 7. Thus, $7 − 7 = 0$. Write the 0 under the 7.

```
    5   7
   6¹7 8¹3 . 4 5
 − 1 8 7 5 . 3 2
   ─────────────
          4 9 0
```

**Step 4:** Go to 3 − 5. Since 1 already has been borrowed, this is 13 − 5. Do not write the 8 yet. Look to the right at 4 − 3. Since this can be subtracted without borrowing from the 13, write the 8 under the 5.

```
    5   7
   6¹7 8¹3 . 4 5
 − 1 8 7 5 . 3 2
   ─────────────
        4 9 0 8 .
```

**Step 5:** Go to 4 − 3, but do not write the 1 yet. Look to the right at 5 − 2. Since this can be subtracted without borrowing from the 4, write the 1 under the 3.

```
    5   7
   6¹7 8¹3 . 4 5
 − 1 8 7 5 . 3 2
   ─────────────
        4 9 0 8 . 1
```

**Step 6:** 5 − 2 = 3. Write the 3 under the 2.

```
    5   7
   6¹7 8¹3 . 4 5
 − 1 8 7 5 . 3 2
   ─────────────
        4 9 0 8 . 1 3
```

Just as in addition, sometimes it is necessary to go two or more places to the right to see if there will be borrowing to be done. When the digits in the combination to the right are the same, go to the next right (or farther) to see if double borrowing is necessary.

*Example:*
```
   81.42
 −51.47
```

**Step 1:** Start with 8 − 5. Before writing the 3, look to the right at 1 − 1. Since these digits are the same, go to the next combination, 4 − 4. Since these digits are also the same, go to the next combination, 2 − 7. In order to subtract this, 1 will have to be borrowed from the 4, changing it to a 3.

In order to subtract 3 − 4, 1 will have to be borrowed from the 1, changing it to a 0.

In order to subtract 0 − 1, 1 will have to be borrowed from the 8, changing it to 7. Thus, 7 − 5 = 2. Write the 2 under the 5.

```
   7¹0  ¹3
   8 1 . 4¹2
 − 5 1 . 4 7
   ──────────
          2
```

**Step 2:** Go to 1 − 1, which is now 10 − 1. Write the 9 under the 1.

```
   7¹0  ¹3
   8 1 . 4¹2
 − 5 1 . 4 7
   ──────────
        2 9 .
```

**Step 3:** Go to 4 − 4, which is now 13 − 4. Write the 9 under the 4.

```
   7¹0  ¹3
   8 1 . 4¹2
 − 5 1 . 4 7
   ──────────
        2 9 . 9
```

**Step 4:** Since 2 − 7 is now 12 − 7, write the 5 under the 7.

```
   7¹0  ¹3
   8 1 . 4¹2
 − 5 1 . 4 7
   ──────────
        2 9 . 9 5
```

Note that while the explanation for the above problem is long, the work can be done mentally very quickly.

**Part C Adding Two Fractions Whose Numerators Are 1**

The sum of two fractions whose numerators are both 1 is a fraction whose numerator is the sum of the two denominators, and whose denominator is the product of the two denominators.

*Examples:*

a. $\frac{1}{3} + \frac{1}{4} = \frac{3 + 4}{3 \times 4} = \frac{7}{12}$

b. $\frac{1}{5} + \frac{1}{9} = \frac{5 + 9}{5 \times 9} = \frac{14}{45}$

When the original two denominators have a common factor, the sum found by using the shortcut is a fraction which can be reduced.

*Examples:*

a. $\frac{1}{4} + \frac{1}{6} = \frac{4+6}{4 \times 6} = \frac{10}{24} = \frac{5}{12}$

b. $\frac{1}{3} + \frac{1}{15} = \frac{3+15}{3 \times 15} = \frac{18}{45} = \frac{2}{5}$

## Part D  Subtracting Two Fractions Whose Numerators Are 1

The difference of two fractions whose numerators are both 1 is a fraction whose numerator is equal to the second denominator minus the first denominator, and whose denominator is the product of the two denominators. As in addition, if the two denominators have a common factor, the difference found by using the shortcut is a fraction which can be reduced.

*Examples:*

a. $\frac{1}{3} - \frac{1}{4} = \frac{4-3}{4 \times 3} = \frac{1}{12}$

b. $\frac{1}{5} - \frac{1}{8} = \frac{8-5}{8 \times 5} = \frac{3}{40}$

c. $\frac{1}{8} - \frac{1}{12} = \frac{12-8}{12 \times 8} = \frac{4}{96} = \frac{1}{24}$

## Part E  Multiplying and Dividing by .1, .01, .001, etc.

The time-saving shortcut to multiply or divide by .1, .01, .001, etc., is to move the decimal point only. If the multiplicand or the dividend is a whole number, put a decimal point after the last digit in order to be able to move the decimal point.

*Multiplying by .1, .01, .001, etc.* When the multiplier is .1, .01, .001, etc., all you need to do is to add the correct number of decimal places to the multiplicand by moving the decimal point to the *left*. The number of places moved depends on the number of decimal places in the multiplier.

When the multiplier is .1, move the decimal point one place to the left.

*Example:* $6.75 \times .1 = .6{\scriptstyle\curvearrowleft}75 = .675$

When the multiplier is .01, move the decimal point two places to the left.

*Example:* $784 \times .01 = 784. \times .01 = 7.84{\scriptstyle\curvearrowleft} = 7.84$

When the multiplier is .001, etc., move the decimal point three places to the left, etc. It may be necessary to add preceding zeros in order to move the correct number of places.

*Example:* $3.4 \times .001 = .003{\scriptstyle\curvearrowleft}4 = .0034$

*Dividing by .1, .01, .001, etc.* When the divisor is .1, .01, .001, etc., to find the quotient, move the decimal point of the dividend as many places to the *right* as there are decimal places in the divisor. The result is the answer.

When the divisor is .1, move the dividend point one place to the right.

*Example:* $38.7 \div .1 = 38{\scriptstyle\curvearrowright}7. = 387$

When the divisor is .01, move the dividend decimal point two places to the right.

*Example:* $7.2 \div .01 = 7{\scriptstyle\curvearrowright}20. = 720$

When the divisor is .001, etc., move the dividend decimal point three places to the right, etc.

*Example:* $.0458 \div .001 = {\scriptstyle\curvearrowright}045.8 = 45.8$

Note that since $.1 = \frac{1}{10}$, dividing any number by $\frac{1}{10}$ is the same as multiplying it by $\frac{10}{1}$, dividing by .01 is the same as multiplying by $\frac{100}{1}$, etc. The quotient always must be larger than the original dividend. Think of dividing $5.00 into dimes (a dime is .10 or $\frac{1}{10}$ of a dollar):

$$\$5 \div \frac{1}{10} = \frac{5}{1} \times \frac{10}{1} = 50 \text{ dimes}$$

Similarly, dividing $5.00 into pennies becomes:

$$\$5 \div .01 = \$5 \div \frac{1}{100} = \frac{5}{1} \times \frac{100}{1} = 500 \text{ pennies}$$

## Part F  Multiplying and Dividing by 50 and 25

A shortcut can be used to multiply and divide by 50 and 25 since they can be expressed as $100 \div 2$ and $100 \div 4$, respectively.

**Multiplying by 50 and 25.** Since 50 equals 100 ÷ 2, to multiply any number by 50, first multiply it by 100 and then divide the result by 2. (Use the shortcuts for multiplying by 100: If the multiplicand is a whole number, add two zeros; if it is a decimal, move the decimal point two places to the right.)

*Examples:*

a. 615 × 50

   615 × 50 = 61,500 ÷ 2 = 30,750

b. 7.032 × 50

   7.032 × 50 = 703.2 ÷ 2 = 351.6

Since 25 equals 100 ÷ 4, to multiply any number by 25, first multiply it by 100 and then divide the result by 4.

*Examples:*

a. 488 × 25

   488 × 25 = 48,800 ÷ 4 = 12,200

b. 5.62 × 25

   5.62 × 25 = 562 ÷ 4 = 140.5

**Dividing by 50 and 25.** In dividing any number by 50, instead of using 100 ÷ 2, use the equivalent fractional form of $\frac{100}{2}$. Remember that to divide any number by a fraction, you invert the divisor and multiply. Therefore, dividing a number by 50 is the same as multiplying it by $\frac{2}{100}$; that is, multiply the number by 2 and then divide the result by 100. (When dividing by 100, move the decimal point two places to the left.)

*Examples:*

a. 409 ÷ 50

   $\frac{409 \times 2}{100}$ = 818 ÷ 100 = 8.18

b. 3.65 ÷ 50

   $\frac{3.65 \times 2}{100}$ = 7.30 ÷ 100 = .073

Similarly, when dividing any number by 25, instead of using 100 ÷ 4, use the equivalent fractional form of $\frac{100}{4}$. Therefore, dividing a number by 25 is the same as multiplying it by $\frac{4}{100}$; that is, multiply the number by 4 and then divide the result by 100.

*Examples:*

a. 4,320 ÷ 25

   $\frac{4,320 \times 4}{100}$ = 17,280 ÷ 100 = 172.8

b. 7.51 ÷ 25

   $\frac{7.51 \times 4}{100}$ = 30.04 ÷ 100 = .3004

*Part*
# G  *Multiplying by 11*

The shortcut for multiplying a two-digit number by 11 is so easy that you should always use it. The answer can be written immediately.

To multiply any two-digit number by 11, do these steps mentally:

**Step 1:** Add the two digits of the multiplicand.

**Step 2:** If the sum of these two digits is 9 or less, place this sum in between the two digits of the multiplicand to form the product.

*Examples:*

a. 43 × 11

   4 + 3 = 7

   43 × 11 = 4<u>7</u>3

b. 54 × 11

   5 + 4 = 9

   54 × 11 = 5<u>9</u>4

**Step 3:** If the sum of the two digits of the multiplicand is 10 or more, add the 1 of this sum to the tens digit of the multiplicand. Then put the remaining digit of this sum in between the *new* tens digit and the units digit of the multiplicand. (When the multiplicand is between 91 and 99 inclusive, the product will have four digits.)

*Examples:*

a. 58 × 11

   5 + 8 = 13

            6
   58 × 11 = 5̶38 = 638

b. 94 × 11

   9 + 4 = 13

            10
   94 × 11 = 9̶34 = 1,034

If either the multiplicand or the multiplier, or both, is a decimal, point off the total number of decimal places in the product.

*Examples:*

a. 6.2 × 11

   6 + 2 = 8

   (62 × 11 = 682); 6.2 × 11 = 68.2

b. 89 × .11

   8 + 9 = 17

            9
   (89 × 11 = 8̶79); 89 × .11 = 9.79

c. .89 × .011

   8 + 9 = 17

            9
   (89 × 11 = 8̶79); .89 × .011 = .00979

The same procedure can be followed for multiplying a number with three or more digits by 11. It is shown here without explanation only for the student's interest.

*Example:* 62,935 × 11

Starting at the right, two digits at a time are added. Their sums are placed in between the first and the last digits of the multiplicand.

$$6 \frown 2 \frown 9 \frown 3 \frown 5$$
$$(+1) \quad (+1)$$
$$6 \quad 9 \quad 2 \quad 2 \quad 8 \quad 5$$

62,935 × 11 = 692,285

Generally it is simpler to multiply in the regular way by copying the multiplicand twice in the correct positions as shown below.

*Example:* 62,935 × 11

$$
\begin{array}{r}
62935 \\
\times \quad 11 \\
\hline
62935 \\
629350 \\
\hline
692285 \\
\end{array}
$$

## Part H Some Miscellaneous Shortcuts

*Adding and subtracting 9 from any number.* The fact that 9 is one less than 10 provides a quick way to add 9 to a number or to subtract 9 from a number.

To add 9 to any number, first add 10 to it and then subtract one.

*Examples:*

a. 84 + 9 = 84 + 10 − 1 = 94 − 1 = 93

b. 67 + 9 = 67 + 10 − 1 = 77 − 1 = 76

To subtract 9 from any number, first subtract 10 from it and then add one.

*Examples:*

a. 76 − 9 = 76 − 10 + 1 = 66 + 1 = 67

b. 34 − 9 = 34 − 10 + 1 = 24 + 1 = 25

This shortcut can be extended to adding or subtracting two-digit numbers ending in 9. You know that 19 is one less than 20, 29 is one less than 30, 39 is one less than 40, etc. In the examples given here, you do not recopy the problems in order to add or subtract in the usual way. Try to do all the work mentally.

*Examples:*

a. 84 + 29

   84 + 30 − 1 = 114 − 1 = 113

b. 67 + 79

   67 + 80 − 1 = 147 − 1 = 146

c. 76 − 39

   76 − 40 + 1 = 36 + 1 = 37

d. 134 − 69

   134 − 70 + 1 = 64 + 1 = 65

***Multiplying a three-digit number by a one-digit number when all the digits are 4 or less.*** When a three-digit number is multiplied by a one-digit number and all the digits are 4 or less, you can write the product almost immediately. Starting at the left, mentally multiply and add as you go along: the hundreds digit by the multiplier, plus the tens digit by the multiplier, plus the units digit by the multiplier. (It sounds more difficult than it really is.)

*Examples:*

a. 421 × 3

  (400 × 3)    + (20 × 3) + (1 × 3)

   1,200     +    60   +   3   = 1,263

b. 232 × 4

  (200 × 4)    + (30 × 4) + (2 × 4)

   800   +   120   +   8    = 928

***Multiplying a two-digit number by another two-digit number.*** The shortcut for multiplying a two-digit number by another two-digit number is very useful, especially if the digits are small. However, to do it easily requires some practice.

The steps in the multiplication are the same as in the long method, but the partial products are added mentally. Study the steps given for the examples shown below.

*Examples:*

a. 43 × 26

$$\times \begin{matrix} 4 & 3 \\ 2 & 6 \end{matrix}$$
$$\overline{11 \quad 1 \quad 8} = 1,118$$

**Step 1:** Multiply 3 × 6 = 18. Write the 8 and carry the 1 mentally.

**Step 2:** Multiply 4 × 6 = 24; 24 + 1 = 25. Multiply 3 × 2 = 6. Mentally add 25 + 6 = 31. Write the 1 in the second position to the left and carry the 3.

**Step 3:** Multiply 4 × 2 = 8; 8 + 3 = 11. Write the 11.

b. 57 × 39

$$\times \begin{matrix} 5 & 7 \\ 3 & 9 \end{matrix}$$
$$\overline{22 \quad 2 \quad 3} = 2,223$$

**Step 1:** Multiply 7 × 9 = 63. Write the 3 and carry the 6 mentally.

**Step 2:** Multiply 5 × 9 = 45; 45 + 6 = 51. Multiply 7 × 3 = 21. Mentally add 51 + 21 = 72. Write the 2 in the second position to the left and carry the 7.

**Step 3:** Multiply 5 × 3 = 15; 15 + 7 = 22. Write the 22.

A word of warning on the shortcuts given in this section and all other shortcuts: You must recognize when they can be used and then be able to use them easily if they are to serve as real shortcuts.

**Complete Assignment 19**

# Assignment 19
# Section 6-1

*Shortcuts in Calculating*

| | Perfect Score | Student's Score |
|---|---|---|
| Part A | 10 | |
| Part B | 10 | |
| Part C | 5 | |
| Part D | 5 | |
| Part E | 20 | |
| Part F | 20 | |
| Part G | 10 | |
| Part H | 20 | |
| TOTAL | 100 | |

## Part A

### Adding from Left to Right

*Directions:* Add from left to right only. ($\frac{1}{2}$ point for each correct answer)

| | | | | | | | |
|---|---|---|---|---|---|---|---|
| **1.** 43 <br> + 16 | | **2.** 25 <br> + 72 | | **3.** 78 <br> + 23 | | **4.** 68 <br> + 34 | |

| | | | |
|---|---|---|---|
| **5.** 2.06 <br> + 1.63 | **6.** 3.24 <br> + 5.62 | **7.** 1.57 <br> + 7.10 | **8.** 9.61 <br> + 3.28 |

| | | | |
|---|---|---|---|
| **9.** 5.37 <br> + 6.94 | **10.** 8.24 <br> + 7.78 | **11.** 67.32 <br> + 15.62 | **12.** 43.85 <br> + 24.15 |

| | | | |
|---|---|---|---|
| **13.** 91.06 <br> + 29.94 | **14.** 41.45 <br> + 38.74 | **15.** 425.91 <br> + 698.63 | **16.** 554.17 <br> + 172.87 |

| | | | |
|---|---|---|---|
| **17.** 985.67 <br> + 567.98 | **18.** 453.67 <br> + 824.59 | **19.** 1,838.59 <br> + 4,901.86 | **20.** 6,251.28 <br> + 9,478.39 |

Student's Score _____

## Part B

### Subtracting from Left to Right

*Directions:* Subtract from left to right only. ($\frac{1}{2}$ point for each correct answer)

| | | | |
|---|---|---|---|
| **21.** 82 <br> − 31 | **22.** 75 <br> − 62 | **23.** 73 <br> − 59 | **24.** 54 <br> − 18 |

| | | | |
|---|---|---|---|
| **25.** 5.27 <br> − .28 | **26.** 7.48 <br> − 1.89 | **27.** 9.02 <br> − 4.13 | **28.** 94.38 <br> − 14.02 |

| 29. | 85.56<br>− 63.07 | 30. | 41.82<br>− 36.57 | 31. | 10.72<br>−  9.89 | 32. | 28.64<br>− 19.82 |
|---|---|---|---|---|---|---|---|
| 33. | 379.14<br>−  69.04 | 34. | 406.75<br>− 235.74 | 35. | 325.95<br>− 137.99 | 36. | 863.47<br>− 692.53 |
| 37. | 390.56<br>− 290.65 | 38. | 1,634.78<br>−  523.67 | 39. | 2,900.09<br>− 1,798.43 | 40. | 8,500.87<br>− 6,257.98 |

*Student's Score* _____

# Part C
## Adding Two Fractions Whose Numerators Are 1

*Directions:* Add by using the shortcut. ($\frac{1}{2}$ point for each correct answer)

41. $\frac{1}{2} + \frac{1}{3}$

42. $\frac{1}{2} + \frac{1}{4}$

43. $\frac{1}{3} + \frac{1}{5}$

44. $\frac{1}{3} + \frac{1}{6}$

45. $\frac{1}{4} + \frac{1}{7}$

46. $\frac{1}{5} + \frac{1}{8}$

47. $\frac{1}{3} + \frac{1}{10}$

48. $\frac{1}{6} + \frac{1}{8}$

49. $\frac{1}{7} + \frac{1}{11}$

50. $\frac{1}{20} + \frac{1}{12}$

*Student's Score* _____

# Part D
## Subtracting Two Fractions Whose Numerators Are 1

*Directions:* Subtract by using the shortcut. ($\frac{1}{2}$ point for each correct answer)

51. $\frac{1}{2} - \frac{1}{3}$

52. $\frac{1}{3} - \frac{1}{4}$

53. $\frac{1}{4} - \frac{1}{6}$

54. $\frac{1}{5} - \frac{1}{8}$

55. $\frac{1}{8} - \frac{1}{12}$

56. $\frac{1}{3} - \frac{1}{9}$

57. $\frac{1}{4} - \frac{1}{20}$

58. $\frac{1}{10} - \frac{1}{12}$

59. $\frac{1}{16} - \frac{1}{20}$

60. $\frac{1}{5} - \frac{1}{30}$

*Student's Score* _____

# Part E
## Multiplying and Dividing by .1, .01, .001, etc.

*Directions:* Multiply by moving the decimal point only. (1 point for each correct answer)

61. $57.535 \times .1$

62. $49.3 \times .1$

63. $419 \times .01$

64. $5,206 \times .01$

Assignment 19

| | | | |
|---|---|---|---|
| **65.** | 4.5427 × .001 | **68.** | 1,318 × .0001 |
| **66.** | 3.19 × .001 | **69.** | 64.5 × .00001 |
| **67.** | 1,098 × .0001 | **70.** | 7.56 × .00001 |

*Directions:* Divide by moving the decimal point only. (1 point for each correct answer)

| | | | |
|---|---|---|---|
| **71.** | .97 ÷ .1 | **76.** | 2.45 ÷ .01 |
| **72.** | 25.9 ÷ .1 | **77.** | 90.8 ÷ .001 |
| **73.** | 86 ÷ .01 | **78.** | 22.3 ÷ .001 |
| **74.** | 317 ÷ .01 | **79.** | 8.87 ÷ .0001 |
| **75.** | 1.0674 ÷ .01 | **80.** | 7.3 ÷ .0001 |

*Student's Score* _____

# Part F

## *Multiplying and Dividing by 50 and 25*

*Directions:* Multiply by using a shortcut. (1 point for each correct answer)

| | | | |
|---|---|---|---|
| **81.** | 64 × 50 | **85.** | 314 × 25 |
| **82.** | 96 × 50 | **86.** | 532 × 25 |
| **83.** | .063 × 50 | **87.** | 7.14 × 25 |
| **84.** | 5.69 × 50 | **88.** | 38.2 × 25 |

*Directions:* Divide by using a shortcut. (1 point for each correct answer)

| | | | |
|---|---|---|---|
| **89.** | 348 ÷ 50 | **95.** | 48 ÷ 25 |
| **90.** | 563 ÷ 50 | **96.** | 32 ÷ 25 |
| **91.** | 18.2 ÷ 50 | **97.** | 56.1 ÷ 25 |
| **92.** | 75.8 ÷ 50 | **98.** | 9.75 ÷ 25 |
| **93.** | 14.23 ÷ 50 | **99.** | 6.085 ÷ 25 |
| **94.** | 71.25 ÷ 50 | **100.** | 47.781 ÷ 25 |

*Student's Score* _____

# Part G

## Multiplying by 11

*Directions:* Multiply by using the shortcut only. (½ point for each correct answer)

| | | | |
|---|---|---|---|
| **101.** 13 × 11 | | **111.** 6.9 × 11 | |
| **102.** 43 × 11 | | **112.** .63 × 11 | |
| **103.** 94 × 11 | | **113.** 9.9 × .11 | |
| **104.** 65 × 11 | | **114.** .00047 × 1.1 | |
| **105.** 84 × 11 | | **115.** .19 × .11 | |
| **106.** 37 × 11 | | **116.** 28 × 1.1 | |
| **107.** 82 × 11 | | **117.** .075 × 11 | |
| **108.** 73 × 11 | | **118.** .016 × 11 | |
| **109.** 39 × 11 | | **119.** 5.9 × .0011 | |
| **110.** 51 × 11 | | **120.** .0035 × 11 | |

*Student's Score* _____

# Part H

## Some Miscellaneous Shortcuts

*Directions:* Add or subtract by using a shortcut. (1 point for each correct answer)

**121.** 56 + 29    **122.** 37 + 69    **123.** 24 + 89    **124.** 63 + 59

**125.** 47 − 19    **126.** 80 − 39    **127.** 151 − 99    **128.** 110 − 79

*Directions:* Multiply from left to right. (1 point for each correct answer)

**129.** 123 × 4    **130.** 245 × 2    **131.** 104 × 5    **132.** 421 × 3

*Directions:* Multiply by using a shortcut. (1 point for each correct answer)

**133.** 25
× 21

**134.** 32
× 43

**135.** 55
× 34

**136.** 23
× 94

**137.** 63
× 26

**138.** 72
× 24

**139.** 6.8
× .042

**140.** 1.7
× .41

*Student's Score* _____

# Section 6-2 Estimating with Rounded-Off Numbers

An **estimate** is about what an answer should be; it is not the exact answer. When estimating, the calculation is done with rounded-off numbers to get a rough idea of what the actual results should be.

Estimates are given in many lines of business such as painting, roofing, all kinds of repairing, etc., to give the customer some idea of costs. Experience in the business is needed to prepare a good estimate. For this reason business estimates are not presented here. Learning how to estimate an answer in business mathematics, however, will help you in the business world.

Up to this point you have rounded off an answer to a certain number of decimal places only. (For rounding off to a particular decimal place, refer to Chapter 1, Section 1-4, Part C.) The same general procedure is used to round off a number to the nearest unit, ten, hundred, thousand, etc. For *any* rounding off, the first two steps are the same. These are:

**Step 1:** Look only at the digit directly to the right of the required place; the rest of the number is not used in rounding off. Until you are sure of yourself, it is a good idea to draw a vertical line after the required place and to underline the digit to its right.

**Step 2:** If the digit after the required place is less than 5, make no change in the required place. It stays the same. If the digit after the required place is 5 or more, add 1 to the required place.

For rounding off to the nearest unit, ten, hundred, thousand, etc., two more steps are needed. These are:

**Step 3:** Drop any decimal places as well as the decimal point.

**Step 4:** For rounding off to the nearest ten, hundred, thousand, etc., whether or not a *one* was added to the required place, change all the digits to the right of the required place to zeros through the units position.

When any rounding off has been completed, always check the result. It should be *about* the same size as the original number; that is, it should be either a little smaller or a little larger.

## Part A  Rounding Off to the Nearest Unit

In business, an amount of money given in dollars and cents is often rounded off to the nearest dollar. Rounding off to the nearest dollar is the same as rounding off to the nearest unit.

By following Step 1 given above for any rounding off, you can tell that the digit to the right of the units place is in the *tenths* position. The application of Steps 2 and 3 is explained in detail in the examples below.

***When the digit in the tenths position is less than 5.*** Make no change in the units digit if the tenths place digit is less than 5. Drop the decimal point and all the decimal places. The rounded-off result is the same as the original whole number part.

*Examples:*

a.  $178.3675 = 178|.\underline{3}675 = 178\cancel{.3675} = 178$

The tenths place digit is 3. Since this is less than 5, make no change in the 8 and drop the decimal point and all the decimal places.

b.  $\$4,653.49 = \$4,653|.\underline{4}9 = \$4,653\cancel{.49} = \$4,653$

***When the digit in the tenths position is 5 or more.*** Add 1 to the units digit if the tenths place digit is 5 or more. Then drop the decimal point and all the decimal places. The rounded-off result is *one* more than the original whole number part.

*Examples:*

a.  $\$999.50 = \$999|.\underline{5}0 = \overset{1000}{\$\cancel{999}\cancel{.50}} = \$1,000$

The tenths place digit is 5. Therefore, add 1 to the last 9, which is the same as adding 1 to $999 to make it $1,000. Drop the decimal point and all decimal places.

b.  $263.82 = 263|.\underline{8}2 = 26\overset{4}{\cancel{3}}\cancel{.82} = 264$

The tenths place digit is 8. Since this is more than 5, add 1 to the 3 to make it 4. Then drop the .82.

# Rounding Off to the Nearest Ten, Hundred, Thousand, etc.

In applying Step 1 given on the previous page for any rounding off, you can tell that:

1. To round off to the nearest ten, you should look only at the digit in the *units* position. The units place digit is the first digit to the left of the decimal point. It is also the last digit in a whole number.

2. To round off to the nearest hundred, you should look at the digit in the *tens* position.

3. To round off to the nearest thousand, you should look at the digit in the *hundreds* position.

All other digits to the right of the required place are disregarded.

In applying Step 2 given for any rounding off, the same procedure holds true: If the digit to the right of the required place is less than 5, make no change in the required place; if it is 5 or more, add 1 to the required place.

In applying Step 3, if the number being rounded off is a decimal mixed number, drop the decimal point and all the decimal places. If the number being rounded off is a whole number, Step 3 is omitted.

Lastly, apply Step 4 as given.

The following examples illustrate in detail the application of Steps 1 through 4 for any rounding off that were given on page 157.

*Examples:*

a. Round off 364.57 to the nearest ten.

$$364.57 = 36 \underline{4}.57 = 364\cancel{.57} = 360$$

The digit in the units position is 4. Since this is less than 5, make no change in the 6. Drop the .57 and change the 4 to 0.

b. Round off $1,276.98 to the nearest ten dollars.

$$\overset{80}{\$1,276.98} = \$1,27 \underline{6}.98 = \$1,27\cancel{6.98} = \$1,280$$

The digit in the units position is 6. Since this is more than 5, add 1 to the 7 to make it 8. Then drop the .98 and change the 6 to 0.

c. Round off 628 to the nearest hundred.

$$\overset{00}{628} = 6 \underline{28} = 6\cancel{28} = 600$$

The digit to the right of the hundreds position is 2. Since this is less than 5, make no change in the 6. Change the 28 to 00.

d. Round off 682 to the nearest hundred.

$$\overset{700}{682} = 6 \underline{82} = \cancel{682} = 700$$

The digit to the right of the hundreds position is 8. Since this is more than 5, add 1 to the 6 to make it 7. Change the 82 to 00.

e. Round off $2,309.45 to the nearest thousand dollars.

$$\overset{000}{\$2,309.45} = \$2, \underline{309}.45 = \$2,\cancel{309.45} = \$2,000$$

The digit to the right of the thousands position is 3. Since this is less than 5, make no change in the 2. Drop the .45 and change the 309 to 000.

f. Round off $19,500 to the nearest thousand dollars.

$$\overset{20,000}{\$19,500} = \$19, \underline{500} = \$\cancel{19,500} = \$20,000$$

The digit to the right of the thousands position is 5. Since this is 5, add 1 to the 19 to make it 20. Change the 500 to 000.

To round off numbers to larger place values, follow the same procedure. For example, 22,998 to the nearest ten thousand is 20,000; 26,298 to the nearest ten thousand is 30,000; 649,999 to the nearest hundred thousand is 600,000; 650,000 to the nearest hundred thousand is 700,000; 7,443,210 to the nearest million is 7,000,000; and 7,543,210 to the nearest million is 8,000,000.

A common error in rounding off to the nearest ten, hundred, thousand, etc., is to move the decimal point of the number to the left so that there are two digits before the point for the nearest ten, three digits for the nearest hundred etc. This is wrong since it changes the value of the number. For correct rounding off, you must follow only the steps that have been given here.

Part C

## Estimating Sums and Differences

An estimate shows only about how much the answer should be. The main reason for getting an estimate is to find out if an answer is about right.

Estimates found by different individuals may vary slightly, depending on how the numbers were rounded off. All may be satisfactory, however, since an estimate is only a rough answer. An estimate will show whether or not an answer is pointed off correctly, but it will not show minor errors in the calculation.

*Estimating sums.* In estimating the sum of a column of figures, generally all the addends are rounded off to the *same* place value—ten, hundred, thousand, etc., whichever is the largest. Then only a single digit from each number needs to be added since the rest of the number consists of zeros. In the rounding off, some of the numbers may not be included in the sum if they are less than half the place value used in the rounding off process. This does not affect the estimate to any extent since other numbers may be rounded up as much or more.

To estimate the sum of a column of figures, round off the addends and add the non-zero digits as you go down this column. In the examples that follow, the rounded-off numbers are given only to show the procedure.

*Examples:*

a.
| $85.07 – – – | 90 | (9) |
|---|---|---|
| 43.29 – – – | 40 | (4) |
| 7.38 – – – | 10 | (1) |
| 62.59 – – – | 60 | (6) |
| 1.46 – – – | 00 | (0) |
| 35.02 – – – | 40 | (4) |
| | 240 | (24) |

b.
| $   68.33 – – – | 100 | ( 1) |
|---|---|---|
| 595.24 – – – | 600 | ( 6) |
| 36.42 – – – | 000 | ( 0) |
| 129.87 – – – | 100 | ( 1) |
| 1,459.95 – – – | 1,500 | (15) |
| 307.06 – – – | 300 | ( 3) |
| | 2,600 | (26) |

Note that in *Example b,* the addends are rounded off to the nearest hundred since there is only one number in the thousands.

c.
| $10,025.93 – – – | 10,000 | (10) |
|---|---|---|
| 68.24 – – – | 0,000 | ( 0) |
| 1.37 – – – | 0,000 | ( 0) |
| 511.55 – – – | 1,000 | ( 1) |
| 432.50 – – – | 0,000 | ( 0) |
| 50.78 – – – | 0,000 | ( 0) |
| | 11,000 | (11) |

Note that in *Example c,* the four numbers that are rounded off to 0,000 are not included in the estimate. Their sum is a little more than 500, which is made up when the 511.55 is rounded up to 1,000. Thus, the estimate is close to the actual total of $11,090.37. Since the first addend is so large, the addends can be rounded off to the nearest thousand.

*Estimating differences.* In estimating the difference between two numbers, the minuend and the subtrahend may be rounded off to *different* place values, depending on the problem. The only requirement is that the rounded-off numbers can be subtracted mentally.

*Examples:*

a.
| 689.76 – – – | 700 |
|---|---|
| −309.32 – – – | 300 |
| | 400 |

b.
| 430.26 – – – | 400 | | 430 |
|---|---|---|---|
| − 49.75 – – – | 50 | *or* | − 50 |
| | 350 | | 380 |

c.
| 8,011.72 – – | 8,000 | | 8,000 |
|---|---|---|---|
| − 75.08 – – | 100 | *or* | − 80 |
| | 7,900 | | 7,920 |

When the minuend is very large as compared to the subtrahend, only that part of the minuend which is directly involved in the subtraction needs to be considered in the rounding off. The digits to its left are brought down to the answer.

*Example:*

$$
\begin{array}{rr}
27{,}492.36 --- & (274)\,90 \\
-\quad 38.67 --- & -\ \ 40 \\
\hline
& 27{,}4\,50
\end{array}
$$

## Part D — Estimating Products

In estimating the product of two numbers, usually the multiplicand and the multiplier are rounded off to *different* place values. Here you will learn how to estimate products under two conditions: (1) when neither the multiplicand nor the multiplier is a decimal fraction, and (2) when either the multiplicand or the multiplier, or both, is a decimal fraction.

***When neither the multiplicand nor the multiplier is a decimal fraction.*** When neither of the numbers to be multiplied is a decimal fraction, round off each number so that only the *first* digit is not zero. Then multiply the first digits mentally and place the correct number of zeros after the product to get the estimate.

*Example:* Estimate the product and compare the estimate with the given product.

$$
\begin{array}{rr}
867 --- & 900 \\
\times\ 93 --- & \times\ \ 90 \\
\hline
& 81{,}000 \text{ (estimated product)}
\end{array}
$$

$867 \times 93 = 80{,}631$ (given product)

Note that the given product is close to the estimated product and is probably correct.

Estimating is valuable because the estimated product serves as a check on the correct placement of the decimal point in the given product. However, the estimated product will not reveal any minor errors that may be made when multiplying the numbers to get the exact product. In the following examples, the given products are intentionally wrong so that you can see what an estimate can and cannot do.

*Examples:* Estimate the product and compare the estimate with the given product.

a. $489.67 \times 2.95$

$$
\begin{array}{rr}
489.67 --- & 500 \\
\times\ \ 2.95 --- & \times\ \ 3 \\
\hline
& 1{,}500 \text{ (estimated product)}
\end{array}
$$

$489.67 \times 2.95 = 1{,}433.5265$ (given product)

Note that the given product is correctly pointed off and is close to the estimate. However, the estimate does not reveal the error made in the multiplication process. The correct product is 1,444.5265.

b. $37.072 \times 5.37\frac{1}{2}$

$$
\begin{array}{rr}
37.072 --- & 40 \\
\times\ 5.37\frac{1}{2} --- & \times\ 5 \\
\hline
& 200 \text{ (estimated product)}
\end{array}
$$

$37.072 \times 5.37\frac{1}{2} = 19.926200$ (given product)

Note that the given product is pointed off incorrectly. You can see that an error was made by including the $\frac{1}{2}$ as a decimal place, for the correct product is 199.26200. But the error should have been seen even without an estimate because the given product is less than the multiplicand. This is not possible when the multiplier contains a whole number.

***When either the multiplicand or the multiplier, or both, is a decimal fraction.*** In estimating a product when at least one of the numbers to be multiplied is a decimal fraction, generally the decimal fraction is rounded off to the nearest tenth, hundredth, thousandth, etc.

*Examples:* Estimate the product and compare the estimate with the given product.

a. $6{,}799.542 \times .0086$

$$
\begin{array}{rr}
6{,}799.542 --- & 7{,}000 \\
\times\ \ \ .0086 --- & \times\ .009 \\
\hline
& 63.000 \text{ (estimated product)}
\end{array}
$$

$6{,}799.542 \times .0086 = 58.4760612$ (given product)

Note that the given product is less than the estimated product. This is because both the multiplicand and the multiplier were rounded *up* to get the estimate.

**b.** 48.95 × .0427

$$\begin{array}{ccc} 48.95 & & 50 \\ \times\ .0427 & --- & \times\ .04 \\ \hline & & 2.00\ \text{(estimated product)} \end{array}$$

48.95 × .0427 = .2090165 (given product)

Note that the given product is pointed off incorrectly. If one less place had been pointed off, the given answer would have been close to the estimate.

## Part E Estimating Quotients

As with estimating products, estimating quotients is important as a check on the size of and the decimal point placement in the given quotient. Also, like any estimated answer, the estimated quotient will not reveal minor errors that might be made when dividing numbers to get the exact quotient.

Here you will learn how to estimate quotients under four conditions: (1) when neither the dividend nor the divisor is a decimal fraction; (2) when the divisor is a decimal fraction and the dividend is a whole or mixed number; (3) when the dividend is a decimal fraction and the divisor is a whole or mixed number; and (4) when both the dividend and the divisor are decimal fractions. Finally, you will also learn how to check a given quotient by finding the estimated dividend.

*When neither the dividend nor the divisor is a decimal fraction.* To estimate the quotient of two numbers, neither of which is a decimal fraction, round off both numbers to such place values that the division can be done mentally or with some quick paper-and-pencil figuring.

*Examples:* Estimate the quotient and compare the estimate with the given quotient.

**a.** 272 ÷ 26

$$\frac{272}{26} \ --- \ \frac{300}{30} = 10\ \text{(estimated quotient)}$$

272 ÷ 26 = 10.461 (given quotient)

Note that the given quotient is pointed off correctly and is close to the estimate.

**b.** 838 ÷ 3.75

$$\frac{838}{3.75} \ --- \ \frac{800}{4} = 200\ \text{(estimated quotient)}$$

838 ÷ 3.75 = 2.235 (given quotient)

Note that the given quotient is pointed off incorrectly. When you carry out the division, you will find that the correct quotient is 223.5.

**c.** 9.05 ÷ 18.32

$$\frac{9.05}{18.32} \ --- \ \frac{9}{18} = \tfrac{1}{2} \text{ or } .5\ \text{(estimated quotient)}$$

9.05 ÷ 18.32 = .944 (given quotient)

Note that the given quotient is pointed off correctly, but it is too large. When you check the division, you will find that the correct quotient is .494. It is possible that, even though the division was done correctly, later on the 4 and the 9 were transposed when the answer had to be copied and written elsewhere. This is a very common error.

*When the divisor is a decimal fraction and the dividend is a whole or mixed number.* In estimating the quotient when the divisor is a decimal fraction and the dividend is a whole or mixed number, round off the decimal fraction (divisor) to the nearest tenth, hundredth, thousandth, etc. Then round off the dividend to the nearest ten, hundred, thousand, etc.

*Example:* Estimate the quotient of 174.61 ÷ .572 and compare the estimate with the given quotient.

$$\frac{174.61}{.572} \ --- \ \frac{180}{.6} = 300\ \text{(estimated quotient)}$$

174.61 ÷ .572 = 305.262 (given quotient)

Note that the given quotient is pointed off correctly and is close to the estimated quotient. Note also that instead of rounding off 174.61 to the nearest hundred (which would be 200), it is rounded to 180. Since .572 is rounded up to .6, the division can be done more easily with 180 and will give a better estimate.

**When the dividend is a decimal fraction and the divisor is a whole or mixed number.** In estimating the quotient when the dividend is a decimal fraction and the divisor is a whole or mixed number, round off the decimal fraction (dividend) to the nearest tenth, hundredth, thousandth, etc. Then round off the divisor to the nearest ten, hundred, thousand, etc.

*Example:* Estimate the quotient of .796 ÷ 185 and compare the estimate with the given quotient.

$$\frac{.796}{185} \ ---\ \frac{.8}{200} = .004 \text{ (estimated quotient)}$$

.796 ÷ 185 = 4.303 (given quotient)

Note that the given quotient is pointed off incorrectly. The decimal point in the dividend was moved three places to the right instead of being left in its original position. It is possible, of course, that the same error may be made in finding the estimated quotient. In that case, the estimate will not reveal the error.

**When both the dividend and the divisor are decimal fractions.** In estimating a quotient when both the dividend and the divisor are decimal fractions, round off each number separately to the nearest tenth, hundred, thousand, etc.

*Example:* Estimate the quotient of .831 ÷ .0049 and compare the estimate with the given quotient.

$$\frac{.831}{.0049} \ ---\ \frac{.8}{.005} = 160 \text{ (estimated quotient)}$$

.831 ÷ .0049 = 169.592 (given quotient)

Note that the given quotient is pointed off correctly and is close to the estimate.

**Checking a given quotient by finding the estimated dividend.** Although it has been said that estimating quotients is valuable as a check on the size of and decimal point placement in the given quotient, it is often easier to check the accuracy of the given quotient by another method. This method consists of finding the estimated dividend.

To find the estimated dividend, follow these three steps:

1. Round off the given quotient.
2. Round off the divisor.
3. Multiply the rounded-off quotient by the rounded-off divisor. The product should be close to the given dividend.

*Examples:* Find the estimated dividend and compare it with the given dividend.

a. 272 ÷ 26 = 10.461 (given quotient)

   10.461 – – – 10
   26      – – – 26
   10 × 26 = 260 (estimated dividend)

Note that the estimated dividend and the given dividend are about the same.

b. 838 ÷ 3.75 = 2.235 (given quotient)

   2.235 – – – 2
   3.75  – – – 4
   2 × 4 = 8 (estimated dividend)

The estimated dividend shows that the given quotient is pointed off incorrectly. The correct quotient is 223.5, which would be rounded off to 200.

c. 9.05 ÷ 18.32 = .944 (given quotient)

   .944  – – –   .9
   18.32 – – – 20
   .9 × 20 = 18 (estimated dividend)

The estimated dividend shows that the given quotient is pointed off correctly, but it is twice as large as it should be. The correct quotient is .494, which would be rounded off to .5.

d. .796 ÷ 185 = 4.303 (given quotient)

   4.303 – – –   4
   185   – – – 200
   4 × 200 = 800 (estimated dividend)

The estimated dividend shows that the given quotient is pointed off incorrectly. The correct quotient is .004303, which would be rounded off to .005.

Complete Assignment 20

## Assignment 20
## Section 6-2

**Estimating with Rounded-Off Numbers**

|  | Perfect Score | Student's Score |
|---|---|---|
| Part A | 10 | |
| Part B | 30 | |
| Part C | 10 | |
| Part D | 20 | |
| Part E | 30 | |
| TOTAL | 100 | |

## Part A

### Rounding Off to the Nearest Unit

*Directions:* Round off to the nearest unit or dollar as indicated. (1 point for each correct answer)

**Nearest Unit**

1. 5.678 _____

2. 4.249 _____

3. 3.1509 _____

4. 78.69 _____

5. 199.499 _____

**Nearest Dollar**

6. $9.4449 _____

7. $86.50 _____

8. $378.002 _____

9. $1,999.995 _____

10. $3,600.497 _____

Student's Score _____

## Part B

### Rounding Off to the Nearest Ten, Hundred, Thousand, etc.

*Directions:* Round off to the nearest ten, hundred, thousand, etc. as indicated. (1 point for each correct answer)

**Nearest Ten**

11. 74.99 _____

12. 16.05 _____

13. 138.99 _____

14. 44.50 _____

15. 199.95 _____

**Nearest Hundred**

21. 580.46 _____

22. 56.63 _____

23. 49.98 _____

24. 1,142.32 _____

25. 350.00 _____

**Nearest $10**

16. $122.32 _____

17. $450.00 _____

18. $799.86 _____

19. $1,274.99 _____

20. $6,126.41 _____

**Nearest $100**

26. $1,549.00 _____

27. $94.95 _____

28. $48.95 _____

29. $1,043.00 _____

30. $1,050.00 _____

31. 750.01 _____          36. $500.00 _____

32. 2,833.75 _____        37. $4,912.54 _____

33. 6,161.32 _____        38. $491.36 _____

34. 7,875.35 _____        39. $11,400.00 _____

35. 499.99 _____          40. $105,500.00 _____

*Student's Score* _____

# Part C

## Estimating Sums and Differences

*Directions:* Estimate the sums or differences as indicated. Show the rounded-off numbers in the spaces at the right. Show the estimated answers in the double-ruled spaces. (1 point for each correct answer)

| 41. | | 42. | | 43. | |
|---|---|---|---|---|---|
| 44.44 | _____ | 247.98 | _____ | 865.10 | _____ |
| 63.45 | _____ | 9.02 | _____ | 1,940.37 | _____ |
| 266.62 | _____ | 63.27 | _____ | 1,079.46 | _____ |
| 113.14 | _____ | 717.00 | _____ | 50.82 | _____ |
| 7.61 | _____ | 820.20 | _____ | 500.00 | _____ |
| + 842.56 | _____ | + 29.63 | _____ | + 263.12 | _____ |

| 44. | | 45. | |
|---|---|---|---|
| 7,000.43 | _____ | 93,012.76 | _____ |
| 69.08 | _____ | 540.17 | _____ |
| 400.00 | _____ | 1,067.65 | _____ |
| 196.78 | _____ | 887.04 | _____ |
| 5.66 | _____ | 7,419.39 | _____ |
| + 651.95 | _____ | 692.58 | _____ |
| | | 418.03 | _____ |
| | | 8,301.85 | _____ |
| | | 900.00 | _____ |
| | | + 4,739.37 | _____ |

| 46. | | 47. | | 48. | |
|---|---|---|---|---|---|
| 87.50 | _____ | 605.47 | _____ | 958.65 | _____ |
| − 18.50 | _____ | − 9.89 | _____ | − 86.80 | _____ |

**49.**   1,187.02   _____
          −   99.51   _____

          ═════════

**50.**   2,108.35   _____
          −  267.44   _____

          ═════════

*Student's Score* _____

# Part D
## Estimating Products

**Directions:** Estimate the products. Show the rounded-off numbers used to find the estimated product. (1 point for each correct answer)

| | Rounded-Off Numbers | | Estimated Product |
|---|---|---|---|
| **51.** $65 \times 49$ | _____ × | _____ = | _____ |
| **52.** $29 \times 8$ | _____ × | _____ = | _____ |
| **53.** $1,876 \times .95$ | _____ × | _____ = | _____ |
| **54.** $405 \times 1.15$ | _____ × | _____ = | _____ |
| **55.** $26,995 \times .007$ | _____ × | _____ = | _____ |
| **56.** $29.68 \times .008$ | _____ × | _____ = | _____ |
| **57.** $82.7 \times .003$ | _____ × | _____ = | _____ |
| **58.** $.006 \times 62.5$ | _____ × | _____ = | _____ |
| **59.** $.45 \times 53.125$ | _____ × | _____ = | _____ |
| **60.** $2.54 \times .16$ | _____ × | _____ = | _____ |
| **61.** $17.5 \times 91\frac{1}{4}$ | _____ × | _____ = | _____ |
| **62.** $308.47 \times 12\frac{1}{2}$ | _____ × | _____ = | _____ |
| **63.** $675,981 \times .08$ | _____ × | _____ = | _____ |
| **64.** $19,607 \times .05$ | _____ × | _____ = | _____ |
| **65.** $543.7 \times .0875$ | _____ × | _____ = | _____ |
| **66.** $.03125 \times 69.5$ | _____ × | _____ = | _____ |
| **67.** $10,932 \times \frac{3}{4}$ | _____ × | _____ = | _____ |
| **68.** $87,000 \times \frac{1}{4}$ | _____ × | _____ = | _____ |
| **69.** $9\frac{1}{12} \times 11\frac{3}{8}$ | _____ × | _____ = | _____ |
| **70.** $5\frac{1}{3} \times 97\frac{4}{5}$ | _____ × | _____ = | _____ |

*Student's Score* _____

# Part E
## *Estimating Quotients*

*Directions:* Estimate the quotients. Show the rounded-off dividends and divisors used. (2 points for each correct answer)

| | Rounded-Off Dividend | | Rounded-Off Divisor | | Estimated Quotient |
|---|---|---|---|---|---|
| 71. $402.278 \div 222$ | _____ | ÷ | _____ | = | _____ |
| 72. $876.05 \div 315$ | _____ | ÷ | _____ | = | _____ |
| 73. $59.34 \div 2.857$ | _____ | ÷ | _____ | = | _____ |
| 74. $80.98 \div 4.126$ | _____ | ÷ | _____ | = | _____ |
| 75. $43.4 \div .096$ | _____ | ÷ | _____ | = | _____ |
| 76. $77.9 \div .038$ | _____ | ÷ | _____ | = | _____ |
| 77. $.159 \div .375$ | _____ | ÷ | _____ | = | _____ |
| 78. $.328 \div .625$ | _____ | ÷ | _____ | = | _____ |
| 79. $4 \div 105$ | _____ | ÷ | _____ | = | _____ |
| 80. $28 \div 316$ | _____ | ÷ | _____ | = | _____ |

*Directions:* Find the estimated dividends. Show the rounded-off quotients and divisors used. If the given quotient is correct, place the symbol "√" in the last column; if the given quotient is wrong, place the symbol "×." (2 points for each correct answer)

| | Rounded-Off Quotient | | Rounded-Off Divisor | | Estimated Dividend | Given Quotient |
|---|---|---|---|---|---|---|
| 81. $248.25 \div 4.6 = 53.967$ | _____ | × | _____ | = | _____ | _____ |
| 82. $275 \div .155 = 1.774$ | _____ | × | _____ | = | _____ | _____ |
| 83. $.57 \div 63 = .905$ | _____ | × | _____ | = | _____ | _____ |
| 84. $194.96 \div 2.437 = 80$ | _____ | × | _____ | = | _____ | _____ |
| 85. $.281 \div .312 = .9$ | _____ | × | _____ | = | _____ | _____ |

*Student's Score* _____

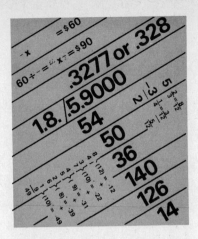

CHAPTER
7

# Keeping a Checking Account

Business firms and most individuals use **checking accounts**, which are simply bank accounts that represent money deposited and against which checks may be drawn. Making payments by check is generally more convenient and safer than paying cash. As a rule, only enough money is kept in a checking account to meet expected current expenses.

Computers, accounting machines, or checkwriting machines are used by large companies to produce both the checks and the necessary records in one single operation. In a small business, however, the checks are typed or hand-written; and the records are kept on the check stubs. The information on the check stubs is transferred to the owner's books of account.

The discussion in Section 7-1 of this chapter applies only to the handling of checks and deposits by individuals or small businesses where a computer is not used. To keep up with the latest developments, however, a brief description of the electronic, checkless method of banking is given at the end of this section. Section 7-2 deals with monthly bank statements and reconciliation statements. These are statements that have to be prepared regularly to check the accuracy of the records maintained on a checking account by both the depositor and the bank.

## Section 7-1  Checks and Deposits

A **check** is a written order to a bank to pay a stated amount of money to the individual or business named. Books of blank checks and deposit tickets are furnished by a bank to individuals or businesses that have money on deposit in a checking account. Usually checkbooks for businesses have three or four checks to a page. Perforations between the checks, as well as between the check and its stub, help in tearing out the checks from the checkbook.

Since most banks use computers in their operations, a magnetized number identifying the bank and the depositor's account appears on each check and deposit ticket.

Part

### A  Completing Check Stubs

For accurate record keeping, the check stub always should be completed whenever a deposit is made and *before* a check is made out. When a deposit is made, it is recorded and added to the last balance which is usually labeled *Balance Forward* on the check stub. The sum is recorded in the space labeled *Total*. Before writing a check, the stub should be filled out with the date, to whom the check is payable, and for what. The amount of the check is recorded and subtracted

Chapter 7 / Keeping a Checking Account

**167**

# Figure 7-1    A Completed Check and Check Stub

| No. 895    $ 80²⁵ | | A. J. MORAN<br>1204 N. Allen St.<br>Milwaukee, WI 53208 | No. 895 | 12 - 79<br>750 |

No. 895    $ 80²⁵
Date Oct. 23, 19 - -
To Carter Supply
Company
For Store
Supplies

|  | Dollars | Cents |
|---|---|---|
| Balance Forward | 1,396. | 89 |
| Deposit | 400. | 00 |
| TOTAL | 1,796. | 89 |
| This Check | 80. | 25 |
| Balance | 1,716. | 64 |

A. J. MORAN
1204 N. Allen St.
Milwaukee, WI 53208

No. 895    12 - 79 / 750

Oct. 23, 19 --

PAY TO THE
ORDER OF Carter Supply Company    $ 80²⁵
Eighty and ²⁵/₁₀₀ _____ DOLLARS

**Grand National Bank**
Milwaukee, Wisconsin 53201

A. J. Moran

⑆0750⑈0079⑆ 02⑈79 7607⑈

from the *Total*. The result is the new balance, which is recorded and also brought forward to the next stub.

Figure 7-1 above shows a check and its stub. The stub shows that on October 23, 19—, A. J. Moran had a balance of $1,396.89 (see the *Balance Forward* line). On the same day Mr. Moran deposited $400 to give a new balance of $1,796.89 (see the *Total* line). He also makes out check #895 for $80.25 to the Carter Supply Company for store supplies. After the $80.25 is subtracted from $1,796.89, the new balance in his checking account is $1,716.64.

## Part B    Making Out Checks

After completing the dateline in making out a check, start as far to the left as possible and write closely together the following items (refer again to Figure 7-1):

1. The name of the **payee**, the individual or business to whom the check is payable. Draw a wavy line or a series of dashes to fill in any blank spaces at the end of the name to prevent possible changing of the rightful payee's name.
2. The amount of the check written in figures.
3. The amount of the check written in words in the line labeled *DOLLARS*. Note that the amount in dollars is always written in words, but the amount in cents is written as a common fraction with a denominator of 100. The word "and" should be used to separate the dollars from the cents to prevent confusion. Here again, draw the wavy line or dashes.

Finally, be sure to sign the check on the line provided at the bottom.

## Part C    Endorsing Checks

Before a check can be cashed or sent to the bank for deposit, the payee must endorse it. **Endorsing** means signing the check on the back, across the short side at the top left.

There are several ways of endorsing a check. In the **blank endorsement** shown in Figure 7-2 on page 169, only the name of the payee is signed. If a check with a blank endorsement is lost or stolen, anybody who is in possession of it may cash it. A better way to endorse a check is with a **restrictive endorsement**. Here the name of the person or business allowed to cash the check is written below the words "Pay to the order of." The second block in Figure 7-2 shows a restrictive endorsement to an individual.

Another form of restrictive endorsement is made when the payee mails the check for deposit. In this case the words "For deposit only" are written above the payee's signature, as shown in the third block in Figure 7-2. Many companies stamp all incoming checks with this form of restrictive endorsement as soon as they are received. Thus, if a check is lost or stolen, it cannot be cashed.

## Part D    Clearing of Checks

After a check has been cashed by the payee, it may take several days or even longer before the check reaches a **clearing house**. A check is

# Figure 7-2 Various Forms of Endorsement

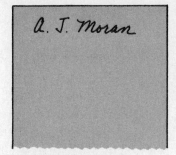

Blank Endorsement

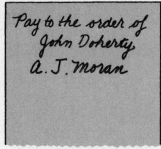

Restrictive Endorsement
to an Individual

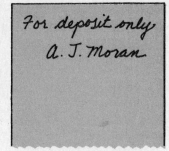

Restrictive Endorsement
for a Mail Deposit

cleared when its amount is charged to the bank against which it was drawn. This bank in turn subtracts the amount of the check from the depositor's account. After this has been done, the check is specially stamped and becomes a **canceled check**.

The American Bankers Association (ABA), the national organization of banking, has devised a numerical coding system so that all banks in the country can be identified by location and by official bank number. The **ABA number** for a particular bank usually is printed in the upper right-hand corner of the check. In Figure 7-1 on page 168, it is 12-79/750. The magnetized numbers at the bottom are used for routing the checks with computerized equipment and for charging the amount to the depositor's account. The right-hand part of the magnetized numbers at the bottom is the depositor's checking account number with the bank. In Figure 7-1 it is 02-79 7607.

## Part E Making Deposits

When a deposit is to be made, a deposit ticket is completed to show the details of the cash and checks being deposited. Usually the deposit ticket is made out in duplicate. If the deposit is made in person, a copy of the deposit ticket is handed back to the depositor. If the deposit is mailed, the original copy is returned by the bank along with the depositor's monthly statement and canceled checks.

Figure 7-3 on page 170 shows a completed deposit ticket. Note that only the totals of the currency and coins are listed; the checks are listed singly. Most deposit tickets have room on the reverse side to list additional checks. The total of the checks listed on the back is brought to the face of the deposit ticket.

Sometimes the ABA number of each check deposited is written to the left of the amount. This procedure is no longer necessary because most banks make a photographic record of all deposits made with them.

## Part F Transferring Funds Electronically

Although electronic banking in itself does not involve business mathematics directly, you should be familiar with its fundamental aspects. If you are interested, you can obtain more information from your bank.

An **Electronic Funds Transfer System (EFTS)** is a new, checkless ("less paper") method of paying for goods or services, making deposits, withdrawing money, etc. It was developed in an effort to reduce the rising costs of processing checks—which is about 20¢ per check. One of the systems now using the EFTS method is the **Automated Clearing House (ACH)**. Stated simply, the information regarding payment is put on magnetic tape. This tape is then run through the bank's computer to complete the desired transfer of funds.

*Uses of the ACH.* Many companies, as well as the federal and most state governments, have switched to the direct method of paying their employees. Instead of issuing pay checks, the company uses magnetic tape to authorize its bank to transfer money from the company's account to accounts in the names of its employees. The

# Figure 7-3 A Completed Deposit Ticket (front and back)

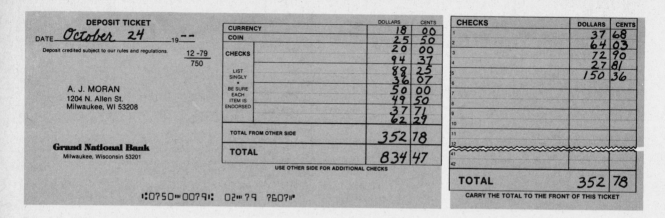

employees can then request electronic transfer of these payroll amounts to their own banks.

Another use of the Automated Clearing House allows an individual who has a bank account to request the bank to pay his or her regular monthly expenses by electronic transfer of funds. Examples of regular monthly expenses are mortgage payments, car installment payments, charge account payments, etc. The individual's monthly bank statement will show all amounts deposited and taken out to pay the pre-authorized expenses.

**The 24-hour teller.** One of the first applications of the EFTS was the installation of the **24-hour teller** by banks and savings and loan associations in the early 70s. The 24-hour teller automated machine is placed in a lobby, on an outside wall, or in a drive-in window. When it is installed in places away from the bank or the savings and loan association—such as in a store or in a shopping center—it is called a **Customer-Bank Communication Terminal (CBCT)**. The auto-

mated teller is activated by the insertion of a plasticized card which has a magnetic strip to identify the individual user. Generally the user must also depress a secret code number on the keyboard. By doing this an individual can make deposits, withdraw cash, or transfer funds to a different account without using checks. Receipts for the transaction are made available. In some cases the transfer of money can be canceled on three days' notice, which is similar to stopping payment on a check.

**A word of caution.** The student should be aware that there are also disadvantages to the electronic transfer of money in spite of the strict rules set up by state banking and savings and loan associations on operating these new money exchange systems. Although EFTS is useful in reducing the total volume of checks, particularly at the consumer level, it does not replace the need for using checks in the operation of most businesses.

Complete Assignment 21

|  | Perfect Score | Student's Score |
|---|---|---|
| Problem 1 | 20 | |
| Problem 2 | 20 | |
| Problem 3 | 20 | |
| Problem 4 | 10 | |
| Problem 5 | 20 | |
| Problem 6 | 10 | |
| TOTAL | 100 | |

# Assignment 21
# Section 7-1

## Checks and Deposits

*Directions:* Complete the check stubs and the checks from the given information in Problems 1, 2, and 3. Assume you are A. J. Moran and sign his name. (20 points for each correctly written check and check stub)

1. Check #896: Date of check is October 24, 19—.
   Balance brought forward from check #895 is $1,716.64.
   Deposit made is $492.65.
   Amount of check is $153.75 made to Jones Brothers for Accounts Payable.

No. _____ $_____
Date _____ 19 _____
To _____
For _____

|  | Dollars | Cents |
|---|---|---|
| Balance Forward | | |
| Deposit | | |
| TOTAL | | |
| This Check | | |
| Balance | | |

A. J. MORAN
1204 N. Allen St.
Milwaukee, WI 53208

No. _____    12 - 79 / 750

_____ 19 _____

PAY TO THE
ORDER OF _____ $_____

_____ DOLLARS

**Grand National Bank**
Milwaukee, Wisconsin 53201

⑈0750⑈0079⑈ 02⑈79 7607⑈

*Student's Score* _____

2. Check #897: Date of check is October 25, 19—.
   Amount of check is $141.19 made to Page Supply Company for Office Supplies.
   (Use the balance from check #896.)

No. _____ $_____
Date _____ 19 _____
To _____
For _____

|  | Dollars | Cents |
|---|---|---|
| Balance Forward | | |
| Deposit | | |
| TOTAL | | |
| This Check | | |
| Balance | | |

A. J. MORAN
1204 N. Allen St.
Milwaukee, WI 53208

No. _____    12 - 79 / 750

_____ 19 _____

PAY TO THE
ORDER OF _____ $_____

_____ DOLLARS

**Grand National Bank**
Milwaukee, Wisconsin 53201

⑈0750⑈0079⑈ 02⑈79 7607⑈

*Student's Score* _____

**3.** Check #898: Date of check is October 26, 19—.
Amount of check is $45.00 made to John Stanford for Miscellaneous Expenses.
(Use the balance from check #897.)

| No. _____ $ _____ | A. J. MORAN | No. _____ | 12 - 79 |
| Date _____ 19 ____ | 1204 N. Allen St. | | 750 |
| To _____ | Milwaukee, WI 53208 | _____ 19 ___ | |
| For _____ | | | |
| | PAY TO THE ORDER OF _____ $ _____ | | |
| | _____ DOLLARS | | |

| | Dollars | Cents |
| --- | --- | --- |
| Balance Forward | | |
| Deposit | | |
| TOTAL | | |
| This Check | | |
| Balance | | |

**Grand National Bank**
Milwaukee, Wisconsin 53201

⑆0750⑈0079⑆ 02⑈79 7607⑈

*Student's Score* _____

**4.** A. J. Moran has received a $65.00 check from a customer. He uses this check to buy $65.00 worth of office supplies from the Page Supply Company. Show the restrictive endorsement to transfer the check. (10 points)

*Student's Score* _____

**5.** On October 28, A. J. Moran makes the following deposit: Currency—$375.00; Coins—$50.00; Checks—$142.98, 16.95, 236.43, and 15.09. Complete the deposit ticket. (20 points)

**DEPOSIT TICKET**

DATE _____ 19 ____

Deposit credited subject to our rules and regulations.  12 -79 / 750

A. J. MORAN
1204 N. Allen St.
Milwaukee, WI 53208

**Grand National Bank**
Milwaukee, Wisconsin 53201

| | | DOLLARS | CENTS |
| --- | --- | --- | --- |
| CURRENCY | | | |
| COIN | | | |
| CHECKS | | | |
| LIST SINGLY • BE SURE EACH ITEM IS ENDORSED | | | |
| | | | |
| | | | |
| TOTAL FROM OTHER SIDE | | | |
| **TOTAL** | | | |

USE OTHER SIDE FOR ADDITIONAL CHECKS

⑆0750⑈0079⑆ 02⑈79 7607⑈

*Student's Score* _____

**6.** Show the restrictive endorsement that should be written on all of the checks deposited in Problem 5. (10 points)

*Student's Score* _____

# Section 7-2 Bank Statements and Reconciliation Statements

A **monthly bank statement** is sent to each depositor who has a checking account. The purpose of this monthly statement is to show the depositor's bank balance as of a given date. As soon as possible after the bank statement has been received, the depositor prepares a **reconciliation statement.** This is a statement in which the depositor's current checkbook balance and the bank balance on the monthly statement as of a given date are compared and adjusted to find the true cash balance in the account.

Canceled checks are returned with the monthly bank statement. Original copies of deposit tickets are also returned if the depositor had made deposits by mail.

## Part A Understanding the Monthly Bank Statement

Every bank has its own form for the monthly statement sent to each depositor, but the information on it is standard. Shown either at the top or at the bottom are the starting balance (or *Balance—Last Statement)*; the total deductions (or *Total Amount—Debits*); the total deposits (or *Total Amount—Credits*); and the ending balance (or *Balance—This Statement*). The main body of the statement shows the following items:

1. Checks which have been returned to the bank and subtracted from the depositor's account.
2. Bank charges and other miscellaneous information which are deducted from the account.
3. Deposits received by the bank and added to the account.
4. The balance at the end of each day in which there was some activity.

In discussing each of the above items, reference will be made to the monthly statement shown in Figure 7-4 on page 174.

*Listing order of checks.* The order in which the checks appear on the monthly statement is immaterial. However, for the depositor's convenience in checking the bank statement, many banks now list the checks in numerical order and show the number, date, and amount for each one. Missing checks (either destroyed by the depositor or not yet returned to the bank) are noted by a series of asterisks or dashes. Note that the ending balance does not include any missing checks.

Other banks list the checks in the order in which they were received and show only the amounts. This form is not as easy to check as that shown in Figure 7-4.

*Bank charges and miscellaneous information.* A few banks impose a monthly service charge and/or a fee for each check drawn. Most banks charge a fee when a deposited check turns out to be **NSF,** *not* sufficient *funds* in the maker's account. The depositor is notified immediately so that the checkbook balance can be reduced by the amount of the returned check and the fee. Figure 7-4 shows two deposited checks returned (in the amounts of $25 and $47); the fee charged for each returned check is $3.00 and is identified by "X." A fee also is charged if the depositor's account is *overdrawn.*

Some banks make no charges of any kind if the checking account being maintained is large enough.

*Deposits added to the account.* In Figure 7-4 the total of four deposits made is $2,552.20. The number of deposits, 4, is recorded in the space labeled *Number of Credits* at the top of the monthly statement; and the total, $2,552.20, is recorded in the space labeled *Total Amount— Credits*.

Also at the top of the statement, in the space labeled *Number of Debits*, is the number 28, which consists of the 24 listed checks, the 2 deposited checks returned, and the 2 fees charged (marked X). The total of all these checks and fees is $2,231.61 and is recorded in the space labeled *Total Amount—Debits*.

The amount of $2,536.10 in the space labeled *Balance—This Statement* is calculated in two steps: (1) add the total amount of credits to the balance of the last statement; and (2) from this sum subtract the total amount of debits. For the interest of accounting students, the debits and credits are from the bank's standpoint. The depositor's account is similar to an account payable as far as the bank is concerned.

## Figure 7-4  A Monthly Bank Statement

### Grand National Bank
Milwaukee, Wisconsin 53201

**Checking Account Statement**

| Date—Last Statement | Number of Debits | Number of Credits | Date—This Statement |
|---|---|---|---|
| 8/13/-- | 28 | 4 | 9/13/-- |

| 2,215.51 | − | 2,231.61 | + | 2,552.20 | − | .00 | = | 2,536.10 |
|---|---|---|---|---|---|---|---|---|
| Balance—Last Statement | | Total Amount—Debits | | Total Amount—Credits | | Service Charge | | Balance—This Statement |

MR.A.J.MORAN
1204 N.ALLEN ST.
MILWAUKEE, WI  53208

Account Number
**02-79-7607**

S — Service charge for
previous period unless
otherwise noted
X — Charge for overdraft
or returned check

| DEPOSITS AND OTHER CREDITS | | CHECKS AND OTHER DEBITS | | | | | | DAILY BALANCE | |
|---|---|---|---|---|---|---|---|---|---|
| DATE | AMOUNT | NO. | DATE | AMOUNT | NO. | DATE | AMOUNT | DATE | AMOUNT |
| 8/16 | 317.24 | 601 | 8/16 | 12.01 | 619 | 8/31 | 80.57 | 8/16 | 2,520.74 |
| 8/23 | 495.21 | 602 | 8/17 | 11.65 | **** | | | 8/17 | 2,379.09 |
| 9/01 | 559.63 | 603 | 8/17 | 130.00 | 621 | 9/01 | 109.06 | 8/18 | 2,343.47 |
| 9/08 | 1,180.12 | 604 | 8/18 | 35.62 | 622 | 9/03 | 72.50 | 8/19 | 2,261.81 |
| | | 605 | 8/19 | 51.96 | 623 | 9/10 | 135.00 | 8/23 | 2,720.96 |
| | | 606 | 8/19 | 29.70 | 624 | 9/10 | 231.28 | 8/24 | 2,647.96 |
| | | **** | | | **** | | | 8/26 | 2,567.22 |
| | | 608 | 8/23 | 4.00 | 626 | 9/10 | 514.62 | 8/27 | 2,542.11 |
| | | 609 | 8/23 | 32.06 | **** | | | 8/30 | 2,053.73 |
| | | 610 | 8/24 | 42.00 | 628 | 9/10 | 59.35 | 8/31 | 1,973.16 |
| | | 611 | 8/24 | 3.00 | 629 | 9/10 | 5.00 | 9/01 | 2,423.73 |
| | | 612 | 8/26 | 98.77 | | | | 9/03 | 2,351.23 |
| | | 613 | 8/26 | 9.97 | OTHER DEDUCTIONS | | | 9/08 | 3,531.35 |
| | | 614 | 8/27 | 25.11 | | | | 9/10 | 2,586.10 |
| | | **** | | | DEPOSITED CHECKS RETURNED | | | 9/13 | 2,536.10 |
| | | 616 | 8/30 | 168.08 | | 8/24 | 25.00 | | |
| | | 617 | 8/30 | 183.74 | | | 3.00X | | |
| | | 618 | 8/30 | 136.56 | | 9/13 | 47.00 | | |
| | | | | | | | 3.00X | | |

Please examine at once and report any differences to our Auditing Department.

**Daily balance.** The daily balance for any date on which some transaction was made is found in two steps: (1) add any deposit made, and (2) deduct the total of all checks written and any bank charges, as notified. The last amount in the *Daily Balance* column is identical with the amount in *Balance—This Statement.*

Note that the notice for the second deposited check returned in Figure 7-4 probably would have been sent out on the same date as the statement. This means that A. J. Moran would not have reduced his checkbook balance as yet for the total amount of $50.

## Part B Preparing the Reconciliation Statement

Most banks print a reconciliation form on the back of the monthly statement. Generally, however, the depositor prepares a separate reconciliation statement.

Banks rarely make mistakes in their statements. Yet, the last balance shown on the monthly statement often does not agree with the depositor's checkbook balance. This may be due to several reasons such as: (1) **outstanding checks,** which are checks that have been subtracted in the checkbook but have not yet been cleared; (2) deposits added in the checkbook but not received or recorded by the bank at the time the statement was prepared; (3) bank service charges or other fees shown on the monthly statement for which the depositor has not yet received notice; (4) checks written by the depositor but not recorded in the checkbook or check stubs; (5) an incorrect deduction by the bank for a check not written by the depositor; and (6) errors in computing the checkbook balance or the bank balance.

***Preliminary work before preparing a reconciliation statement.*** There are five items to be checked or compared before preparing a reconciliation statement. These are:

1. Amounts on canceled checks with amounts listed on the monthly statement.
2. Amounts on canceled checks with amounts recorded on the check stubs.
3. Amounts of outstanding checks.
4. Amounts on returned deposit tickets or on the monthly statement with amounts recorded on the check stubs.
5. Any additions or deductions listed on the monthly statement for which notice has not been received.

The detailed procedure for checking each of the above items is best understood by working out an example. Assume you are A. J. Moran whose monthly statement is shown in Figure 7-4 on page 174. Also assume that your checkbook balance on September 13 is $1,821.08 and that the canceled checks are in numerical order. Note that possible errors will be introduced intentionally in order to show how you can correct them. Before doing this preliminary work, take a separate sheet and label it "CORRECTIONS." Under this label put three subheadings: *Checkbook Balance, Bank Balance,* and *Outstanding Checks.*

1. If the amounts on the canceled checks match the amounts listed on the monthly statement, put a small checkmark next to the amount on the statement. If they do not match, circle any errors on the statement and note the date, check number, and amount for later corrections.

In our example, assume there are no errors.

2. If the amounts on the canceled checks match the amounts recorded on the check stubs, place a checkmark after the amount on the stub. If they do not match, circle any errors on the stubs and note the corrections to be made, either as additions or as deductions to the checkbook balance. If a canceled check has not been recorded on the check stub and therefore not subtracted from the checkbook balance, note the check number and the amount to be deducted.

In our example you find two errors: (1) your check stub #610 shows that $98.00 was subtracted instead of the $42.00 shown on the check. Further, you discover that the check is not yours. On the CORRECTIONS sheet under *Bank Balance,* write "Incorrect charge— + $42.00"; (2) on check stub #616 you find that you subtracted $168.80 instead of $168.08, which is a common transposition error. On the CORRECTIONS sheet under *Checkbook Balance,* write "+.72" which is the difference between the two numbers.

Note that if the amount subtracted on the stub is larger than the amount on the check, the difference is an *Add* item under *Checkbook Balance.* If the amount subtracted is smaller than the amount on the check, the difference is a *Subtract* item.

3. On the CORRECTIONS sheet under *Outstanding Checks,* list all the check numbers and amounts which have not been checked off on the stubs. Then find their total, which will be subtracted from the bank balance on the reconciliation statement.

In our example you have 10 outstanding checks whose amounts total $1,406.30, as shown in Figure 7-5 on page 176. (If you used an adding machine, save the tape for attachment to the reconciliation statement.)

4. Compare the four deposits listed on the monthly statement with the first four deposits recorded on the check stubs. If they match, check them off on the monthly statement. List all deposits which the bank has not recorded. Find their total for later addition to the bank balance on the reconciliation statement.

# Figure 7-5 A Reconciliation Statement

| Outstanding Checks | |
|---|---|
| **Check No.** | |
| 607 | $ 176.60 |
| 610 | 98.00 |
| 615 | 544.00 |
| 620 | 133.00 |
| 625 | 23.10 |
| 627 | 35.76 |
| 630 | 338.93 |
| 631 | 32.07 |
| 632 | 13.97 |
| 633 | 10.87 |
| | |
| | |
| | |
| | |
| **Total** | **$1,406.30** |

**A. J. Moran**
Reconciliation Statement
September 13, 19--

Checkbook balance......................................$1,821.08
Add:
   Error on #616.............................. .72
                                   $1,821.80

Subtract:
   Returned check and fee..... $50.00
   Error on #624.............. 100.00
              Total........................... 150.00
Adjusted checkbook balance......................$1,671.80

Bank balance........................................$2,536.10
Add:
   Unrecorded deposit, Sept.13...$500.00
   Incorrect charge, Aug.24...... 42.00
              Total........................... 542.00
                                   $3,078.10
Subtract:
   Outstanding checks...................... 1,406.30
Adjusted bank balance...........................$1,671.80

In our example a $500 deposit made on Sept. 13 is not listed on the monthly statement. On the CORRECTIONS sheet under Bank Balance, write "Unrecorded deposit—+ $500."

5. Note for later correction any additions or deductions listed on the monthly statement for which notice has not been received.

In our example you have just received the notice on the deposited check returned and fee of Sept. 13. On the CORRECTIONS sheet under *Checkbook Balance,* write "Returned check and fee— − $50.00."

From all the above data, you can now make the following rough reconciliation:

Checkbook balance on 9/13 ........ $1,821.08
Error on check #616 .............. + .72
Returned check and fee .......... − 50.00
  Adjusted checkbook balance ..... $1,771.80

Bank balance on 9/13 ............ $2,536.10
Unrecorded deposit of 9/13 ........ + 500.00
Incorrect charge ................. + 42.00
Outstanding checks .............. − 1,406.30
  Adjusted bank balance .......... $1,671.80

The two adjusted balances should be the same, but your rough reconciliation shows that the checkbook balance is $100 more than the bank balance. First, check that all figures were copied correctly. Then check the arithmetic on the rough reconciliation. You find no errors. Now double-check the addition and subtraction on the check stubs.

In our example you find the error on stub # 624. The amount of $100 becomes a *Subtract* item under *Checkbook Balance.* (If there had been no error, the bank monthly statement is checked last. Notify the bank immediately if errors are found on the statement.)

*Form of the reconciliation statement.* When the two adjusted balances are the same, you can now prepare the reconciliation statement. There are various forms, but the one shown in Figure 7-5 is used most widely. Note that, except for outstanding checks, when there are two or more items to be added or subtracted, they are listed separately. Their total, however, is written in the last column rather than underneath the items. If there is only one item, the amount is placed directly in the last column.

**Complete Assignment 22**

# Assignment 22
# Section 7-2

## Bank Statements and Reconciliation Statements

|  | Perfect Score | Student's Score |
|---|---|---|
| Problem 1 | 25 | |
| Problem 2 | 25 | |
| Problem 3 | 50 | |
| TOTAL | 100 | |

1. Prepare a bank reconciliation statement for A. J. Moran from the following information. Use the space below. (25 points)

| | |
|---|---|
| Checkbook balance, March 15 ................................................ | $2,336.52 |
| Bank balance, March 13, per monthly statement ................................... | 2,197.24 |
| Deposit, March 14 ........................................................ | 400.00 |

Outstanding checks:  #405 ............ $ 40.66
#410 ............ 32.42
#412 ............ 80.35
#413 ............ 130.29
#414 ............ 8.00

Service charge ............................................................. 4.00
Check #396 shows the amount as $74.00; the checkbook deduction shows $47.00.

2. Prepare a bank reconciliation statement for A. J. Moran from the following information. Use the space below. (25 points)

| | |
|---|---:|
| Checkbook balance, May 16 | $3,629.10 |
| Bank balance, May 14, per monthly statement | 3,870.55 |
| Deposit, May 15 | 762.80 |

Outstanding checks:
| | |
|---|---:|
| #604 | $499.75 |
| #606 | 348.50 |
| #607 | 182.57 |
| #608 | 117.43 |
| Deposited check return | 60.00 |
| Charge for the NSF check | 4.00 |

A check for $100.00 was incorrectly charged to A. J. Moran.
Check #596 shows the amount as $370.00; the checkbook deduction shows $390.00.

**3.** The October bank statement received by A. J. Moran on October 14 shows a starting balance of $2,318.26 and an ending balance of $2,795.77. The deposits, checks, and service charge from the bank statement and the checkbook stubs from September 11 through October 14 are shown below. The amounts on 19 canceled checks and 5 returned deposit tickets agree with those on the statement. A comparison of the canceled checks and returned deposit tickets with the checkbook stubs shows that four checks and one deposit ticket were not returned and that two amounts were transposed on the check stubs. A rough reconciliation shows that the adjusted bank balance and the adjusted checkbook balance do not agree. Further checking reveals three more errors on the check stubs.

Locate all errors on the check stubs and note the corrections to be made. Adjust the October 14 checkbook balance for the errors and the service charge. Then, on the next page prepare a reconciliation statement as of October 14. (50 points)

| Deposits and Other Credits | | Checks and Other Debits | | | | | | | Daily Balance | |
|---|---|---|---|---|---|---|---|---|---|---|
| Date | Amount | No. | Date | Amount | No. | Date | Amount | | Date | Amount |
| 9/14 | 1,366.38 | 765 | 9/14 | 641.81 | 776 | 10/01 | 111.58 | | 9/14 | 2,528.44 |
| 9/17 | 240.00 | 766 | 9/14 | 514.39 | 777 | 10/05 | 526.00 | | 9/17 | 2,726.44 |
| 9/29 | 1,387.10 | 767 | 9/17 | 32.00 | **** | | | | 9/21 | 2,467.25 |
| 10/01 | 1,263.31 | 768 | 9/17 | 10.00 | 779 | 10/05 | 620.00 | | 9/24 | 1,975.35 |
| 10/09 | 1,361.38 | 769 | 9/21 | 7.64 | 780 | 10/08 | 33.55 | | 9/29 | 2,796.43 |
| | | 770 | 9/21 | 131.55 | 781 | 10/08 | 19.02 | | 9/30 | 2,667.86 |
| | | 771 | 9/21 | 120.00 | **** | | | | 10/01 | 3,806.59 |
| | | 772 | 9/24 | 491.90 | 783 | 10/08 | 538.78 | | 10/05 | 2,660.59 |
| | | 773 | 9/29 | 566.02 | 784 | 10/12 | 513.05 | | 10/08 | 2,069.24 |
| | | 774 | 9/30 | 128.57 | 785 | 10/12 | 120.00 | | 10/09 | 3,430.62 |
| | | 775 | 10/01 | 13.00 | | OTHER DEDUCTIONS | | | 10/12 | 2,795.77 |
| | | | | | | 10/12 | 1.80S | | | |

### Checkbook Stubs

| | | | | | | | | | | | |
|---|---|---|---|---|---|---|---|---|---|---|---|
| Bal. | 9/11 | 2,318.26 | Bal. | 9/21 | 2,561.25 | Bal. | 10/01 | 3,952.59 | Bal. | 10/09 | 2,896.62 |
| Dep. | 9/14 | 1,366.38 | 771 | 9/21 | 120.00 | 777 | 10/05 | 526.00 | 784 | 10/12 | 513.05 |
| | | 3,684.64 | | | 2,441.25 | | | 3,426.59 | | | 2,383.57 |
| 765 | 9/14 | 641.81 | 772 | 9/24 | 419.90 | 778 | 10/05 | 175.39 | 785 | 10/12 | 120.00 |
| | | 3,042.83 | | | 2,021.35 | | | 3,251.20 | | | 2,163.57 |
| 766 | 9/14 | 541.39 | Dep. | 9/29 | 1,387.10 | 779 | 10/05 | 620.00 | 786 | 10/12 | 33.80 |
| | | 2,501.44 | | | 3,408.45 | | | 2,631.20 | | | 2,129.77 |
| Dep. | 9/17 | 240.00 | 773 | 9/29 | 566.02 | 780 | 10/05 | 33.55 | Dep. | 10/13 | 1,324.98 |
| | | 2,741.44 | | | 2,942.43 | | | 2,597.65 | | | 3,454.75 |
| 767 | 9/17 | 32.00 | 774 | 9/30 | 128.57 | 781 | 10/08 | 19.02 | 787 | 10/14 | 123.05 |
| | | 2,709.44 | | | 2,813.86 | | | 2,578.63 | | | 3,331.70 |
| 768 | 9/17 | 10.00 | Dep. | 10/01 | 1,263.31 | 782 | 10/08 | 504.61 | | | |
| | | 2,699.44 | | | 4,077.17 | | | 2,074.02 | | | |
| 769 | 9/21 | 7.64 | 775 | 10/01 | 13.00 | 783 | 10/08 | 538.78 | | | |
| | | 2,692.80 | | | 4,064.17 | | | 1,535.24 | | | |
| 770 | 9/21 | 131.55 | 776 | 10/01 | 111.58 | Dep. | 10/09 | 1,361.38 | | | |
| | | 2,561.25 | | | 3,952.59 | | | 2,896.62 | | | |

A.J.Moran
Reconciliation Statement
_____

Checkbook balance............................. $_____

   Add:
      Errors on
        #_____ $_____
        #_____ _____
        #_____ _____
        #_____ _____
            Total................... _____

                              $_____

   Subtract:
      Service charge $_____
      Errors on
        #_____ _____
        #_____ _____
        #_____ _____
        #_____ _____
             Total................... _____

Adjusted checkbook balance................... $_____

Bank balance................................. $_____
   Add:
      Unrecorded deposit, 10/13.............. _____

                          $_____

   Subtract:
      Outstanding checks..................... _____

Adjusted bank balance........................ $_____

Outstanding checks
No.        Amount
_____
_____
_____
_____
_____
_____
_____
_____
_____
_____
    Total $_____

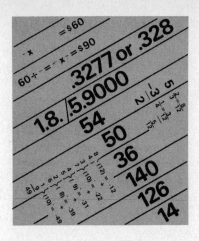

**Interest** is the charge which is paid for the use of money. Banks, savings and loan associations, finance companies, and credit unions are in business primarily to lend money. Many department stores have revolving charge accounts on which interest is charged on balances not paid within 30 days. Most business firms also charge interest on overdue accounts.

In figuring interest there are three elements to consider. These are: (1) the **principal**, or the amount of money borrowed; (2) the **rate**, or the percent charged for the use of the principal for one year (per annum); and (3) the **time**, or the period of days, months, years, or combinations of these, for which interest must be paid.

Because finding the due date and the exact time for which interest must be paid generally pose a problem, Section 8-1 of this chapter is devoted to this topic. Section 8-2 deals with calculating **simple interest**, which is interest figured on only the principal. Generally simple interest is charged on **short-term loans**, or loans made for less than one year. Section 8-3 deals with calculating **compound interest**, which is often charged on **long-term loans**, or loans made for one or more years. When charging compound interest, the interest for one period is added to the principal before the interest for the next period is figured.

## Section *8-1*   *The Time Element*

There are various ways of expressing the time. However, when an amount of interest is required, the time must be expressed in *years* or a *fractional part of a year*.

To find the fractional part of a year, when the time expressed is an exact number of months, divide the number of months by 12. When the time is not expressed as an exact number of years or months, then the **exact time**, or actual number of days in the interest period, must be found. The number of days is then changed into a fractional part of a year.

Finding the exact time is necessary when figuring interest on short-term loans, as well as on many types of long-term loans. But other methods of finding the time are used when figuring interest on long-term loans where the principal and interest are paid off on a regular basis, such as real-estate loans and installment purchase loans. These other methods, however, are not discussed here.

Counting the actual number of days in the interest period means that you have to know the number of days in each month and take leap years into consideration. All months have the same number of days from year to year, with the exception of February which has 28 days in non-leap years and 29 days in leap years.

There are two ways to find out if a particular year is a leap year: (1) Look at the *last two digits*. If they are exactly divisible by 4, then the year is a leap year. (2) If the last two digits are 00, then look at the *first two digits*. If they are exactly divisible by 4, then the year is a leap year. Thus, 1900 was not a leap year but 2000 will be. Note that, unless otherwise specified, February is taken as having 28 days when the year is not given.

## Part A Finding the Exact Time Between Two Dates

An easy way to count the actual number of days between two dates is to take the following steps:

1. Subtract the first date from the number of days in that month.
2. Add the exact number of days in each of the months in between.
3. Then add the days in the second date.

*Examples:*

a. Find the exact time between April 24 and October 3.

| | |
|---|---|
| April ................ | 30 − 24 = 6 |
| May ................. | 31 |
| June ............... | 30 |
| July ............... | 31 |
| August ............ | 31 |
| September .......... | 30 |
| October ............ | 3 |
| Total ............. | 162 days |

b. Find the exact time between January 31 and May 16 in a leap year.

| | |
|---|---|
| January ............. | 31 − 31 = 0 |
| February ........... | 29 |
| March .............. | 31 |
| April ............... | 30 |
| May ................ | 16 |
| Total ............. | 106 days |

## Part B Finding the Due Date and Exact Time When the Given Time Is in Days

Usually a borrower obtains a loan on the basis of signing a **promissory note**, which is simply a written promise to pay the amount borrowed within a specified time. The interest period on the note is often given in days from the **date of origin**, or the date on which the note is made. The **due date** is the date on which the loan must be paid off.

To find the due date, follow these steps:

1. Subtract the date or origin from the number of days in that month.
2. To this difference, keep adding the exact number of days in the months that follow until you find a total that is *equal* to the given number of days or is *less than one month* from the given number of days.
3. If the total found is equal to the given number of days, the due date is the last month and day in the "added" months that follow. If the total found is less than one month from the number of days given, count forward into the next month the number of days that are left. That next month and number of days left becomes the due date.

*Examples:*

a. A 120-day note is dated April 2. Find the due date.

| | |
|---|---|
| April 30 − 2 = 28 | |
| May ............ | 31 (Subtotal = 59 days) |
| June ............ | 30 (Subtotal = 89 days) |
| July ............ | 31 |
| Total ........ | 120 days |

Since the total is exactly 120 days, the due date is July 31.

b. A 90-day note is dated June 14. Find the due date.

| | |
|---|---|
| June 30 − 14 = 16 | |
| July ............ | 31 (Subtotal = 47 days) |
| August .......... | 31 |
| Total ........ | 78 days |

90 days − 78 days = 12 days

Counting forward into September, the due date is September 12.

### When the due date falls on a nonbusiness day.

Nonbusiness days are Saturdays, Sundays, and legal holidays. The actual dates for several legal holidays, such as Labor Day and Thanksgiving, vary from year to year. In addition, some traditional holiday dates, such as Washington's Birthday and Memorial Day, have been changed to provide three-day holiday weekends. The following legal holidays continue to be celebrated on the traditional dates: New Year's Day, January 1st; Independence Day, July 4th; and Christmas Day, December 25th.

For the student's information, the federal government each year sets the legal holiday dates for federal employees only. Individual states set their own legal holidays which may be different from the federal holidays.

In actual business practice, when the due date falls on a nonbusiness day, it is changed to the next business day. This means that interest may be charged for the additional time involved; that is, the actual interest period is no longer the exact number of days that fall between the date of origin and the calculated due date.

### How legal holidays are counted.

When a legal holiday falls in between dates, it is counted as any other day. Note that in *Examples a* and *b* on the previous page, July 4 is part of the 31 days in July.

When a legal holiday falls on a Sunday, the next day is considered to be the legal holiday.

### Examples:

a. A 60-day note is dated October 26. Find the due date and the exact time in the interest period.

| | |
|---|---|
| October ............. | $31 - 26 = 5$ |
| November .......... | 30 |
| Total .............. | 35 days |

60 days − 35 days = 25 days

Counting forward into December, the due date is December 25. Since this is a legal holiday, the due date is changed to December 26 and the exact time becomes 61 days.

b. A 45-day note is dated May 20. Find the due date and the exact time in the interest period.

| | |
|---|---|
| May ................. | $31 - 20 = 11$ |
| June ............... | 30 |
| Total .............. | 41 days |

45 days − 41 days = 4 days

Counting forward into July, the due date is July 4. Since this is a legal holiday, the due date is changed to July 5 and the exact time becomes 46 days.

When a legal holiday falls on a Friday, with Saturday and Sunday being nonbusiness days, two more days must be added to the exact number of days in the interest period. Thus, in *Example a* above, the due date would become December 28 and the exact time would be 63 days. In *Example b,* the due date would become July 7 and the exact time would be 48 days.

### Part C
## Finding the Due Date and Exact Time When the Given Time Is in Months

The time period on a loan may be expressed as a given number of months from the date of the note. To find the due date, as a general rule count forward the given number of months and use the same day of the month as the date or origin.

*Example:* Find the due date of a three-month note dated August 7.

Counting forward three months, the due date is November 7.

There are three exceptions to the general rule just given: (1) If the date or origin is the 31st and the due month has only 30 days, the due date is the 30th of the due month.

*Example:* Find the due date of a three-month note dated March 31.

The due month is June, which has only 30 days. The due date is June 30.

(2) If the date of origin is the 29th, 30th, or 31st and the due month is February of a non-leap year,

the due date is February 28. In a leap year, the due date becomes February 29.

*Example:* Find the due date of a three-month note dated November 30.

The due month is February, and the due date is February 28 in a non-leap year.

(3) If the due date falls on a known legal holiday or a known nonbusiness day, the next business day is used.

*Example:* Find the due date of a four-month note dated September 1.

The due month is January. January 1 is a legal holiday; so the due date becomes January 2.

Although the time period on a short-term loan may be given in months, the exact number of days between the date of origin and the due date (exact time) is used to figure the interest.

*Examples:*

a. Find the due date and the exact time in the interest period on a one-month note dated August 21.

The due date is September 21. The exact time between August 21 and September 21 is 31 days, computed as follows:

August .............. 31 − 21 = 10
September ........... 21
  Total .............. 31 days

b. Find the due date and the exact time in the interest period on a two-month note dated December 31.

The due date is February 28. The exact time between December 31 and February 28 is 59 days, computed as follows:

December :........... 31 − 31 = 0
January ............. 31
February ............ 28
  Total .............. 59 days

In a leap year the date would be February 29, and the exact time would be 60 days.

c. Find the due date and the exact time in the interest period on a four-month note dated March 4.

Since four months from March 4 is July 4, a legal holiday, the due date becomes July 5. The exact time between March 4 and July 5 is 123 days, computed as follows:

March ............... 31 − 4 = 27
April ................ 30
May ................. 31
June ................ 30
July ................. 5
Total ............... 123 days

**Complete Assignment 23**

## Assignment 23
## Section 8-1

| | Perfect Score | Student's Score |
|---|---|---|
| Part A | 40 | |
| Part B | 40 | |
| Part C | 20 | |
| TOTAL | 100 | |

*The Time Element*

## Part A
### Finding the Exact Time Between Two Dates

**Directions:** Find the exact time from the first date to the second date. Use the work space at the right and write your answers in the spaces provided. (4 points for each correct answer)

| From | To | Exact Time | WORK SPACE |
|---|---|---|---|
| 1. January 12 | February 21 | _____ | |
| 2. December 1 | March 25 | _____ | |
| 3. November 14 | January 8 | _____ | |
| 4. February 18 (leap year) | August 18 | _____ | |
| 5. April 2 | June 11 | _____ | |
| 6. March 29 | July 1 | _____ | |
| 7. May 11 | August 30 | _____ | |
| 8. June 15 | October 19 | _____ | |
| 9. July 24 | November 5 | _____ | |
| 10. January 31 (leap year) | May 24 | _____ | |

*Student's Score* _____

# Part B

## Finding the Due Date and Exact Time When the Given Time Is in Days

**Directions:** Find the due date and the exact time in the period of interest. Use the work space at the right and write your answers in the spaces provided. (4 points for each correct answer)

| Date of Note | Time | Due Date | Exact Time | WORK SPACE |
|---|---|---|---|---|
| 11. May 15 | 15 days | _____ | _____ | |
| 12. May 20 | 45 days | _____ | _____ | |
| 13. February 15 (leap year) | 30 days | _____ | _____ | |
| 14. August 27 | 40 days | _____ | _____ | |
| 15. December 15 | 45 days | _____ | _____ | |
| 16. June 19 | 75 days | _____ | _____ | |
| 17. September 26 | 90 days | _____ | _____ | |
| 18. May 13 | 100 days | _____ | _____ | |
| 19. February 5 | 120 days | _____ | _____ | |
| 20. March 3 | 135 days | _____ | _____ | |

*Student's Score* _____

# Part C

## Finding the Due Date and Exact Time When the Given Time Is in Months

**Directions:** Find the due date and the exact time in the period of interest. Use the work space at the right and write your answers in the spaces provided. (4 points for each correct answer)

| Date of Note | Time | Due Date | Exact Time | WORK SPACE |
|---|---|---|---|---|
| 21. March 17 | 1 month | _____ | _____ | |
| 22. July 31 | 2 months | _____ | _____ | |
| 23. April 4 | 3 months | _____ | _____ | |
| 24. August 27 | 4 months | _____ | _____ | |
| 25. September 23 | 6 months | _____ | _____ | |

*Student's Score* _____

Assignment 23

# Section 8-2  Calculating Simple Interest

There are two ways of figuring simple interest, depending upon the number of days that the business year is considered to have. **Ordinary interest** is based on a 360-day year and is used in many interest calculations. **Exact interest** is based on a 365-day year and is used by the federal government as well as by some lending agencies. Generally both ordinary and exact interest are computed with exact time for periods of less than one year. In most simple interest problems, ordinary interest is found unless exact interest is specified.

To find the amount of simple interest, either ordinary or exact, multiply the principal by the rate by the time. The formula is:

$$I = prt$$

where I = interest, p = principal, r = rate, and t = time. As indicated in Section 8-1, time must be expressed in years or a fractional part of a year. Up to six decimal places are used in the calculations, and only the final result is rounded off.

## Part
# A  Ordinary Interest

To find the amount of ordinary interest by direct application of the formula, first find the product of the principal times the rate, which is changed to its decimal form. Then multiply this product by the years or the fractional part of a year to get the amount of interest, I.

*Example:* Find the interest on $650 at 5¾% for 2½ years.

$$I = (\$650 \times .0575) \times 2.5$$
$$= \$37.375 \times 2.5 = 93.4375 = \$93.44$$

***Shorter methods of figuring ordinary interest.*** Under certain conditions there are three shorter methods of figuring ordinary interest. These conditions and the applicable shorter methods are: (1) When the time is given in months, it is not necessary to find the fractional part of the year *in a separate step.* To figure the ordinary interest, simply multiply the principal by the rate by the number of months; then divide the product by 12.

*Example:* Find the interest on $750 at 7½% for 16 months.

$$I = (\$750 \times .075) \times 16 \div 12$$
$$= (\$56.25 \times 16) \div 12$$
$$= \$900 \div 12 = \$75$$

(2) When the time is given in days, again it is not necessary to find the fractional part of the year in a separate step. To figure the ordinary interest, multiply the principal by the rate by the number of days; then divide the product by 360.

*Example:* Find the interest on $530 at 8% for 75 days.

$$I = (\$530 \times .08) \times 75 \div 360$$
$$= (\$42.40 \times 75) \div 360$$
$$= \$3,180 \div 360 = \$8.833333 = \$8.83$$

Note that, if the three examples just given are worked on a calculator, the entire computation can be done in sequence as shown in the first step of each example. The separate products do not have to be found.

(3) When the numbers in a calculation are such that cancellations can be foreseen, use the cancellation method.

*Examples:*

a. $500 at 6% for 2 years.

$$I = \frac{\overset{5}{\cancel{500}}}{1} \times \frac{6}{\underset{1}{\cancel{100}}} \times \frac{2}{1} = \$60$$

b. $400 at 8% for 30 months

$$I = \frac{\overset{4}{\cancel{400}}}{1} \times \frac{\overset{4}{\cancel{8}}}{\underset{1}{\cancel{100}}} \times \frac{\overset{5}{\cancel{30}}}{\underset{\underset{1}{2}}{\cancel{12}}} = \$80$$

c. $800 at 7% for 30 days

$$I = \frac{\overset{2}{\cancel{\overset{8}{\cancel{800}}}}}{1} \times \frac{7}{\underset{1}{\cancel{100}}} \times \frac{\overset{1}{\cancel{30}}}{\underset{\underset{3}{12}}{\cancel{360}}} = \frac{14}{3} = 4.666667$$

= $4.67

If the interest to be found is interest on a short-term promissory note, the exact time used must be checked to make sure that the due date does not fall on a legal holiday or other nonbusiness day. The exact time on a note is the number of days from the date of origin to the due date.

*Example:* Find the interest on a $400, 6%, 90-day note dated April 5 and paid on the due date.

90 days after April 5 is July 4, a legal holiday. The due date is changed to July 5, and the exact time for which interest is charged becomes 91 days. Thus:

$$I = \frac{\overset{1}{\cancel{\overset{4}{\cancel{400}}}}}{1} \times \frac{\overset{1}{\cancel{6}}}{\underset{1}{\cancel{100}}} \times \frac{91}{\underset{\underset{15}{\cancel{60}}}{\cancel{360}}} = \frac{91}{15} = 6.066667$$

= $6.07

*Finding the maturity value of a note.* The **maturity value** of a note is the amount to be paid to the lender on the due date, or maturity date. When there is an interest charge, the maturity value is the sum of the principal plus the interest. In the case of a noninterest-bearing note, the maturity value is the same as the principal. Notes are discussed more fully in Chapter 12.

*Example:* Find the maturity value of an $800, 6%, 60-day note dated October 15.

The due date is December 14, which is not a legal holiday. The exact time is 60 days. Thus:

$$I = \frac{\overset{8}{\cancel{800}}}{1} \times \frac{\overset{1}{\cancel{6}}}{\underset{\underset{1}{\cancel{6}}}{\cancel{100}}} \times \frac{\overset{1}{\cancel{60}}}{\underset{1}{\cancel{360}}} = \$8$$

Maturity value = $800 + $8 = $808

## Part B  Exact Interest

Although both ordinary and exact interest are found by using the simple interest formula, exact interest differs from ordinary interest in two ways: (1) Exact time is used; that is, the period of interest must be stated as an exact number of days. (2) The number of days is divided by the actual number of days in the calendar year, 365 (366 in a leap year), instead of 360.

As with figuring ordinary interest, there are shorter methods of figuring exact interest. That is, it is not necessary to find the fractional part of a year in a separate step when the time is given in days. The shorter cancellation method is also applicable in finding the exact interest.

*Examples:*

a. $530 at 8% for 75 days

$$\begin{aligned} I &= (\$530 \times .08) \times 75 \div 365 \\ &= (\$42.40 \times 75) \div 365 \\ &= \$3,180 \div 365 = 8.712329 = \$8.71 \end{aligned}$$

Note that, for the above example, ordinary interest would be $8.83. Exact interest is always smaller than ordinary interest on the same principal, rate, and time.

b. $500 at 6% for 30 days

$$I = \frac{\overset{5}{\cancel{500}}}{1} \times \frac{6}{\underset{1}{\cancel{100}}} \times \frac{30}{\underset{73}{\cancel{365}}} = \frac{180}{73} = 2.465753$$

= $2.47

c. $1,250 at 6% from June 21 to October 3.

The exact time from June 21 to October 3 is 104 days. Thus:

$$I = \frac{\overset{5}{\cancel{25}}\ \overset{\cancel{1250}}{\cancel{1250}}}{1} \times \frac{\overset{3}{\cancel{6}}}{\cancel{100}} \times \frac{104}{\cancel{365}} = \frac{1560}{73}$$

$$= 21.369863 = \$21.37$$

## Part C
## Ordinary Interest at 6% for 60 Days and for 6 Days

The ordinary interest on any principal at 6% for 60 days can be stated as:

$$I = p \times \frac{6}{100} \times \frac{60}{360}$$

$$= p \times \frac{\overset{1}{\cancel{6}}}{100} \times \frac{\overset{1}{\cancel{60}}}{\underset{\underset{1}{\cancel{6}}}{\cancel{360}}}$$

$$= p \times \frac{1}{100}$$

Since multiplying by 1/100 is the same as dividing by 100, the above equation becomes:

$$I = p \div 100$$

The shortcut rule is: To find the ordinary interest when the rate is 6% and the time is 60 days, divide the principal by 100 by moving the decimal point two places to the left.

### Examples:

a. $324 at 6% for 60 days

$$I = \$3.24_x = \$3.24$$

b. $78.94 at 6% for 60 days

$$I = \$0.78_x94 = \$0.79$$

c. $10,639.45 at 6% for 60 days

$$I = \$106.39_x45 = \$106.39$$

d. $9.42 at 6% for 60 days

$$I = \$0.09_x42 = \$0.09$$

Following the same procedure, the ordinary interest on any principal at 6% for 6 days can be stated as:

$$I = p \times \frac{6}{100} \times \frac{6}{360}$$

$$= p \times \frac{\overset{1}{\cancel{6}}}{100} \times \frac{\overset{1}{\cancel{6}}}{\underset{\underset{10}{\cancel{60}}}{\cancel{360}}}$$

$$= p \times \frac{1}{1,000}$$

Since multiplying by 1/1,000 is the same as dividing by 1,000, the above equation becomes:

$$I = p \div 1,000$$

The shortcut rule is: To find the ordinary interest on any principal when the rate is 6% and the time is 6 days, divide the principal by 1,000 by moving the decimal point three places to the left.

### Examples:

a. $245 at 6% for 6 days

$$I = \$0.245_x = \$0.25$$

b. $39.50 at 6% for 6 days

$$I = \$0.039_x50 = \$0.04$$

c. $6,678.29 at 6% for 6 days

$$I = \$6.678_x29 = \$6.68$$

d. $21,890 at 6% for 6 days

$$I = \$21.890_x = \$21.89$$

## Part D
## Applications of the 6%, 60-day Method

The 6%, 60-day method is a shortcut for computing ordinary interest at 6% for *any number of days*. It involves the use of parts or multiples of 60 days and/or 6 days. While there may be more steps in this method, the arithmetic is so much simpler that there is less chance of making errors. These steps are:

1. Express the given number of days in the interest period as a part or a multiple of 60 or 6 days, or as a combination of parts and multiples.
2. Figure the interest for 60 days or 6 days, or both. Then compute the corresponding interest for each part or multiple with respect to the interest for 60 days or 6 days.
3. When using a combination of parts and multiples, find the total interest for all the parts and multiples.

The following examples use only one part or one multiple and therefore illustrate only the first two steps. (An example illustrating all three steps by using a combination of parts and multiples will be given later.)

**Examples:**

**a.** $200 at 6% for 30 days

Step 1: 30 days = $\frac{1}{2}$ × 60 days
Step 2: I for 60 days = $2.00
I for 30 days = $\frac{1}{2}$ × $2.00 = $1.00

**b.** $562.89 at 6% for 20 days

Step 1: 20 days = $\frac{1}{3}$ × 60 days
Step 2: I for 60 days = $5.6289
I for 120 days = $\frac{1}{3}$ × $5.6289
= $1.8763 = $1.88

**c.** $2,654.98 at 6% for 120 days

Step 1: 120 days = 2 × 60 days
Step 2: I for 60 days = $26.5498
I for 120 days = 2 × $26.5498
= $53,0996 = $53.10

**d.** $126.75 at 6% for 3 days

Step 1: 3 days = $\frac{1}{2}$ × 6 days
Step 2: I for 6 days = $0.12675
I for 3 days = $\frac{1}{2}$ × $0.12675
= $0.063375 = $0.06

The following are useful parts and multiples of 60 days and 6 days. Multiples of the parts, such as 2 × 20 days for 40 days, also may be used.

| Parts | Multiples |
|---|---|
| 30 da = $\frac{1}{2}$ × 60 da | 120 da = 2 × 60 da |
| 20 da = $\frac{1}{3}$ × 60 da | 180 da = 3 × 60 da |
| 15 da = $\frac{1}{4}$ × 60 da | 240 da = 4 × 60 da |
| 10 da = $\frac{1}{6}$ × 60 da | 12 da = 2 × 6 da |
| 3 da = $\frac{1}{2}$ × 6 da | 18 da = 3 × 6 da |
| 2 da = $\frac{1}{3}$ × 6 da | 24 da = 4 × 6 da |
| 1 da = $\frac{1}{6}$ × 6 da | |

The following example uses a combination of parts and multiples, thus illustrating all three steps given above.

*Example:* $237.81 at 6% for 167 days

Step 1: 167 days = 120 + 30 + 15 + 2 days
Step 2: I for 60 days = $2.3781
I for 6 days = $0.23781

Using parts and multiples:

120 da = 2 × $2.3781 = $4.7562
30 da = $\frac{1}{2}$ × 2.3781 = 1.18905
15 da = $\frac{1}{4}$ × 2.3781 = .594525
2 da = $\frac{1}{3}$ × .23781 = .07927
Step 3: 167 da ................ $6.619045
I for 167 days = $6.62

Note that 167 days can be separated in other ways also, such as 120 da + 40 da + 6 da + 1 da or even 180 da − 12 da − 1 da.

The 6%, 60-day method can also be used to find the interest at *rates other than 6%*. To do this, the interest at 6% for the given number of days is found first. Then the adjustment for the given rate is made on this amount. This method is illustrated below only for the student's interest, for other methods are definitely preferable to it.

*Example:* $237.81 at 8% for 167 days

8% = 6% + 2% (which is 1/3 of 6%)
I at 6% for 167 da = $6.619045
I at 2% for 167 da = 2.206348
I at 8% ............ $8.825393 = $8.83

**Complete Assignment 24**

## Assignment 24
## Section 8-2

### Calculating Simple Interest

|         | Perfect Score | Student's Score |
|---------|---------------|-----------------|
| Part A  | 32            |                 |
| Part B  | 32            |                 |
| Part C  | 16            |                 |
| Part D  | 20            |                 |
| TOTAL   | 100           |                 |

# Part A
### Ordinary Interest

**Directions:** Solve the problems. Show all work and write your answers in the spaces provided. (4 points for each correct answer)

1. Find the ordinary interest on $560 at 6% for 2 years.

   Ans._____

2. Find the ordinary interest on $480 at 7% for 3 years 6 months.

   Ans._____

3. Find the ordinary interest on $480 at 8% for 15 months.

   Ans._____

4. Find the ordinary interest on $720 at 6% for 20 months.

   Ans._____

5. Find the ordinary interest on $800 at 5% for 72 days.

   Ans._____

6. Find the ordinary interest on $720 at 7½% for 40 days.

   Ans._____

7. Find the maturity value of a $600 note at 9% for 4 months, dated June 14, paid on due date.

   Ans._____

8. Find the total payment made on a note dated April 10 for $800 at 7½%, paid on August 8.

   Ans._____

*Student's Score* _____

# Part B
## *Exact Interest*

*Directions:* Solve the problems. Show all work and write your answers in the spaces provided. (4 points for each correct answer)

9. Find the exact interest on $1,460 at 6% for 95 days.

    Ans._____

13. Find the exact interest on $500 at 6¾% from November 28 to February 9.

    Ans._____

10. Find the exact interest on $730 at 7½% for 100 days.

    Ans._____

14. Find the exact interest on $1,000 at 6½% from April 8 to September 1.

    Ans._____

11. Find the exact interest on $239.50 at 5% for 146 days.

    Ans._____

15. How much more than the exact interest is the ordinary interest on $1,200 at 6% for 72 days?

    Ans._____

12. Find the exact interest on $365 at 8% for 75 days.

    Ans._____

16. How much more than the exact interest is the ordinary interest on $800 at 10% for 146 days?

    Ans._____

*Student's Score* _____

# Part C

## *Ordinary Interest at 6% for 60 Days and for 6 Days*

*Directions:* Find the ordinary interest at 6% for the days indicated. Use shortcuts only. Write your answers in the spaces provided. (½ point for each correct answer)

| Principal | 60 days | Principal | 6 days |
|---|---|---|---|
| 17. $  450.00 | _____ | 33. $  768.48 | _____ |
| 18.    962.47 | _____ | 34.    894.32 | _____ |
| 19.  1,200.00 | _____ | 35.      9.63 | _____ |
| 20.     36.53 | _____ | 36.    475.00 | _____ |
| 21.      5.98 | _____ | 37.  1,575.08 | _____ |
| 22.    457.51 | _____ | 38.    459.25 | _____ |
| 23.  7,629.34 | _____ | 39.    203.75 | _____ |
| 24.    525.18 | _____ | 40.  3,999.12 | _____ |
| 25.    324.39 | _____ | 41.     86.38 | _____ |
| 26.     79.06 | _____ | 42.      4.86 | _____ |
| 27.    504.87 | _____ | 43.  3,454.40 | _____ |
| 28.  6,072.95 | _____ | 44.    908.31 | _____ |
| 29.    784.50 | _____ | 45.     40.67 | _____ |
| 30.      6.95 | _____ | 46.    878.10 | _____ |
| 31.     97.86 | _____ | 47.     98.64 | _____ |
| 32.    244.39 | _____ | 48.    125.50 | _____ |

*Student's Score* _____

# Part D

## Applications of the 6%, 60-day Method

**Directions:** Find the ordinary interest at 6% by using the 6%, 60-day method. Show all work and write your answers in the spaces provided. (1 point for each correct answer)

49. $675.42 for 30 days   _____

50. $856.48 for 30 days   _____

51. $78.90 for 120 days   _____

52. $219.46 for 120 days   _____

53. $39.73 for 90 days   _____

54. $450.00 for 90 days   _____

55. $340.20 for 12 days   _____

56. $256.80 for 12 days   _____

57. $109.32 for 3 days   _____

58. $678.90 for 3 days   _____

59. $622.35 for 15 days   _____

60. $208.75 for 15 days   _____

61. $73.09 for 90 days   _____

62. $89.03 for 90 days   _____

63. $320.97 for 96 days   _____

64. $892.36 for 96 days   _____

65. $726.90 for 129 days   _____

66. $501.35 for 150 days   _____

67. $1,298.60 from May 5 to _____
August 24

68. $932.50 from March 16 to _____
September 2

*Student's Score* _____

# Section 8-3   Calculating Compound Interest

In finding simple interest over a period of time, the *same* original principal is used for each interest period. In finding compound interest over a period of time, a *new* principal is used for each interest period. The new principal is the **amount** from the last period. The amount (A) at the end of a particular period is the sum of the principal used at the beginning of the period plus the interest for that period. Thus, compound interest is "interest on interest." The compound interest for a given period of time is the difference between the amount at the end of the time minus the original principal.

## Part A   Compounding Interest at Different Periods

Interest may be compounded annually, semiannually, quarterly, monthly, or daily.

***Interest compounded annually.*** To compound interest **annually**, compute the ordinary interest for the first year. Add this interest to the principal to give the amount at the end of the first year. This amount becomes the new principal for computing the interest for the second year. The sum of the first-year amount and the interest for the second year becomes the amount at the end of the second year. Repeat this procedure as many times as the given number of years. Do not round off until you have the final answer.

*Example:* Find the amount and the compound interest at the end of 3 years on $500 invested at 5% compounded annually.

**End of 1st year:**

$$I = \$500 \times .05 \times 1 \text{ (year)} = \$\ 25$$
$$A = \$500 + \$25 = \$525$$

**End of 2nd year:**

$$I = \$525 \times .05 \times 1 \text{ (year)} = \$\ 26.25$$
$$A = \$525 + \$26.25 = \$551.25$$

**End of 3rd year:**

$$I = \$551.25 \times .05 \times 1 \text{ (year)} = \$\ 27.5625$$
$$A = \$551.25 + \$27.5625 = \$578.8125$$
$$= \$578.81$$

**Compound Interest for the 3-year period:**

$$\$578.81 - \$500.00 = \$78.81$$

On most hand calculators with a percent key, the example above can be worked by using a particular series of operations. The intermediate results displayed correspond to those shown in the example. There are several ways of doing this, depending upon the kind of calculator used. The two most common sequences are:

1. $500 \times 5\% + \times 5\% + \times 5\% + (578.8125)$

2. $500 + 5\% = + 5\% = + 5\% = (578.8125)$

***Interest compounded semiannually.*** To compound interest **semiannually** (twice a year), follow the same general procedure for computing interest compounded annually. Now, however, use the **semiannual rate** (half the given rate) for *twice* the number of given years.

*Example:* Find the amount at the end of two years on $600 invested at 6% compounded semiannually.

Semiannual rate $= \frac{1}{2} \times 6\% = 3\%$
Number of periods $= 2 \times 2 = 4$ half-years

**End of 1st half-year:**

$$A = \$600 + (\$600 \times 3\%) = \$600 + \$18 = \$618$$

**End of 2nd half-year:**

$$A = \$618 + (\$618 \times 3\%) = \$618 + \$18.54$$
$$= \$636.54$$

**End of 3rd half-year:**

$$A = \$636.54 + (\$636.54 \times 3\%)$$
$$= \$636.54 + \$19.0962 = \$655.6362$$

**End of 4th half-year:**

$$A = \$655.6362 + (\$655.6362 \times 3\%)$$
$$= \$655.6362 + \$19.669086 = \$675.305286$$
$$= \$675.31$$

**Interest compounded quarterly.** To compound interest **quarterly** (four times a year), use the **quarterly rate** (one-fourth of the given rate) for *four times* the number of given years.

**Interest compounded monthly.** To compound interest **monthly**, use the **monthly rate** (one-twelfth the given rate) for *12 times* the number of given years. Interest compounded monthly is used mostly for real estate loans.

**Interest compounded daily.** To compound interest **daily**, use the **daily rate** of 1/365 (or 1/366 in a leap year) for 365 (or 366) times the number of years. With the advent of the computer, many banks now offer daily compounding on savings account deposits. In most cases the computer updates the amount daily, so that the interest earned on savings is always available.

For the interested student, the daily amount and compound interest can be found easily by using a sophisticated calculator. A simpler calculator which has a power key (to multiply a number by itself the necessary number of times) also can be used. The steps to find the daily amount are illustrated with the example below.

**Example:** Find the amount and compound interest on $500 at 5% compounded daily from April 8 to July 27 (110 days).

**Step 1:** Change the rate to a decimal, add 365 (366) to it, and divide the sum by 365 (366).

$$(.05 + 365) \div 365 = 1.000136986$$

**Step 2:** Raise this quotient to the power that is the number of days in the interest period.

$$(1.000136986)^{110} = 1.015181548$$

**Step 3:** Multiply the result by the given principal to find the amount.

A = $1.015181548 \times \$500$
  = $\$507.5907738 = \$507.59$
Compound interest = $\$507.59 - \$500 = \$7.59$

Note that the amount and compound interest may vary by a penny or two from those found by a computer. This is due to differences in the number of decimal places used.

## Part B Using Compound Interest Tables

Because of the lengthy computations necessary to find the compound interest, tables are available and used to find the amount for interest compounded annually, semiannually, quarterly, and monthly. There are no tables for daily compounding.

Compound interest tables show the amount of $1 for rates starting as low as $\frac{1}{4}$% and for periods that may be over 200 for the fractional percents. Table 8-1 on page 197 is a partial table of compound amounts.

Referring to Table 8-1, $n$ stands for the number of interest periods. For example, in quarterly compounding for five years, $n$ is $4 \times 5$ or 20 periods. The amounts under the rate column are figured on an annual basis. If periods of compounding are other than annual, the rate must be converted. For example, for 8% compounded quarterly, the converted rate to be used from Table 8-1 is $\frac{1}{4} \times 8\%$, or 2%.

**Using tables when interest is compounded annually.** To find the amount when the interest is compounded annually, find the number of years in the $n$ column and go across the row to the given rate. Where the row and the column meet is the **accumulation factor**, which is the amount to which $1 accumulates at the given rate for the given number of years. Multiply the accumulation factor by the principal to find the required amount. The compound interest is the difference between this amount and the original principal.

**Examples:** Find the amount and the compound interest.

a. $1,000 at 6% compounded annually for 5 years

Find 5 in the $n$ column and go across that row to the 6% column. The accumulation factor is 1.338226.

A = $\$1,000 \times 1.338226 = \$1,338.226$
  = $\$1,338.23$

Compound interest = $\$1,338.23 - \$1,000.00$
  = $\$338.23$

# Table 8-1 Compound Interest Table

| | | | Amount of $1 at Compound Interest | | | | |
|---|---|---|---|---|---|---|---|
| $n$ | $\frac{1}{2}$% | 1% | 2% | 3% | 4% | 5% | 6% |
| 1 | 1.005000 | 1.010000 | 1.020000 | 1.030000 | 1.040000 | 1.050000 | 1.060000 |
| 2 | 1.010025 | 1.020100 | 1.040400 | 1.060900 | 1.081600 | 1.102500 | 1.123600 |
| 3 | 1.015075 | 1.030301 | 1.061208 | 1.092727 | 1.124864 | 1.157625 | 1.191016 |
| 4 | 1.020150 | 1.040604 | 1.082432 | 1.125509 | 1.169859 | 1.215506 | 1.262477 |
| 5 | 1.025251 | 1.051010 | 1.104081 | 1.159274 | 1.216653 | 1.276282 | 1.338226 |
| ---- | ---------- | ---------- | ---------- | ---------- | ---------- | ---------- | ---------- |
| ---- | ---------- | ---------- | ---------- | ---------- | ---------- | ---------- | ---------- |
| 10 | 1.051140 | 1.104622 | 1.218994 | 1.343916 | 1.480244 | 1.628895 | 1.790848 |
| ---- | ---------- | ---------- | ---------- | ---------- | ---------- | ---------- | ---------- |
| ---- | ---------- | ---------- | ---------- | ---------- | ---------- | ---------- | ---------- |
| 20 | 1.104896 | 1.220190 | 1.485947 | 1.806111 | 2.191123 | 2.653298 | 3.207135 |
| ---- | ---------- | ---------- | ---------- | ---------- | ---------- | ---------- | ---------- |
| ---- | ---------- | ---------- | ---------- | ---------- | ---------- | ---------- | ---------- |
| 50 | 1.283226 | 1.644632 | 2.691588 | 4.383906 | 7.106683 | 11.467400 | 18.420154 |
| ---- | ---------- | ---------- | ---------- | ---------- | ---------- | ---------- | ---------- |
| ---- | ---------- | ---------- | ---------- | ---------- | ---------- | ---------- | ---------- |
| 100 | 1.646668 | 2.704814 | 7.244646 | 19.218632 | 50.504948 | 131.501258 | 339.302084 |

b. $2,000 at 5% compounded annually for 3 years

Find 3 in the $n$ column and go across the row to the 5% column. The accumulation factor is 1.157625.

A = $2,000 × 1.157625 = $2,315.25

Compound interest = $2,315.25 − $2,000
= $315.25

*Using tables when interest is compounded semiannually.* To find the amount when the interest is compounded semiannually, double the number of years for the periods to be found in the $n$ column. Take half of the given rate to get the converted rate to be found in the table.

*Examples:* Find the amount and the compound interest.

a. $1,000 at 8% compounded semiannually for 5 years.

Semiannual rate = $\frac{1}{2}$ × 8% = 4%
Number of periods = 2 × 5 = 10 periods

Find 10 in the $n$ column and go across that row to the 4% column. The accumulation factor is 1.480244.

A = $1,000 × 1.480244 = $1,480.244
= $1,480.24

Compound interest = $1,480.24 − $1,000
= $480.24

**b.** $350 at 6% compounded semiannually for 2 years

Semiannual rate = $\frac{1}{2} \times 6\% = 3\%$
Number of periods = $2 \times 2 = 4$ periods

Find 4 in the $n$ column and go across that row to the 3% column. The accumulation factor is 1.125509.

A = $350 \times 1.125509 = \$393.92815 = \$393.93$

Compound interest = $393.93 − $350.00
 = $43.93

**Using tables when interest is compounded quarterly.** To find the amount when the interest is compounded quarterly, multiply the number of years by 4 for the periods to be found in the $n$ column. Take one-fourth of the given rate to get the converted rate to be found in the table.

*Examples:* Find the amount and the compound interest.

**a.** $500 at 4% compounded quarterly for 5 years

Quarterly rate = $\frac{1}{4} \times 4\% = 1\%$
Number of periods = $4 \times 5 = 20$ periods

Find 20 in the $n$ column and go across that row to the 1% column. The accumulation factor is 1.220190.

A = $500 \times 1.22019 = \$610.095 = \$610.10$

Compound interest = $610.10 − $500
 = $110.10

**b.** $3,000 at 8% compounded quarterly for $2\frac{1}{2}$ years

Quarterly rate = $\frac{1}{4} \times 8\% = 2\%$
Number of periods = $2\frac{1}{2} \times 4 = 10$ periods

Find 10 in the $n$ column and go across that row to the 2% column. The accumulation factor is 1.218994.

A = $3,000 \times 1.218994 = \$3,656.982$
 = $3,656.98

Compound interest = $3,656.98 − $3,000
 = $656.98

**Using tables when interest is compounded monthly.** To find the amount when the interest is compounded monthly, multiply the number of full years by 12 and add any extra months for the number of periods to be found in the $n$ column. Take one-twelfth of the given rate to get the converted rate to be found in the table.

*Examples:* Find the amount and the compound interest.

**a.** $400 at 12% compounded monthly for 4 years and 2 months.

Monthly rate = $\frac{1}{12} \times 12\% = 1\%$
Number of periods = $4 \times 12 + 2 = 50$ periods

Find 50 in the $n$ column and go across that row to the 1% column. The accumulation factor is 1.644632.

A = $400 \times 1.644632 = \$657.8528 = \$657.85$

Compound interest = $657.85 − $400
 = $257.85

**b.** $2,500 at 6% compounded monthly for 8 years and 4 months

Monthly rate = $\frac{1}{12} \times 6\% = \frac{1}{2}\%$
Number of periods = $12 \times 8 + 4 = 100$ periods

Find 100 in the $n$ column and go across that row to the $\frac{1}{2}\%$ column. The accumulation factor is 1.646668.

A = $2,500 \times 1.646668 = \$4,116.67$

Compound interest = $4,116.67 − $2,500
 = $1,616.67

**Complete Assignment 25**

## Assignment 25
## Section 8-3

|  | Perfect Score | Student's Score |
|---|---|---|
| Part A | 20 | |
| Part B | 80 | |
| TOTAL | 100 | |

### Calculating Compound Interest

# Part A
## Compounding Interest at Different Periods

*Directions:* Without using a table, find the amount and the compound interest. Show all work and write your answers in the spaces provided. (10 points for each correct problem)

1. $1,000 at 7% compounded annually for 3 years:

   Amount_____  Compound int._____

2. $400 at 7% compounded semiannually for $1\frac{1}{2}$ years:

   Amount_____  Compound int._____

Student's Score _____

# Part B
## Using Compound Interest Tables

*Directions:* Using Table 8-1 on page 197, find the amount and the compound interest. Show all work and write your answers in the spaces provided. (8 points for each correct problem)

3. $500 at 6% compounded annually for 4 years:

   Amount_____  Compound int._____

5. $1,000 at 8% compounded semiannually for 10 years:

   Amount_____  Compound int._____

4. $1,000 at 5% compounded annually for 3 years:

   Amount_____  Compound int._____

6. $2,000 at 6% compounded semiannually for $2\frac{1}{2}$ years:

   Amount_____  Compound int._____

7. $400 at 8% compounded quarterly for 5 years:

Amount＿＿＿＿＿ Compound int.＿＿＿＿＿

9. $800 at 6% compounded monthly for one year eight months:

Amount＿＿＿＿＿ Compound int.＿＿＿＿＿

8. $800 at 4% compounded quarterly for 25 years:

Amount＿＿＿＿＿ Compound int.＿＿＿＿＿

10. $500 at 12% compounded monthly for 8 years 4 months:

Amount＿＿＿＿＿ Compound int.＿＿＿＿＿

**Directions:** A full table is used to find the amounts. Show the table rates and number of periods used, but do not work the problems. Write your answers in the spaces provided. (2 points for each correct problem)

11. $2,500 at 7½% compounded annually for 14 years:

Rate＿＿＿＿＿ No. of Periods＿＿＿＿＿

15. $1,999 at 10% compounded quarterly for 12 years:

Rate＿＿＿＿＿ No. of Periods＿＿＿＿＿

12. $700 at 9% compounded annually for 25 years:

Rate＿＿＿＿＿ No. of Periods＿＿＿＿＿

16. $785 at 9% compounded quarterly for 15 years:

Rate＿＿＿＿＿ No. of Periods＿＿＿＿＿

13. $10,000 at 6½% compounded semiannually for 18 years:

Rate＿＿＿＿＿ No. of Periods＿＿＿＿＿

17. $980 at 10% compounded monthly for 20 years:

Rate＿＿＿＿＿ No. of Periods＿＿＿＿＿

14. $8,000 at 4¾% compounded semiannually for 11 years:

Rate＿＿＿＿＿ No. of Periods＿＿＿＿＿

18. $550 at 7% compounded monthly for 15 years 6 months:

Rate＿＿＿＿＿ No. of Periods＿＿＿＿＿

*Student's Score* ＿＿＿＿＿

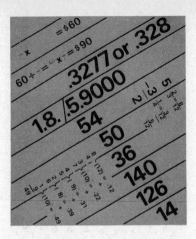

CHAPTER
9

*Figuring Cash and Trade Discounts*

Before discussing cash and trade discounts, Section 9-1 in this chapter first considers two forms important in business transactions: purchase orders and invoices. A **purchase order** is an order by a buyer for certain items to be bought from a seller. When supplies are needed, the purchasing department is informed. On the basis of this information, a purchase order is prepared for the chosen supplier. After the ordered goods have been shipped or mailed to the purchaser, the supplier sends a bill, or **invoice**, for the cost of the goods. The supplier, or seller, is often called a **vendor**.

Section 9-2 deals with **cash discounts** and the terms under which they are offered by many companies if an invoice is paid within a specified number of days. Figuring various forms of **trade discounts**, which are reductions from the suggested retail price in a catalog, is discussed in Section 9-3.

## Section 9-1  Purchase Orders and Invoices

In a large firm a purchasing department is responsible for buying all the supplies and materials that are needed for conducting company business. In a small firm usually only one person does the buying.

The basis for a purchase order is a request from an individual or a department for the needed supplies. This request is called a purchase requisition. It lists the materials wanted and the date required. Generally it must be approved by a supervisor before it is sent to the purchasing department.

### Part A  *Preparing and Checking Purchase Orders*

An order for goods may be given directly to a supplier's representative, placed by telephone or telegram, or mailed out. Many companies use their own printed forms for ordering.

A purchase order shows the particular goods that are wanted and specifies quantities and unit prices. Also included are details on how and when the order is to be shipped, as well as the terms and conditions to which the vendor must agree in accepting the order.

The purchase order must then be signed by the purchasing agent or another responsible person. Several copies are prepared for future reference.

A purchase order is illustrated in Figure 9-1 on page 202. Note that the purchaser, the ABC Company, uses it own printed form. After its purchasing department received the approved Requisition No. 24578, it prepared Purchase Order No. 83250 on March 3.

Purchase Order No. 83250 shows that the order is to be shipped by United Parcel Service by March 25. The company's purchasing agent is R.H. Ellis. The order is to be shipped to the N. First Street address. The vendor to whom the purchase order is sent is the A. J. Moran Company.

## Figure 9-1 A Purchase Order

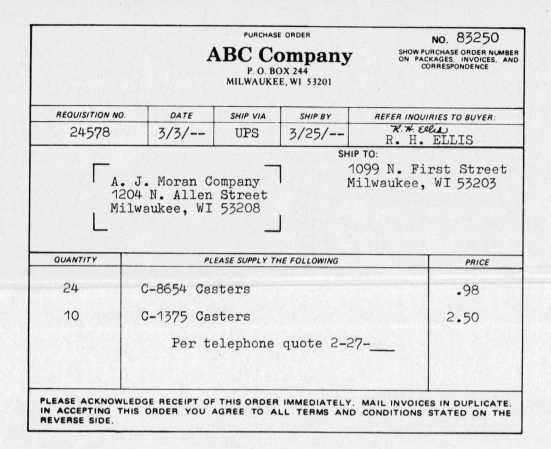

PURCHASE ORDER

# ABC Company
P. O. BOX 244
MILWAUKEE, WI 53201

NO. 83250
SHOW PURCHASE ORDER NUMBER ON PACKAGES, INVOICES, AND CORRESPONDENCE

| REQUISITION NO. | DATE | SHIP VIA | SHIP BY | REFER INQUIRIES TO BUYER: |
|---|---|---|---|---|
| 24578 | 3/3/-- | UPS | 3/25/-- | *R. H. Ellis* R. H. ELLIS |

SHIP TO:

A. J. Moran Company
1204 N. Allen Street
Milwaukee, WI 53208

1099 N. First Street
Milwaukee, WI 53203

| QUANTITY | PLEASE SUPPLY THE FOLLOWING | PRICE |
|---|---|---|
| 24 | C-8654 Casters | .98 |
| 10 | C-1375 Casters | 2.50 |
| | Per telephone quote 2-27-___ | |

PLEASE ACKNOWLEDGE RECEIPT OF THIS ORDER IMMEDIATELY. MAIL INVOICES IN DUPLICATE. IN ACCEPTING THIS ORDER YOU AGREE TO ALL TERMS AND CONDITIONS STATED ON THE REVERSE SIDE.

The quantities, descriptions of the items, and the unit prices are listed in the main part of the order form.

The printed statement at the bottom shows that the vendor must acknowledge receipt of the order and that two copies of the invoice are to be sent. It also calls attention to the terms and conditions—printed on the other side—to which the vendor must agree if the order is accepted.

When the order is delivered, a clerk in the receiving department checks the goods against the purchase order. If the vendor has included a **bill of lading**, which is a description of the shipment without any prices, that also is checked. The clerk then makes out a **receiving record** of the goods delivered and informs the purchasing and accounting departments if any items are missing or damaged or if the wrong items or quantities have been sent.

When the invoice for the goods is received, an accounting clerk goes over it for any errors reported by the receiving clerk and then checks all extensions and the total. If there are any errors

either in the order itself or on the invoice, the vendor is notified immediately so that the necessary adjustments can be made as soon as possible.

## Part B  Preparing and Checking Invoices

Many companies use printed invoice forms designed to fit their particular needs. In a small company, invoices may be prepared on a billing machine or a typewriter; or they may be done by hand. In a large concern they are often produced by a computer.

A distinction is sometimes made between a bill and an invoice: An invoice is a statement for goods that have been sold, while a **bill** is a statement for services that have been performed.

Most companies use a standard invoice form although the individual designs vary considerably. The upper part of the invoice shows the vendor's name and address, the purchaser's name and address, the order number, and the invoice date. In addition, it may show the terms of payment,

## Figure 9-2  An Invoice

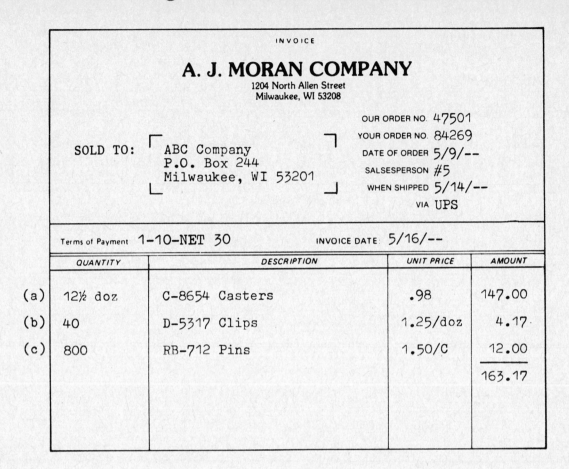

INVOICE

# A. J. MORAN COMPANY
1204 North Allen Street
Milwaukee, WI 53208

| | |
|---|---|
| | OUR ORDER NO. 47501 |
| | YOUR ORDER NO. 84269 |
| SOLD TO: ABC Company | DATE OF ORDER 5/9/-- |
| P.O. Box 244 | SALESPERSON #5 |
| Milwaukee, WI 53201 | WHEN SHIPPED 5/14/-- |
| | VIA UPS |

Terms of Payment 1-10-NET 30    INVOICE DATE 5/16/--

| | QUANTITY | DESCRIPTION | UNIT PRICE | AMOUNT |
|---|---|---|---|---|
| (a) | 12½ doz | C-8654 Casters | .98 | 147.00 |
| (b) | 40 | D-5317 Clips | 1.25/doz | 4.17 |
| (c) | 800 | RB-712 Pins | 1.50/C | 12.00 |
| | | | | 163.17 |

shipping details, the salesperson's name or number, the purchase order number, and such other information as is necessary.

The lower part of the invoice has separate columns for the quantity, description, unit price, amount, and other particular information needed. Most manufacturers and distributors identify each product or item with a separate stock number. The stock number is included in the description column, and it does not affect the cost of the item in any way.

Usually computer- or billing machine-prepared invoices omit the dollar signs on prices and amounts. For the most part, handwritten or typewritten invoices still use dollar signs for the first prices and amounts in a column and for the total.

An invoice is illustrated in Figure 9-2. This invoice was prepared for Order No. 47501 of the A. J. Moran Company which was sent to the ABC Company in accordance with its Purchase Order No. 84269 given to Salesperson #5. The goods were shipped on May 14 via United Parcel Service. The invoice date is May 16, the date on which it was prepared. The terms of payment (a topic discussed in Section 9-2) are 1-10-NET 30.

Generally the quantity ordered by the purchaser is expressed in the same unit as that used in the price quoted by the vendor. If the quantity ordered is given in a different unit, it is changed to that in the unit price when the extensions are made. To illustrate such extensions, the three items on the invoice in Figure 9-2 are calculated as follows:

(a) $12\frac{1}{2}$ doz = $12\frac{1}{2} \times 12$ = 150 pieces
150 pieces $\times$ \$0.98 = \$147.00

(b) $40 \div 12 = 3\frac{1}{3}$ doz
$3\frac{1}{3}$ doz $\times$ \$1.25 = \$4.17

(c) $800 \div 100 = 8$ C
   $8$ C $\times \$1.50 = \$12.00$

Note that the total is placed under the last extension. On some invoices there is a separate column for the total.

A reminder: While many companies are now packaging their small items in lots of 10, 25, 50, 100, or more with the unit price set per package, some are continuing to use unit prices per dozen or per gross.

Complete Assignment 26

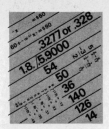

# Assignment 26
# Section 9-1

|  | Perfect Score | Student's Score |
|---|---|---|
| Part A | 30 | |
| Part B | 70 | |
| TOTAL | 100 | |

## Purchase Orders and Invoices

# Part A

### Preparing and Checking Purchase Orders

On the basis of an approved requisition, #25116, the buyer, R. H. Ellis, ordered these supplies:

2 AC-54 panels, 2′ × 8′, at $19.76 each
4 doz B-8614 bolts at 14¢ each
150 C-5623 screws at $12.53 per C
1 gross L-9006 washers at 95¢ per doz
40 D-6311 dividers, 14″ × 12″, at 75¢ each

The unit prices were given to Mrs. Ellis by telephone on June 9 by the area salesperson, R. B. Ross. The order is to be shipped by July 1 via the Lane Express Company to the plant at 1099 N. First Street, Milwaukee, WI 53203. The vendor is the A. J. Moran Company, 1204 N. Allen Street, Milwaukee, WI 53208.

From the information given, complete Purchase Order #84289, dated June 14, in the form provided below. (30 points)

PURCHASE ORDER

## ABC Company
P. O. BOX 244
MILWAUKEE, WI 53201

NO.

SHOW PURCHASE ORDER NUMBER ON PACKAGES, INVOICES, AND CORRESPONDENCE

| REQUISITION NO. | DATE | SHIP VIA | SHIP BY | REFER INQUIRIES TO BUYER: |
|---|---|---|---|---|
| | | | | |

SHIP TO:

| QUANTITY | PLEASE SUPPLY THE FOLLOWING | PRICE |
|---|---|---|
| | | |

PLEASE ACKNOWLEDGE RECEIPT OF THIS ORDER IMMEDIATELY. MAIL INVOICES IN DUPLICATE. IN ACCEPTING THIS ORDER YOU AGREE TO ALL TERMS AND CONDITIONS STATED ON THE REVERSE SIDE.

*Student's Score* _____

# Part B

## Preparing and Checking Invoices

*Directions:* Make the extensions and find the totals. Write your answers in the spaces provided. (2 points for each correct answer in the two problems)

| Quantity | Unit Price | Amount | | Quantity | Unit Price | Amount |
|---|---|---|---|---|---|---|
| 1. 40 | $37.50 | _____ | 2. | 1,600 lb | $62.50/cwt | _____ |
| 24 | 87.50 | _____ | | 2,500 lb | 9.25/cwt | _____ |
| 2 doz | 11.00 each | _____ | | 3,000 | 80.00/M | _____ |
| 50 | 1.80/doz | _____ | | 8 doz | .45 each | _____ |
| 3 doz | 7.50 each | _____ | | 27 doz | 1.50/gross | _____ |
| 150 | 48.00/doz | _____ | | 14 | .65 | _____ |
| 8 | 3.75 | _____ | | 68 doz | 36.00/gross | _____ |
| 87 | 6.40/doz | _____ | | 5 gross | 8.50/doz | _____ |
| 2 gross | .50 each | _____ | | 400 | 24.00/gross | _____ |
| | Total | _____ | | | Total | _____ |

3. The purchase order in Part A of this assignment was received on June 16. Thereafter, the vendor's order #47954 was shipped on June 21. Complete the invoice for the vendor's order as of June 22 with terms of 1-10, NET 30. (30 points)

INVOICE

# A. J. MORAN COMPANY
1204 North Allen Street
Milwaukee, WI 53208

SOLD TO:

OUR ORDER NO.

YOUR ORDER NO.

DATE OF ORDER

SALSESPERSON

WHEN SHIPPED

VIA

Terms of Payment:                           INVOICE DATE:

| QUANTITY | DESCRIPTION | UNIT PRICE | AMOUNT |
|---|---|---|---|
| | | | |

*Student's Score* _____

# Section 9-2   Cash Discounts

The **terms**, or **terms of payment**, usually found in the upper part of an invoice state the time within which the purchaser can pay the total of the invoice without penalty. Ordinarily 30 days are allowed, but the time may vary depending upon company policy. If the terms are COD (cash on delivery), payment must be made on delivery of the goods. The payment for purchased goods is often called the **remittance**. If the terms include a cash discount, the cash discount is stated as a percent followed by the number of days allowed. Although the vendor gives this discount primarily to encourage prompt payment of an invoice, the discount itself reduces the cost of the goods to the purchaser.

An account is overdue, or **past due**, if the remittance has not been sent by the last day allowed in the terms. In this regard, many companies have a printed statement of their policy on the invoice. Some examples of company policies are: "6% charge on past due accounts"; "Interest at the rate of 1% per month is charged on past due accounts"; and "Any invoice not paid by the 25th of the month following the date of the invoice will be subject to a $1\frac{1}{2}\%$ finance charge. This is an annual percentage rate of 18%."

## Part A   Terms of Payment with Cash Discounts

There are several ways of showing the time in the discount period.

*Ordinary dating.* In **ordinary dating**, the rate and number of days in the cash discount period are followed by the total number of days allowed for paying the invoice without penalty. For example, **2-10, n-30** means that 2% of the net amount, or invoice total, may be deducted if payment is made on or before the 10th day after the invoice date; the net amount (n) or **net** is due within 30 days after the invoice date. Other ways of expressing these terms are: 2/10, N-30; 2%-10-30; or 2-10, NET 30.

Some companies offer two or more possible dates for taking advantage of the cash discount, such as 5-10, 2-20, n-60. These terms mean that 5% of the net may be deducted from payment within 10 days; 2%, if paid within 20 days; and the net is due in 60 days.

When the last day allowed for discount or for payment of the net falls on a nonbusiness day or a legal holiday, the next business day is used. The extra days are not counted. And if a shipment is delayed, the purchaser can use the date of receipt of the goods—rather than the invoice date—to figure the discount period.

*Examples:* Find the time between the invoice date and the date of payment. Indicate the percent of discount allowed.

a. $\frac{1}{2}$-10, n-30; date of invoice, Jan. 23; date of payment, Feb. 2

   Time between dates is 10 days; cash discount is $\frac{1}{2}\%$.

b. 1%-10-30; date of invoice, June 24; date of payment, July 5

   Time between dates is 11 days, but discount date is July 4, a legal holiday. The extra day is allowed; cash discount is 1%.

c. 5/10, 2/20, n/60; date of invoice, Feb. 5; date of payment, Feb. 25

   Time between dates is 20 days; cash discount is 2%.

d. 3-10, NET 30; date of invoice, Apr. 16; date of payment, May 16

   Time between dates is 30 days; no cash discount.

e. 2/10, n/30; date of invoice, Oct. 19; date of payment, Nov. 30

   Time between dates is 42 days; no cash discount. The invoice is past due and subject to penalty.

*Extra dating.* When goods are sold before they are in season, the period allowed for taking the cash discount may be extended. This is called **extra dating**. Thus, 2/10 − 90 extra means that a 2% cash discount can be taken if the invoice is paid within 10 + 90, or 100 days, from the date of the invoice. Instead of "extra," the symbol "X" is often used; for example, 2/10 − 90X. If the cash discount is not taken, generally the net amount is due 20 days after the discount date.

*Example:* The terms on an invoice dated Apr. 19 are 3/10 − 60X. Find the last date of the discount period and the last date for paying the invoice without penalty.

The discount period is 10 + 60, or 70 days. The last day of the discount period is June 28, which is 70 days after Apr. 19. The invoice is due 20 days after June 28, or July 18.

**ROG dating.** When a vendor knows that shipments may be delayed, **receipt-of-goods (ROG) dating** is often used instead of ordinary dating. Under these terms the date of the receipt of the goods is used as the first day of the discount period rather than the invoice date. Usually the net period is not stated but is assumed to be 30 days after the receipt of goods; for example, 2-10 ROG.

*Examples:* Find the number of days between the first day of the discount period and the date of payment. Indicate the percent of discount allowed.

a. 3-10 ROG (received Nov. 27); date of invoice, Oct. 25; date of payment, Dec. 7

Time between Nov. 27 and Dec. 7 is 10 days; cash discount is 3%.

b. 2/10 ROG (received June 25); date of invoice, June 1; date of payment, July 30

Time between June 25 and July 30 is 35 days. The invoice is past due and subject to penalty.

**EOM dating.** In **end-of-month (EOM) dating,** the discount period starts immediately after the end of the month in which the invoice has been dated. The usual discount period is 10 days. For example, on an invoice dated March 2 with terms of **2-10 EOM,** the last day for taking advantage of the cash discount is April 10, which is 10 days after March 31.

If the invoice date is the 26th or any later date in the month, most companies allow an extra month for discounting. For example, on an invoice

dated March 26 with terms of 2-10 EOM, the discount period ends on May 10.

If the cash discount is not taken, usually the date for payment without penalty is the 30th of the month of discount. In some cases the last day of the month is considered as the due date of the invoice. For example, the due date for payment without penalty of an invoice dated March 26 with terms of 2-10 EOM would be May 31.

Instead of "EOM," **prox.** is sometimes used. This stands for the Latin *proximo mense,* which means "in the next month."

*Examples:* Determine if a cash discount can be taken.

a. 1-10 EOM; date of invoice, March 1; date of payment, April 10

April 10 is 10 days after March 31; cash discount of 1% can be taken.

b. 8-10 EOM; date of invoice, Oct. 27; date of payment, Dec. 10

Because the invoice date is after the 26th, an extra month is allowed. Cash discount of 8% can be taken.

c. 3-20 prox.; date of invoice, Feb. 3; date of payment, March 30

March 10 is the last day for taking advantage of the cash discount. March 30 is the due date of the net amount.

**Other ways of expressing terms of payment.** In the last few years there has been a trend to eliminate the formal terms of payment in the top part of the invoice. Instead, a printed statement is placed at the bottom of the invoice in which the last date for taking the cash discount and the amount of the cash discount are inserted.

*Examples:*

a. IF PAID BY THIS DATE _____10/10/—_____.
   TAKE THIS DISCOUNT_____$1.83_____.

b.             Cash discount as marked, if paid by 10th.

     TERMS   Net if paid by the last date of that month.

                  Add 1% per month service charge if paid thereafter.

IF INVOICE IS PAID BEFORE 10th OF NEXT MONTH, YOU SAVE ____$4.78____.

Note that terms in *Examples a* and *b* are similar to EOM since generally the 10th of the month following the date of the invoice is used.

Two other terms of payment are mentioned here only for the student's interest since they are no longer widely used. Generally an explanatory statement follows the terms.

### Examples:

a. 1% 10th and 25th, NET 30 days

To earn a discount, invoices dated between the 1st and 15th (both dates inclusive) must be paid by the 25th of the same month. Those dated between the 16th and the end of the month (both dates inclusive) must be paid by the 10th of the following month.

b. NET 10th and 25th

Invoices dated between the 1st and 15th inclusive must be paid by the 25th of the same month. Those dated between the 16th and the end of the month must be paid by the 10th of the following month.

## Part B — Figuring Cash Discounts

When the amount due on an invoice is paid within the cash discount period, the purchaser deducts the amount of discount when making the payment. To find the amount of cash discount, multiply the cash discount percent by the amount of the net invoice.

**Examples:** Find the remittance sent in payment of the invoices.

a. Invoice for $325.00 dated June 2 with terms of 2-10-30 and paid on June 12.

Cash discount = $325.00 × 2% = $6.50
Payment = $325.00 − $6.50 = $318.50

b. Invoice for $569.75 dated July 25 with terms of 3/10-90X and paid on Oct. 23.

Cash discount = $569.75 × 3% = $17.09
Payment = $569.75 − $17.09 = $552.66

c. Invoice for $286.73 dated Sept. 12 with terms of 2/10 ROG and paid on Nov. 5. Goods were received on Oct. 26.

Cash discount = $286.73 × 2% = $5.73
Payment = $286.73 − $5.73 = $281.00

d. Invoice for $1,238.82 dated May 26 with terms of 1/10 EOM and paid on July 10.

Cash discount = $1,238.82 × 1% = $12.39
Payment = $1,238.82 − $12.39 = $1,226.43

On most calculators with a percent key, the cash discount and the net payment can be found in sequence without clearing in between. Depending upon the calculator, generally either of these sequences can be used:

1. Invoice total × discount rate −

Note that after the (%) key is depressed, the amount displayed equals the cash discount. After the (−) key is depressed, the amount displayed is the payment.

2. Invoice total − discount rate =

Note that after the (%) key is depressed, the amount displayed equals the cash discount. After the (=) key is depressed, the amount displayed is the payment.

**When a portion of the goods is returned.** A cash discount is allowed only on goods actually purchased. If some goods that have been returned are included in the invoice total, these must be subtracted from the total before the cash discount is calculated.

**Example:** An invoice for $578.90 with terms of 2/10, n/30 includes returned goods worth $47.65. Find the remittance if the invoice is paid within the discount period.

Actual purchases   = \$578.90 − \$47.65
                   = \$531.25
Cash discount  = \$531.25 × 2% = \$10.625
Payment  = \$531.25 − \$10.625 = \$520.625
          = \$520.63

Note that when the cash discount ends with a 5 in the third decimal place, it is not rounded off. In all other cases, however, the cash discount generally is rounded off since the final answer is the same whether the rounding off is done before or after the subtraction.

**When prepaid freight charges are paid by the purchaser.** It sometimes happens that a vendor includes prepaid freight charges in the invoice total. The prepaid freight charges must be deducted from the invoice total before the cash discount is figured since no cash discount is allowed on freight charges. The cash discount is calculated on the remainder and subtracted from the value of the goods purchased. The freight charge is then added back to get the amount of the payment.

*Example:*  An invoice for \$806.12 with terms of 3-10 EOM includes a freight charge of \$59.75. Find the remittance if the invoice is paid within the discount price.

Value of goods = \$806.12 − \$59.75 = \$746.37
Cash discount = \$746.37 × 3% = \$22.39
Payment = \$746.37 − \$22.39 + \$59.75
          = \$783.73

**When only a portion of the invoice is paid within the discount period.** If only a specified part of the invoice is to be paid within the discount period, cash discount is figured on only that part. The remittance equals the part minus the cash discount. The balance due on the account is the original invoice minus the part on which the discount was taken.

*Example:*  An invoice for \$1,756.33 has terms of 2/10, n/30. The payment to be sent within the discount period is to apply on only \$756.33, leaving a balance of \$1,000 to be paid later. Find the remittance.

Cash discount = \$756.33 × 2% = \$15.13
Payment = \$756.33 − \$15.13 = \$741.20

For some final words about cash discounts, the student should know that most vendors accept a cash discount invoice even though it is several days late, as long as the remittance is dated on the last day of the discount period. In small companies the invoices often are placed in a file with dividers numbered 1 through 31 for the due dates. If the terms specify a cash discount, the invoice is filed behind the last date of the discount period. If it is not paid by that date, the invoice is refiled behind the net due date.

Complete Assignment 27

# Assignment 27
# Section 9-2

|  | Perfect Score | Student's Score |
|---|---|---|
| Part A | 40 |  |
| Part B | 60 |  |
| TOTAL | 100 |  |

## Cash Discounts

# Part A

### Terms of Payment with Cash Discounts

**Directions:** Place a check mark in the column which shows the kind of payment made as determined by the date of payment. (2 points for each correct answer)

| Terms | Date of Invoice | Date of Payment | Cash Discount | Net | Past Due |
|---|---|---|---|---|---|
| 1. 1/10, n/30 | Mar. 28 | Apr. 7 | _____ | _____ | _____ |
| 2. 1-10-30 | Jan. 15 | Feb. 16 | _____ | _____ | _____ |
| 3. 5/10, 2/20, n/60 | June 17 | July 7 | _____ | _____ | _____ |
| 4. 3-10, 1-20, n-30 | Oct. 9 | Nov. 8 | _____ | _____ | _____ |
| 5. 2/10 - 90 Extra | Feb. 3 | May 14 | _____ | _____ | _____ |
| 6. 2-10 - 60X | Apr. 4 | June 30 | _____ | _____ | _____ |
| 7. 2/10 ROG (received June 5) | May 3 | June 15 | _____ | _____ | _____ |
| 8. 1-10 ROG (received Feb. 15) | Jan. 8 | Mar. 17 | _____ | _____ | _____ |
| 9. 2/10 ROG (received Dec. 16) | Oct. 3 | Jan. 20 | _____ | _____ | _____ |
| 10. 4/10 EOM | Feb. 26 | Apr. 10 | _____ | _____ | _____ |
| 11. 8/10 EOM | Sept. 9 | Nov. 10 | _____ | _____ | _____ |
| 12. 5/10 EOM | Jan. 25 | Feb. 10 | _____ | _____ | _____ |
| 13. 1-10, n-30 | Nov. 12 | Dec. 12 | _____ | _____ | _____ |
| 14. 4/10, 2/20, n/60 | June 12 | June 30 | _____ | _____ | _____ |
| 15. 3/10 prox. | July 28 | Sept. 10 | _____ | _____ | _____ |
| 16. 2/10 - 90X | Apr. 19 | July 30 | _____ | _____ | _____ |
| 17. 1/10 ROG (received Aug. 31) | Aug. 17 | Sept. 30 | _____ | _____ | _____ |
| 18. 1-10-30 | Dec. 15 | Dec. 26 | _____ | _____ | _____ |
| 19. 5-10, 2-20, n/30 | June 4 | July 5 | _____ | _____ | _____ |
| 20. 4/10 prox. | Sept. 25 | Nov. 10 | _____ | _____ | _____ |

*Student's Score* _____

# Part B

## Figuring Cash Discounts

*Directions:* Assume that payment on the invoice is to be made within the discount period. Find the last day on which the discount can be taken, the amount of the cash discount, and the amount of the payment. Write your answers in the spaces provided, and show your calculations in the space below. (2 points for each correct answer)

| Terms | Invoice Total | Portion Paid | Date of Invoice | Date of Payment | Cash Discount | Amount of Payment |
|---|---|---|---|---|---|---|
| 21. ½-10, n-30 | $ 437.91 | All | May 29 | _____ | _____ | _____ |
| 22. 1-10 - 90X | 1,165.08 (includes freight charge of $150) | All | Feb. 6 | _____ | _____ | _____ |
| 23. 1-10 ROG | 2,589.95 | All | Aug. 8 (received Aug. 30) | _____ | _____ | _____ |
| 24. 2/10 ROG | 1,601.36 | $ 601.36 | Nov. 12 (received Dec. 22) | _____ | _____ | _____ |
| 25. 3/10 EOM | 8,500 (includes return of $500) | All | Mar. 27 | _____ | _____ | _____ |
| 26. 5-10 EOM | 287.40 | All | June 5 | _____ | _____ | _____ |
| 27. 3-30, NET 60 | 1,550.00 | 550.00 | Oct. 22 | _____ | _____ | _____ |
| 28. ½-10 ROG | 825.37 | 575.37 | May 10 (received June 21) | _____ | _____ | _____ |
| 29. 2-10-30 | 10,425.50 | 5,425.50 | July 23 | _____ | _____ | _____ |
| 30. 8/10 prox. | 3,311.63 | 2,311.63 | Nov. 10 | _____ | _____ | _____ |

*Student's Score* _____

Assignment 27

# Section 9-3  Trade Discounts

Most manufacturers and distributors state their unit prices in dollars and cents. Another way of stating the unit price, however, is in terms of a suggested retail price less one or more trade discounts. Trade discounts are deductions from the list price for retailers. The result often is called the **wholesale price**. Trade discounts are not the same as cash discounts since they do not reduce the cost to the purchaser.

For this method of quoting prices, a catalog containing pictures, descriptions, and stock or model numbers for the products manufactured or distributed is sent to retailers. A suggested retail price, which is called the **catalog** or **list price**, also is given. In addition to the catalog, separate sheets which show the trade discount rates offered on the products are sent to the retailer. For example, a refrigerator may be listed at $498 in the catalog, with a trade discount of 40% on the discount sheet. The retailer can find the **net price** or **net cost** by deducting the trade discount from the list price; in this case; $498.00 − $199.20 = $298.80, the cost to the retailer.

There are several advantages in quoting unit prices by this method. Retailers can use the catalog to place an order for specific items by their stock numbers and, in the absence of a salesperson, can find their cost by applying the trade discounts. Retailers can also show the catalog to their customers for items which they do not carry, without disclosing the prices they would have to pay for such items.

As market prices vary throughout the year, new catalogs are not necessary. All that the manufacturer or distributor must do is change the trade discount rates offered and send out new discount sheets effective as of a particular date. If a price goes up, the discount rate is decreased in order to increase the net price to the retailer. If a price goes down, the discount rate is increased, or an extra discount is added, to decrease the net price. New discount sheets may also be sent out to reduce prices on unpopular items.

The invoice sent to the retailer or purchaser shows the list price, the discount rate or rates allowed, and the net price. In modern business practice the amount of trade discount does not appear on the invoice.

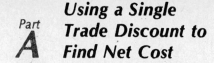

## Part A  Using a Single Trade Discount to Find Net Cost

There are two ways to find the net cost when a single trade discount is offered. The first way consists of the following two steps:

1. Multiply the list price by the trade discount rate to find the amount of the trade discount.
2. Subtract the trade discount from the list price to find the net cost.

*Examples:*  Find the net cost.

a.  A clock radio listed at $69.95 less a trade discount of 40%

Trade discount = $69.95 × 40% = $27.98
Net cost = $69.95 − $27.98 = $41.97

b.  A calculator listed at $45.50 less a trade discount of 35%

Trade discount = $45.50 × 35% = $15.925
Net cost = $45.50 − $15.925 = $29.575
　　　　 = $29.58

Note in *Example b* that when the trade discount ends in an exact half cent, it is the net cost that is rounded off and not the trade discount.

On most calculators with a percent key, the trade discount and the net cost can be found in sequence without clearing in between. Depending upon the calculator, generally either of these sequences can be used:

1.  List price × discount rate −

Note that after the (%) key is depressed, the amount displayed is the trade discount. After the (−) key is depressed, the amount displayed is the net cost.

2.  List price − discount rate =

Note that when the (%) key is depressed, the amount displayed is the trade discount. After the (=) key is depressed, the amount displayed is the net cost.

The second way to find the net cost when there is a single trade discount is to subtract the trade discount rate from 100% and then multiply the result by the list price. The difference is called the **complement** of the discount rate.

*Examples:* Find the net cost.

a. A camera listed at $98.75 less a trade discount of 55%

Complement of 55% = 100% − 55% = 45%
Net cost = $98.75 × 45% = $44.4375 = $44.44

b. A power drill listed at $49.95 less a trade discount of 40%

Complement of 40% = 100% − 40% = 60%
Net cost = $49.95 × 60% = $29.97

When a group of items have the same trade discount rate, on the invoice the rate is shown next to the last item in the group. The net cost is found by multiplying the complement of the rate by the total of the list prices. In the example tabulated below, note that the invoice is designed specifically to show list prices, total list, trade discount rate, and the net cost of each group of items. The first trade discount of 33⅓% is taken on the sum of the first two items, and their net cost is placed in the net column.

## Part B Using Chain Discounts to Find Net Price

Trade discounts sometimes are offered as a series of discounts, or **chain discounts**. They may be written in several ways: 40%, 20%, 10%; 40%-20%-10%; or 40/20/10. Only the first method is used here.

As mentioned earlier, chain discounts provide a means for changing a net price. They are also useful when the size of the order is a factor in the discount allowed. For example, 40% may be given on orders under $100; 40%, 20% for orders from $100 to $500; and 40%, 20%, 10% for orders more than $500.

Just as in finding the net cost using single trade discounts, there are two ways of finding the net price using chain discounts. (In Part A of this section, the term "net cost" was used; in this Part, the term "net price," which has the same meaning to the purchaser, is used.) The first method consists of the following steps:

1. Multiply the first discount rate by the list price and subtract this amount from the list price.
2. Multiply the second rate by the remainder and subtract this amount from the first remainder. Repeat this procedure until all the discounts have been deducted. To find the total amount of the trade discount, subtract the net price from the list price.

All decimals through the sixth place are carried until the final answer is reached. Since the order of multiplication does not matter, the discounts may be taken in any convenient order, not necessarily as listed. The same net price will result.

*Examples:* Find the net price.

a. A sprayer listed at $39.50 less 20% and 10%

1st discount = $39.50 × 20% = $7.90
1st net remainder = $39.50 − $7.90 = $31.60

2nd discount = $31.60 × 10% = $3.16
Net price = $31.60 − $3.16 = $28.44

Total trade discount = $39.50 − $28.44
                     = $11.06

*Example:*

| Quantity | Description | List | Total List | Discount | Net |
|---|---|---|---|---|---|
| 2 | 6″ No. 40 Diagonal Cutting Pliers | $3.95 ea. | $ 7.90 | | |
| 2 | 10″ No. 51 Water Pump Nut Pliers | 3.42 ea. | 6.84 | 33⅓% | |
| | | | 14.74 | | $ 9.83 |
| 500 | No. 4 × ¼″ Pan Head Tapping Screws | .76 C | 3.80 | 30% | 2.66 |
| | | | | | $12.49 |

**b.** A bundle of casters listed at $75.00 less 40%, 10%, 5%

1st discount = $75 × 40% = $30
1st net remainder = $75 − $30 = $45

2nd discount = $45 × 10% = $4.50
2nd net remainder = $45 − $4.50 = $40.50

3rd discount = $40.50 × 5% = $2.025
Net price = $40.50 − $2.025 = $38.475
         = $38.48

Total trade discount = $75.00 − $38.48
                     = $36.52

On a calculator with a percent key, extend the procedure for a single trade discount (see page 213) to the remaining discounts. Always continue the sequence at the second step.

The second method of finding the net price using chain discounts is to start with the list price and multiply by the complement of each rate in succession, rather than multiplying by the rate and then subtracting. The same examples as above are used so that you can compare the two methods.

**Examples:** Find the net price.

**a.** A sprayer listed at $39.50 less 20% and 10%

Complement of 20% = 100% − 20% = 80%
Complement of 10% = 100% − 10% = 90%

1st net remainder = $39.50 × 80% = $31.60
Net price = $31.60 × 90% = $28.44

**b.** A bundle of casters listed at $75.00 less 40%, 10%, 5%

Complement of 40% = 100% − 40% = 60%
Complement of 10% = 100% − 10% = 90%
Complement of  5% = 100% −  5% = 95%

1st net remainder = $75 × 60% = $45
2nd net remainder = $45 × 90% = $40.50
Net price = $40.50 × 95% = $38.475 = $38.48

## Part C Using Net Cost Factors

When the same chain discounts occur repeatedly, it saves time to use the **net cost factor** for the series. The net cost factor is a decimal such that when the list price is multiplied by this decimal the result is the net cost. Actually the net cost factor is the net cost of $1.00 less the series of discounts. The product of the complements of the rates gives the same decimal result.

**Example:** Show that $1.00 less 30% and 20% is the same as the product of the complements of 30% and 20%.

$1.00 × 70% = $0.70
$0.70 × 80% = $0.56

Product of complements = 70% × 80% = 56%
                                         or .56

Therefore, to find the net cost factor for a series of trade discounts, first find the complement of each rate and then find the product of the complements.

**Using the net cost factor when one item is listed with chain discounts.** To find the net cost of an item listed with chain discounts, multiply the list price by the net cost factor for the series.

**Example:** Find the net cost of a gage listed at $19.50 less 30%, 20%, 10% by using the net cost factor.

Complement of 30% = 100% − 30% = 70% = .7
Complement of 20% = 100% − 20% = 80% = .8
Complement of 10% = 100% − 10% = 90% = .9

Net cost factor = .7 × .8 × .9 = .504

Net cost = $19.50 × .504 = $9.828 = $9.83

**Using the net cost factor when several items have the same series of discounts.** When a number of items have the same series of discounts, multiply the total list price of the items by the net cost factor. On an invoice the chain discounts appear under the last item in the group. The net cost for the group is put in the net column.

# Table *9-1*   *Partial Net Cost Factor Table*

| Rate % | 5% | 10% | 15% | 20% | 25% |
|--------|------|--------|--------|------|--------|
| 5 | .9025 | .855 | .8075 | .76 | .7125 |
| 5-5 | .85738 | .81225 | .76713 | .722 | .67688 |
| 10 | | .81 | .765 | .72 | .675 |
| 10-5 | | .7695 | .72675 | .684 | .64125 |
| 10-10 | | .729 | .6885 | .648 | .6075 |

*Example:* Extend the items on the invoice and find the net invoice due by using the net cost factor.

| Qty. | Description | Unit Price | Amount | Net |
|------|-------------|-----------|--------|-----|
| 40 | 295-C Casters | $ 3.50 | $140.00 | |
| 2 | 63-G Gage | 15.95 | 31.90 | |
| 1 | 601-P Panel | 29.50 | 29.50 | |
| | | | $201.40 | |
| | Less 30%, 20%, 10% | | | $101.51 |

Net cost factor = .7 × .8 × .9 = .504
Net cost = $201.40 × .504 = $101.51

*Finding the equivalent single discount of a series.*
Occasionally a purchaser may be interested in the single discount which is equivalent to a series. To find the **equivalent single discount** of a series, first find the net cost factor for the series and change it to a percent. Then subtract this from 100%. Thus, the equivalent single discount of the 30%, 20%, 10% chain used in the examples above is:

$$100\% - 50.4\% = 49.6\%$$

*Using a net cost factor table.* A net cost factor (NCF) table often is used to compute the net cost of an item on which chain discounts are offered. Table 9-1 above shows a partial net cost factor table.

In a net cost factor table a single discount heads each column, and various combinations of discounts are listed in the column at the extreme left. To find the NCF for a series, first locate any one of the series discount rates in the top row. Then in the column at the left, find the combination that contains the remaining discount rates. Go across that row to the column that contains the first discount rate you located. The number you find at that intersection is the NCF.

*Examples:*

a. Find the net cost factor for 20%, 10%, 5%.

Go down the 20% column and across on the 10-5 row at the extreme left. The NCF is .684.

b. Find the net cost of a projector listed at $150 less 15%, 5%, 5%.

NCF = .76713 (from Table 9-1)

Net cost = $150 × .76713 = $115.07

**Complete Assignment 28**

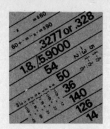

## Assignment 28
## Section 9-3

*Trade Discounts*

# Part A
### Using a Single Trade Discount to Find Net Cost

*Directions:* Find the net cost by using the method indicated. Show all calculations in the work space and write your answers in the spaces provided. (2 points for each correct answer)

Multiplying by the rate:

| | List Price | Trade Discount | Amount of Discount | Net Price |
|---|---|---|---|---|
| 1. | $ 69.95 | 20% | _____ | _____ |
| 2. | 200.00 | 35 | _____ | _____ |
| 3. | 37.50 | 25 | _____ | _____ |
| 4. | 349.50 | 45 | _____ | _____ |
| 5. | 499.98 | 40 | _____ | _____ |

**WORK SPACE**

Multiplying by the complement of the rate:

| | List Price | Trade Discount | Net Price |
|---|---|---|---|
| 6. | $875.00 | $33\frac{1}{3}\%$ | _____ |
| 7. | 89.98 | 40 | _____ |
| 8. | 99.50 | 60 | _____ |
| 9. | 229.95 | 30 | _____ |
| 10. | 688.00 | $62\frac{1}{2}$ | _____ |

*Student's Score* _____

# Part B

## Using Chain Discounts to Find Net Price

*Directions:* Find the net price by using the method indicated. Show all calculations in the work space and write your answers in the spaces provided. (2 points for each correct answer)

Multiplying by the discounts:

| | List Price | Chain Discounts | Amount of Trade Discount | Net Price | WORK SPACE |
|---|---|---|---|---|---|
| 11. | $ 2.40 | 20%, 10% | _____ | _____ | |
| 12. | 52.70 | 25%, 20% | _____ | _____ | |
| 13. | 7.60 | 15%, 7½% | _____ | _____ | |
| 14. | 89.00 | 30%, 20%, 10% | _____ | _____ | |
| 15. | 325.00 | 40%, 10%, 10%, 5% | _____ | _____ | |

Multiplying by the complements of the discounts:

| | List Price | Chain Discounts | Net Price |
|---|---|---|---|
| 16. | $ 3.30 | 33⅓%, 5% | _____ |
| 17. | 17.60 | 37½%, 10% | _____ |
| 18. | 48.30 | 40%, 15%, 5% | _____ |
| 19. | 64.25 | 30%, 20%, 10% | _____ |
| 20. | 191.00 | 40%, 10%, 5%, 5% | _____ |

*Student's Score* _____

# Part C
## Using Net Cost Factors

*Directions:* Extend the items and find the net invoice due. Write your answers in the spaces provided. (1 point for each correct answer)

**21.**

| Quantity | Description | Unit Price | Amount | Net |
|---|---|---|---|---|
| 300 | 14-2 Toggle bolts | 16.34/C | _____ | |
| 500# | 1¼″ Steel wire nails—shingle | 76.40/cwt | _____ | |
| 600# | 1″ Steel wire nails—roofing | 58.70/C | _____ | |
| | | (Total) | _____ | |
| | Less 50%, 10%, 5% . . . . . . . . . . . . . . . . . . . . . . . . . . | | | _____ |
| 10 | 832MC Micrometers | 47.60 | _____ | |
| 10 | 832MD Micrometers | 59.50 | _____ | |
| | | (Total) | _____ | |
| | Less 40%, 25% . . . . . . . . . . . . . . . . . . . . . . . . . . . | | | _____ |
| | Net Invoice Due . . . . . . . . . . . . . . . . . . . . . . . . . . . | | | _____ |

**22.**

| Quantity | Description | Unit Price | Amount | Net |
|---|---|---|---|---|
| 5 | 350-H Yankee ratchets | 6.20 | _____ | |
| 10 | 163-T Tap wrenches | 3.00 | _____ | |
| 10 boxes | C-87 Drill bits | 27.25/box | _____ | |
| | | (Total) | _____ | |
| | Less 40%, 25% . . . . . . . . . . . . . . . . . . . . . . . . . | | | _____ |
| 2 ctns. | 1816 Steel abrasives | 6.30/ctn. | _____ | |
| 10 | 4670 Disc pads | 7.50 | _____ | |
| | | (Total) | _____ | |
| | Less 50%, 10%, 5% . . . . . . . . . . . . . . . . . . . . . . . . | | | _____ |
| | Net Invoice Due . . . . . . . . . . . . . . . . . . . . . . . . . . | | | _____ |

**Directions:** Find the net cost factors and the net prices. Use Table 9-1 on page 216 where applicable. Show all calculations in the work space, and write your answers in the spaces provided. (1 point for each correct answer)

| | List Price | Chain Discounts | Net Cost Factor | Net Price |
|---|---|---|---|---|
| 23. | $ 2.00 | 15%, 10% | | |
| 24. | 3.60 | 10%, 10% | | |
| 25. | 4.70 | 5%, 5% | | |
| 26. | 1.50 | 25%, 5% | | |
| 27. | 64.00 | 10%, 5% | | |
| 28. | 50.00 | 20%, 10%, 5% | | |
| 29. | 1,000.00 | 33⅓%, 20%, 10% | | |
| 30. | 300.00 | 40%, 15%, 10% | | |
| 31. | 500.00 | 50%, 20%, 10% | | |
| 32. | 600.00 | 40%, 20%, 10% | | |

## WORK SPACE

*Student's Score* _____

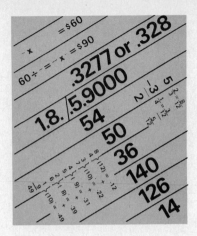

# 10 Selling Goods

Manufacturers, wholesale distributors, and retailers are in business to sell their products at a profit. The total sales must be high enough to cover not only the cost of the goods and the expenses related to selling them, but also the desired net profit.

Section 10-1 deals with **markup**, or the difference between what goods sell for and what they cost. Other names for it are **markon**, **margin on sales**, or **gross profit**. Markup consists of two parts: (1) **operating expenses**, which includes such items as wages and salaries of office and sales personnel, advertising, office and selling supplies, utilities, etc.; and (2) **net profit**.

Stated in another way, the cost of the goods plus the markup added to it equal the sales. The markup may be expressed as a percent of either the cost or the selling price of the goods.

Any business must determine on a periodic basis what its net profit or net loss is. This is the subject of Section 10-2.

## Section 10-1 Markup

Markup is usually expressed as a percent of a **base**, which can be either the cost or the selling price. However, selling price is used more widely than cost.

Generally cost is used as the base by wholesale and retail distributors of large or expensive products such as furniture, appliances, jewelry, etc. Some drug companies and manufacturers also use it. Most other lines of business, especially retailing, find it more practical to use selling price as the base for markup.

The **basic markup equation** (or formula) applies to both ways. It is:

$$\text{Selling Price} = \text{Cost} + \text{Markup}$$

To find the amount of markup, multiply the markup percent by either the cost or the selling price, depending upon which is used as the base.

## Part A Cost as the Base for Markup

*Finding the selling price.* When the cost and the desired percent of markup based on cost are known, the selling price is found in two steps:

1. First find the amount of markup by multiplying the cost by the markup percent.
2. Add the amount of markup to the cost.

Expanding the basic markup equation, this becomes:

$$\text{Selling Price} = \text{Cost} + (\text{Cost} \times \text{Markup}\%)$$
$$\text{SP} = \text{C} + (\text{C} \times \text{M}\%)$$

*Examples:* Find the selling price when the markup is based on cost.

a. Cost is $5.40; markup is 16⅔%.

$$M = \$5.40 \times 16\tfrac{2}{3}\% = \$0.90$$
$$SP = \$5.40 + \$0.90 = \$6.30$$

b. Cost is $36; 30% is allowed for operating expenses and 5% for net profit.

$$M\% = 30\% + 5\% = 35\%$$
$$M = \$36 \times 35\% = \$12.60$$
$$SP = \$36.00 + \$12.60 = \$48.60$$

The selling price can be found by another method without having to find the amount of markup. By this method the cost is considered as 100% of itself. That is, since 100% = 1, this is the same as saying 1 × the cost. Thus, in terms of the cost, the selling price equals 100% × Cost plus Markup Percent × Cost. As a formula, this becomes:

*or*
$$SP = 100\% \times C + M\% \times C$$
$$SP = C \times (100\% + M\%)$$

*Example b* above could be worked by this method as follows:

$$SP = \$36 \times (100\% + 35\%) = \$36 \times 135\%$$
$$= \$48.60$$

**Finding the percent of markup.** Sometimes the selling price originally set for an item is changed so that it will be in line with competitors' prices. When the cost and the selling price are known, the percent of markup is found in two steps:

1. First find the amount of markup by subtracting the cost from the selling price.
2. Divide the amount of markup by the cost and convert the result to a percent.

The formula for finding the percent of markup then becomes:

$$M\% = \frac{SP - C}{C}$$

*Examples:* Find the markup percent based on cost.

a. Cost is $12; selling price is $16.

$$\text{Amount of Markup} = \$16 - \$12 = \$4$$
$$\text{Markup \%} = \$4 \div \$12 = \tfrac{1}{3} \text{ or } 33\tfrac{1}{3}\%$$

b. Cost is $55.71; selling price is $89.50.

$$\text{Amount of Markup} = \$89.50 - \$55.71$$
$$= \$33.79$$
$$\text{Markup \%} = \$33.79 \div \$55.71$$
$$= .6065 = 60.7\%$$

c. Cost is $319.67; selling price is $700.

$$\text{Amount of Markup} = \$700 - \$319.67$$
$$= \$380.33$$
$$\text{Markup \%} = \$380.33 \div \$319.67$$
$$= 1.1897 = 119.0\%$$

Note that when the amount of markup is larger than the cost, as in *Example c*, the percent of markup based on cost is over 100%. Note further that, as in *Examples b* and *c*, generally one decimal place in the percent is sufficient.

**Finding the cost.** Occasionally records containing cost data may be lost or destroyed and the cost must be determined from the known selling price and markup based on cost. Since the known markup percent is based on an unknown cost, the amount of markup cannot be found directly in this case. The cost, however, can be found by reworking the second formula for finding the selling price, which is given in the left-hand column of this page.

$$\frac{SP}{(100 + M\%)} = \frac{C \times (\cancel{100\% + M\%})}{(\cancel{100\% + M\%})}$$

Dividing both sides of the equation by (100% + M%) gives the following formula to find the cost:

$$C = \frac{SP}{(100\% + M\%)} \text{ or } C = SP \div (100\% + M\%)$$

This type of problem can be checked by going in reverse. That is, multiply the cost by the markup percent to find the amount of markup. Then add the amount of markup to the cost. The result should be the given selling price.

*Examples:* Find the cost when markup is based on cost.

a. Selling price is \$31.25; markup is 25%.

$$100\% + 25\% = 125\%$$
$$C = \$31.25 \div 125\% = \$25.00$$

**Check:** $\$25 \times 25\% = \$6.25$
$\$25 + \$6.25 = \$31.25$, given SP

b. Selling price is \$259.98; markup is 160%.

$$100\% + 160\% = 260\%$$
$$C = \$259.98 \div 260\% = \$99.99$$

**Check:** $\$99.99 \times 160\% = \$159.98$
$\$99.99 + \$159.98 = \$259.97$, given SP

Note that the check in *Example b* gives a selling price which is 1¢ less than the given selling price. This is due to the decimals dropped in rounding off the cost.

## Part B Selling Price as the Base for Markup

*Finding the cost.* When the selling price and the desired percent of markup based on the selling price are known, the cost is found in two steps:

1. First find the amount of markup by multiplying the selling price by the markup percent.
2. Subtract the markup amount from the selling price.

Expanding the basic markup equation, this becomes:

$$C = SP - (SP \times M\%)$$

*Examples:* Find the cost when the markup is based on the selling price.

a. Selling price is \$10.89; markup is 33⅓%.

$$M = \$10.89 \times 33\tfrac{1}{3}\% = \$3.63$$
$$C = \$10.89 - \$3.63 = \$7.26$$

b. Selling price is \$72; markup is 37½%.

$$M = \$72 \times \$37\tfrac{1}{2}\% = \$27$$
$$C = \$72 - \$27 = \$45$$

On a calculator the same procedure that is used to find cash or trade discounts and net prices can be used to find the markup and the cost.

Another method can be used to find the cost without having to find the amount of markup. By this method the selling price is considered as 100% of itself. Thus, in terms of the selling price, the cost equals 100% × Selling Price less Markup Percent × Selling Price. As a formula, this becomes:

$$C = 100\% \times SP - M\% \times SP$$
$$or \quad C = SP \times (100\% - M\%)$$

This formula may be stated in another way: The cost equals the selling price times the complement of the markup percent.

*Examples:* Find the cost when markup is based on selling price.

a. Selling price is \$40; markup is 25%.

$$100\% - 25\% = 75\%$$
$$C \qquad = \$40 \times 75\% = \$30$$

b. Selling price is \$59.97; markup is 45%.

$$100\% - 45\% = 55\%$$
$$C \qquad = \$59.97 \times 55\% = \$32.98$$

*Finding the percent of markup.* When the cost and the selling price are known, the percent of markup based on the selling price is found in two steps:

1. First find the amount of markup by subtracting the cost from the selling price.
2. Divide the amount of markup by the selling price and convert the result to a percent.

The formula for finding the markup percent then becomes:

$$M\% = M \div SP$$

*Examples:* Find the markup percent based on selling price.

a. Cost is \$28; selling price is \$42.

Amount of Markup = \$42 − \$28 − \$14
Markup % = $\$14 \div \$42 = \tfrac{1}{3}$ or 33⅓%

b. Cost is $50; markup is $29.

SP $= \$50 + \$29 = \$79$
M% $= \$29 \div \$79 = .3670 = 36.7\%$

c. Cost is $118; selling price is $295.

Amount of Markup $= \$295 - \$118 = \$177$
M% $\quad\quad\quad = \$177 \div \$295$
$\quad\quad\quad = .6 = 60\%$

Note that when markup is based on cost, the markup percent can be greater than 100%. But when markup is based on selling price, the markup percent cannot be more than 100% since the markup is a part of the selling price.

*Finding the selling price.* In retailing generally the selling price is used as the base for determining the markup rate, on the theory that there can be no real profit until the goods are sold. In actual business practice **markup tables** or **markup wheels** are used. They show what the selling price should be for a given unit cost and a given markup percent based on the selling price.

A formula for finding the selling price can be developed from the second formula for finding the cost given on page 223:

$$C = SP \times (100\% - M\%)$$

Dividing both sides of the equation by (100% − M%)

$$\frac{C}{(100\% - M\%)} = \frac{SP\,(\cancel{100\% - M\%})}{(\cancel{100\% - M\%})}$$

gives the following formula for finding the selling price:

$$SP = C \div (100\% - M\%)$$

The (100% − M%), which is the complement of the markup rate, also is the percent that the cost is of the selling price. Therefore, the formula also can be expressed as: Selling price equals the cost divided by the cost percent.

The amount of markup is not found by the use of the above formula. It can be found after the selling price has been determined.

This type of problem also is checked by going in reverse. Multiply the selling price by the markup percent based on the selling price. Then subtract the markup from the selling price. The result should be the given cost.

*Examples:* Find the selling price when the markup is based on the selling price.

a. Cost is $60; markup is 40%.

$100\% - 40\% = 60\%$
SP $\quad\quad = \$60 \div 60\% = \$100$

**Check:** $\$100 \times 40\% = \$40$
$\quad\quad\quad \$100 - \$40 = \$60$, the given cost

b. Cost is $3.09; markup is 70%.

$100\% - 70\% = 30\%$
SP $\quad\quad = \$3.09 \div 30\% = \$10.30$

**Check:** $\$10.30 \times 70\% = \$7.21$
$\quad\quad\quad \$10.30 - \$7.21 = \$3.09$, the given cost

*Changing the markup percent from one base to the other.* The markup rate can be changed from one base to the other by assuming that the original base equals $100. It is illustrated here only for the student's interest and is not included in the Assignment.

*Examples:*

a. Change the markup of 40% on selling price to its equivalent rate based on cost.

SP $= \$100$
M $= \$100 \times 40\% = \$40$
C $= \$100 - \$40 = \$60$
Markup on cost $= \$40 \div \$60 = \frac{2}{3} = 66\frac{2}{3}\%$

b. Change the markup of 25% on cost to its equivalent rate based on selling price.

C $= \$100$
M $= \$100 \times 25\% = \$25$
SP $= \$100 + \$25 = \$125$
Markup on selling price $= \$25 \div \$125 = .20$
$\quad\quad\quad\quad\quad\quad\quad\quad = 20\%$

Complete Assignment 29

## Assignment 29
## Section 10-1

|  | Perfect Score | Student's Score |
|---|---|---|
| Part A | 50 |  |
| Part B | 50 |  |
| TOTAL | 100 |  |

*Markup*

# Part A

### Cost as the Base for Markup

**Directions:** In the following problems markup is based on cost. Find the parts indicated by the column headings, and write your answers in the spaces provided. (1 point for each correct answer in Problems 1-10; 3 points for each correct answer in Problems 11-20)

| Cost | Markup % | Amount of Markup | Selling Price | | Selling Price | Markup % | Cost |
|---|---|---|---|---|---|---|---|
| 1. $ 2.75 | 25 | _____ | _____ | | 11. $ 1.09 | 15 | _____ |
| 2. 4.00 | 40 | _____ | _____ | | 12. 5.85 | 54 | _____ |
| 3. 92.80 | 75 | _____ | _____ | | 13. 42.50 | $33\frac{1}{3}$ | _____ |
| 4. 294.84 | 140 | _____ | _____ | | 14. 498.00 | 25 | _____ |
| 5. 145.71 | $166\frac{2}{3}$ | _____ | _____ | | 15. 185.50 | 70 | _____ |
| | | | | | 16. 139.98 | $37\frac{1}{2}$ | _____ |
| | | | | | 17. 47.80 | 75 | _____ |
| | | | | | 18. 910.00 | $133\frac{1}{3}$ | _____ |

| Cost | Selling Price | Amount of Markup | Markup % |
|---|---|---|---|
| 6. $ 1.70 | $ 2.50 | _____ | _____ |
| 7. 4.80 | 5.95 | _____ | _____ |
| 8. 32.50 | 79.95 | _____ | _____ |
| 9. 165.00 | 330.00 | _____ | _____ |
| 10. 300.00 | 800.00 | _____ | _____ |

| Selling Price | Markup % | Cost |
|---|---|---|
| 19. 149.50 | 160 | _____ |
| 20. 1,595.00 | 180 | _____ |

*Student's Score* _____

# Part B

## Selling Price as the Base for Markup

**Directions:** In the following problems markup is based on selling price. Find the parts indicated by the column headings, and write your answers in the spaces provided. (1 point for each correct answer in Problems 21-30; 3 points for each correct answer in Problems 31-40)

| | Selling Price | Markup % | Amount of Markup | Cost | | | Cost | Markup % | Selling Price |
|---|---|---|---|---|---|---|---|---|---|
| 21. | $ 21.59 | 20 | _____ | _____ | | 31. $ | 0.75 | 5 | _____ |
| 22. | 19.98 | 33⅓ | _____ | _____ | | 32. | 1.33 | 12½ | _____ |
| 23. | 43.20 | 37½ | _____ | _____ | | 33. | 12.84 | 25 | _____ |
| 24. | 223.75 | 45 | _____ | _____ | | 34. | 22.80 | 16⅔ | _____ |
| 25. | 798.00 | 60 | _____ | _____ | | 35. | 46.20 | 40 | _____ |
| | | | | | | 36. | 235.60 | 37½ | _____ |
| | | | | | | 37. | 146.66 | 66⅔ | _____ |

| | Cost | Selling Price | Amount of Markup | Markup % | | | Cost | Markup % | Selling Price |
|---|---|---|---|---|---|---|---|---|---|
| | | | | | | 38. | 588.00 | 75 | _____ |
| | | | | | | 39. | 1,250.00 | 60 | _____ |
| 26. | $ 19.16 | $ 23.95 | _____ | _____ | | 40. | 1,889.00 | 80 | _____ |
| 27. | 189.50 | 350.00 | _____ | _____ | | | | | |
| 28. | 400.00 (Less 40% and 20%) | 400.00 | _____ | _____ | | | | | |
| 29. | 6.48 | 14.85 | _____ | _____ | | | | | |
| 30. | 15.46 | 30.00 | _____ | _____ | | | | | |

*Student's Score* _____

# Section 10-2  Profit and Loss

In connection with the selling of goods, some general considerations on profit and loss and on marking goods are in order. The cost of the goods sold and the operating expenses necessary to sell the goods determine whether there is a net profit or a net loss.

When the selling price is fixed the first time, part of the markup added to the cost is the expected net profit. However, if the goods do not sell well or if a special sale is planned, the goods may be *marked down* to a lower selling price. As a result the profit is decreased; or there may be a net loss instead of a profit.

### Part A  Net Profit

In Section 10-1 it was pointed out that markup often is a predetermined percent of the cost or of the selling price. The markup percent is broken down into the percent alloted to operating expenses (OE) and the percent for the desired net profit (NP). The base used may be either cost or selling price. Generally the base is determined when sales and costs are being analyzed.

The basic markup equation given on page 221 may be expanded to:

$$SP = C + OE + NP$$

*Examples:* Find the selling price.

a. Cost is $11.64; OE is $3.92; NP is $0.93.

  $SP = \$11.64 + \$3.92 + \$0.93 = \$16.49$

b. Cost is $562.04; OE is $340.46; NP is $47.50.

  $SP = \$562.04 + \$340.46 + \$47.50 = \$950.00$

The expanded markup equation given above can be reworked so that cost, operating expenses, and net profit also can be expressed in terms of the other parts. In other words, when any three parts of the equation are known, the fourth one can be found. Simply start with the basic equation for the selling price; then subtract from both sides the parts necessary to have the required part stand alone.

To find the cost when the other three parts are known, subtract the operating expenses and net

profit from both sides of the equation so that cost is left on one side and the known three parts are on the other.

$$
\begin{aligned}
SP &= C + OE + NP \\
SP - OE - NP &= C + OE + NP \\
&\quad - OE - NP \\
C &= SP - OE - NP
\end{aligned}
$$

*Examples:* Find the cost.

a. SP is $9.95; OE is $3.48; NP is $0.50.

  $C = \$9.95 - \$3.48 - \$0.50 = \$5.97$

b. SP is $125.00; OE is $39.50; NP is $10.50.

  $C = \$125.00 - \$39.50 - \$10.50 = \$75.00$

To find the operating expenses when the other three parts are known, subtract the cost and the net profit from both sides of the equation so that operating expenses are alone on one side of the equation.

$$
\begin{aligned}
SP &= C + OE + NP \\
SP - C - NP &= C + OE + NP \\
&\quad - C - NP \\
OE &= SP - C - NP
\end{aligned}
$$

*Examples:* Find the operating expenses.

a. SP is $28.50; C is $18.68; NP is $1.27.

  $OE = \$28.50 - \$18.68 - \$1.27 = \$8.55$

b. SP is $298.95; C is $194.42; NP is $14.84.

  $OE = \$298.95 - \$192.42 - \$14.84 = \$89.69$

To find the net profit when the other three parts are known, subtract the cost and the operating expenses from both sides of the equation so that net profit is alone on one side.

$$
\begin{aligned}
SP &= C + OE + NP \\
SP - C - OE &= C + OE + NP \\
&\quad - C - OE \\
NP &= SP - C - OE
\end{aligned}
$$

*Examples:* Find the net profit.

a. SP is $39.97; C is $23.80; OE is $14.97.

   NP = $39.97 − $23.80 − $14.97 = $1.20

b. SP is $455.00; C is $256.60; OE is $171.10.

   NP = $455.00 − $256.60 − $171.10 = $27.30

## Part B Net Loss

After a selling price has been reduced, the sum of the cost and the operating expenses may be greater than the selling price. This means that there is a net loss (NL) instead of a net profit.

The selling price may be less than the cost itself, or it may be larger than the cost but less than the cost and operating expenses together. In either case, the equation for the selling price becomes:

$$SP = C + OE - NL$$

*Examples:* Find the selling price.

a. Cost is $11.35; OE is $3.72; NL is $4.07.

   SP = $11.35 + $3.72 − $4.07 = $11.00

b. Cost is $256.32; OE is $110.17; NL is $66.49.

   SP = $256.32 + $110.17 − $66.49 = $300.00

Just as when there is a net profit, the selling price equation can be reworked when there is a net loss. That is, cost, operating expenses, and net loss can be expressed in terms of the other parts. In cases of net loss, however, both addition and subtraction are necessary to have the required part stand alone.

To find the cost when the other three parts are known, subtract the operating expenses from both sides of the equation but add the net loss to both sides so that the cost is left alone on one side.

$$\begin{aligned} SP &= C + OE - NL \\ SP - OE + NL &= C + OE - NL \\ &\quad - OE + NL \\ C &= SP - OE + NL \end{aligned}$$

*Examples:* Find the cost.

a. SP is $12.50; OE is $3.79; NL is $4.27.

   C = $12.50 − $3.79 + $4.27 = $12.98

b. SP is $28.75; OE is $6.03; NL is $2.82.

   C = $28.75 − $6.03 + $2.82 = $25.54

To find the operating expenses when the other three parts are known, subtract the cost from both sides of the equation but add the net loss to both sides so that the operating expenses are alone on one side.

$$\begin{aligned} SP &= C + OE - NL \\ SP - C + NL &= C + OE - NL \\ &\quad - OE + NL \\ OE &= SP - C + NL \end{aligned}$$

*Examples:* Find the operating expenses.

a. SP is $64.00; C is $67.80; NL is $23.33.

   OE = $64.00 − $67.80 + $23.33
      = $64.00 + $23.33 − $67.80 = $19.53

Note that the $64.00 and $23.33 are added first in order to subtract the $67.80. This regrouping is unnecessary if the problem is worked on a calculator which can perform the calculation in the first sequence.

b. SP is $75.00; C is $54.63; NL is $7.44.

   OE = $75.00 − $54.63 + $7.44 = $27.81

To find the net loss when the other three parts are known, subtract the selling price from both sides of the equation but add the net loss to both sides so that the net loss is alone on one side.

$$\begin{aligned} SP &= C + OE - NL \\ SP - SP + NL &= C + OE - NL \\ &\quad - SP + NL \\ NL &= C + OE - SP \end{aligned}$$

*Examples:* Find the net loss.

a. SP is $5.49; C is $6.32; OE is $1.98.

   NL = $6.32 + $1.98 − $5.49 = $2.81

b. SP is $15.95; C is $13.70; OE is $4.36.

NL = $13.70 + $4.36 − $15.95 = $2.11

At this point the student should be aware that the mathematics of retailing is far more complex than the basic concepts presented here.

| | Cost Plus Markup | | Adjusted Selling Price |
|---|---|---|---|
| a. | 8¢ | .................. | 8¢ |
| b. | 23¢ | .................. | 25¢ |
| c. | 67¢ | .................. | 69¢ |
| d. | $ 2.44 | .................. | $ 2.49 |
| e. | $ 5.07 | .................. | $ 5.39 |
| f. | $ 6.73 | .................. | $ 6.98 |
| g. | $ 12.36 | .................. | $ 12.49 |
| h. | $ 23.64 | .................. | $ 23.98 |
| i. | $ 32.17 | .................. | $ 34.98 |
| j. | $ 46.90 | .................. | $ 49.98 |
| k. | $ 80.06 | .................. | $ 79.98 |
| l. | $271.82 | .................. | $279.98 |

## Part C  Adjusting the Selling Price

Up to this point the selling price has been taken as the cost plus the desired markup. Most manufacturers and wholesale distributors use this as the unit price quoted for a product. Most retailers, however, adjust this unit price to "even money" or to the more popular prices ending in 5, 7, 8, or 9. For example, if the cost plus markup on a product amounts to $26.32, a retailer may offer the product at an adjusted selling price of $26.00, $26.35, $26.57, $26.98, or even $26.99, depending upon the store's policy and the prices used by competitors.

Table 10-1 below illustrates an adjustment policy used by some retailers. To use the table, find the given cost plus markup in one of the price ranges at the left, and then adjust the selling price according to the ending given at the right.

*Examples:* Adjust the selling price according to Table 10-1.

Items under 50¢ often are priced in quantity on the basis of the adjusted price. For example, two items may be priced at twice the adjusted price less 1¢, such as 25¢ each or 2 for 49¢; three items at three times the adjusted price less 2¢, such as 19¢ each or 3 for 55¢ ($3 \times 19¢ − 2¢$); and four items at four times the adjusted price less 3¢, such as 13¢ each or 4 for 49¢ ($4 \times 13¢ − 3¢$).

*Examples:* Adjust the given quantity prices according to the policies stated above.

| | Cost Plus Markup | Adjusted Unit Selling Price | Adjusted Quantity Price |
|---|---|---|---|
| a. | 8¢ | 8¢ | 2 for 15¢ |
| b. | 22¢ | 25¢ | 2 for 49¢ |
| c. | 18¢ | 19¢ | 3 for 55¢ |
| d. | 37¢ | 39¢ | 3 for $1.15 |
| e. | 13¢ | 13¢ | 4 for 49¢ |
| f. | 24¢ | 25¢ | 4 for 97¢ |

## Table 10-1  Adjustment Policy

| Cost Plus Markup | Adjusted Selling Price |
|---|---|
| 15¢ or under .............................. | same as determined |
| 16¢ to 99¢ .............................. | ends in the next nearest 5¢ or 9¢ |
| $1 to $ 4.99.............................. | ends in the next 9¢ |
| $5 to $ 9.99.............................. | ends in the next nearest .39, .69, or .98 |
| $10 to $19.99.............................. | ends in the next nearest .49 or .98 |
| $20 to $29.99.............................. | ends in the next .98 |
| $30 to $49.99.............................. | ends in the next nearest 4.98 or 9.98 |
| $50 and up.............................. | ends in 9.98, either up or down |

Occasionally a retailer tempts a customer to buy in quantities that provide no real savings. For example, 25¢ each or 4 for $1.00 and 15¢ each or 10 for $1.50 are the same price whether bought singly or in quantity. In packaged or bottled goods that are sold by weight or fluid measure, the larger sizes sometimes are priced higher than the smaller sizes. For example, 16 ounces or 454 grams at 69¢ costs more per unit of measure than 12 ounces or 340 grams at 49¢. The alert consumer should be able to figure out which prices actually provide savings.

# Part D Using Price Tag Codes

Some merchandise, such as coats, dresses, jewelry, furniture, large appliances, etc., have the selling price on a separate tag. The price tag may include the cost in letters or in code. In the case of some items, such as expensive jewelry, both the cost and the selling price may be given in code. Having the cost on the tag enables the retailer to change the marked selling price without going below the cost. It is also helpful at inventory time.

A code may consist of a word or phrase which has a combination of 10 different letters, such as PURCHASING, ENOUGH TALK, BOY AND GIRL, etc. The first letter is used for 1, the second for 2, etc. The last letter is for 0. An additional different letter may be used as a repeater when the same digit occurs in succession in the marked price.

*Examples:* Using PURCHASING as the code with B for a repeater, write the given numbers in code.

P U R C H A S I N G
1 2 3 4 5 6 7 8 9 0

a. $5.63 ............................. HAR

b. $10.74 ........................... PGSC

c. $881.22 .......................... IBPUB

A numerical code may also be used in which the cost figures are manipulated according to a scheme devised by the company. For example, a cost of $34.71 may be coded 724963 according to the following scheme: Double the cost, reverse the digits of the result, and then place these digits between any two meaningless digits which are never the same.

*Examples:* Write the given numbers in the numerical code given above.

a. $8.36 ........................... 427615

b. $97.70 .......................... 6045913

c. $72.25 .......................... 1054417

Complete Assignment 30

# Assignment 30
# Section 10-2

## Profit and Loss

|         | Perfect Score | Student's Score |
|---------|---------------|-----------------|
| Part A  | 30            |                 |
| Part B  | 30            |                 |
| Part C  | 30            |                 |
| Part D  | 10            |                 |
| TOTAL   | 100           |                 |

## Part A

### Net Profit

**Directions:** Fill in the missing amount. Write your answers in the spaces provided. (3 points for each correct answer)

|     | Cost      | Operating Expenses | Net Profit | Selling Price |
|-----|-----------|--------------------|------------|---------------|
| 1.  | $  26.70  | $_____        | $  1.45    | $  34.50      |
| 2.  | _____ | 6.75              | 1.06       | 18.95         |
| 3.  | 19.47     | 3.04              | 2.25       | _____    |
| 4.  | 294.11    | 156.32            | _____ | 487.50        |
| 5.  | 8.74      | 2.38              | 0.88       | _____    |
| 6.  | 72.00     | _____        | 3.00       | 106.00        |
| 7.  | 21.45     | 13.47             | _____ | 36.89         |
| 8.  | _____ | 7.83             | 5.40       | 75.38         |
| 9.  | 71.32     | 8.95              | 5.76       | _____    |
| 10. | 115.09    | 51.06             | _____ | 179.50        |

*Student's Score* _____

## Part B

### Net Loss

**Directions:** Fill in the missing amounts. Write your answers in the spaces provided. (3 points for each correct answer)

|     | Cost      | Operating Expenses | Net Loss   | Selling Price |
|-----|-----------|--------------------|------------|---------------|
| 11. | $_____ | $  0.81          | $  1.24    | $  7.69       |
| 12. | 12.39     | 1.84              | 3.73       | _____    |
| 13. | 28.00     | _____        | 5.11       | 25.69         |
| 14. | 46.78     | 6.30              | 9.90       | _____    |
| 15. | 61.31     | 10.22             | _____ | 61.95         |
| 16. | _____ | 3.64             | .99        | 57.96         |
| 17. | 74.50     | 9.86              | _____ | 76.50         |
| 18. | 3.19      | _____        | .27        | 3.59          |
| 19. | _____ | 21.50            | 14.68      | 159.00        |
| 20. | 821.40    | 97.00             | _____ | 840.00        |

*Student's Score* _____

# Part C

## Adjusting the Selling Price

*Directions:* Find the adjusted selling price according to the schedule given below in the right-hand column. Write your answers in the spaces provided. (2 points for each correct answer)

| | Cost | Adjusted Selling Price | Cost Plus Markup | Adjusted Selling Price |
|---|---|---|---|---|
| 21. | $ 0.026 | _____ | 0 to .15 | nearest cent |
| 22. | .17 | _____ | .16 to .19 | 19¢ |
| | | | .20 to .25 | 25¢ |
| 23. | .24 | _____ | .26 to .29 | 29¢ |
| 24. | .375 | _____ | .30 to .35 | 35¢ |
| | | | .36 to .39 | 39¢ |
| 25. | .61 | _____ | .40 to .45 | 45¢ |
| | | | .46 to .49 | 49¢ |
| 26. | .77 | _____ | .50 to .55 | 55¢ |
| | | | .56 to .59 | 59¢ |
| 27. | .93 | _____ | .60 to .65 | 65¢ |
| 28. | 2.05 | _____ | .66 to .69 | 69¢ |
| | | | .70 to .75 | 75¢ |
| 29. | 6.53 | _____ | .76 to .79 | 79¢ |
| 30. | 14.78 | _____ | .80 to .85 | 85¢ |
| | | | .86 to .89 | 89¢ |
| 31. | 90.60 | _____ | .90 to .95 | 95¢ |
| | | | .96 to .99 | 99¢ |
| 32. | 135.74 | _____ | $ 1 to $4.99 ending in next 9¢ |
| 33. | .11 | 2 for _____ | $ 5 to $9.99 ending in next .49 or .99 |
| 34. | .13 | 3 for _____ | $10 to $19.99 ending in next .99 |
| 35. | .23 | 4 for _____ | $20 and up ending in next nearest 4.95 or 9.95 |

For quantities of 2:  (2 × adjusted price) − 1¢
For quantities of 3:  (3 × adjusted price) − 2¢
For quantities of 4:  (4 × adjusted price) − 3¢

*Student's Score* _____

# Part D

## Using Price Tag Codes

*Directions:* In the spaces provided write the codes for the given costs. For the numerical code, double the given cost, reverse it, and place the result between meaningless digits. (2 points for each correct answer)

| | | | |
|---|---|---|---|
| 36. | $ 25.76 | REPUBLICAN (Repeater Q) | _____ |
| 37. | 673.81 | COME AND BUY (Repeater L) | _____ |
| 38. | 499.05 | REDISCOUNT (Repeater P) | _____ |
| 39. | 63.15 | (Numerical) | _____ |
| 40. | 240.79 | (Numerical) | _____ |

*Student's Score* _____

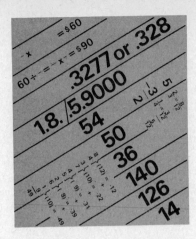

# CHAPTER 11

# Figuring Gross Pay for Payrolls

A **payroll** is a record of the earnings paid to individuals classified as employees. Various terms are used in place of the word "earnings." Generally the term **wages** refers to payment for total hours of work at a given hourly rate, for total pieces produced at a given rate per piece, or for a combination of both. The term **salary** refers to payment set for a week, a month, or a year. The term **commission** refers to payment based on dollar sales made by the individual within a specified period of time.

**Gross pay** is the total amount earned before any deductions are made. It is the amount on which the employee's taxes are figured. The deductions from the employee's gross pay may consist of such items as income and social security taxes, which the employer must withhold by law; union dues; hospital and life insurance premiums; pensions; and so forth. The **net pay** is the amount paid to the employees after all required and authorized deductions have been subtracted from the gross pay.

Preparing a payroll in a large company is often done by means of a computer. In some cases a company may utilize the payroll service offered by many banks. A bank that offers this service charges a fee based on the number of employees on the company's payroll. It also reconciles the separate checking account kept by the company for payroll purposes. Many companies, however, still prepare their own payrolls without using a computer or a banking service. Since the forms and methods used in preparing a payroll vary from company to company and from state to state, only certain common features will be discussed in this chapter.

The principal methods of paying employees are based on any one of the following elements: time, piecework, or commission. Payment may also be made on the basis of various combinations of these elements. Section 11-1 deals with the time basis, in which payment may be based on an hourly, weekly, biweekly (every two weeks), semimonthly (twice a month), or monthly rate. At the end of this section is a brief discussion of payroll deductions that are required by law. Section 11-2 covers the methods of payment based on piecework and on commission.

## Section 11-1    Time Basis Payment and Payroll Deductions

A **time card**, or a **time sheet**, is used to keep a record of the total hours worked by an employee paid on a time basis. Where a time clock is used, each company has its own policy on the time limits for punching in and out without penalty for the regular work period. **Overtime**, which is time worked beyond the regular hours, is punched in separate columns.

## Part A *Straight Time (or Day Rate) Pay*

When the hours worked are all regular, or **straight time**, the gross pay equals the number of hours worked times the given hourly rate. This hourly rate often is called the **day rate**, especially in combination with a piecework payment plan.

*Example:* Eva Thompson is paid $3.25 an hour for straight time. Find her gross pay for a week in which she worked 40 hours.

Gross pay = 40 × $3.25 = $130.00

## Part B *Overtime Pay on a Weekly Basis*

A **standard workweek** usually is 40 hours, but it may be longer or shorter. The **regular pay** is the pay for the standard workweek hours at the given rate. When an overtime rate is paid for hours worked beyond the standard workweek, this is called **overtime on a weekly basis**. The **overtime pay** is the pay for the overtime hours at the overtime rate.

In accordance with the Federal Wage and Hour Law, companies which engage in interstate commerce must pay time and a half for all hours over 40 worked in one week. State laws and most union contracts also specify when overtime must be paid.

Most companies pay overtime at one and a half times the regular rate (time and a half), but may pay two or three times the regular rate for work done on Saturdays, Sundays, or holidays.

To find the overtime rate, multiply the hourly rate by $1\frac{1}{2}$ (or 2 or 3). To find the overtime pay, multiply the number of overtime hours by the overtime rate. The gross pay is the sum of the regular pay and the overtime pay.

*Examples:*

a. John Doherty earns $4.00 per hour for a 40-hour standard workweek and time and a half for overtime. Find his gross pay for a week in which he worked 45 hours.

Overtime rate = $4 × $1\frac{1}{2}$ = $6.00 per hr

| | | | |
|---|---|---|---|
| Regular pay | = 40 × $4 | = $160.00 |
| Overtime pay | = 5 × $6 | = 30.00 |
| Gross pay | | = $190.00 |

b. Geraldine Brent earns $4.50 per hour, with overtime paid on a weekly basis. According to the union contract, all hours over 40 worked on Monday through Friday are paid at time and a half; all hours on Saturday at double time; and all hours on Sunday or a holiday at triple time. Find her gross pay for a week in which she worked these hours:

| S | M | T | W | Th | F | S |
|---|---|---|---|----|---|---|
| 4 | 8 | 8 | 0 | 10 | 8 | 4 |

| | |
|---|---|
| Monday through Friday | = 42 hours |
| Straight time | = 40 hours |
| Overtime at time and a half | = 2 hours |
| Overtime at double time (Sat.) | = 4 hours |
| Overtime at triple time (Sun.) | = 4 hours |

| | | |
|---|---|---|
| Overtime rate at time and a half ..... | $4.50 × $1\frac{1}{2}$ = | $ 6.75 |
| Overtime rate at double time ........ | $4.50 × 2 = | $ 9.00 |
| Overtime rate at triple time ......... | $4.50 × 3 = | $ 13.50 |

| | | | |
|---|---|---|---|
| Regular pay: | 40 × $4.50 | = $180.00 |
| Overtime pay: | 2 × $6.75 | = 13.50 |
| | 4 × $9.00 | = 36.00 |
| | 4 × $13.50 | = 54.00 |
| Gross pay | | = $283.50 |

Originally overtime pay was figured by taking the actual overtime hours and multiplying them by $1\frac{1}{2}$, or "time and a half," (in *Example a* this would be 5 hours × $1\frac{1}{2}$, or $7\frac{1}{2}$ hours) and then multiplying the total overtime hours by the regular hourly rate ($7\frac{1}{2}$ × $4.00 = $30.00). This method is rarely used today.

## Part C *Overtime Pay on a Daily Basis*

A company may pay for **overtime on a daily basis**, which means that all hours worked over the regular workday hours (usually 8) are paid at the overtime rate. In the examples below, a regular workday of 8 hours is used.

By federal law, companies that have federal contracts must pay time and a half for any hours over 8 worked in a day or over 40 in one week, *whichever is greater*. Many union contracts specify that all time over the regular workday hours in the standard workweek (usually Monday through Friday, but not including holidays) and all time worked on the remaining two days (usually Saturday and Sunday) and on holidays must be paid at the overtime rate. Even though the total hours worked are less than 40, the overtime rate must be paid as specified.

## Examples:

a. Joyce Miller is paid $5.00 per hour, with overtime on a daily basis at time and a half. Find her gross pay for the following time worked:

| | S | M | T | W | Th | F | S | |
|---|---|---|---|---|---|---|---|---|
| | 0 | 6 | 6 | 10 | 10 | 8 | 0 | |
| Straight time: | 0 | 6 | 6 | 8 | 8 | 0 | | = 36 |
| Overtime: | | 0 | 0 | 0 | 2 | 2 | 0 | 0 | = 4 |

Overtime rate = $5.00 × $1\frac{1}{2}$ = $7.50

| | | |
|---|---|---|
| Regular pay | = 36 × $5.00 | = $180.00 |
| Overtime pay | = 4 × $7.50 | = 30.00 |
| Gross pay | | = $210.00 |

b. Charles Adams is paid $5.25 per hour, with overtime on a daily basis at time and a half for Monday through Friday, but double time for Saturday, Sunday, or a legal holiday. Find his gross pay for the following time worked:

| | S | M | T | W | Th | F | S |
|---|---|---|---|---|---|---|---|
| | 0 | 8 | 9 | 9 | 8 | 0 | 8 |
| Straight time: | 0 | 8 | 8 | 8 | 8 | 0 | 0 |
| Overtime: | 0 | 0 | 1 | 1 | 0 | 0 | 8 |

Overtime rate at
time and a half ....$5.25 × $1\frac{1}{2}$ = $ 7.875
Overtime rate at
double time .......$5.25 × 2 = $10.50

| Regular pay: | 32 × $5.25 | = $168.00 |
|---|---|---|
| Overtime pay: | 2 × $7.875 | = 15.75 |
| | 8 × $10.50 | = 84.00 |
| Gross pay | | = $267.75 |

Note that if a rate has an exact half-cent ending, such as $7.875, generally the three decimal places are used.

## Part D Overtime Pay for Salaried Employees

Salaried employees above a certain management level are classified as **exempt** and do not receive overtime pay. However, there are many non-exempt salaried employees who are also eligible for overtime pay. The salary per week or per month is converted to an hourly rate. The overtime hours are figured on either a weekly or a daily basis, depending upon the company's policy.

To find the hourly rate for a *weekly* salary, divide the salary by the number of hours in the regular workweek.

*Example:* Richard Braun is paid $225 for a regular workweek of $37\frac{1}{2}$ hours, with overtime paid at time and a half. Find his gross pay for a week in which he had $4\frac{1}{2}$ hours of overtime.

Hourly rate = $225 ÷ $37\frac{1}{2}$ = $6.00 per hr
Overtime rate = $6 × $1\frac{1}{2}$ = $9.00 per hr

| Regular pay: | = $225.00 |
|---|---|
| Overtime pay: $4\frac{1}{2}$ × $9.00 | = 40.50 |
| Gross pay | $265.50 |

For payroll purposes, generally a month is considered to have $4\frac{1}{3}$ weeks. To find the hourly rate for a *monthly* salary, divide the salary by the product of the hours in the regular workweek times $4\frac{1}{3}$.

*Example:* Judy Ross earns $900 a month and is paid semimonthly. The regular workweek is 40 hours, with overtime paid at time and a half. Find her gross pay for a half-month in which she had 10 hours of overtime.

Hourly rate = $900 ÷ (40 × $4\frac{1}{3}$) hr
= $900 ÷ $173\frac{1}{3}$ = $5.19 per hr
Overtime rate = $7.785

Regular pay: $\frac{1}{2} \times \$900$     = $450.00
Overtime pay: $10 \times \$7.785$     = 77.85
Gross pay     = $527.85

## Part E   Payroll Deductions

Only deductions required by law or union contracts and those authorized by the individual employee should be taken from the gross pay. Because of the many variations in employee deductions and in the payroll records kept by employers, only deductions required by law and a few general points on the subject are discussed here. For this reason, *net pay* problems are not included in the Assignments for this chapter.

*FICA taxes.* The Federal Insurance Contributions Act (FICA), commonly called Social Security, applies to most people who work in the United States. Individuals who are classified as employees in the covered occupations of this Act must have a social security number and must pay a certain percent of their gross pay toward Social Security and Medicare. The employer is required to deduct the FICA tax from the employee's earnings and to match it in an equal amount.

Self-employed people also are covered by FICA but must send in their own contributions. Booklets explaining the provisions of the FICA are available without charge from the Social Security Administration (SSA).

The U.S. Congress has increased the FICA tax rate and maximum earnings base many times since Social Security went into effect in 1937. To have the correct figures, get the current rates and maximum earnings base either from your instructor or the SSA.

*Federal income taxes.* The employer also is required to withhold, or deduct, federal income taxes for employees in occupations covered by law. The amount deducted each pay period depends upon the employee's gross earnings, the current income tax rate, and the number of exemptions declared by the employee on a W-4 form. The W-4 form must be filled out each time an employee starts a new job.

*State and city income taxes.* Not all states and cities impose income taxes. But where such taxes

are required, deductions for them are withheld from the employee's gross earnings. In addition, deductions are also required for employee contributions toward accident or disability funds where they are in effect.

*Annual tax guides.* The Internal Revenue Service (IRS) prepares an annual Employer's Tax Guide which shows the amounts by wage brackets that should be withheld for federal income taxes and FICA taxes. The revenue departments of those states and cities in which income taxes must be withheld from an employee's gross earnings also prepare annual tax guides. Many companies which use a computer for payroll, however, use simplified tables or formulas, rather than the tax guides, to compute the income taxes and FICA taxes to be withheld.

*Employer's tax reports.* Employers are required to deposit in an authorized bank, within a specific time, all amounts withheld for income taxes and Social Security, as well as their matching FICA contributions. They must also file with IRS a quarterly report which shows the wages paid to each employee during the quarter. As employers, they must pay federal and state taxes for unemployment and disability funds and file the necessary quarterly returns. The state rates for these funds vary considerably; for the past few years, the federal rate has been .7% on a maximum of $4,200, but this is subject to change as necessary.

*Employee's earnings record.* Because of the required government reports, most employers keep an Employee's Earnings Record for each employee, in addition to other payroll records. This record shows the employee's name, address, social security number, number of exemptions claimed, rate of pay, gross earnings, deductions, net pay for each pay period, and the total to date of the gross earnings and the taxes withheld. Shortly after the end of the year, the employer is required by law to give two or more copies of a W-2 form to each employee. The W-2 form shows the total amounts of gross pay and taxes withheld, and it must be attached to income tax returns.

Complete Assignment 31

# Assignment 31
# Section 11-1

| | Perfect Score | Student's Score |
|---|---|---|
| Parts A & B | 40 | |
| Part C | 40 | |
| Part D | 20 | |
| TOTAL | 100 | |

*Time Basis Payment and Payroll Deductions*

## Parts A and B

### Straight Time Pay and Overtime Pay on a Weekly Basis

The Abbot Company has a regular workweek of 40 hours with overtime paid on a weekly basis at time and a half. Find the overtime rate, the overtime hours, the regular pay, the overtime pay, and the gross pay for each employee. (2 points for each correct answer)

| Name and Time Worked | Hourly Rate | Overtime Rate | Overtime Hours | Regular Pay | Overtime Pay | Gross Pay |
|---|---|---|---|---|---|---|
| 1. William Boyle | $4.20 | _____ | _____ | _____ | _____ | _____ |
| M T W Th F S<br>7 9 10 10 8 10 | | | | | | |
| 2. Annette Felippo | 3.80 | _____ | _____ | _____ | _____ | _____ |
| M T W Th F S<br>8 10 8 0 8 0 | | | | | | |
| 3. James Grabowski | 5.65 | _____ | _____ | _____ | _____ | _____ |
| M T W Th F S<br>8 8 9 8 8 4 | | | | | | |
| 4. Freda Huss | 4.90 | _____ | _____ | _____ | _____ | _____ |
| M T W Th F S<br>8 6 10 0 8 8 | | | | | | |

*Student's Score* _____

## Part C

### Overtime Pay on a Daily Basis

The Lemon Products Company pays overtime on a daily basis at time and a half for all work over 8 hours per day, Monday through Friday, and at double time for all work on Saturdays, Sundays, or legal holidays. Find the overtime rate at time and a half, the overtime rate at double time, the regular pay, the overtime pay, and the gross pay for each employee. (2 points for each correct answer)

| | Hourly Rate | Time and a Half Rate | Double Time Rate | Regular Pay | Overtime Pay | Gross Pay |
|---|---|---|---|---|---|---|
| 5. Richard Morton | $5.50 | _____ | _____ | _____ | _____ | _____ |
| S M T W Th F S<br>0 8 10 8 6 8 0 | | | | | | |
| 6. Barbara Chan | 4.76 | _____ | _____ | _____ | _____ | _____ |
| S M T W Th F S<br>8 0 8 8 8 8 8 | | | | | | |
| 7. Robert Ryczek | 5.00 | _____ | _____ | _____ | _____ | _____ |
| S M T W Th F S<br>0 4 8 8 10 8 4 | | | | | | |
| 8. Elizabeth Wallner | 0.50 | _____ | _____ | _____ | _____ | _____ |
| S M T W Th F S<br>0 8 8 9 9 11 4  (Monday was a legal holiday) | | | | | | |

*Student's Score* _____

# Part D

## *Overtime Pay for Salaried Employees*

9. Jane Jansen earns $220 for a regular work-week of 38 hours. Overtime is paid at time and a half. Find her gross pay for a week in which she had 8 hours of overtime. Write your answer in the space provided. (5 points)

Gross Pay_____

10. William Cuerva earns $280 for a regular workweek of 40 hours. Overtime is paid at time and a half for all overtime Monday through Friday, and double time for all work on Saturday and Sunday. Find his gross pay for a week in which he had a total of 6 hours of overtime Monday through Friday and 4 hours on Saturday. Write your answer in the space provided. (5 points)

Gross Pay_____

11. Kevin Krohn earns $980 a month and is paid semimonthly. The regular workweek is 36 hours with overtime paid at time and a half. Find his gross pay for a half-month in which he worked a total of 20 hours overtime. Write your answer in the space provided. (5 points)

Gross Pay _____

12. Paula Winters earns $825 a month and is paid semimonthly. All work over 8 hours, Monday through Friday, and all work on Saturdays or legal holidays is paid at time and a half. Find her gross pay for a period in which she worked the hours listed below. Write your answer in the space provided. (5 points)

| S | M | T | W | Th | F | S |
|---|---|---|---|---|---|---|
| | | | | 8 | 8 | 4 |
| 0 | 8 | 9 | 6 | 0 | 8 | 4 |
| 0 | 8 | 8 | 8 | 9 | | |

Gross Pay_____

*Student's Score* _____

# Section 11-2 Piecework and Commission Methods of Payment

Part A of this section deals with the various methods of figuring wages based on piecework production. The different methods of paying for earnings on a commission basis are discussed in Part B.

## Part A Various Plans of Piecework Payment

Piecework payment can be based on straight piecework, on a combination of piecework with bonus, or on piecework with an hourly base rate.

For each of these three plans, daily reports of the work done by each employee are necessary not only for computing the payroll but also to find total labor expenses for pricing the finished products. The most common form of record is called a **time** or **labor ticket**. This record contains all the information needed for payroll and cost purposes such as the employee's name, clock number, date, rate, time worked, pieces produced, order number, job number, job code, etc. The time on each job, the number of pieces produced, and all other necessary information are recorded by the employee or a production clerk. The labor ticket must be signed by the employee's supervisor.

In the problems given in this Part, the employee is assumed to produce pieces at only one rate. In many shops, however, the employee may work at several jobs that have different rates in the course of one day. The labor ticket in Figure 11-1 below is an example of a job in which 7 pieces were produced in 3.5 hours at a rate of $2.01 per piece.

Many companies now use a computerized production control card instead of separate labor tickets. The computer prints out all the information necessary to process an order. There are enough spaces on the face and the back of the card to record the production of all the employees who have worked on the order. Upon completion, the information is fed into the computer for payroll and accounting purposes.

*Straight piecework.* When payment is made for the total number of pieces produced in a regular workday—which is usually 8 hours—the gross daily wages equal the number of pieces produced times the rate per piece. Many companies, however, combine piecework with a day rate so that the employee receives whichever amount is greater as the wages for the day.

*Examples:*

a. Richard Brown receives 21¢ for each piece assembled in a regular 8-hour day or a day rate of $5.50 per hour, whichever is greater. Find his gross wages for the week in which he produced the following:

## Figure 11-1 Labor Ticket

**LABOR TICKET**

Order No. _07-892-0056_   Quantity Required _10_   Drawing No. _4-155-1049_ Part _Shaft_
Clock No. _5047_
Name _Arthur Willis_                              Date _8/29/--_

| Job No. | Description of Work | Hours | Rate | Amount | IN | OUT |
|---------|--------------------|-------|------|--------|-----|------|
| 6 | Center and turn | 3.5 | 2.01 | 7 | 12:00 | 3:30 |
| | | | | | | |
| | | | | | | |

Balance Pieces Due ___3___          Supervisor _J. F. Green_

```
   M    T    W    Th   F
  240  250  200  230  220
```

Earnings at day rate = 8 × $5.50 = $44.00

```
M  − 240 ×  $0.21            = $ 50.40
T  − 250 ×   0.21            =   52.50
W  − 200 ×   0.21            =   4̶2̶.̶0̶0̶
   (Day rate is used for W.)  =   44.00
Th − 230 ×   0.21            =   48.30
F  − 220 ×   0.21            =   46.20
Gross wages                  = $241.40
```

**b.** Diane Wells receives 70¢ for each piece produced in a regular 8-hour day or a day rate of $4.50 per hour, whichever is greater. Find her gross wages for the week in which she produced the following:

```
M  T  W  Th  F
56 60 51 50 55
```

Earnings at day rate = 8 × $4.50 = $36.00

```
M  − 56 ×  $0.70             = $ 39.20
T  − 60 ×   0.70             =   42.00
W  − 51 ×   0.70             =   3̶5̶.̶7̶0̶
   (Day rate is used for W.)  =   36.00
Th − 50 ×   0.70             =   3̶5̶.̶0̶0̶
   (Day rate is used for Th.) =   36.00
F  − 55 ×   0.70             =   38.50
Gross wages                  = $191.70
```

**Piecework with bonus.** A straight piecework plan may be combined with a bonus rate for all pieces produced beyond a standard minimum per day. This plan provides an incentive to employees to produce more pieces in a workday.

The daily wages earned in this plan equal the total pieces produced times the straight piecework rate, plus the number of pieces over the standard minimum times the bonus rate.

*Example:* Sarah Zimmerman receives 35¢ for each piece assembled in a regular 8-hour day, plus a 10¢ bonus for each piece assembled over the standard minimum of 100 pieces per day. Find her gross wages for the week in which she produced the following:

```
 M   T   W   Th   F
120  90 130 150  128
```

```
M − 120 × $0.35 = $42.00
     20 ×  0.10 = + 2.00      $ 44.00
T −  90 ×  0.35 =               31.50
W − 130 ×  0.35 =   45.50
     30 ×  0.10 = + 3.00        48.50
Th− 150 ×  0.35 =   52.50
     50 ×  0.10 = + 5.00        57.50
F − 128 ×  0.35 =   44.80
     28 ×  0.10 = + 2.80        47.60
Gross Wages     =             $229.10
```

**Piecework with an hourly base rate.** A piecework plan of payment may include time basis payment at an hourly base rate. The hourly base rate is not to be confused with the straight time or day rate; it is generally much lower than the hourly day rate.

Under this plan the daily gross earnings equal the number of hours worked in the regular workday times the base rate, plus the number of pieces produced times the piece rate. If there is overtime, both the base rate and the piece rate are multiplied by 1½ (or 2 or 3) for payment of the overtime hours and the pieces produced in that time. This plan may also be combined with a day rate; that is, when an employee does not "make out" on piecework, he or she is paid the day rate for eight hours.

**Examples:**

**a.** William Manske receives $1.92 for each piece produced in a regular 8-hour workday and a base rate of $2.00 per hour. Overtime is paid at time and a half. Find his gross wages for Monday and Tuesday on which he produced the following:

```
M − 12 pieces in 8 hours
T − 13 pieces in 8 hours and
        3 pieces in 2 hours of overtime
```

Overtime base rate = $2.00 × 1½ = $3.00
Overtime piece rate = $1.92 × 1½ = $2.88

```
M − Reg. time pay:    8 × $2.00 = $16.00
                     12 ×  1.92 =   23.04
T − Reg. time pay:    8 ×  2.00 =   16.00
                     13 ×  1.92 =   24.96
    Overtime pay:     2 ×  3.00 =    6.00
                      3 ×  2.88 =    8.64
Gross wages for M and T         = $94.64
```

b. Mary Balistrieri receives 62¢ for each piece produced in a regular 7-hour workday and a base rate of $2.40 per hour. Overtime is paid at time and a half. Find her gross wages for Wednesday and Thursday on which she produced the following:

W — 46 pieces in 7 hours and
10 pieces in 2 hours of overtime
Th — 50 pieces in 7 hours and
14 pieces in 3 hours of overtime

Overtime base rate = $2.40 × 1½ = $3.60
Overtime piece rate = $0.62 × 1½ = $0.93

| | | | | |
|---|---|---|---|---|
| W — Reg. time pay: | 7 × | $2.40 | = | $ 16.80 |
| | 46 × | 0.62 | = | 28.52 |
| Overtime pay: | 2 × | 3.60 | = | 7.20 |
| | 10 × | 0.93 | = | 9.30 |
| Th — Reg. time pay: | 7 × | 2.40 | = | 16.80 |
| | 50 × | 0.62 | = | 31.00 |
| Overtime pay: | 3 × | 3.60 | = | 10.80 |
| | 14 × | 0.93 | = | 13.02 |
| Gross wages for W and Th | | | = | $133.44 |

## Part B — Various Plans of Commission Payment

A commission basis is used frequently to pay salespeople in both wholesale and retail lines. A **commission** generally is a percent of the individual's sales for a given period, but it may also be a set amount per item sold.

If traveling expenses for the salesperson are involved, the company usually advances a **drawing account**, which is a set amount allowed for payment of expenses as they occur. Whether or not there is a drawing account, an expense sheet must be submitted by the individual since travel expenses are paid by the company apart from the commission.

Salespeople find their total sales for a given period from copies of the invoices or sales slips on orders which were placed with them. From these documents they can figure the commissions due them. When figuring gross amounts due, the travel expenses are added to the commission and the drawing account is subtracted from the total.

Methods of payment may be based on straight commission, on commission and bonus, or on salary and commission.

*Straight commission plan.* In a straight commission basis for payment, the earnings are calculated as a given percent of the total sales for the period.

*Examples:*

a. James Reed receives a 5% commission on his total monthly sales. Find his gross earnings for the month in which his sales were $26,500.

Commission = $26,500 × 5% = $1,325

b. Janis Stover earns a 4% commission on her total sales. Travel expenses are paid by the company, and she is given a drawing account of $600 a month. Find her gross amount (before deductions) for a month in which her sales totaled $32,000 and her expense sheet totaled $619.42.

| | | |
|---|---|---|
| Commission = $32,000 × 4% | = | $1,280.00 |
| Travel expenses | = | + 619.42 |
| Total | = | 1,899.42 |
| Drawing account | = | − 600.00 |
| Gross amount | = | $1,299.42 |

*Commission and bonus plan.* In a commission and bonus basis for payment, a straight commission is given on sales up to a given amount, plus graded bonus commissions for sales above that amount. The gross earnings equal the total of the commissions calculated for each bracket.

*Examples:*

a. Ester Mendoza receives a 3% commission on the first $20,000 of monthly sales; 3½% on the next $10,000; and 4% on all sales beyond $30,000. Find her gross earnings for a month in which her sales totaled $36,496.34.

| | | |
|---|---|---|
| $20,000 × 3% | = | $ 600.00 |
| 10,000 × 3½% | = | 350.00 |
| 6,496.34 × 4% | = | 259.85 |
| Gross earnings | = | $1,209.85 |

b. Thomas Militzer receives a 4% commission on the first $15,000 of monthly sales; 4½% on the next $10,000; and 5% on all sales beyond $25,000. He receives an advance drawing account of $700 a month. Find his gross amount for a month in which his sales were $27,639.80 and his travel expenses were $732.85.

| | | | |
|---|---|---|---|
| $15,000 × 4% | = | $ | 600.00 |
| 10,000 × 4½% | = | | 450.00 |
| 2,639.80 × 5% | = | | 131.99 |
| Total commission earned | = | | 1,181.99 |
| Travel expenses | = | + | 732.85 |
| Total | = | | 1,914.84 |
| Drawing account | = | − | 700.00 |
| Gross amount | = | $ | 1,214.84 |

**Commission and salary plan.** On a salary and commission basis, the gross earnings are the total of a base salary plus the commission earned on total sales.

*Example:* Marian McGee receives a base salary of $150 a week plus a 2% commission on her total weekly sales. Find her gross earnings for a week in which her sales totaled $4,658.31.

| | | | |
|---|---|---|---|
| Commission = $4,658.31 × 2% | = | $ | 93.17 |
| Base salary | = | + | 150.00 |
| Gross earnings | = | $ | 243.17 |

Note that some retail stores pay a commission only on sales above the quota established for the particular department.

Complete Assignment 32

## Assignment 32
## Section 11-2

| | Perfect Score | Student's Score |
|---|---|---|
| Part A | 70 | |
| Part B | 30 | |
| TOTAL | 100 | |

*Piecework and Commission*
*Methods of Payment*

# Part A
### Various Forms of Piecework Payment

The E. G. Williams Company pays its employees on a straight piecework basis for all pieces produced in an 8-hour day or at a given day rate, whichever is greater. Find the daily wages of each employee. (2 points for each correct answer)

| Employee and No. of Pieces | Piece Rate | Day Rate | Daily Wages | | | | |
|---|---|---|---|---|---|---|---|
| | | | Monday | Tuesday | Wednesday | Thursday | Friday |
| 1. John Cord | $0.98 | $4.50 | _____ | _____ | _____ | _____ | _____ |
| M – 54 | | | | | | | |
| T – 42 | | | | | | | |
| W – 40 | | | | | | | |
| Th – 35 | | | | | | | |
| F – 48 | | | | | | | |
| 2. Paula Ross | .30 | 5.75 | _____ | _____ | _____ | _____ | _____ |
| M – 157 | | | | | | | |
| T – 165 | | | | | | | |
| W – 140 | | | | | | | |
| Th – 163 | | | | | | | |
| F – 159 | | | | | | | |

The Jones Electronics Company pays a bonus for all pieces over a standard minimum set for the job. Find the daily earnings of each employee. (5 points for each correct answer)

| Employee | Piece Rate | Bonus Rate | Standard Minimum | Pieces Produced | Daily Earnings |
|---|---|---|---|---|---|
| 3. Kay de Caria | $0.20 | $0.10 | 200 | 250 | _____ |
| 4. Allen Jankowski | .82 | .30 | 50 | 60 | _____ |
| 5. Eva Jones | .64 | .25 | 70 | 80 | _____ |
| 6. Fred Krahn | .25 | .18 | 150 | 208 | _____ |
| 7. Edward Raschka | .93 | .35 | 45 | 52 | _____ |

The Groth Gasket Company pays its employees on a piecework basis combined with an hourly base rate for work produced in an 8-hour day. Overtime is paid at 1½ times the piece rate and the base rate. Find the daily earnings of each employee. (5 points for each correct answer)

| | Regular Time | | | Overtime | | |
|---|---|---|---|---|---|---|
| Employee | Piece Rate | Base Rate | Pieces Produced | Hours | Pieces Produced | Daily Earnings |
| 8. Fran Gregory | $0.25 | $2.00 | 100 | | | _____ |
| 9. Roberto Alvarez | .35 | 1.75 | 90 | | | _____ |
| 10. Barbara Klein | .32 | 2.50 | 115 | | | _____ |
| 11. Jo Lund | .24 | 2.10 | 120 | 2 | 30 | _____ |
| 12. Todd Miller | .28 | 2.90 | 110 | 4 | 50 | _____ |

*Student's Score* _____

# Part B

## *Various Forms of Commission Payment*

The Randolph Company pays its salespeople on a commission basis. A drawing account of $700 a month is allowed for travel expenses. Find the gross amount for each salesperson. (5 points for each correct answer)

| Employee | Sales | Commission | Travel Expenses | Base Salary | Gross Amount |
|---|---|---|---|---|---|
| 13. Donald Ames | $25,000 | 5% | | | _____ |
| 14. Richard Cottam | 35,000 | 3½% | $669.24 | | _____ |
| 15. Kevin Joorabchi | 46,000 | 2% —first $20,000<br>2½%—next $10,000<br>3% —all sales over $30,000 | 718.72 | | _____ |
| 16. Linda Moy | 23,000 | 5% —first $10,000<br>6% —next $10,000<br>6½%—all sales over $20,000 | 754.94 | | _____ |
| 17. Mildred Niesen | 12,000 | 4½% | | $500.00 | _____ |
| 18. George Tanaka | 37,000 | 2% | 692.35 | 600.00 | _____ |

*Student's Score* _____

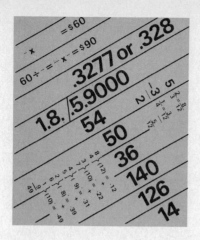

# Figuring Time Payment Plans and Short-Term Loans

**12**

Many retailers offer credit plans to "buy now and pay later." These allow a buyer to take possession of goods or receive services and pay for them over an extended period of time. Usually the deferred payment price consists of the cash price plus a **finance charge**. The finance charge covers such items as: (1) the interest for the loan of money to the customer in the form of goods or services, (2) bookkeeping expenses for recording payments, (3) losses on the goods if payments are not made, and (4) insurance on the goods. In general, three kinds of credit plans are available for deferred payments.

1. A time payment plan in which the buyer makes equal and regular monthly or weekly payments, called **installments**, for a specified number of months or weeks. A down payment often is required.
2. A revolving charge account in which the buyer has the option of paying the full amount due within 30 days without a finance charge or making minimum monthly payments with a finance charge based on the average daily balance. The payments vary with the balance in the account.
3. A 90-day period for payment with a **service charge**, which is usually $1.00, rather than a finance charge.

**Consumer loans**, which are personal, family, or household loans, are often repaid with time payment plans. The monthly or weekly payments cover the amount of the loan plus a finance charge. Section 12-1 deals with figuring finance charges, amounts of the installments, and the annual percentage rates in time payment plans.

As distinguished from a consumer loan, a **commercial loan** is one that is made to a business. Usually the entire amount of a commercial loan plus interest is paid at the end of the time period; in some cases, however, it can be repaid in installments just like consumer loans. Section 12-2 focuses on the discounting of short-term commercial loans.

## Section 12-1  Time Payment Plans

The Consumer Credit Protection Act, better known as Truth-in-Lending, went into effect on July 1, 1969. Those extending credit or giving consumer loans with repayment on an installment basis must give a **disclosure statement** which contains the following information in writing before the sale or the loan is completed:

1. The cash price
2. The down payment required
3. The total amount of the unpaid balance (which is cash price minus the down payment)
4. Any additional charges to be financed
5. The total amount to be financed
6. The actual dollar amount of the finance charge
7. The amount of each installment payment
8. The charges for late payments
9. The true annual percentage rate (APR) based on the reduced balances.

Violators of the Truth-in-Lending Act are subject to penalties.

The term **annual percentage rate** is used rather than "interest rate" because the finance charge includes charges other than interest rates. The percentage rate must be given on an annual basis so that the charge is clearly understood. For example, a rate of $1\frac{1}{2}\%$ per month sounds much less than 18% per year—which is the same rate on an annual basis.

A percentage rate stated for a period other than a year can be converted to an annual percentage rate by multiplying the given rate by the number of times the given period is contained in one year. Thus, a rate given per month is multiplied by 12; a rate per quarter is multiplied by 4, etc.

*Examples:*

a. 1% per month = 1% × 12 = 12% per year
b. 4% per quarter = 4% × 4 = 16% per year
c. $4\frac{1}{2}\%$ semiannually = $4\frac{1}{2}\%$ × 2 = 9% per year

**Usury** is an interest charge that is higher than the legal rate. All states have usury laws which establish the maximum annual interest rates that may be charged.

## Part A  Finding the Amount of the Finance Charge

The total time payment price of goods bought on a time payment plan is found by multiplying the number of payments by the amount of the required installment and then adding the down payment if there is one. The finance charge is the difference between the total time payment price and the cash price of the goods.

*Example:* A department store advertises a television set for $500 or 10% down and $33.60 for 15 months. What is the finance charge?

| | | |
|---|---|---|
| Total installments | = 15 × $33.60 | = $504 |
| Down payment | = $500 × 10% | = 50 |
| Total time payment price | | = $554 |
| Finance charge | = $554 − $500 | = $54 |

The total cost of a consumer loan is the product of the number of installment payments times the amount of each payment. The finance charge is the difference between the total amount repaid and the amount of the loan.

*Example:* A $600 loan is repaid in 6 monthly installments of $103.50. What is the finance charge?

| | | |
|---|---|---|
| Total payments | = 6 × $103.50 | = $621 |
| Amount of loan | | = − 600 |
| Finance charge | | $ 21 |

Note that only monthly payments are considered here, as most time payment plans are on a monthly basis. The same procedure, however, applies to weekly payment plans.

## Part B  Finding the Amount of the Monthly Installment

The monthly installment consists of two parts: (1) the finance charge divided by the number of months of payment, and (2) the unpaid cash balance (cash price minus the down payment) divided by the number of months of payment.

In order to find the amount of the monthly installment, the total finance charge (FC) must be known. The finance charge for each month can be found in the same way as interest. Since the principal owed (the unpaid cash balance remaining) is reduced after each installment paid, the actual finance charge is smaller with each succeeding month. The total finance charge is the sum of the monthly finance charges.

*Computing the total monthly finance charges.* Computing the monthly finance charges separately and then finding their sum is a time-consuming process. A simple formula can be used to find the total of the monthly finance charges:

$$FC = \frac{\text{1st month's charge} \times (\text{no. of payments} + 1)}{2}$$

The following example will illustrate a step-by-step procedure in finding the total finance charge.

**Example:** A television set is advertised for $500 cash or 10% down and the balance to be paid in 15 equal monthly payments. The finance charge is $1\frac{1}{2}$% per month on the reduced balances. Find the total finance charge.

**Step 1:** Find the unpaid cash balance.

$$\$500 - \$50 = \$450$$

**Step 2.** Find the APR.

$$1\frac{1}{2}\% \times 12 = 18\%$$

**Step 3.** Find the first month's finance charge by using the interest formula, I = prt.

$$I = \$450 \times 18\% \times \tfrac{1}{12} = \$6.75$$

**Step 4.** Find the total finance charge.

$$FC = \frac{\$6.75 \times (15 + 1)}{2} = \$54$$

Although the actual finance charge on the unpaid cash balance is reduced each month, in most time payment plans the total finance charge is divided by the months of payment so that the charge, as well as the unpaid cash balance, can be repaid in equal installments. Occasionally, when rounded numbers are used, the last payment may be a few cents *more* or *less* to adjust to the total amount due.

***Computing the monthly installment amount.***
Generally the amount of the monthly installment is found by dividing the sum of the finance charge and the unpaid cash balance by the number of months scheduled for payment.

*Examples:*

a. A chair is advertised for $350 cash or $50 down and the balance to be paid in 12 monthly installments. The finance charge is $1\frac{1}{3}$% per month on the reduced balances. Find the monthly payment.

**Step 1.** Find the unpaid cash balance.

$$\$350 - \$50 = \$300$$

**Step 2.** Find the APR.

$$1\tfrac{1}{3}\% \times 12 = 16\%$$

**Step 3.** Find the first month's charge.

$$\$300 \times 16\% \times \tfrac{1}{12} = \$4.00$$

**Step 4.** Find the total FC.

$$FC = \frac{\$4 \times (12 + 1)}{2} = \$26$$

**Step 5.** Find the sum of the finance charge and the unpaid cash balance.

$$\$26 + \$300 = \$326$$

**Step 6.** Monthly payment $= \$326 \div 12$
$$= \$27.17$$

Since $\$27.17 \times 12 = \$326.04$, the last payment is reduced to $27.13.

b. An $800 loan is to be repaid in 10 equal monthly installments. The finance charge is 1% per month on the reduced cash balances. Find the monthly installment.

**Step 1.** Unpaid cash balance = $800

**Step 2.** APR = $1\% \times 12 = 12\%$

**Step 3.** 1st month's charge $= \$800 \times 12\% \times \tfrac{1}{12}$
$$= \$8.00$$

**Step 4.** $FC = \dfrac{\$8 \times (10 + 1)}{2} = \$44$

**Step 5.** FC + unpaid cash balance
$$\$44 + \$800 = \$844$$

**Step 6.** Monthly payment $= \$844 \div 10$
$$= \$84.40$$

## Part C — Finding the Annual Percentage Rate (APR)

The usual method of finding an interest rate ($r = I \div pt$) cannot be used to find the true annual percentage rate since the principal is reduced after each payment. There are several ways to find the annual percentage rate. The following formula is easy to use for time payment plans paid in monthly installments and is accurate enough for most purposes:

$$APR = \frac{24 \times \text{finance charge}}{\text{unpaid cash bal.} \times (\text{no. of payments} + 1)}$$

In the case of weekly installments, use 104, or $2 \times 52$, in the numerator instead of 24.

Note, however, that APR tables or a computer generally are used to get more accurate results than those found by using this simple formula.

Before the formula can be applied, the unpaid cash balance (cash price minus the down payment, if there is one) and the total finance charge must be found for goods bought on time. In the case of consumer loans, the unpaid cash balance is the amount of the loan.

To find the annual percentage rate, follow these five steps:

1. Find the total amount of payments (monthly installment times the number of months of payment).
2. Find the total time payment price (total amount of installments plus down payment). Omit this step for consumer loans.
3. Find the total finance charge (total time payment price minus the cash price, or total time payment price minus the amount of the loan).
4. Find the unpaid cash balance (cash price minus down payment, or the amount of the loan). Note that the unpaid cash balance does *not* include the finance charge.
5. Find the APR by substituting the correct figures in the formula given above.

### Examples:

a. A television set sells for $500 cash or $20 down and $27.36 a month for 20 months. Find the annual percentage rate charged.

Step 1. Find the total amount of payments.

$27.36 \times 20 = $547.20$

Step 2. Find the total time payment price.

$547.20 + $20 = $567.20$

Step 3. Find the total finance charge.

$567.20 - $500.00 = $67.20$

Step 4. Find the unpaid cash balance.

$500 - $20 = $480$

Step 5. Find the annual percentage rate.

$$APR = \frac{24 \times \$67.20}{\$480 \times (20 + 1)} = .16 \text{ or } 16\%$$

On a calculator, the sequence of steps to find the APR is: $24 \times 67.2 \div 480 \div 21$.

b. A $900 loan is to be repaid in 11 equal monthly installments of $81.34 and $81.31 for the last payment. Find the annual percentage rate charged.

Step 1. Find the total amount of payments.

$(\$81.34 \times 11) + \$81.31 = \$976.05$

Step 2. Find the total time payment price.

(This is the same as Step 1.)

Step 3. Find the total finance charge.

$976.05 - $900 = $76.05$

Step 4. Find the unpaid cash balance.

$900, the amount of the loan.

Step 5. Find the annual percentage rate.

$$APR = \frac{24 \times \$76.05}{\$900 \times (12 + 1)} = .156 \text{ or } 15.6\%$$

Complete Assignment 33

# Assignment 33
# Section 12-1

| | Perfect Score | Student's Score |
|---|---|---|
| Part A | 20 | |
| Part B | 40 | |
| Part C | 40 | |
| TOTAL | 100 | |

**Time Payment Plans**

## Part A

### Finding the Amount of the Finance Charge

*Directions:* Find the total time payment prices and the finance charges. Write your answers in the spaces provided. (1 point for each correct answer)

| | Cash Price | Down Payment | Monthly Payment | Number of Payments | Total Time Payment Price | Finance Charge |
|---|---|---|---|---|---|---|
| 1. | $ 169.00 | $ 69.00 | $ 9.25 | 12 | _____ | _____ |
| 2. | 59.95 | 5.00 | 7.33 | 8 | _____ | _____ |
| 3. | 537.50 | 10% | 30.70 | 18 | _____ | _____ |
| 4. | 1,260.00 | 260.00 | 91.46 | 12 | _____ | _____ |
| 5. | 2,500.00 | 10% | 156.56 | 16 | _____ | _____ |

*Directions:* Find the total cost of each loan and the finance charge. Write your answers in the spaces provided. (1 point for each correct answer)

| | Amount of Loan | Monthly Payment | Number of Payments | Total Cost of Loan | Finance Charge |
|---|---|---|---|---|---|
| 6. | $ 400.00 | $43.30 | 10 | _____ | _____ |
| 7. | 500.00 | 23.44 | 24 | _____ | _____ |
| 8. | 700.00 | 63.07 | 12 | _____ | _____ |
| 9. | 950.00 | 68.40 | 15 | _____ | _____ |
| 10. | 1,125.00 | 60.19 | 20 | _____ | _____ |

*Student's Score* _____

# Part B

## Finding the Amount of the Installment

*Directions:* Find the finance charges and the monthly payments. Write your answers in the spaces provided and put an asterisk (*) after any monthly payment in which the last payment must be adjusted. (2 points for each correct answer)

| | Cash Price or Amount of Loan | Down Payment | Number of Payments | Rate per month | Finance Charge | Monthly Payment |
|---|---|---|---|---|---|---|
| 11. | $ 498.00 | $50.00 | 18 | $1\frac{1}{2}$% | _____ | _____ |
| 12. | 895.00 | 95.00 | 24 | 1 | _____ | _____ |
| 13. | 390.00 | 30.00 | 10 | $1\frac{1}{3}$ | _____ | _____ |
| 14. | 2,400.00 | 10% | 36 | $\frac{7}{8}$ | _____ | _____ |
| 15. | 648.00 | 10% | 15 | $1\frac{2}{3}$ | _____ | _____ |
| 16. | 800.00 | | 16 | $1\frac{1}{2}$ | _____ | _____ |
| 17. | 3,000.00 | | 36 | $\frac{3}{4}$ | _____ | _____ |
| 18. | 750.00 | | 21 | 1 | _____ | _____ |
| 19. | 200.00 | | 6 | $1\frac{1}{2}$ | _____ | _____ |
| 20. | 1,760.00 | | 30 | $1\frac{1}{4}$ | _____ | _____ |

*Student's Score* _____

# Part C

## Finding the Annual Percentage Rate (APR)

*Directions:* Find the finance charges and the annual percentage rates to the nearest .1%. Write your answers in the spaces provided. (2 points for each correct answer)

| | Cash Price or Amount of Loan | Down Payment | Monthly Payment | Number of Payments | Finance Charge | Annual Percentage Rate |
|---|---|---|---|---|---|---|
| 21. | $ 320.00 | $20.00 | $32.20 | 10 | _____ | _____ |
| 22. | 400.00 | 40.00 | 33.25 | 12 | _____ | _____ |
| 23. | 650.00 | 50.00 | 43.20 | 15 | _____ | _____ |
| 24. | 800.00 | 10% | 44.75 | 18 | _____ | _____ |
| 25. | 750.00 | 10% | 31.00 | 24 | _____ | _____ |
| 26. | 360.00 | | 42.00 | 9 | _____ | _____ |
| 27. | 400.00 | | 26.86 | 16 | _____ | _____ |
| 28. | 200.00 | | 18.29 | 12 | _____ | _____ |
| 29. | 1,200.00 | | 71.42 | 18 | _____ | _____ |
| 30. | 3,000.00 | | 96.18 | 36 | _____ | _____ |

*Student's Score* _____

# Section 12-2 Short-Term Commercial Loans

A *commercial loan* is made for business purposes, as distinguished from a consumer loan made for personal use. Commercial loans can be short-term (for less than one year) or long-term (for one or more years). Because of the wide variation among long-term loans such as bonds, debentures, mortgages, etc., and the complicated nature of their repayment, long-term loans are not discussed here.

Short-term commercial loans usually require a note that is **negotiable**, or transferable to another person, to confirm the debt. The promissory note, which was defined on page 182 in Chapter 8 and is illustrated below, is an example of a negotiable instrument. (Most lending agencies, however, use a longer form with detailed legal specifications.)

Notes may also be required from purchasers who are late in settling their accounts. The bank to which payment is to be made often is specified on such notes. Other negotiable instruments used in connection with short-term commercial loans are trade acceptances, bills of exchange, and drafts.

When a commercial loan is made, the borrower or signer of the note is called the **maker**; the lender is called the **payee**. The amount of the loan is the **face value**, or **face**, of the note. Sometimes the maker may be required to furnish **collateral**, which is something of value such as stocks, equipment, accounts receivable, real estate, etc. The collateral is evidence of the maker's ability to pay, and the lender has the right to sell it if the note is not paid.

A note may be **non-interest bearing** or **interest-bearing**. As mentioned on page 188 in Chapter 8, the maturity value of a non-interest bearing note is the same as the principal, or the face of the note. When a note is interest-bearing, it must show the rate of the interest charge which is to be paid at maturity or as specified. The maturity value of an interest-bearing note equals the face value plus the interest.

## Part A — Finding the Interest Charge, Due Date, and Maturity Value

Interest rates on short-term commercial loans vary considerably and often depend on the circumstances or uses for the loans. The **prime rate** is the rate charged by leading banks to their low-risk, top customers. As a rule of thumb, the higher the risk, the higher the rate. In computing the interest, on either a 360- or 365-day basis, the exact number of days of the loan is used. For ease of computation, in this section **banker's interest** (360 days) is used in all examples.

In consumer loans which are repaid in installments, the finance charge (which includes the interest charge) is part of each payment. In contrast, the interest on short-term commercial loans usually is payable on the due date of the note. For this reason, the interest on short-term commercial loans is often called **interest due at maturity**, **interest after date**, or **interest to follow**. The maturity value of the note is paid on the due date.

Finding the due date, the interest charge, and the maturity value of the notes in the examples given below should serve as a review of the things you learned about figuring interest in Chapter 8.

## Figure 12-1 Promissory Note

$ 1,000.00          Milwaukee, Wisconsin, March 3, 19 – –

For value received, Sixty days after date I promise to pay

to the order of Grand National Bank

One thousand and no/100 ———————— DOLLARS,

with interest at the rate of 7 percent.

No. 374          Due May 2, 19 – –          A. J. Moran

*Examples:*

a. Find the due date, the interest charge, and the maturity value of a 90-day note dated January 15 for $500 with interest at 6½% annually.

Jan. . . . . . . . . . . . . . . . . . . . . . . . . . . 16 days
Feb. . . . . . . . . . . . . . . . . . . . . . . . . . 28
March . . . . . . . . . . . . . . . . . . . . . . . . <u>31</u>
75
April . . . . . . . . . . . . . . . . . . . . . . . . . <u>15</u>
90 days

Due date is April 15.

$$\text{Interest} = \$500 \times 6\tfrac{1}{2}\% \times \frac{90}{360} = \$8.13$$

$$\text{Maturity value} = \$500 + \$8.13 = \$508.13$$

b. Find the due date, the interest charge, and the maturity value of a three-month note dated July 8 for $600 with interest at 7% annually.

Due date is October 8.

Interest period:  July . . . . . . . 23 (31 − 8)
Aug. . . . . . . . 31
Sept. . . . . . . . 30
Oct. . . . . . . . . <u>8</u>
92 days

$$\text{Interest} = \$600 \times 7\% \times \frac{92}{360} = \$10.73$$

$$\text{Maturity value} = \$600 + \$10.73 = \$610.73$$

## Part B  Discounting Non-Interest Bearing Notes

Although the interest on most short-term loans is not payable until the due date of the note, some banks may require that the interest on the face value of a note be paid in advance, that is, at the time the loan is made. The amount of interest usually is deducted from the face value, and the borrower receives the difference. This kind of interest, paid in advance, is called **bank discount**, and the note is said to be **discounted**. The amount of money received by the borrower is called the **proceeds** of the note. Actually bank discount is

"interest on interest" since the charge is figured on the entire face value and not on the smaller amount of the proceeds.

The rate charged on discounted notes is called the **discount rate**, and the time is called the **discount period**. The bank discount is figured in the same way as banker's interest.

There are two kinds of short-term, non-interest-bearing notes which can be discounted: (1) a note payable signed by the maker, with the bank as the payee, and (2) a note receivable which a company has received from a customer in settlement of an account. From the accounting point of view, a note is called a **note payable** by the maker of the note and a **note receivable** by the lender.

*Finding the proceeds of discounted notes payable.* A note payable signed by the maker, with the bank as the payee, is considered to be non-interest-bearing because the interest is paid in advance in the form of bank discount. The discount period is the time of the note; the maturity value is the face of the note.

*Examples:*

a. On May 6, B. R. Brown has his own $600, 90-day note discounted at his bank at 6%. Find the proceeds.

$$\text{Bank discount} = \$600 \times 6\% \times \frac{90}{360} = \$9$$

$$\text{Proceeds} \quad = \$600 - \$9 = \$591$$

b. On October 18, Angela Troy has her own $800, 60-day note discounted at her bank at 6½%. Find the proceeds.

$$\text{Bank discount} = \$800 \times 6\tfrac{1}{2}\% \times \frac{60}{360} = \$8.67$$

$$\text{Proceeds} \quad = \$800 - \$8.67 = \$791.33$$

*Finding the proceeds of discounted notes receivable.* When a company has a non-interest-bearing note receivable discounted at a bank, it is the same as "selling" the note, for the bank becomes the new payee. In this case the fee charged for this service is the bank discount.

If the note is brought in on the same day that it was drawn, the discount period is the same as the time of the note. More often, however, the discount date is some time after the date of origin. In this case the discount period runs from the date of discount to the due date. There is no charge for the days preceding the date of discount.

To find the proceeds of a non-interest bearing note receivable which is discounted, follow these four steps:

1. Find the due date if it does not appear on the note.
2. Find the number of days in the discount period. Remember that the discount period starts on the date that the note was discounted. In most cases this is not the same as the date of the note.
3. Find the bank discount by multiplying the face value by the discount rate by the discount period.
4. Find the proceeds by subtracting the bank discount from the face value.

## Examples:

a. Brenda Matthew accepted a 60-day, non-interest-bearing note for $400 on September 20 in settlement of a customer's account. She had it discounted at her bank on October 15 at 8%. Find the proceeds.

**Step 1.** Find the due date.

Sept. . . . . . . . . . . . . . . . . . . . 10 days
Oct. . . . . . . . . . . . . . . . . . . . 31
Nov. . . . . . . . . . . . . . . . . . . . $\underline{19}$
60 days

Due date is November 19.

**Step 2.** Find the discount period.

Oct. . . . . . . . . . . . . . . . . . . . 16 days
Nov. . . . . . . . . . . . . . . . . . . . $\underline{19}$
35 days

**Step 3.** Find the bank discount.

$$400 \times 8\% \times \frac{35}{360} = \$3.11$$

**Step 4.** Find the proceeds.

$$400 - \$3.11 = \$396.89$$

b. Allen Zickert accepted a 45-day, non-interest-bearing note for $700 on July 24 in settlement of a customer's account. He had it discounted at his bank on August 16 at 7½%. Find the proceeds.

**Step 1.** July . . . . . . . . . . . . . . . 7
Aug. . . . . . . . . . . . . . . 31
Sept. . . . . . . . . . . . . . . $\underline{7}$ (due date)
45

**Step 2.** Aug. . . . 15
Sept. . . . $\underline{7}$
22 days (discount period)

**Step 3.** $700 \times 7½\% \times \frac{22}{360} = \$3.21$ (bank discount)

**Step 4.** $700 - \$3.21 = \$696.79$ (proceeds)

## Part C — Discounting Interest-Bearing Notes

A note given to a company by a customer in settlement of an overdue account usually is interest-bearing. It can be discounted either on the date it was made or later. The procedure for discounting is much the same as for non-interest-bearing notes receivable.

The bank discount is computed on the maturity value of the note since this is what the bank collects on the due date. The face value of the note is used only to find the amount of interest. To find the proceeds, the bank discount is subtracted from the maturity value, not the face value.

The step-by-step procedure in finding the proceeds of an interest-bearing note receivable is given below.

1. Find the due date if it does not appear on the note.
2. Find the maturity value of the note. If the time of the note is expressed in months, the exact number of days between the date of origin and the due date must be used in figuring the interest, not the number of months. For example, a two-month note which is dated June 21 is due on August 21 and the exact time of interest is 61 days.

3. Find the number of days in the discount period. This should be the exact time from the date of discount to the due date. Remember that there is no charge for the time before the date of discount.
4. Find the bank discount. Multiply the maturity value by the rate of discount by the discount period.
5. Find the proceeds by subtracting the bank discount from the maturity value.

## Examples:

a. Eugene Morgan accepted a 60-day, 7% interest-bearing note for $500 on March 12 in settlement of a customer's account. The note was discounted on March 28 at 6%. Find the proceeds.

**Step 1.** Find the due date.

March .......... 19 days
April ........... 30
May ........... 11
         60 days

Due date is May 11.

**Step 2.** Find the maturity value.

$$\text{Interest} = \$500 \times 7\% \times \frac{60}{360}$$
$$= \$5.83$$

Maturity value = $500 + $5.83
              = $505.83

**Step 3.** Find the discount period.

March .......... 3 days
April ........... 30
May ........... 11
         44 days

**Step 4.** Find the bank discount.

$$\$505.83 \times 6\% \times \frac{44}{360} = \$3.71$$

**Step 5.** Find the proceeds.

$$\$505.83 - \$3.71 = \$502.12$$

b. Alice Barnes accepted a three-month, 6% interest-bearing note for $1,200 on July 8 in settlement of a customer's account. She took it to her bank on July 12 for discounting at 7%. Find the proceeds.

**Step 1.** Due date is October 8.

**Step 2.** July ............ 23 days
Aug. ............ 31
Sept. ............ 30
Oct. ............. 8
Time of note ..... 92 days

$$\text{Interest} = \$1,200 \times 6\% \times \frac{92}{360}$$
$$= \$18.40$$

Maturity value = $1,200 + $18.40
              = $1,218.40

**Step 3.** July ............ 19 days
Aug. ............ 31
Sept. ............ 30
Oct. ............. 8
Discount period .. 88 days

**Step 4.** Bank discount = $1,218.40 × 7%
$$\times \frac{88}{360}$$
$$= \$20.85$$

**Step 5.** Proceeds = $1,218.40 − $20.85
            = $1,197.55

Note in *Example b* that, in order to get needed cash, Ms. Barnes loses the $18.40 interest on the note and pays an additional bank discount of $20.85 − $18.40 = $2.45.

In modern business practice, very little discounting of notes receivable is done. Rather than accepting a note in settlement of an account, the vendor may charge interest on the overdue amount, ask the purchaser to borrow money from the bank to make the payment, or, as a last resort, turn the account over to a collection agency.

**Complete Assignment 34**

## Assignment 34
## Section 12-2

*Short-Term Commercial Loans*

|  | Perfect Score | Student's Score |
|---|---|---|
| Part A | 30 | |
| Part B | 30 | |
| Part C | 40 | |
| TOTAL | 100 | |

# Part A

### *Finding the Interest Charge, Due Date, and Maturity Value*

*Directions:* The interest is due at maturity in the following notes. Find the due date, the interest charge, and the maturity value for each. Write your answers in the spaces provided. (1 point for each correct answer)

1. 30-day note dated June 5 for $7,500 with interest at 6%.

    Due date _____
    Interest charge _____
    Maturity value _____

2. 60-day note dated October 20 for $700 with interest at 7%.

    Due date _____
    Interest charge _____
    Maturity value _____

3. 45-day note dated August 4 for $500 with interest at $7\frac{1}{2}\%$.

    Due date _____
    Interest charge _____
    Maturity value _____

4. 90-day note dated December 23 for $775 with interest at 6%.

    Due date _____
    Interest charge _____
    Maturity value _____

5. 75-day note dated April 14 for $400 with interest at $6\frac{1}{2}\%$.

    Due date _____
    Interest charge _____
    Maturity value _____

6. 15-day note dated February 27 for $1,200 with interest at 5%.

    Due date _____
    Interest charge _____
    Maturity value _____

7. 240-day note dated March 31 for $1,000 with interest at 8%.

    Due date _____
    Interest charge _____
    Maturity value _____

8. 135-day note dated May 26 for $850 with interest at 9%.

    Due date _____
    Interest charge _____
    Maturity value _____

9. 80-day note dated January 8 for $5,000 with interest at $8\frac{1}{2}\%$.

    Due date _____
    Interest charge _____
    Maturity value _____

10. 120-day note dated February 17 for $300 with interest at $10\frac{1}{2}\%$.

    Due date _____
    Interest charge _____
    Maturity value _____

*Student's Score* _____

# Part B

## Discounting Non-Interest-Bearing Notes

*Directions:* The following notes payable are signed by the maker with a bank as the payee, and are discounted on the dates of origin at the given rates. Find the bank discount and the proceeds for each. Write your answers in the spaces provided. (½ point for each correct answer)

11. 90-day note dated September 18 for $500 discounted at 6%.

    Bank discount _____
    Proceeds _____

16. 60-day note dated July 24 for $1,500 discounted at 6¼%.

    Bank discount _____
    Proceeds _____

12. 30-day note dated August 30 for $2,000 discounted at 6½%.

    Bank discount _____
    Proceeds _____

17. 15-day dated February 27 for $5,000 discounted at 10%.

    Bank discount _____
    Proceeds _____

13. 80-day note dated July 12 for $850 discounted at 7½%.

    Bank discount _____
    Proceeds _____

18. 40-day note dated October 1 for $375 discounted at 9%.

    Bank discount _____
    Proceeds _____

14. 45-day note dated September 1 for $600 discounted at 8%.

    Bank discount _____
    Proceeds _____

19. 75-day note dated July 28 for $400 discounted at 10%.

    Bank discount _____
    Proceeds _____

15. 120-day note dated November 8 for $950 discounted at 7%.

    Bank discount _____
    Proceeds _____

20. 135-day note dated December 4 for $2,400 discounted at 6¾%.

    Bank discount _____
    Proceeds _____

***Directions:*** The following non-interest-bearing notes receivable are discounted on the given dates at the given rates. Find the due date, the discount period, the bank discount, and the proceeds for each. (½ point for each correct answer)

21. 90-day note dated July 19 for $500 discounted on August 12 at 6%.

Due date _____
Discount period _____
Bank discount _____
Proceeds _____

26. 80-day note dated October 9 for $900 discounted on November 22 at 9½%.

Due date _____
Discount period _____
Bank discount _____
Proceeds _____

22. 60-day note dated March 15 for $650 discounted on April 14 at 9%.

Due date _____
Discount period _____
Bank discount _____
Proceeds _____

27. 30-day note dated April 13 for $600 discounted on April 25 at 8½%.

Due date _____
Discount period _____
Bank discount _____
Proceeds _____

23. 75-day note dated November 3 for $1,000 discounted on December 8 at 6%.

Due date _____
Discount period _____
Bank discount _____
Proceeds _____

28. 15-day note dated January 18 for $3,000 discounted on January 23 at 10%.

Due date _____
Discount period _____
Bank discount _____
Proceeds _____

24. 45-day note dated September 7 for $500 discounted on October 2 at 7%.

Due date _____
Discount period _____
Bank discount _____
Proceeds _____

29. 50-day note dated February 6 for $1,600 discounted on March 13 at 6¼%.

Due date _____
Discount period _____
Bank discount _____
Proceeds _____

25. 135-day note dated July 11 for $400 discounted on September 9 at 6½%.

Due date _____
Discount period _____
Bank discount _____
Proceeds _____

30. 120-day note dated August 10 for $4,000 discounted on September 9 at 7½%.

Due date _____
Discount period _____
Bank discount _____
Proceeds _____

*Student's Score* _____

# Part C

## Discounting Interest-Bearing Notes Receivable

*Directions:* The following interest-bearing notes receivable are discounted on the given dates at the given rates. Find the due date, the maturity value, the discount period, the bank discount and the proceeds for each. Write your answers in the spaces provided. (1 point for each correct answer)

**31.** 60-day, 6% interest-bearing note dated July 2 for $750 discounted on August 1 at 6%.

Due date _____
Maturity value _____
Discount period _____
Bank discount _____
Proceeds _____
_____

**35.** 30-day, 6½% interest-bearing note dated September 5 for $200 discounted on September 10 at 7½%.

Due date _____
Maturity value _____
Discount period _____
Bank discount _____
Proceeds _____

**32.** 120-day, 5% interest-bearing note dated November 9 for $600 discounted on December 9 at 6%.

Due date _____
Maturity value _____
Discount period _____
Bank discount _____
Proceeds _____

**36.** Four-month, 9% interest-bearing note dated June 4 for $6,000 discounted on August 17 at 7%.

Due date _____
Maturity value _____
Discount period _____
Bank discount _____
Proceeds _____

**33.** Three-month, 6% interest-bearing note dated June 19 for $1,200 discounted on July 15 at 7%.

Due date _____
Maturity value _____
Discount period _____
Bank discount _____
Proceeds _____

**37.** 45-day, 8% interest-bearing note dated April 3 for $800 discounted on May 3 at 10%.

Due date _____
Maturity value _____
Discount period _____
Bank discount _____
Proceeds _____

**34.** 60-day, 7% interest-bearing note dated January 16 for $500 discounted on February 25 at 8%.

Due date _____
Maturity value _____
Discount period _____
Bank discount _____
Proceeds _____

**38.** 75-day, 7% interest-bearing note dated June 30 for $525 discounted on July 30 at 7¼%.

Due date _____
Maturity value _____
Discount period _____
Bank discount _____
Proceeds _____

*Student's Score* _____

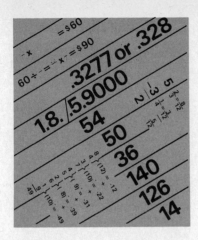

# Inventory Valuation, Cost of Goods Sold, and Depreciation

CHAPTER 13

An important function of accounting is to provide the information needed for preparing a company's financial statements. A **fiscal period** is that period of doing business, such as a month, a quarter, a half-year, or a year, at the conclusion of which the operations are summarized and presented in financial statements for analysis.

The cost of the goods that have been sold during the period determines the gross profit (or markup) for the fiscal period. In order to find the cost of the goods sold, it is necessary to know three things: (1) the value of the inventory at the beginning of the fiscal period, (2) the net cost of the goods purchased, and (3) the value of the inventory at the end of the fiscal period. Finding the ending inventory value and the cost of the goods sold are discussed in Section 13-1.

Most of the fixed assets used in a business, such as machinery, furniture, trucks, buildings, etc., decrease in value as they get older. Their cost cannot be declared as a business expense in the year they were acquired, but much of it can be charged off systematically during their years of useful life. This charging-off is an allowable business expense called **depreciation**. The three methods of calculating depreciation expense that are commonly used are discussed in Section 13-2.

## Section 13-1  Inventory Valuation and Cost of Goods Sold

**Merchandise inventory** is the term given to all the goods owned by a business and available for sale in the hope of making a profit. Most companies keep a running inventory, or **perpetual inventory**, of the stock on hand. In a large company, this is kept in the computer; in a small company, generally it is kept on stock record cards. As a check on the perpetual inventory and for a more accurate record, a **physical inventory**, in which each item in stock is counted, weighed, or measured, is taken at least once a year.

The value of the merchandise in stock may be computed on the *unit cost* of the goods or on their *current market value*. Only a physical inventory at cost is considered in this chapter.

While quantities can be found easily, the unit costs to be assigned to the counted goods are more difficult to determine. This is because the items in the ending inventory usually consist of purchases made at varying costs during the period. The problem thus becomes one of finding what unit costs should be assigned to them.

There are four methods of inventory valuation in common use, with the choice of method depending upon the kind of business. These methods are:

1. specific identification
2. first-in, first-out (FIFO)
3. last-in, first-out (LIFO)
4. weighted average cost

## Part A  Specific Identification

The **specific identification method** is used if the actual cost of each unit in the ending inventory is available. For example, each item may have an attached price tag which has the cost in code or has a specific invoice reference. Finding the ending inventory cost is then only a matter of extending the inventory and finding the total. (Refer to Section 1-4, Part F, page 30.)

*Example:* Find the cost of the ending inventory by specific identification.

$$15 \text{ units @ } \$25 \text{ each} = \$ \ 375$$
$$24 \text{ units @ } \$27 \text{ each} = \ \ 648$$
$$16 \text{ units @ } \$28 \text{ each} = \ \ 448$$
$$\text{Total} = \$1,471$$

## Part B  First-In, First-Out (FIFO)

In the **first-in, first-out** method it is assumed that the merchandise is sold in the order in which it has been received. That is, the oldest goods on hand at the beginning of the fiscal period (first-in) are sold (first-out); then the goods bought during the fiscal period are sold, also in the order of their acquisition. Thus, the unsold units at the end of the fiscal period, when the ending inventory is taken, are assumed to consist of the latest purchases.

In order to show the different inventory values obtained by using the three methods (first-in, first-out; last-in, first-out; and weighted average cost), the same problem given below will be used to illustrate each method.

In this problem it is assumed that by physical count the units in the ending inventory = 125.

| Item 674-A | Number of Units | Unit Cost |
|---|---|---|
| Beginning inventory ....... | 75 | $10.00 |
| Purchase 1 ................. | 200 | 11.00 |
| Purchase 2 ................. | 100 | 12.00 |
| Purchase 3 ................. | 500 | 11.50 |
| Purchase 4 ................. | 100 | 12.50 |

*Example:* Find the cost of the ending inventory by using FIFO.

The 125 units in the ending inventory consist of 100 units from Purchase 4 and 25 units from Purchase 3.

$$100 \times \$12.50 = \$1,250.00$$
$$25 \times \$11.50 = \ \ 287.50$$
$$\text{Cost of ending inventory} = \$1,537.50$$

## Part C  Last-In, First-Out (LIFO)

In the **last-in, first-out** method it is assumed that the latest merchandise purchased (last-in) has been sold (first-out) and that the ending inventory consists of the oldest stock. Since market prices have been rising for many years, the use of LIFO gives a more realistic amount for the cost of the goods that are bought to replenish the stock that has been sold. Another consideration in favor of LIFO is that a lower ending inventory value results in a higher cost of goods sold, and thus a lower net profit for tax purposes.

*Example:* Find the cost of the ending inventory by using LIFO.

The 125 units in the ending inventory consist of the 75 units in the beginning inventory and 50 units from Purchase 1.

$$75 \times \$10.00 = \$ \ 750.00$$
$$50 \times \$11.00 = \ \ 550.00$$
$$\text{Cost of ending inventory} = \$1,300.00$$

It is easy to confuse the procedures used in the FIFO and LIFO methods to find the ending inventory cost. It may be helpful to lightly cross out those units that are assumed to have been sold and thus are not in the physical inventory count.

In the FIFO method, cross out the units in the beginning inventory and in at least the earliest purchase. Consider these as "first-sold" (first-out). Continue to cross out, in the order of their purchase, further units that are assumed to be sold and not in the inventory count, until a critical figure is reached. The same FIFO problem in Part B is used on page 261 so that you can compare the two ways.

*Example:* Find the cost of the ending inventory by using FIFO.

| Item 674-A | Number of Units | Unit Cost | |
|---|---|---|---|
| ~~Beginning inventory~~ | ~~75~~ | ~~$10.00~~ | |
| ~~Purchase 1~~ | ~~200~~ | ~~11.00~~ | |
| ~~Purchase 2~~ | ~~100~~ | ~~12.00~~ | |
| Purchase 3 | 500 | 11.50 | 25 |
| Purchase 4 | 100 | 12.50 | 100 |
| | | | 125 |

$$25 \times \$11.50 = \$ \ 287.50$$
$$100 \times \ 12.50 = \ 1,250.00$$
$$\text{Cost of ending inventory} = \underline{\underline{\$1,537.50}}$$

In the LIFO method, cross out the units in the last purchase (last-in) and consider these as "first-sold" (first-out). Continue to cross out, in reverse order of their purchase, further units that are assumed to be sold and not in the inventory count, until a critical figure is reached. The same LIFO problem used previously in this part is used for purposes of comparison.

*Example:* Find the cost of the ending inventory by using LIFO.

| Beginning inventory | 75 | $10.00 | 75 |
|---|---|---|---|
| Purchase 1 | 200 | 11.00 | 50 |
| ~~Purchase 2~~ | ~~100~~ | ~~12.00~~ | 125 |
| ~~Purchase 3~~ | ~~500~~ | ~~11.50~~ | |
| ~~Purchase 4~~ | ~~100~~ | ~~12.50~~ | |

$$50 \times \$11.00 = \$ \ 550.00$$
$$75 \times \ 10.00 = \ 750.00$$
$$\text{Cost of ending inventory} = \underline{\underline{\$1,300.00}}$$

## Part D Weighted Average Cost

The unit cost of an item may vary somewhat from purchase to purchase. By using the **weighted average cost** method, an average cost per item is found in which the larger purchases affect the average cost more than the smaller purchases. Thus, the "weighted average" is more realistic than just the average of all unit costs.

To find the weighted average cost per unit, the total cost of the merchandise available for sale is divided by the total number of units available for sale. This weighted average cost per unit is then multiplied by the number of units in the ending inventory to find the value of the ending inventory.

*Example:* Find the cost of the ending inventory by using the weighted average cost method.

| | | |
|---|---|---|
| 75 × $10.00 = | $ | 750 |
| 200 × $11.00 | | 2,200 |
| 100 × $12.00 | | 1,200 |
| 500 × $11.50 | | 5,750 |
| 100 × $12.50 | | 1,250 |
| 975 | | $11,150 |

$11,150 ÷ 975 = $11.44, weighted average cost per unit

125 × $11.44 = $1,430.00, cost of ending inventory

An error in the physical count affects the ending inventory value. As a result, the cost of goods sold may be overstated or understated, and, in turn, the net profit may be understated or overstated.

## Part E Estimated Inventory Value

There are times in the operation of a business, other than at the end of a fiscal period, that the value of the ending inventory is needed. A physical inventory may be too time-consuming, expensive, or even impossible, as in the case of fire. There are two ways commonly used to estimate the inventory at cost without taking a physical count.

*Gross profit (or markup) method.* In accounting, the term "gross profit" is used instead of "markup." The gross profit method is based on the following markup equation:

$$\text{Sales} - \text{Markup} = \text{Cost}$$

To estimate the cost of the ending inventory by the gross profit method, follow these four steps:

1. Find the approximate amount of gross profit to date by multiplying the percent of gross profit from the previous fiscal period by the net sales to date.

2. Find the cost of goods sold to date by subtracting the approximate amount of gross profit to date (result obtained in Step 1) from the net sales to date.

3. Find the cost of goods available for sale to date by adding the cost of the beginning inventory and the net purchases to date.

4. Find the cost of the ending inventory by subtracting the cost of goods sold to date from the cost of goods available for sale to date (Step 3 minus Step 2).

### Examples:

a. Using the same problem illustrated in Parts B, C, and D, assume that the gross profit rate from the previous fiscal period is 25% and that net sales to date = $13,000. Find the estimated inventory value at cost.

Step 1:  $13,000
       × .25
       $ 3,250 (Estimated gross profit to date)

Step 2:  $13,000
       − 3,250
       $ 9,750 (Cost of goods sold to date)

Step 3:  $ 750
       + 10,400
       $11,150 (Cost of goods available for sale to date)

Step 4:  $11,150
       − 9,750
       $ 1,400 (Estimated ending inventory value at cost)

b. Find the estimated inventory value at cost from the following information:

Beginning inventory ............ $24,000
Net purchases to date .......... 41,000
Net sales to date .............. 60,000
Estimated gross profit .......... 30%

Step 1:  $60,000
       × .3
       $18,000 (Estimated gross profit to date)

Step 2:  $60,000
       − 18,000
       $42,000 (Cost of goods sold to date)

Step 3:  $24,000
       + 41,000
       $65,000 (Cost of goods available for sale to date)

Step 4:  $65,000
       − 42,000
       $23,000 (Estimated ending inventory value at cost)

**Retail method** Most department stores, supermarkets, and other retail enterprises prepare monthly income statements in order to analyze sales. The retail method is used to estimate the cost of the ending inventory.

As goods are received, they are marked with the expected retail prices. Records are kept to show both the net purchases and the expected sales on this merchandise.

To estimate the cost of the ending inventory by the retail method, follow these five steps:

1. Find the cost of goods available for sale by adding the beginning inventory at cost and the net purchases to date.

2. Find the goods available for sale at retail by adding the beginning inventory at retail and the net purchases at retail.

3. Find the cost/selling price ratio by dividing the cost of goods available for sale by the goods available for sale at retail.

4. Find the ending inventory at retail by subtracting the net sales to date from goods available for sale at retail.

5. Find the ending inventory at cost by multiplying the cost/selling price ratio by the ending inventory at retail.

### Examples:

a. Use the retail method to estimate the ending inventory cost from the following information:

|                          | Cost      | Retail     |
|--------------------------|-----------|------------|
| Beginning inventory ..   | $ 72,000  | $111,000   |
| Net purchases to date    | 136,000   | 204,000    |
| Net sales to date .....  |           | 210,000    |

Step 1:  $ 72,000
        + 136,000
        ─────────
         $208,000 (Cost of goods available
                  for sale)

Step 2:  $111,000
        + 204,000
        ─────────
         $315,000 (Goods available for sale
                  at retail)

Step 3: $208,000
        ──────── = .66 (Cost/selling price
        $315,000           ratio)

Step 4:  $315,000
        − 210,000
        ─────────
         $105,000 (Ending inventory at re-
                  tail)

Step 5:  $105,000
        ×     .66
        ─────────
         $ 69,300 (Estimated ending in-
                  ventory value at cost)

b. Use the retail method to estimate the ending inventory cost from the following information:

|                          | Cost      | Retail     |
|--------------------------|-----------|------------|
| Beginning inventory ..   | $23,000   | $ 38,000   |
| Net purchases to date    | 97,000    | 162,000    |
| Net sales to date .....  |           | 164,000    |

Step 1:  $ 23,000
        +  97,000
        ─────────
         $120,000 (Cost of goods available
                  for sale)

Step 2:  $ 38,000
        + 162,000
        ─────────
         $200,000 (Goods available for sale
                  at retail)

Step 3: $120,000
        ──────── = .6 or 60% (Cost/selling
        $200,000               price ratio)

Step 4:  $200,000
        − 164,000
        ─────────
         $ 36,000 (Ending inventory at re-
                  tail)

Step 5:  $36,000
        ×    .6
        ───────
         $21,600 (Estimated ending inven-
                 tory value at cost)

Other factors, such as markups and markdowns, also affect the ending inventory cost; however, they are not considered in this chapter.

## Part F  Finding Cost of Goods Sold

In order to find the gross profit on sales, it is necessary to find the cost of goods sold. The formula for **cost of goods sold (CGS)** is:

CGS = Beginning inventory + Net purchases
      − Ending inventory

Net purchases equal the Purchases less the sum of the Purchases returns and allowances and the Purchases discount. The Ending inventory may be found by any one of the methods given in the preceding parts of this section.

*Example:* Find the cost of goods sold from the following information:

Inventory, January 1, 19— ............ $19,800
Purchases .......................... 28,500
Purchases returns & allowances ....... 200
Purchases discount .................. 1,000
Inventory, December 31, 19— ........ 18,800

         $28,500
        −  1,200
        ────────
         $27,300 (Net purchases)

         $19,800
        + 27,300
        − 18,800
        ────────
         $28,300 (Cost of goods sold)

Figure 13-1 on page 264 shows this example in income statement form.

Complete Assignment 35

## Figure *13-1*  A Partial Income Statement

**ROBINSON'S SPORTING GOODS**
**Income Statement**
**For Year Ended December 31, 19—**

Income:
  Sales ........................................... $61,230
  Less: Sales returns and allowances ................ 1,230
    Net sales ............................................. $60,000

Cost of goods sold:
  Inventory, January 1, 19— ....................... $19,800
  Purchases ............................. $28,500
  Less: Purchases returns and
       allowances .............. $ 200
       Purchases discount ...... 1,000    1,200
  Net purchases ...................................... 27,300
  Goods available for sale .......................... $47,100
  Less: Inventory, December 31, 19— ............... 18,800
    Cost of goods sold ....................................... 28,300

Gross profit on sales ......................................... $31,700

# Assignment 35
# Section 13-1

| | Perfect Score | Student's Score |
|---|---|---|
| Part A | 8 | |
| Parts B, C, D | 48 | |
| Part E | 24 | |
| Part F | 20 | |
| TOTAL | 100 | |

*Inventory Valuation and
Cost of Goods Sold*

## Part A

### Specific Identification

**Directions:** Find the ending inventory cost by the specific identification method. (4 points for each correct answer)

1.  8 units @ $56.50 . . . . . . . . . . . . .  _____
   64 units @ 37.50 . . . . . . . . . . . . .  _____
  157 units @ 40.00 . . . . . . . . . . . . .  _____
   20 units @ 9.00 . . . . . . . . . . . .  _____

   Ending inventory cost . . . . . . . . . .  _____

2. 210 units @ $13.60 . . . . . . . . . . . .  _____
    48 units @ 5.75 . . . . . . . . . . . . .  _____
    60 units @ 12.50 . . . . . . . . . . . . .  _____
   355 units @ 4.00 . . . . . . . . . . . . .  _____

   Ending inventory cost . . . . . . . . . .  _____

*Student's Score* _____

## Parts B, C, D

### First-In, First-Out; Last-In, First-Out; Weighted Average Cost

**Directions:** Find the ending inventory value at cost by FIFO, LIFO, and weighted average cost. Show all work under the given headings. (4 points for each correct answer)

| | Number of Units | Unit Cost |
|---|---|---|
| Inventory, January 1, 19— . . . . . . . . . . . . . . . . . . . . | 300 | $2.00 |
| Purchase 1 . . . . . . . . . . . . . . . . . . . . . . . . . . . . . . . | 100 | 2.10 |
| Purchase 2 . . . . . . . . . . . . . . . . . . . . . . . . . . . . . . . | 300 | 2.15 |
| Purchase 3 . . . . . . . . . . . . . . . . . . . . . . . . . . . . . . . | 200 | 2.20 |
| Purchase 4 . . . . . . . . . . . . . . . . . . . . . . . . . . . . . . . | 100 | 2.25 |
| Physical count on December 31, 19—, is 350 units | | |

3. FIFO                4. LIFO                5. Weighted Average Cost

|  | Number of Units | Unit Cost |
|---|---|---|
| Inventory, July 1, 19— ........................ | 500 | $4.50 |
| Purchase 1 ................................... | 300 | 4.60 |
| Purchase 2 ................................... | 600 | 4.40 |
| Purchase 3 ................................... | 200 | 4.65 |
| Purchase 4 ................................... | 400 | 4.70 |
| Physical count on December 31, 19—, is 600 units | | |

6. FIFO                    7. LIFO                    8. Weighted Average Cost

|  | Number of Units | Unit Cost |
|---|---|---|
| Inventory, April 1, 19 ...................... | 100 | $5.00 |
| Purchase 1 ................................... | 100 | 5.50 |
| Purchase 2 ................................... | 150 | 6.00 |
| Purchase 3 ................................... | 150 | 6.20 |
| Purchase 4 ................................... | 200 | 6.10 |
| Physical count on June 30, 19—, is 250 units | | |

9. FIFO                    10. LIFO                    11. Weighted Average Cost

|  | Number of Units | Unit Cost |
|---|---|---|
| Inventory, October 1, 19— ................... | 150 | $8.00 |
| Purchase 1 ................................... | 100 | 8.50 |
| Purchase 2 ................................... | 250 | 8.25 |
| Purchase 3 ................................... | 200 | 8.75 |
| Purchase 4 ................................... | 100 | 9.00 |
| Physical count on December 31, 19—, is 200 units | | |

12. FIFO                    13. LIFO                    14. Weighted Average Cost

*Student's Score* _____

# Part E

## Estimated Inventory Value

*Directions:* Find the estimated inventory value by the method indicated. Show all work. (4 points for each correct answer)

### Gross Profit Method

**15.**

| | |
|---|---:|
| Net sales to date ............... | $60,000 |
| Inventory, January 1, 19— ....... | 24,000 |
| Purchases ...................... | 42,000 |
| Purchases returns & allowances .. | 1,000 |
| Gross profit % from last period ... | 40% |

Estimated inventory value = _____

**16.**

| | |
|---|---:|
| Net sales to date .............. | $120,000 |
| Inventory, July 1, 19— ........ | 15,000 |
| Purchases ..................... | 87,500 |
| Purchases returns & allowances . | 2,000 |
| Purchases discount ............. | 500 |
| Gross profit % from last period .. | 25% |

Estimated inventory value = _____

**17.**

| | |
|---|---:|
| Net sales to date .............. | $200,000 |
| Inventory, January 1, 19— ...... | 20,000 |
| Purchases ..................... | 132,000 |
| Purchases returns & allowances . | 1,500 |
| Purchases discount ............. | 500 |
| Gross profit % from last period... | 36% |

Estimated inventory value = _____

### Retail Method

**18.**

| | Cost | Retail |
|---|---:|---:|
| Inventory, Jan. 1, 19— | $36,000 | $ 56,000 |
| Net purchases to date . | 68,000 | 100,000 |
| Net sales to date .............. | | 105,000 |

Estimated inventory value = _____

**19.**

| | Cost | Retail |
|---|---:|---:|
| Inventory, July 1, 19— | $14,000 | $ 20,000 |
| Net purchases to date . | 63,000 | 90,000 |
| Net sales to date .............. | | 85,000 |

Estimated inventory value = _____

**20.**

| | Cost | Retail |
|---|---:|---:|
| Inventory, Mar. 1, 19— | $ 5,400 | $ 10,400 |
| Net purchases to date . | 43,600 | 83,800 |
| Net sales to date .............. | | 79,000 |

Estimated inventory value = _____

*Student's Score* _____

# Part F

## Finding the Cost of Goods Sold

*Directions:* Find the cost of goods sold. Show your work in income-statement form below each problem. (4 points for each correct answer)

21. Inventory, January 1, 19— ....... $34,000
    Inventory, December 31, 19— .... 30,000
    Net purchases .................. 90,000

    Cost of goods sold = _____

24. Inventory, July 1, 19— .......... $12,300
    Inventory, December 31, 19— .... 14,500
    Purchases ...................... 87,000
    Purchases returns & allowances .. 2,100
    Purchases discount ............. 900

    Cost of goods sold = _____

22. Inventory, April 1, 19— .......... $21,400
    Inventory, September 30, 19— .... 18,600
    Purchases ...................... 69,700
    Purchases discount ............. 800

    Cost of goods sold = _____

25. Inventory, January 1, 19— ....... $18,000
    Inventory, March 15, 19— ....... 16,500
    Purchases to date ............... 78,000
    Purchases returns & allowances .. 3,600
    Purchases discount ............ 1% of purchases

    Cost of goods sold = _____

23. Inventory, January 1, 19— ....... $10,300
    Inventory, December 31, 19— .... 8,900
    Purchases ...................... 51,200
    Purchases returns & allowances .. 2,800
    Purchases discount ............. 400

    Cost of goods sold = _____

*Student's Score* _____

# Section 13-2  Calculating Depreciation

All plant assets which are necessary for a business, such as equipment, furniture, and trucks, eventually wear out or become obsolete. Their cost can be charged off periodically as depreciation expense. Three of the more common methods of determining depreciation are straight-line, declining-balance, and sum-of-the-years-digits. Each has certain advantages and disadvantages.

Three essentials must be available in order to determine depreciation, no matter which method is used. These are:

1. The original cost of the asset. This includes not only the purchase cost but also any costs resulting from shipping charges or installation charges.
2. The estimated salvage value. This is an estimate of the asset's worth at the end of its useful life. This often is called **scrap or resale value**.
3. The estimated life of the asset. This is usually stated in years, but occasionally may be stated in other units such as miles (for trucks or buses) or pieces produced (for machines).

The **book value** of an asset equals the original cost minus the accumulated depreciation. Note that salvage value is not deducted. The last book value cannot be less than the estimated salvage value. Book value, as such, does not appear in any account, but must be calculated separately.

## Part A  Straight-Line Method of Figuring Depreciation

In the **straight-line method**, the cost of the asset minus its estimated salvage value is charged off in *equal amounts* over its estimated useful life. The formula for determining the dollar amount of allowable depreciation is:

$$\frac{\text{Annual}}{\text{Depreciation}} = \frac{\text{Original Cost} - \text{Salvage Value}}{\text{Estimated Life}}$$

*Examples:*

a. Determine the annual depreciation by the straight-line method for a delivery truck whose original cost is $8,500, estimated salvage value is $1,000, and estimated useful life is 5 years.

$$\frac{\text{Annual}}{\text{Depreciation}} = \frac{\$8,500 - \$1,000}{5} = \$1,500$$

b. Find the book value for each year for the delivery truck in *Example a*.

| Year | Accumulated Depreciation | Book Value |
|------|------|------|
| 1 | $1,500 | $8,500 − $1,500 = $7,000 |
| 2 | 3,000 | 8,500 − 3,000 = 5,500 |
| 3 | 4,500 | 8,500 − 4,500 = 4,000 |
| 4 | 6,000 | 8,500 − 6,000 = 2,500 |
| 5 | 7,500 | 8,500 − 7,500 = 1,000 |

## Part B  Declining-Balance Method of Figuring Depreciation

The **declining-balance method** is an accelerated method of computing depreciation since the depreciation is larger in the early life of the asset and then declines sharply. One of the advantages of an accelerated method is that as the allowable depreciation is decreased, repair and maintenance expenses are increased to even out the business expense.

In this method, a constant or *fixed rate* is multiplied by a base that is reduced each year by the amount of depreciation taken the previous year. Thus, the base used is the book value of the asset at the beginning of the fiscal period. Note that the term "declining-balance" refers to the book value which decreases each year. The maximum fixed rate allowed is twice the quotient of 100% divided by the estimated life. The formula is:

$$\text{Fixed rate} = 2 \times \frac{100\%}{\text{Estimated life}}$$

A lower rate also may be used, but it *must* be used if the asset acquired is not new.

*Example:* Determine the depreciation by the declining-balance method for each year for the delivery truck used in the Part A examples.

$$\text{Fixed rate} = 2 \times \frac{100\%}{5} = 40\%$$

| | | |
|---|---|---|
| $8,500 × 40% | = $3,400 | (1st year dep.) |
| $8,500 − $3,400 | = $5,100 | (1st year b. v.) |
| $5,100 × 40% | = $2,040 | (2d year dep.) |
| $8,500 − $5,440 | = $3,060 | (2d year b. v.) |
| $3,060 × 40% | = $1,224 | (3d year dep.) |
| $8,500 − $6,664 | = $1,836 | (3d year b. v.) |

$1,836 × 40% = $734.40 (4th year dep.)
$8,500 − $7,398.40 = $1,101.60 (4th year b. v.)
$1,101.60 − $1,000 = $101.60 (5th year dep.)
$8,500 − $7,500 = $1,000 (Est. salvage value)

Note that the beginning book value is always the original cost. Salvage value is *not* deducted. Note also that the 5th year calculated depreciation amount would be $440.64, but only $101.60 can be used because the book value for the last year cannot fall below the $1,000 estimated salvage value.

## Part C Sum-of-the-Years-Digits Method of Figuring Depreciation

Like the declining-balance method, the sum-of-the-years-digits (SOYD) method allows a larger dollar amount of depreciation in the early years of the asset's life. Each year, as the asset gets older, the amount of allowable depreciation becomes smaller.

To determine the amount of depreciation allowable under the SOYD method, several steps have to be followed:

1. Find the sum-of-the-years-digits of the estimated life of the asset. For the delivery truck whose estimated life is 5 years, the SOYD = 5 + 4 + 3 + 2 + 1 = 15.

An easy way to find the SOYD is to use the following formula:

$$SOYD = \frac{n(n+1)}{2} \text{ where n = Estimated life}$$

2. Find the rate of depreciation for each year. The rate is a changing fraction which is formed by using the SOYD as the denominator; the numerator needed is the number of years of estimated life that remain for the asset. For example, the rate for the 1st year's depreciation of the delivery truck mentioned above is 5/15. The rate for the 2d year's depreciation is 4/15. This process is continued until the last year. (The annual *difference* is always $\frac{1}{SOYD}$ × Cost − Salvage value. This provides a check on the annual amounts calculated.)

3. Multiply the rate (fraction) for each year by the original cost of the asset minus the estimated salvage value.

*Example:* Determine the depreciation and book value by the SOYD method for each year for the truck whose original cost is $8,500; estimated salvage value, $1,000; and estimated life, 5 years.

Step 1: $\frac{5(5+1)}{2} = 15$

Step 2: Rate for 1st year = 5/15
Rate for 2d year = 4/15
Rate for 3d year = 3/15
Rate for 4th year = 2/15
Rate for 5th year = 1/15

Step 3:

| | |
|---|---|
| 5/15 × $7,500 | = $2,500 (1st year dep.) |
| $8,500 − $2,500 | = $6,000 (1st year b. v.) |
| 4/15 × $7,500 | = $2,000 (2d year dep.) |
| $8,500 − $4,500 | = $4,000 (2d year b. v.) |
| 3/15 × $7,500 | = $1,500 (3d year dep.) |
| $8,500 − $6,000 | = $2,500 (3d year b. v.) |
| 2/15 × $7,500 | = $1,000 (4th year dep.) |
| $8,500 − $7,000 | = $1,500 (4th year b. v.) |
| 1/15 × $7,500 | = $ 500 (5th year dep.) |
| $8,500 − $7,500 | = $1,000 (Est. salvage value) |

## Part D Comparison of Depreciation Methods

The same delivery truck is used to compare the three methods of determining depreciation. Sometimes it is easier to compare the different methods if the depreciation amounts are presented in the following form.

Original cost......................... $8,500
Estimated salvage value ............ 1,000
Estimated life ..................... 5 years

| Year | Straight-Line Method | Declining-Balance Method | SOYD Method |
|---|---|---|---|
| 1 | $1,500 | $3,400.00 | $2,500 |
| 2 | 1,500 | 2,040.00 | 2,000 |
| 3 | 1,500 | 1,224.00 | 1,500 |
| 4 | 1,500 | 734.40 | 1,000 |
| 5 | 1,500 | 101.60* | 500 |

* This figure results because the last year book value cannot fall below $1,000.

Complete Assignment 36

Chapter 13 / Inventory Valuation, Cost of Goods Sold, and Depreciation

## Assignment 36
## Section 13-2

*Calculating Depreciation*

| | Perfect Score | Student's Score |
|---|---|---|
| Part A | 30 | |
| Part B | 30 | |
| Part C | 24 | |
| Part D | 16 | |
| TOTAL | 100 | |

# Part A

### Straight-Line Method of Figuring Depreciation

*Directions:* Use the straight-line method to calculate the annual depreciation for the given year, the accumulated depreciation (annual depreciation × year of depreciation), and the book value at the end of the given year (original cost − accumulated depreciation). Show all work. (1 point for each correct answer)

| | Original Cost | Estimated Life | Estimated Salvage Value | Year of Depreciation | Annual Depreciation | Accumulated Depreciation | Book Value End of Year |
|---|---|---|---|---|---|---|---|
| 1. | $ 675 | 5 yrs. | $ 50 | 1st | _____ | _____ | _____ |
| 2. | 2,400 | 10 yrs. | 300 | 2d | _____ | _____ | _____ |
| 3. | 1,650 | 8 yrs. | 0 | 3d | _____ | _____ | _____ |
| 4. | 2,710 | 5 yrs. | 200 | 2d | _____ | _____ | _____ |
| 5. | 230 | 4 yrs. | 40 | 1st | _____ | _____ | _____ |
| 6. | 960 | 7 yrs. | 50 | 2d | _____ | _____ | _____ |
| 7. | 4,800 | 4 yrs. | 650 | 3d | _____ | _____ | _____ |
| 8. | 3,950 | 8 yrs. | 0 | 6th | _____ | _____ | _____ |
| 9. | 150 | 10 yrs. | 0 | 5th | _____ | _____ | _____ |
| 10. | 540 | 3 yrs. | 75 | 2d | _____ | _____ | _____ |

*Student's Score* _____

# Part B

## Declining-Balance Method of Figuring Depreciation

**Directions:** Use the declining-balance method to calculate the annual depreciation for the given year, the accumulated depreciation, and the book value at the end of the given year. Show all work. (1 point for each correct answer)

| | Original Cost | Estimated Life in Years | Salvage Value | Year of Use | Annual Depreciation | Accumulated Depreciation | Book Value |
|---|---|---|---|---|---|---|---|
| 11. | $2,100 | 5 | $100 | 1st | _____ | _____ | _____ |
| 12. | 1,500 | 10 | 100 | 2d | _____ | _____ | _____ |
| 13. | 400 | 4 | 0 | 3d | _____ | _____ | _____ |
| 14. | 4,900 | 4 | 430 | 4th | _____ | _____ | _____ |
| 15. | 6,800 | 5 | 600 | 5th | _____ | _____ | _____ |
| 16. | 850 | 10 | 50 | 3d | _____ | _____ | _____ |
| 17. | 600 | 6 | 25 | 2d | _____ | _____ | _____ |
| 18. | 1,350 | 8 | 150 | 4th | _____ | _____ | _____ |
| 19. | 5,200 | 4 | 500 | 3d | _____ | _____ | _____ |
| 20. | 2,300 | 10 | 200 | 2d | _____ | _____ | _____ |

*Student's Score* _____

# Part C
## Sum-of-the-Years-Digits Method of Figuring Depreciation

*Directions:* Use the sum-of-the-years-digits method to calculate the annual depreciation for the given year, the accumulated depreciation, and the book value at the end of the given year. Show all work. (1 point for each correct answer)

| Original Cost | Estimated Life in Years | Salvage Value | Year of Use | Annual Depreciation | Accumulated Depreciation | Book Value |
|---|---|---|---|---|---|---|
| 21. $ 500 | 5 | $ 20 | 1st | _____ | _____ | _____ |
| 22. 1,500 | 6 | 100 | 2d | _____ | _____ | _____ |
| 23. 875 | 5 | 50 | 3d | _____ | _____ | _____ |
| 24. 1,250 | 8 | 100 | 2d | _____ | _____ | _____ |
| 25. 5,400 | 6 | 500 | 4th | _____ | _____ | _____ |
| 26. 1,100 | 4 | 100 | 3d | _____ | _____ | _____ |
| 27. 400 | 8 | 40 | 5th | _____ | _____ | _____ |
| 28. 600 | 10 | 50 | 6th | _____ | _____ | _____ |

*Student's Score* _____

# Part D

## Comparison of Depreciation Methods

*Directions:* Calculate by all three methods the maximum depreciation allowable on a machine purchased for $6,500 with an estimated life of 5 years and an estimated salvage value of $500. Round off answers to whole dollars. Show all work. (1 point for each correct answer)

| | Year | Straight-Line | Declining-Balance | Sum-of-the-Years-Digits |
|---|---|---|---|---|
| 29. | 1 | _____ | _____ | _____ |
| 30. | 2 | _____ | _____ | _____ |
| 01. | 0 | _____ | _____ | _____ |
| 32. | 4 | _____ | _____ | _____ |
| 33. | 5 | _____ | _____ | _____ |

34. Which method results in the highest accumulated depreciation for the first three years?_____

*Student's Score* _____

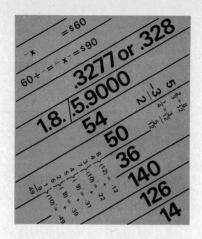

# Binary and Hexadecimal Number Systems

CHAPTER **14**

A **number system** can be defined as a scheme which provides an orderly arrangement of figures or letters to represent numbers. In the **Roman number system**, definite values are given to seven capital letters as follows:

| I | V | X | L | C | D | M |
|---|---|---|---|---|---|---|
| one | five | ten | fifty | one hundred | five hundred | one thousand |

These letters are variously arranged to represent numbers. For example, XXI is twenty-one. A line above the arrangement multiplies the number by 1,000. For example, $\overline{VI}$ is six thousand.

A more logical system has regularly-weighted positional values derived from its base. Such a system uses as many single digits or letters, called *characters*, as there are units in the base. For example, the Hindu-Arabic or decimal number system, which we have used so far in this text-workbook, has ten as its *base*. This base consists of two characters: 10. The 1 stands for 1 set of base units: [1, 1, 1, 1, 1, 1, 1, 1, 1, 1] and the 0 shows that there are no other units in the base. Exactly 10 sets of 10 units equal 100 units, and 10 × 10 sets of 10 units equals 1,000, etc. Each place value is 10 times the place value to its right. There are 10 single digits in the system: 0, 1, 2, 3, 4, 5, 6, 7, 8, and 9. The full value of a digit in a particular position, or place, is found by multiplying the digit by its place value. The sum of all the full values of the digits in the number constitutes the total units in the number. For example:

$$845 = \frac{8}{(100)} \quad \frac{4}{(10)} \quad \frac{5}{(1)}$$

$$
\begin{array}{rcl}
8 \times 100 & = & 800 \text{ units} \\
4 \times 10 & = & 40 \text{ units} \\
5 \times 1 & = & \underline{5} \text{ units} \\
& & 845 \text{ units}
\end{array}
$$

There are other logical number systems which do not use 10 as their base. In this chapter you will work with two *other-base* systems: **binary** or base-2, and **hexadecimal** ("hex") or base-16, both of which are used in computers. To denote a number in these other-base systems, a **subscript** (a small number below and to the right) is used. For example, $101_2$ is a binary number.

# Binary Number System (Base 2)

The binary system is a base-2 system. The two digits used are 0 and 1, which are often called **bits** instead of binary digits. Most computers do not use a binary system as such, but they use a number system or **code** based on the binary system. The computer can recognize only "Power On," or 1, and "Power Off," or 0. Only the pure binary system is given here.

In the decimal number system, the positional values are . . . , 10,000, 1,000, 100, 10, 1. Note that each position equals the base (10) times the value

of the number to its right. The last position, whose value is 1, is used to show the number of units less than the base, 10, that are left over.

The positional values in binary are: . . . , 512, 256, 128, 64, 32, 16, 8, 4, 2, 1, with each position equaling the base (2) times the value of the number to its right. A binary number consists of only 0's and 1's since these are the only digits in the system.

***Converting a binary number to its decimal system equivalent.*** To find the decimal system equivalent of a binary number, write the positional value under each digit, multiply each binary digit by its positional value, and find the sum of the products. See the examples below.

## *Examples:*

| | **Binary Number** | **Decimal System Equivalent** |
|---|---|---|

a. $1_2 = \dfrac{0}{(2)} + \dfrac{1}{(1)}$

$\quad\quad\quad\; 0 \;+\; 1$ ......................................... 1

b. $10_2 = \dfrac{1}{(2)} + \dfrac{0}{(1)}$

$\quad\quad\quad\; 2 \;+\; 0$ ......................................... 2

c. $11_2 = \dfrac{1}{(2)} + \dfrac{1}{(1)}$

$\quad\quad\quad\; 2 \;+\; 1$ ......................................... 3

d. $100_2 = \dfrac{1}{(4)} + \dfrac{0}{(2)} + \dfrac{0}{(1)}$

$\quad\quad\quad\; 4 \;+\; 0 \;+\; 0$ ................................... 4

e. $101_2 = \dfrac{1}{(4)} + \dfrac{0}{(2)} + \dfrac{1}{(1)}$

$\quad\quad\quad\; 4 \;+\; 0 \;+\; 1$ ................................... 5

f. $1101_2 = \dfrac{1}{(8)} + \dfrac{1}{(4)} + \dfrac{0}{(2)} + \dfrac{1}{(1)}$

$\quad\quad\quad\; 8 \;+\; 4 \;+\; 0 \;+\; 1$ ............................ 13

g. $111010_2 = \dfrac{1}{(32)} + \dfrac{1}{(16)} + \dfrac{1}{(8)} + \dfrac{0}{(4)} + \dfrac{1}{(2)} + \dfrac{0}{(1)}$

$\quad\quad\quad\; 32 \;+\; 16 \;+\; 8 \;+\; 0 \;+\; 2 \;+\; 0$ .......... 58

h. $1111111_2 = \dfrac{1}{(64)} + \dfrac{1}{(32)} + \dfrac{1}{(16)} + \dfrac{1}{(8)} + \dfrac{1}{(4)} + \dfrac{1}{(2)} + \dfrac{1}{(1)}$

$\quad\quad\quad\; 64 \;+\; 32 \;+\; 16 \;+\; 8 \;+\; 4 \;+\; 2 \;+\; 1$ .. 127

***Converting a decimal number to its binary system equivalent.*** A simple illustration may help you to understand the process of converting a decimal number to its binary system equivalent.

Think of the number 25 in the decimal number system as:

$$\frac{2}{(10)} \qquad \frac{5}{(1)}$$

Break up the two sets of ten into twenty single units or 1's and add the five 1's so that there are now twenty-five 1's.

Now take out 1 set of sixteen 1's to form the first digit of the binary equivalent:

$$\frac{1}{(16)}$$

There are nine 1's left. The positional value to the right of 16 in the binary system is 8, so take out 1 set of eight 1's to form the second digit. The binary equivalent so far is:

$$\frac{1}{(16)} \qquad \frac{1}{(8)}$$

Now there is only one 1 left. The next two positional values to the right of 8 are 4 and 2, but no sets of 4 or 2 can be taken out of the remaining 1. Zeros are written above the 4 and 2 positional values. The remaining 1 is written above the last positional value, 1. The binary equivalent now is complete:

$$\frac{1}{(16)} \qquad \frac{1}{(8)} \qquad \frac{0}{(4)} \qquad \frac{0}{(2)} \qquad \frac{1}{(1)}$$

Note that in the illustration above, the total number of units in the decimal number were redistributed into such sets of the binary positional values that were contained in the decimal number.

The general procedure to change any decimal number to its equivalent in another base is repeated division by the positional values of the other base. Specifically, to convert a decimal number to its binary system equivalent, divide the decimal number by the largest binary positional value contained in that number. This gives the first digit of the binary number. Then divide the remainder by the next binary positional value to get the second digit of the binary number,

either 1 or 0. Continue this with each positional value through the units. If a particular remainder does not contain the next positional value, a 0 must be placed in that position in the binary number.

*Example:* Convert 215 to its binary system equivalent by using repeated division.

The positional values needed start with 128.

$$\begin{array}{r} 1 \\ 128\overline{\smash{\big)}\,215} \\ \underline{128} \\ 87 \end{array}$$ There is 1 "128" and 87 units are left over.

$$\begin{array}{r} 1 \\ 64\overline{\smash{\big)}\,87} \\ \underline{64} \\ 23 \end{array}$$ There is 1 "64" and 23 units are left over. There is 0 "32" and 23 units are left over.

$$\begin{array}{r} 1 \\ 16\overline{\smash{\big)}\,23} \\ \underline{16} \\ 7 \end{array}$$ There is 1 "16" and 7 units are left over. There is 0 "8" and 7 units are left over.

$$\begin{array}{r} 1 \\ 4\overline{\smash{\big)}\,7} \\ \underline{4} \\ 3 \end{array}$$ There is 1 "4" and 3 units are left over.

$$\begin{array}{r} 1 \\ 2\overline{\smash{\big)}\,3} \\ \underline{2} \\ 1 \end{array}$$ There is 1 "2" and 1 unit left over. There is 1 "1."

Therefore, $215 = 11010111_2$.

Since the quotient digits by the above method of repeated division can be only 0 or 1, a second method of converting a decimal system number to its binary system equivalent consists of repeated subtraction. To do this, subtract the positional values in order, starting with the largest value contained in the decimal method. (This method of repeated subtraction can be used easily only in converting a decimal number to its binary equivalent.) The same example used in the first method is used to illustrate the second method.

*Example:* Convert 215 to its binary system equivalent by using repeated subtraction.

The positional values needed start with 128.

$$215$$
$$- \ 128 \quad \text{There is 1 ``128'' and}$$
$$\overline{\quad 87} \quad \text{87 units are left over.}$$

$$87$$
$$- \ 64 \quad \text{There is 1 ``64'' and}$$
$$\overline{\quad 23} \quad \text{23 units are left over.}$$
There is 0 "32" and
23 units are left over.

$$23$$
$$- \ 16 \quad \text{There is 1 ``16'' and}$$
$$\overline{\quad 7} \quad \text{7 units are left over.}$$
There is 0 "8" and
7 units are left over.

$$7$$
$$- \ 4 \quad \text{There is 1 ``4'' and}$$
$$\overline{\quad 3} \quad \text{3 units are left over.}$$

$$3$$
$$- \ 2 \quad \text{There is 1 ``2'' and}$$
$$\overline{\quad 1} \quad \text{1 unit is left over.}$$
There is 1 "1".

Therefore, $215 = 11010111_2$.

## Part B  Hexadecimal Number System (Base 16)

Almost all computers use a code which is based on 16. A converter changes the decimal system numbers on magnetic tape or on punched cards to base-16 numbers for work in the computer. The process is then reversed for the printout. Some special printouts, however, may be in base-16, such as locations or instructions which apply only to internal operations in the computer.

Since the hexadecimal number system has a base of 16, there must be 16 single digits in the system. The decimal system digits 0 through 9 can be used to represent the same quantities in hexadecimal; but for the quantities between 9 and the base, there must be only a *single* figure for each of the numbers. Capital letters are used for these digits.

| Hexadecimal | Decimal |
|---|---|
| A | 10 |
| B | 11 |
| C | 12 |
| D | 13 |
| E | 14 |
| F | 15 |

The sixteen characters in the hexadecimal number system are: 0, 1, 2, 3, 4, 5, 6, 7, 8, 9, A, B, C, D, E, F. There is no letter for 16, since this is written $10_{16}$. Sixteen sets of 16 are written $100_{16}$, with the 1 having the value of 256 units in the decimal number system. Two hundred fifty-six sets of 16 are written as $1000_{16}$, etc. Each positional value in the hexadecimal system is sixteen times the one to its right. The positional values are:

| 4,096 | 256 | 16 | 1 |
|---|---|---|---|
| (256 × 16) | (16 × 16) | (1 × 16) | (units) |

*Converting a hexadecimal number to its decimal system equivalent.* To find the decimal system equivalent of a hexadecimal number, write the positional value under each digit, multiply each hexadecimal digit by its positional value, and then find the sum of the products. See the examples at the top of page 279.

*Converting a decimal number to its hexadecimal system equivalent.* To change a decimal number to a hexadecimal, repeated division is used just as in the binary number system. When the positional value is contained 10 to 15 times, the quotient is changed to the correct capital letter. Each positional value can have only a single digit in that place.

*Examples:*

a. Convert 199 to a hexadecimal number.

The positional values needed are:

$$\overline{(16)} \qquad \overline{(1)}$$

$$\begin{array}{r} 12 \\ 16\overline{)199} \\ \underline{16} \\ 39 \\ \underline{32} \\ 7 \end{array}$$
There are C (12) "16's" and 7 units left over.

Therefore, $199 = C7_{16}$.

*Examples:*

|  | Decimal System Equivalent |
|---|---|
| **Hexadecimal Number** |  |

a. $\quad 1A_{16} = \dfrac{1}{(16)} + \dfrac{A}{(1)}$

$\qquad\qquad 16 \;+\; 10$ ........................................ $\qquad 26$

b. $\quad 789_{16} = \dfrac{7}{(256)} + \dfrac{8}{(16)} + \dfrac{9}{(1)}$

$\qquad\qquad 1{,}792 \;+\; 128 \;+\; 9$ ............................... $\qquad 1{,}929$

c. $\quad BCDE_{16} = \dfrac{B}{(4{,}096)} + \dfrac{C}{(256)} + \dfrac{D}{(16)} + \dfrac{E}{(1)}$

$\qquad\qquad\qquad\; \times\,11 \quad\; \times\,12 \quad\; \times\,13 \quad\; \times\,14$

$\qquad\qquad 45{,}056 \;+\; 3{,}072 \;+\; 208 \;+\; 14$ ................ $\qquad 48{,}350$

---

b. Change 3,739 to a hexadecimal number.

The positional values needed are:

$\overline{\;(256)\;} \qquad \overline{\;(16)\;} \qquad \overline{\;(1)\;}$

$\begin{array}{r} 14 \\ 256\,\overline{\smash{)}\,3739} \\ \underline{256} \\ 1179 \\ \underline{1024} \\ 155 \end{array}$  There are E (14) "256's" and 155 units left over.

$\begin{array}{r} 9 \\ 16\,\overline{\smash{)}\,155} \\ \underline{144} \\ 11 \end{array}$  There are 9 "16's" and B (11) units left over.

Therefore, 3,739 = $E9B_{16}$.

As mentioned earlier, computers recognize only two signals: 0 and 1. Therefore, when a decimal number is converted to hexadecimal, each character is represented by its four-bit binary equivalent, although it is still considered a single character. If the binary equivalent has fewer than four bits, preceding zeros are used to make the four places. Inside the computer, two four-bit numbers are stacked vertically to form a *byte*.

*Examples:*

a. $226 = E2_{16}$

$E_{16} = 14$ units $= 1110_2$

$2_{16} = 2$ units $= 0010_2 \quad$ byte $= \dfrac{\begin{array}{c}1\\1\\1\\0\end{array}}{\begin{array}{c}0\\0\\1\\0\end{array}}$

b. $19{,}231 = 4B1F_{16}$

$4_{16} = 4$ units $= 0100_2$

$B_{16} = 11$ units $= 1011_2 \quad$ 2 bytes $= \dfrac{\begin{array}{cc}0 & 0\\1 & 0\\0 & 0\\0 & 1\end{array}}{\begin{array}{cc}1 & 1\\0 & 1\\1 & 1\\1 & 1\end{array}}$

$1_{16} = 1$ unit $= 0001_2$

$F_{16} = 15$ units $= 1111_2$

## Part C  Using a Hexadecimal and Decimal Conversion Table

A conversion table often is used to convert a hexadecimal system number to a decimal system number and to convert a decimal system number to a hexadecimal system number. Now refer to Table 14-1 on page 280. There are three main columns, each of which has a hexadecimal column and a decimal column, for use with three-byte numbers. The decimal column shows the decimal system equivalent of the hexadecimal character in its particular position in the

# Table 14-1  Hexadecimal and Decimal Conversion Table

| BYTE | | BYTE | | BYTE | | | | | | | |
|---|---|---|---|---|---|---|---|---|---|---|---|
| HEX | DEC | HEX | DEC | HEX | DEC | HEX | DEC | HEX | DEC | HEX | DEC |
| 0 | 0 | 0 | 0 | 0 | 0 | 0 | 0 | 0 | 0 | 0 | 0 |
| 1 | 1,048,576 | 1 | 65,536 | 1 | 4,096 | 1 | 256 | 1 | 16 | 1 | 1 |
| 2 | 2,097,152 | 2 | 131,072 | 2 | 8,192 | 2 | 512 | 2 | 32 | 2 | 2 |
| 3 | 3,145,728 | 3 | 196,608 | 3 | 12,288 | 3 | 768 | 3 | 48 | 3 | 3 |
| 4 | 4,194,304 | 4 | 262,144 | 4 | 16,384 | 4 | 1,024 | 4 | 64 | 4 | 4 |
| 5 | 5,242,880 | 5 | 327,680 | 5 | 20,480 | 5 | 1,280 | 5 | 80 | 5 | 5 |
| 6 | 6,291,456 | 6 | 393,216 | 6 | 24,576 | 6 | 1,536 | 6 | 96 | 6 | 6 |
| 7 | 7,340,032 | 7 | 458,752 | 7 | 28,672 | 7 | 1,792 | 7 | 112 | 7 | 7 |
| 8 | 8,388,608 | 8 | 524,288 | 8 | 32,768 | 8 | 2,048 | 8 | 128 | 8 | 8 |
| 9 | 9,437,184 | 9 | 589,824 | 9 | 36,864 | 9 | 2,304 | 9 | 144 | 9 | 9 |
| A | 10,485,760 | A | 655,360 | A | 40,960 | A | 2,560 | A | 160 | A | 10 |
| B | 11,534,336 | B | 720,896 | B | 45,056 | B | 2,816 | B | 176 | B | 11 |
| C | 12,582,912 | C | 786,432 | C | 49,152 | C | 3,072 | C | 192 | C | 12 |
| D | 13,631,488 | D | 851,968 | D | 53,248 | D | 3,328 | D | 208 | D | 13 |
| E | 14,680,064 | E | 917,504 | E | 57,344 | E | 3,584 | E | 224 | E | 14 |
| F | 15,728,640 | F | 983,040 | F | 61,440 | F | 3,840 | F | 240 | F | 15 |
| (1,048,576) | | (65,536) | | (4,096) | | (256) | | (16) | | (1) | |
| Column 6 | | Column 5 | | Column 4 | | Column 3 | | Column 2 | | Column 1 | |

hexadecimal number. The place values of the hexadecimal system are shown in parentheses at the bottom.

### Examples:

a. D in the third HEX column from the right shows 3,328 in the adjacent DEC column.

**Check:**  $D_{16} = 13$
$13 \times 256 = 3,328$

b. 9 in the fifth HEX column from the right shows 589,824 in the adjacent DEC column.

**Check:** $9 \times 65,536 = 589,824$

**Converting hexadecimal to decimal.** To find the decimal system equivalent of a hexadecimal number, find each HEX character in the proper column and its adjacent DEC equivalent. Then find the sum of the decimal numbers.

### Examples:

a. Find the decimal system equivalent of $C7A_{16}$.

$$
\begin{array}{rr}
C \text{ (column 3)} = & 3,072 \\
7 \text{ (column 2)} = & 112 \\
A \text{ (column 1)} = & \underline{10} \\
C7A_{16} = & 3,194
\end{array}
$$

b. Find the decimal system equivalent of $6B9DC_{16}$.

$$
\begin{array}{rr}
6 \text{ (column 5)} = & 393,216 \\
B \text{ (column 4)} = & 45,056 \\
9 \text{ (column 3)} = & 2,304 \\
D \text{ (column 2)} = & 208 \\
C \text{ (column 1)} = & \underline{12} \\
6B9DC_{16} = & 440,796
\end{array}
$$

**Converting decimal to hexadecimal.** To find the hexadecimal system equivalent of a decimal system number, search the DEC columns for a number that is either *equal* to the given number or *a little less*. The HEX character to the left is the first character in the hexadecimal equivalent.

If the number in the DEC column is equal to the given number, the hexadecimal equivalent consists of the first character followed by as many zeros as there are remaining columns.

*Example:* Find the hexadecimal system equivalent of 917,504.

Search the DEC columns and locate 917,504 in column 5. The HEX character to its left is E. Since the two decimal numbers are equal:

$$917,504 = E0000_{16}$$

If the table decimal number is smaller than the given number, follow these steps:

1. Locate the smaller table decimal number. The HEX character to its left becomes the first character in the hexadecimal equivalent.

2. Find the difference between the table decimal number and the given number. In the next column to the *right*, locate a decimal number that is equal to or smaller than this difference. The HEX character to its left becomes the second character in the hexadecimal equivalent.

3. Continue this procedure until the entire hexadecimal equivalent is found. Note that when the next smaller number is 0, the HEX character is also 0.

*Examples:*

a. Find the hexadecimal system equivalent of 15,261.

**Step 1:** Locate the smaller table decimal number, 12,288, in column 4. The HEX character to its left, $3_{16}$, becomes the first character in the hexadecimal equivalent.

**Step 2:** The difference between 15,261 and 12,288 is 2,973. Locate the smaller table decimal number, 2,816, in column 3. The HEX character to its left, $B_{16}$, becomes the second character in the hexadecimal equivalent.

**Step 3:** The difference between 2,973 and 2,816 is 157. Locate the smaller table decimal number, 144, in column 2. The HEX character to its left, $9_{16}$, becomes the third character in the hexadecimal equivalent.

**Step 4:** The difference between 157 and 144 is 13. Locate 13 in column 1. The HEX character to its left, $D_{16}$, becomes the fourth character in the hexadecimal equivalent.

Therefore, $15,261 = 3B9D_{16}$.

b. Find the hexadecimal equivalent of 10,522,117.

**Step 1:** Locate 10,485,760 in column 6 to get $A_{16}$ as the first HEX character.

**Step 2:** $10,522,117 - 10,485,760 = 36,357$. Locate 0 in column 5 to get $0_{16}$ as the second HEX character.

**Step 3:** $36,357 - 0 = 36,357$. Locate 32,768 in column 4 to get $8_{16}$ as the third HEX character.

**Step 4:** $36,357 - 32,768 = 3,589$. Locate 3,584 in column 3 to get $E_{16}$ as the fourth HEX character.

**Step 5:** $3,589 - 3,584 = 5$. Locate 0 in column 2 to get $0_{16}$ as the fifth HEX character.

**Step 6:** $5 - 0 = 5$. Locate 5 in column 1 to get $5_{16}$ as the sixth HEX character.

Therefore, $10,522,117 = A08E05_{16}$.

For hexadecimal numbers of more than six characters and for decimal numbers larger than the largest value in column 6, a powers of 16 table must be used to supplement Table 14-1. Because of the complexity of these conversions, they are not presented here.

## Part D  Arithmetic Operations in Binary and Hexadecimal Systems

The rules for arithmetic operations are the same in all number systems. Each number system has its own tables for addition, subtraction, multiplication, and division; and the operations can be performed on the basis of these tables, just as in our decimal number system. This is difficult to do without a thorough knowledge of the particular system.

Generally a combination of performing the calculation in the decimal number system and then converting to the other base is used. In the binary number system, the digits have the same values as in the decimal system. In the hexadecimal number system, the first ten digits are the same as the first ten digits in the decimal number system, and the decimal values of the letters are used for the remaining six characters. Each part of an operation is done in the decimal system, and the conversion is made immediately after completing the calculation.

The operation is checked by converting the given other-base numbers to their decimal system equivalents and performing the operation in the decimal system. The answer in the given other-base is then converted to the decimal system to provide the check.

A complete explanation of the fundamental operations in other number systems is beyond the scope of this book, but examples of each operation and a brief explanation will show the basic procedures involved in the operation and the check. In hexadecimal, the procedures used by a computer in addition and subtraction also are shown.

*Addition in binary and hexadecimal systems.* After each step is completed in decimals, change the sum to its other-base equivalent. Any carryover is added to the result in the next step.

*Examples:*

a.
$$\begin{array}{r} 1011_2 \\ + \ 111_2 \\ \hline 10010_2 \end{array}$$

**Step 1:** Add $1 + 1 = 2$. Change the 2 units to binary: $10_2$. Write the 0 and carry the 1.

**Step 2:** Add $1 + 1 + 1 = 3 = 11_2$. Write the 1 and carry the 1.

**Step 3:** Add $0 + 1 + 1 = 2 = 10_2$. Write the 0 and carry the 1.

**Step 4:** Add $1 + 1 = 2 = 10_2$. Write the 10.

**Check:**
$$\begin{array}{r} 1011_2 = 11 \\ + \ 111_2 = \ 7 \\ \hline 10010_2 = 18 \end{array}$$

$10010_2 = (1 \times 16) + (1 \times 2) = 18$

b.
$$\begin{array}{r} A9B_{16} \\ + \ 3CF_{16} \\ \hline E6A_{16} \end{array}$$

**Step 1:** Add B (11) + F (15) = 26 = $1A_{16}$. Write the A and carry the 1.

**Step 2:** Add $9 + C (12) + 1 = 22 = 16_{16}$. Write the 6 and carry the 1.

**Step 3:** Add A (10) $+ 3 + 1 = 14 = E_{16}$. Write the E.

**Check:**
$$\begin{array}{r} A9B_{16} = 2{,}715 \\ + \ 3CF_{16} = \ 975 \\ \hline E6A_{16} = 3{,}690 \end{array}$$

$$\begin{aligned} E6A_{16} &= (14 \times 256) + (6 \times 16) + 10 \\ &= 3{,}584 + 96 + 10 = 3{,}690 \end{aligned}$$

In the computer, a hexadecimal number is in byte form, with each character represented by its four-bit binary equivalent. The longitudinal byte form is changed here to a horizontal form, with a space in between each equivalent so that the addition can be explained more easily. The addition is the same as shown in the binary example. Any carryover goes to the combination at the left, including the next equivalent.

c.
$$\begin{array}{r} A9B_{16} = 1010 \quad 1001 \quad 1011 \\ + \ 3CF_{16} = 0011 \quad 1100 \quad 1111 \\ \hline 1110 \quad 0110 \quad 1010 \\ (E) \quad\ \ (6) \quad\ \ (A) \end{array}$$

**Step 1:** Start at the extreme right. Add $1 + 1 = 2 = 10_2$. Write the 0 and carry the 1.

**Step 2:** Add $1 + 1 + 1 = 3 = 11_2$. Write the 1 and carry the 1.

**Step 3:** Add $0 + 1 + 1 = 2 = 10_2$. Write the 0 and carry the 1.

**Step 4:** Add $1 + 1 + 1 = 3 = 11_2$. Write the 1 and carry the 1 to the next four-bit equivalent.

**Step 5:** Add $1 + 0 + 1 = 2 = 10_2$. Write the 0 and carry the 1.

**Step 6:** $0 + 0 + 1 = 1$. Write the 1. Etc.

**Step 7:** After completing the binary addition, convert each four-bit equivalent first to its decimal system equivalent and then to hexadecimal.

$$\begin{array}{ccc} 1110 & 0110 & 1010 \\ (14) & (6) & (10) \\ E & 6 & A \end{array}$$

**Check:** Same as in the regular addition.

*Subtraction in binary and hexadecimal systems.* When the subtrahend digit is larger than the minuend digit, a 1 is borrowed from the column at the left. It may be necessary to go more than one column to the left and then borrow from each column in between. In the decimal number system, the borrowed 1 equals 10 units which are automatically added to the minuend digit by placing the borrowed one in front of it.

*Example:*
$$\begin{array}{r} 1 \\ \cancel{2}^1 6 \dots 10 + 6 = 16 \\ - \quad 7 \\ \hline 1\ 9 \end{array}$$

The same procedure is used in other-base number systems when the subtrahend digit is larger than the minuend digit. However, since the actual subtraction is done in the decimal system, the borrowed 1 must be changed to the number of units in the base and then added to the minuend digit. In binary, the borrowed 1 equals 2 units; and in hexadecimal, 16 units.

*Examples:*

a. $10001_2 - 111_2$

$$\begin{array}{r} 0\ 1\ 1 \\ \cancel{1}\cancel{0}\cancel{0}0\ 1_2 \\ - \quad\ \ 1\ 1\ 1_2 \\ \hline 1\ 0\ 1\ 0_2 \end{array}$$

**Step 1:** $1 - 1 = 0$. Write the 0.

**Step 2:** Since 1 cannot be taken from 0, it is necessary to borrow. Since the next two digits to the left are 0's, borrow from the 1 to their left. Each 0 becomes $10_2 = 2$. When a 1 is borrowed from 2, 1 is left. (Note the triple borrowing in the example.) Take 1 from $10_2$ (2). $2 - 1 = 1$. Write the 1.

**Step 3:** $1 - 1 = 0$. Write the 0.

**Step 4:** Since there are no more subtrahend digits, bring down the 1 to the answer.

**Check:**
$$\begin{array}{r} 10001_2 = 17 \\ -\quad 111_2 = \ \ 7 \\ \hline 1010_2 = 10 \end{array}$$

$$1010_2 = (1 \times 8) + (1 \times 2) = 10$$

b. $CA4_{16} - 2BD_{16}$

$$\begin{array}{r} B^1 9 \\ \cancel{C}\ \cancel{A}\ ^1 4_{16} \\ - \quad 2\ B\ D_{16} \\ \hline 9\ E\ 7_{16} \end{array}$$

**Step 1:** Since D (13) cannot be taken from 4, borrow 1 from the A. ($A_{16} - 1 = 9$). Change the borrowed 1 to 16 units and add it to the 4 to make 20 units ($14_{16} = 20$). $20 - 13 = 7$. Write the 7.

**Step 2:** Since B cannot be taken from 9, borrow 1 from the C. Change the borrowed 1 to 16 units and add it to the 9 to make 25 units. ($19_{16} = 25$). $25 - 11 = 14 = E$. Write the E.

**Step 3:** $B (11) - 2 = 9$. Write the 9.

**Check:**
$$\begin{array}{r} CA4_{16} = (12 \times 256) + (10 \times 16) + \ \ 4 \\ -\ 2BD_{16} = (\ 2 \times 256) + (11 \times 16) + 13 \\ \hline 9E7_{16} \end{array}$$

$$\begin{array}{r} = 3,236 \\ = \ \ 701 \\ \hline 2,535 \end{array}$$

$$9E7_{16} = (9 \times 256) + (14 \times 16) + 7$$
$$= 2,304 + 224 + 7 = 2,535$$

Basically, the computer can perform only one operation: binary addition. For subtraction, a method called *base-minus-one complementation* is used.

In general, the base-minus-one complement of a number in any number system is found by taking each digit from the largest digit in the number system. In the binary number system, each digit is taken from 1. The result is always the opposite digit: $1 - 0 = 1$ and $1 - 1 = 0$.

The base-minus-one complement is then added to the minuend. The left-most digit in the result is always 1. This 1 is crossed out and added to the last digit in the result ("end-over-one-carry").

Just as in addition, the longitudinal byte form is changed to a horizontal form with a space in between each four-bit equivalent so that the subtraction can be explained more easily.

c.    $CA4_{16}$ = 1100 1010 0100
    − $2BD_{16}$ = 0010 1011 1101

$$
\begin{array}{r}
1100 \quad 1010 \quad 0100 \\
+\ 1101 \quad 0100 \quad 0010 \\
\cancel{0010} \quad \cancel{1011} \quad \cancel{1101} \\
\hline
\cancel{1}\ 1001 \quad 1110 \quad 0110 \\
+\ 1 \\
\hline
1001 \quad 1110 \quad 0111 \\
(9) \quad\ (E) \quad\ (7)
\end{array}
$$

**Step 1:** Find the base-minus-one complement of the subtrahend and write it above the subtrahend.

**Step 2:** Add the base-minus-one complement to the minuend. The addition is done in the same way as in hexadecimal addition in the computer.

**Step 3:** Convert each four-bit equivalent first to its decimal system equivalent and then to hexadecimal.

**Check:** Same as in the regular subtraction.

*Multiplication in binary and hexadecimal systems.* The actual multiplication of each set of two digits is done in the decimal system. The result is converted immediately to the other base to form the partial products. The digits in the partial products also are added first in the decimal system and then converted to the given base.

*Examples:*

a.
$$
\begin{array}{r}
11101_2 \\
\times \quad 11011_2 \\
\hline
11101 \\
111010 \\
1010111 \\
11101000 \\
100111111 \\
111010000 \\
\hline
1100001111_2
\end{array}
$$

Note that in binary multiplication, when the multiplier digit is 1, the partial product is the multiplicand. When the multiplier digit is 0, no partial product is written. Care must be taken to position the partial products correctly. Generally as soon as there are two numbers in the partial product positions, their sum is found before continuing.

**Step 1:** Since the first multiplier digit is 1, copy the multiplicand.

**Step 2:** Since the next multiplier digit stands for 10, copy the multiplicand with one 0 after it.

**Step 3:** Find the sum of the two partial products: 1010111.

**Step 4:** Since the third multiplier digit is 0, go to the fourth multiplier digit. Since the 1 stands for 1000, copy the multiplicand with three 0's after it under the first sum.

**Step 5:** Add this partial product to the first sum to get the second sum: 100111111.

**Step 6:** Since the fifth multiplier digit stands for 10000, copy the multiplicand with four 0's after it under the second sum.

**Step 7:** Add this partial product to the second sum to get the answer: $1100001111_2$.

**Check:**
$$
\begin{array}{r}
11101_2 = 29 \\
\times \quad 11011_2 = 27 \\
\hline
1100001111_2 = 783
\end{array}
$$
$1100001111_2 = 512 + 256 + 8 + 4 +$
               $2 + 1$
        $= 783$

b.
$$
\begin{array}{r}
3A6_{16} \\
\times \quad 5B_{16} \\
\hline
2822 \\
123E0 \\
\hline
14C02_{16}
\end{array}
$$

**Step 1:** Multiply $6 \times B\,(11) = 66$. Convert the 66 to hexadecimal: $42_{16}$. Write the 2 and carry the 4.

**Step 2:** Multiply A (10) by B (11) and add the carryover 4 = 114 = $72_{16}$. Write the 2 and carry the 7.

**Step 3:** Multiply 3 by B (11) and add the carryover 7 = 40 = $28_{16}$. Write the 28.

**Step 4:** Since the 5 stands for 50, write a 0 under the 2. Multiply 6 by 5 = 30 = $1E_{16}$. Write the E to the left of the 0 and carry the 1.

**Step 5:** Multiply A (10) by 5 and add the carryover 1 = 51 = $33_{16}$. Write the 3 and carry the 3.

**Step 6:** Multiply 3 by 5 and add the carryover 3 = 18 = $12_{16}$. Write the 12.

**Step 7:** Add the two hexadecimal partial products by first adding each combination in decimal and then converting immediately to hexadecimal.

**Check:**

$$\begin{array}{r} 3A6_{16} = 934 \\ \times\ 5B_{16} = \times\ 91 \\ \hline 14C02_{16} = 84{,}994 \end{array}$$

$$\begin{aligned} 14C02_{16} &= (1 \times 65{,}536) + (4 \times 4{,}096) \\ &\quad + (12 \times 256) + 2 \\ &= 65{,}536 + 16{,}384 + 3{,}072 \\ &\quad + 2 \\ &= 84{,}994 \end{aligned}$$

**Division in binary and hexadecimal systems.** Both the divisor and the partial dividend that is used must be changed to their decimal system equivalents to find the quotient digits. The multiplication and subtraction procedures are the same as explained previously.

Because of the difficulty of division in other-base systems, division is not included in the assignment and is not a course requirement. Division in binary and hexadecimal systems is illustrated without explanation below. It is shown only for the student's interest.

*Examples:*

a.

$$\begin{array}{r} 100111_2 \\ 11001_2\ \overline{)\ 1111001111_2} \\ \underline{11001} \\ 101011 \\ \underline{11001} \\ 100101 \\ \underline{11001} \\ 11001 \\ \underline{11001} \end{array}$$

**Check:** $1111001111_2 = 512 + 256 + 128 +$
$64 + 8 + 4 + 2 + 1$
$= 975$
$11001_2 = 16 + 8 + 1 = 25$
$975 \div 25 = 39$
$100111_2 = 32 + 4 + 2 + 1$
$= 39$

b.

$$\begin{array}{r} 82_{16} \\ 4E_{16}\ \overline{)\ 279C_{16}} \\ \underline{270} \\ 9C \\ \underline{9C} \end{array}$$

**Check:** $279C_{16} = (2 \times 4{,}096) + (7 \times$
$256) + (9 \times 16) + 12$
$= 8{,}192 + 1{,}792 + 144$
$+ 12$
$= 10{,}140$
$4E_{16} = (4 \times 16) + 14$
$= 64 + 14$
$= 78$
$10{,}140 \div 78 = 130$
$82_{16} = (8 \times 16) + 2$
$= 128 + 2$
$= 130$

**Complete Assignment 37**

## Assignment 37

### Binary and Hexadecimal Number Systems

|  | Perfect Score | Student's Score |
|---|---|---|
| Part A | 16 | |
| Part B | 24 | |
| Part C | 24 | |
| Part D | 36 | |
| TOTAL | 100 | |

## Part A

### Binary Number System (Base 2)

*Directions:* Perform the indicated conversions. Show all necessary work. Write your answers in the spaces provided. (2 points for each correct answer)

**Binary to Decimal**

1. $11110_2$ = _____

2. $110111_2$ = _____

3. $11000110_2$ = _____

4. $1111001111_2$ = _____

**Decimal to Binary**

5. 77 = _____$_2$

6. 150 = _____$_2$

7. 318 = _____$_2$

8. 945 = _____$_2$

*Student's Score* _____

## Part B

### Hexadecimal Number System (Base 16)

*Directions:* Perform the indicated conversions. Show all necessary work. Write your answers in the spaces provided. (2 points for each correct answer)

**Hexadecimal to Decimal**

9. $24_{16}$ = _____

10. $C5_{16}$ = _____

11. $1A9_{16}$ = _____

12. $BDF_{16}$ = _____

**Decimal to Hexadecimal**

13. 44 = _____$_{16}$

14. 686 = _____$_{16}$

15. 991 = _____$_{16}$

16. 2,748 = _____$_{16}$

*Directions:* Change the hexadecimal numbers to their longitudinal byte forms. (2 points for each correct answer)

17. $F9_{16}$ =

18. $1B8_{16}$ =

19. $37AC_{16}$ =

20. $2D40E_{16}$ =

*Student's Score* _____

# Part C

## Using a Hexadecimal and Decimal Conversion Table

*Directions:* Use the table on page 280 to perform the indicated conversions. Show all necessary work, and write your answers in the spaces provided. (3 points for each correct answer)

**Hexadecimal to Decimal**

21. $5CA_{16}$ = _____

22. $ABDF_{16}$ = _____

23. $4E607_{16}$ = _____

24. $135FDE_{16}$ = _____

**Decimal to Hexadecimal**

25. 10,593 = _____ $_{16}$

26. 173,920 = _____ $_{16}$

27. 367,693 = _____ $_{16}$

28. 10,713,278 = _____ $_{16}$

*Student's Score* _____

# Part D

## *Arithmetic Operations in Binary and Hexadecimal Systems*

**Directions:** Perform the indicated operations in the given bases. Check by converting each problem to the decimal system and show that the answers are equivalent. (2 points for each correct answer)

Check:                                                                 Check:

29.  $101011_2$                                         34.  $11001_2$
  +  $11101_2$                                              ×  $10101_2$


30.  $1101111_2$                                        35.  $32A_{16}$
  +  $110011_2$                                            +  $8C_{16}$


31.  $11101_2$                                          36.  $FED_{16}$
  −  $1011_2$                                             +  $BC_{16}$


32.  $1110100_2$                                        37.  $587_{16}$
  −  $101011_2$                                           −  $29A_{16}$


33.  $11011_2$                                          38.  $C9A_{16}$
  ×  $1101_2$                                             −  $ABF_{16}$

39.     $3A_{16}$                                               40.     $C6_{16}$
    $\times$  $\underline{B4_{16}}$                                              $\times$  $\underline{5D_{16}}$

*Directions:* Perform the indicated operations using the computer procedure. Write the byte forms horizontally. (3 points for each correct answer)

41.     $89A_{16}$                                              43.     $AB8_{16}$
    $+$  $\underline{4D_{16}}$                                              $-$  $\underline{86D_{16}}$

42.     $ACE_{16}$                                              44.     $BC3_{16}$
    $+$  $\underline{BDF_{16}}$                                             $-$  $\underline{91D_{16}}$

*Student's Score* _____

# ANSWERS TO ODD-NUMBERED PROBLEMS

## Chapter 1
### Working with Decimals

## Assignment 1

### Part A

1. Six hundred forty-one
3. Ninety thousand fifty-eight
5. Six million thirty-five

### Part B

7. 89,100  9. 2,000,002

### Part C

11. Two hundred forty and seven hundred ninety-three thousandths
13. Four thousand and four ten-thousandths
15. Six and forty-three and three-fourths thousandths

### Part D

17. 400,045.0404  19. $6.016\frac{2}{3}$

### Part E

21. $.022\frac{1}{2}$  31. 79.34
23. $16.00\frac{2}{3}$  33. 1.495
25. $687.000\frac{1}{4}$  35. $.041\frac{2}{3}$
27. $.0\frac{1}{4}$  37. .0023
29. $.000\frac{2}{3}$  39. 8.000008

### Part F

41. .078  71. 444
43. .355      400.40
45. .01      344
47. .5 = .500      44.4
49. .330          4.440
51. .2          4.4
53. .801 = .80100          3.44
55. .6751          .44
57. .675001  73. 872.94
59. 301.025      870.49
61. 80.60      827.94
63. 61.77      827.49
65. 43.76      784.29
67. 712,590      782.54
69. 5.4183      782.49
          728.54

75. 980.3
    980.29
    520.5
    520.15
    520.05
    520
    173.08
    173.008
    .4164
    .4146

## Assignment 2

### Part A

1. 2.30  5. 446.0806
3. 2.14585  7. 770.74382

### Part B

9. $3,149.27  11. $4,293.99

### Part C

13. 955.14  19. 1,779.35
15. 2,910.93  21. 1,163.19
17. 1,874.43

23. $14,976.48  41. √
25. $3,281.40  43. √
27. X  45. X
29. X  47. X
31. X  49. X
33. X  51. √
35. X  53. X
37. X  55. √
39. X

### Part D

## Assignment 3

### Part A

1. 1.83  11. 8,784.10
3. 39.95  13. 27,646.65
5. 220.04  15. 18,964.71
7. 4,178.29  17. 6.203
9. 1,844.99  19. 85.7217

21. 38.28
23. 96.06

25. 682.04

### Part B

27. 3.7

29. 727.184

### Part C

31. 26.59
33. 38.03

35. 49.25

### Part D

37. $54.05 (inc.)
39. $621.49 (dec.)
41. $1,859.05 (dec.)
43. $7,247.04 (dec.)

45. + $833.25
47. −$2,934.58
49. +$1,522.61

# Assignment 4

### Part A

1. 4.2
3. 200.∅
5. .2613
7. 9.72
9. 4.71086

11. 44.9384
13. 210.752
15. 42.5722
17. 43.62336
19. 59.267013

### Part B

21. .048
23. .0356
25. .005670

27. .0099882
29. .00693183

### Part C

31. 3.4
33. .1
35. 11.0
37. .02
39. 1.65

41. 36.637
43. .001
45. 11.000
47. .3000
49. 99.9999

### Part D

51. 2.0500
53. 1.8125
55. 2.5532500

57. 3.017996982
59. 750.0515001

### Part E

61. 786
63. 2.35
65. 5
67. 90

69. 135
71. 2,300
73. .29
75. 7,300

77. 6,000
79. 2,150,000
81. 800
83. 76.8

85. 19.17
87. 9,035
89. 476,500

### Part F

91. $307.50
93. $50.63
95. $156.00

97. $359.40
99. $21.25

# Assignment 5

### Part A

1. 174
3. 1,022

5. 432
7. 6,708

### Part B

9. 18
11. 46.783
13. 200
15. .081

17. 356.4
19. 70
21. .147
23. .194

### Part C

25. .414

27. .023

### Part D

29. 3.333
31. 6,800

33. 128
35. 900

### Part E

37. .08
39. 5.2083

41. .3889
43. .5333

### Part F

45. 50

47. 3.722

### Part G

49. 47.3
51. .639
53. .00844
55. .00576

57. .0005
59. 67.540
61. .00945
63. .004

### Part H

65. 87.3

# Chapter 2
## Working with Fractions

## Assignment 6

### Part A

1. $\frac{8}{16}$
3. $\frac{36}{54}$
5. $\frac{96}{120}$
7. $\frac{21}{49}$
9. $\frac{120}{135}$
11. $\frac{99}{121}$
13. $\frac{84}{91}$
15. $\frac{143}{165}$
17. $\frac{56}{160}$
19. $\frac{128}{216}$

### Part B

21. $\frac{3}{4}$
23. $\frac{2}{3}$
25. $\frac{5}{8}$
27. $\frac{3}{7}$
29. $\frac{2}{3}$
31. $\frac{1}{3}$
33. $\frac{65}{114}$
35. $\frac{14}{23}$
37. $\frac{29}{250}$
39. $\frac{3}{125}$

### Part C

41. $\frac{11}{3}$
43. $\frac{97}{5}$
45. $\frac{129}{7}$
47. $\frac{32}{9}$
49. $\frac{173}{16}$
51. $8\frac{1}{2}$
53. $6$
55. $1\frac{2}{3}$
57. $27\frac{7}{9}$
59. $34\frac{4}{19}$

### Part D

61. $\frac{1}{20}$
63. $\frac{1}{8}$
65. $\frac{1}{16}$
67. $\frac{71}{125}$
69. $\frac{4399}{10,000}$

## Assignment 7

### Part A

1. $6\frac{2}{3}$
3. $16\frac{1}{100}$
5. $16\frac{3}{8}$

### Part B

7. $1\frac{1}{2}$
9. $26$

### Part C

11. $\frac{1}{2}$
13. $1\frac{5}{6}$
15. $2\frac{37}{60}$

### Part D

17. $21\frac{11}{20}$
19. $89\frac{17}{90}$

### Part E

21. $1.5\emptyset$
23. $189.72\frac{11}{12}$
25. $227.33\frac{1}{3}$

### Part F

27. $79\frac{3}{4}$
29. $52\frac{7}{40}$

### Part G

31. $277\frac{3}{4}$

## Assignment 8

### Part A

1. $\frac{2}{3}$
3. $5\frac{1}{2}$
5. $15\frac{7}{16}$
7. $\frac{1}{6}$
9. $2\frac{13}{24}$

### Part B

11. $2\frac{1}{4}$
13. $12\frac{3}{7}$
15. $31\frac{19}{30}$
17. $35\frac{7}{24}$
19. $28\frac{16}{45}$

### Part C

21. $60\frac{7}{12}$
23. $87\frac{1}{6}$
25. $17\frac{3}{8}$

## Assignment 9

### Part A

1. $\frac{1}{8}$
3. $\frac{3}{80}$
5. $\frac{15}{32}$
7. $\frac{7}{16}$
9. $\frac{3}{14}$

### Part B

11. $1$
13. $4\frac{4}{5}$
15. $7\frac{1}{5}$

### Part C

17. $\frac{7}{8}$
19. $27$
21. $48$
23. $29\frac{13}{15}$
25. $16\frac{8}{9}$

### Part D

27. $58\frac{1}{3}$
29. $8.03\frac{1}{3}$

### Part E

31. 342
32. 97.8Ø
35. $1.5866\frac{2}{3}$

### Part F

37. \$156.90
39. \$66.90

## Assignment 10

### Part A

1. $\frac{2}{3}$
3. $1\frac{1}{5}$
5. $2\frac{1}{3}$
7. $17\frac{1}{2}$
9. $3\frac{3}{5}$
11. 9
13. 80
15. 38

### Part B

17. $\frac{1}{16}$
19. $\frac{2}{7}$

### Part C

21. $\frac{5}{54}$
23. $\frac{3}{8}$
25. $\frac{8}{15}$
27. $1\frac{1}{5}$
29. $5\frac{5}{8}$
31. $1\frac{3}{19}$
33. $1\frac{29}{34}$
35. $\frac{7}{16}$
37. 2
39. 78

### Part D

41. $\frac{3}{4}$
43. $1\frac{5}{8}$
45. $\frac{5}{24}$

### Part E

47. \$2.67

# Chapter 3
## Working with Equivalents

## Assignment 11

### Part A

1. .0833
3. .4583
5. .2813
7. 7.08
9. .0406

### Part B

11. $\frac{1}{20}$
13. $\frac{173}{500}$
15. $\frac{1}{200}$
17. $\frac{1}{400}$
19. $\frac{3}{16}$

### Part C

21. $\frac{4}{15}$
23. $\frac{1}{40}$
25. $\frac{5}{24}$
27. $\frac{2}{15}$
29. $\frac{4}{7}$

### Part D

31. \$0.60
33. \$0.08
35. \$0.065
37. \$0.0333
39. \$0.0025

### Part E

41. $2.75 + 59.625$
43. $75.5 - 43.75$
45. $4{,}860 \times .333333$
47. $8.5625 \times 3.75$
49. $3.083333 \div 11.625$

## Assignment 12

### Part A

1. $\frac{3}{8}$
3. $\frac{1}{2}$
5. $\frac{4}{5}$
7. $\frac{5}{8}$
9. $33\frac{1}{3}$¢
11. $.58\frac{1}{3}$
13. 25¢

### Part B

15. \$31.00
17. \$320.00
19. 90
21. 160
23. \$279.00
25. 288
27. \$102.00
29. \$3,920.00
31. \$30.50

### Part C

33. \$742.00
35. \$1,598.00
37. \$1,435.00

### Part D

39. 32
41. 224.00
43. 600

### Part E

45. 1,600
47. 635
49. \$63.00

# Chapter 4
## Working with Percents

## Assignment 13

### Part A

1. .25
3. .01
5. .18
7. .475
9. .045
11. .0225
13. .875

15. .006667
17. .001
19. .0098
21. 2.25
23. 5
25. 1.1333

### Part B

27. $\frac{1}{4}$
29. $\frac{7}{100}$
31. $\frac{13}{20}$
33. $\frac{1}{16}$
35. $\frac{19}{200}$
37. $\frac{5}{8}$

39. $\frac{1}{200}$
41. $\frac{1}{250}$
43. $\frac{7}{1000}$
45. $2\frac{2}{5}$
47. $2\frac{3}{4}$
49. $1\frac{1}{8}$

### Part C

51. 25%
53. 1%
55. 40%
57. 16.5%
59. $1\frac{2}{3}$%
61. $2\frac{1}{4}$%
63. $7\frac{1}{2}$%

65. .5% or $\frac{1}{2}$%
67. .04%
69. 125%
71. 200%
73. 380%
75. $266\frac{2}{3}$%

### Part D

77. 50%
79. 75%
81. $83\frac{1}{3}$%
83. $77\frac{7}{9}$%
85. $91\frac{2}{3}$%
87. $31\frac{1}{4}$%

89. 3%
91. $\frac{2}{3}$% or $.66\frac{2}{3}$%
93. $\frac{3}{4}$% or .75%
95. 125%
97. 350%
99. $566\frac{2}{3}$%

## Assignment 14

### Part A

1. 3.53
3. .09
5. $8.50
7. .63
9. $0.06

11. 3.87
13. $23.75
15. $0.84
17. $44.58
19. $1,176.00

21. 127
23. 1,200
25. $320.00
27. $5.05
29. $13.97

### Part B

31. 4,900
33. .15
35. $53.40
37. $40.00
39. .01

### Part C

41. 1.95
43. 10
45. $7.50
47. $0.03

49. 1.27
51. $9.60
53. $0.01
55. 4.8

### Part D

57. $11.54
59. .72
61. 3.53
63. $292.50

65. $4,320.00
67. 2,300
69. $10.76

### Part E

71. Dept A — $ 3,252.60  
      B — 1,737.50  
      C — 2,981.55  
      D — 3,711.30  
      E — 708.90  
      F — 3,475.00  
      G — 4,649.55  
      H — 333.60  
      $20,850.00

## Assignment 15

### Part A

1. 8%
3. 5.5% or $5\frac{1}{2}$%
5. 9.3% or $9\frac{1}{3}$%

7. 75%
9. 40.4%

### Part B

11. .5% or $\frac{1}{2}$%
13. .4%
15. .35%

17. .25% or $\frac{1}{4}$%
19. $.83\frac{1}{3}$% or $\frac{5}{6}$%

### Part C

21. 200%

23. 400%

25. 175%      29. 227.32%        9. $33.00        13. .6
27. 350%                        11. 2            15. .33⅓ or ⅓

### Part D

| Amount of Change | Percent of Change |
|---|---|
| 31. $2,000 | − 10.0 |
| 33. 3,000 | + 12.0 |
| 35. 2,000 | − 7.7 |

17. $300.00        19. $600.00

### Part C

21. 1              27. $49.12
23. 2,400          29. $888.89
25. $0.90

## Assignment 16

### Part A

1. 2,400       5. $88.98       31. $750.40        35. $2,600.00
3. 126         7. $20.00       33. $5.50

### Part D

# Chapter 5
## Working with Weights and Measures

## Assignment 17

### Part F

51. 4 lb 5 oz        55. 0.295 kg
53. 1 yd 2 ft 3 in.

### Part A

1. 36 t          11. ¾ lb
3. 88 oz         13. 19/30 h (.63)
5. 9 min         15. 3⅔ cu yd
7. 1,500 lb      17. 8.632 L
9. 2 ft 3 in.    19. 750 mL

## Assignment 18

### Part A

1. 410 ft        7. $1,620.00
3. 69.5 m²       9. 18.75 gal
5. $112.00

### Part B

21. 4.575 m       27. 11.34 dag
23. 8.172 qt      29. 4 424.49 cm³
25. 1.361 kg

### Part B

11. $22.75        21. $308.00
13. $3.42         23. $66.60
15. $4.72         25. $4.55
17. $133.40       27. $405.00
19. $10.63        29. $1.77

### Part C

31. 1 h 22 min
33. 8 sq yd 5 sq ft 95 sq in.
35. 990 cm

### Part C

31. $60.00        41. $41.60
33. $105.00       43. $82.16
35. $65.00        45. $394.50
37. $1.30         47. $33.60
39. $30.25        49. $26.88

### Part D

37. 8 cu yd 18 cu ft 1,168 cu in.
39. 1 225 cm

### Part E

41. 2 da 7 h 12 min
43. 7 sq yd 1 sq ft 6 sq in.
45. 4 cu ft 1,488 cu in.
47. 2.94 L
49. 2.88 m²

### Part D

51. $65.88        59. $12.50
53. $16.80        61. $19.96
55. $6.50         63. $151.20
57. $16.25        65. $1,235.52

# Chapter 6
## Shortcuts and Estimating with Rounded-Off Numbers

## Assignment 19

### Part A

1. 59
3. 101
5. 3.69
7. 8.67
9. 12.31
11. 82.94
13. 121.00
15. 1,124.54
17. 1,553.65
19. 6,740.45

### Part B

21. 51
23. 14
25. 4.99
27. 4.89
29. 22.49
31. .83
33. 310.10
35. 187.96
37. 99.91
39. 1,101.66

### Part C

41. $\frac{5}{6}$
43. $\frac{8}{15}$
45. $\frac{11}{28}$
47. $\frac{13}{30}$
49. $\frac{18}{77}$

### Part D

51. $\frac{1}{6}$
53. $\frac{1}{12}$
55. $\frac{1}{24}$
57. $\frac{1}{5}$
59. $\frac{1}{80}$

### Part E

61. 5.7535
63. 4.19
65. .0045427
67. .1098
69. .000645
71. 9.7
73. 8,600
75. 106.74
77. 90,800
79. 88,700

### Part F

81. 3,200
83. 3.15
85. 7,850
87. 178.5
89. 6.96
91. .364
93. .2846
95. 1.92
97. 2.244
99. .2434

### Part G

101. 143
103. 1,034
105. 924
107. 902
109. 429
111. 75.9
113. 1.089
115. .0209
117. .825
119. .00649

### Part H

121. 85
123. 113
125. 28
127. 52
129. 492
131. 520
133. 525
135. 1,870
137. 1,638
139. .2856

## Assignment 20

### Part A

1. 6
3. 3
5. 199
7. $87.00
9. $2,000.00

### Part B

11. 70
13. 140
15. 200
17. $450.00
19. $1,270.00
21. 600
23. 000
25. 400
27. $100.00
29. $1,000.00
31. 1,000
33. 6,000
35. 0,000
37. $5,000.00
39. $11,000.00

### Part C

41. 1,300
43. 4,800 or 5,000
45. 118,000
47. 595
49. 1,100

### Part D

51. 3,500
53. 2,000
55. 189 or 210
57. .24
59. 25
61. 1,800
63. 67,600
65. 45
67. 7,700 or 8,800
69. 99

### Part E

71. 2
73. 20
75. 430
77. .5
79. .04
81. 250 √
83. 54 x
85. .27 √

# Chapter 7
## Keeping a Checking Account

Assignment **21**

### Problem 1

| No. 896 $153 75 | | A. J. MORAN | No. 896 | 12 - 79 |
|---|---|---|---|---|

No. **896** $**153** **75**
Date **Oct. 24** 19 **--**
To **Jones Brothers**

For **Accounts**
**Payable**

| | Dollars | Cents |
|---|---|---|
| Balance Forward | 1716 | 64 |
| Deposit | 492 | 65 |
| TOTAL | 2209 | 29 |
| This Check | 153 | 75 |
| Balance | 2055 | 54 |

A. J. MORAN
1204 N. Allen St.
Milwaukee, WI 53208

No. **896**    12 - 79 / 750

**October 24** 19 **--**

PAY TO THE
ORDER OF **Jones Brothers** ———— $ **153 75**

**One hundred fifty-three and 75/100** DOLLARS

**Grand National Bank**
Milwaukee, Wisconsin 53201

**A. J. Moran**

⑊0750⑊0074⑊ ⑊2⑊79 7607⑊

### Problem 3

No. **898** $**45 00**
Date **Oct. 26** 19 **--**
To **John Stanford**

For **Misc. Expenses**

| | Dollars | Cents |
|---|---|---|
| Balance Forward | 1914 | 35 |
| Deposit | — | |
| TOTAL | 1914 | 35 |
| This Check | 45 | — |
| Balance | 1869 | 35 |

A. J. MORAN
1204 N. Allen St.
Milwaukee, WI 53208

No. **898**    12 - 79 / 750

**October 26** 19 **--**

PAY TO THE
ORDER OF **John Stanford** ———— $ **45 00**

**Forty - five only** ———— DOLLARS

**Grand National Bank**
Milwaukee, Wisconsin 53201

**A. J. Moran**

⑊0750⑊0074⑊ ⑊2⑊79 7607⑊

## Problem 5

**DEPOSIT TICKET**

DATE _October 28_ 19_- -_

Deposit credited subject to our rules and regulations.

12 - 79
——
750

**A. J. MORAN**
1204 N. Allen St.
Milwaukee, WI 53208

**Grand National Bank**
Milwaukee, Wisconsin 53201

| | | DOLLARS | CENTS |
|---|---|---|---|
| CURRENCY | | 375 | 00 |
| COIN | | 50 | 00 |
| CHECKS | | 142 | 98 |
| | | 16 | 95 |
| LIST SINGLY • BE SURE EACH ITEM IS ENDORSED | | 236 | 43 |
| | | 15 | 09 |
| | | | |
| | | | |
| TOTAL FROM OTHER SIDE | | | |
| TOTAL | | 836 | 45 |

USE OTHER SIDE FOR ADDITIONAL CHECKS

⑆0750⑈00791⑆ 02⑈79 76071⑈

# Assignment 22

## Problem 1

### A. J. Moran
### Reconciliation Statement
### March 15, 19—

Checkbook balance ............................................................. $2,336.52

Subtract:
  Service charge ..................... $ 4.00
  Error on #396 ..................... 27.00
    Total ......................................................................... 31.00

Adjusted checkbook balance ......................................................... $2,305.52

Bank balance ....................................................................... $2,197.24

Add:
  Unrecorded deposit, March 14 ............................................... 400.00
    Total ........................................................................ $2,597.24

Subtract:
  Outstanding checks
    #405 ........................ $ 40.66
    #410 ........................ 32.42
    #412 ........................ 80.35
    #413 ........................ 130.29
    #414 ........................ 8.00
      Total ...................................................................... 291.72

Adjusted bank balance ............................................................. $2,305.52

## Problem 3

**A. J. Moran**
**Reconciliation Statement**
**October 14, 19—**

| | | |
|---|---|---:|
| Checkbook balance | | $3,331.70 |
| Add: | | |
| Errors on #766 and #785 | | 127.00 |
| Total | | $3,458.70 |
| Subtract: | | |
| Service charge | $ 1.80 | |
| Errors on #769, #772, and #773 .. | 173.00 | |
| Total | | 174.80 |
| Adjusted checkbook balance | | $3,283.90 |
| Bank balance | | $2,795.77 |
| Add: | | |
| Unrecorded deposit, October 13 | | 1,324.98 |
| Total | | $4,120.75 |
| Subtract: | | |
| Outstanding checks | | |
| #778 | $175.39 | |
| #782 | 504.61 | |
| #786 | 33.80 | |
| #787 | 123.05 | |
| Total | | 836.85 |
| Adjusted bank balance | | $3,283.90 |

# Chapter 8
## Figuring Interest

## Assignment 23

### Part A

| | |
|---|---|
| 1. 40 days | 7. 111 days |
| 3. 55 days | 9. 104 days |
| 5. 70 days | |

### Part B

| Due Date | Exact Time |
|---|---|
| 11. May 30 | 15 days |
| 13. March 16 | 30 days |
| 15. Jan. 29 | 45 days |
| 17. Dec. 26 | 91 days |
| 19. June 5 | 120 days |

### Part C

| Due Date | Exact Time |
|---|---|
| 21. April 17 | 31 days |
| 23. July 5 | 92 days |
| 25. March 23 | 181 days |

## Assignment 24

### Part A

| | |
|---|---|
| 1. $67.20 | 5. $8.00 |
| 3. $48.00 | 7. $618.30 |

### Part B

| | |
|---|---|
| 9. $22.80 | 13. $6.75 |
| 11. $4.79 | 15. $0.20 |

## Part C

| | |
|---|---|
| 17. $4.50 | 33. $0.77 |
| 19. $12.00 | 35. $0.01 |
| 21. $0.06 | 37. $1.58 |
| 23. $76.29 | 39. $0.20 |
| 25. $3.24 | 41. $0.09 |
| 27. $5.05 | 43. $3.45 |
| 29. $7.85 | 45. $0.04 |
| 31. $0.98 | 47. $0.10 |

## Part D

| | |
|---|---|
| 49. $3.38 | 59. $1.56 |
| 51. $1.58 | 61. $1.10 |
| 53. $0.60 | 63. $5.14 |
| 55. $0.68 | 65. $15.63 |
| 57. $0.05 | 67. $24.02 |

# Assignment 25

## Part A

| | Amount | Compound Interest |
|---|---|---|
| 1. | $1,225.04 | $225.04 |

## Part B

| | Amount | Compound Interest |
|---|---|---|
| 3. | $ 631.24 | $ 131.24 |
| 5. | 2,191.12 | 1,191.12 |
| 7. | 594.38 | 194.38 |
| 9. | 883.92 | 83.92 |

| | Rate | No. of Periods |
|---|---|---|
| 11. | $7\frac{1}{2}\%$ | 14 |
| 13. | $3\frac{1}{4}\%$ | 36 |
| 15. | $2\frac{1}{2}\%$ | 48 |
| 17. | $\frac{5}{6}\%$ | 240 |

# Chapter 9
## Figuring Cash and Trade Discounts

# Assignment 26

### Part A

PURCHASE ORDER

# ABC Company
P. O. BOX 244
MILWAUKEE, WI 53201

NO. 84289

SHOW PURCHASE ORDER NUMBER ON PACKAGES, INVOICES, AND CORRESPONDENCE

| REQUISITION NO. | DATE | SHIP VIA | SHIP BY | REFER INQUIRIES TO BUYER: |
|---|---|---|---|---|
| 25116 | 6/14/-- | Lane Express | 7/1/-- | R. H. Ellis |

SHIP TO:

A. J. Moran Company
1204 N. Allen Street
Milwaukee, WI 53208

1099 N. First Street
Milwaukee, WI 53203

| QUANTITY | PLEASE SUPPLY THE FOLLOWING | PRICE |
|---|---|---|
| 2 | AC-54 Panels, 2' x 8' | 19.76 |
| 4 doz | B-8614 Bolts | .14 |
| 150 | C-5623 Screws | 12.53/C |
| 1 gross | L-9006 Washers | .95/doz |
| 40 | D-6311 Dividers, 14" x 12" | .75 |
| | Per telephone quote 6/9/-- | |

PLEASE ACKNOWLEDGE RECEIPT OF THIS ORDER IMMEDIATELY. MAIL INVOICES IN DUPLICATE. IN ACCEPTING THIS ORDER YOU AGREE TO ALL TERMS AND CONDITIONS STATED ON THE REVERSE SIDE.

## Part B

1. $1,500.00
   2,100.00
   264.00
   7.50
   270.00
   600.00
   30.00
   46.40
   144.00
   ―――――
   $4,961.90

## Problem 3

INVOICE

# A. J. MORAN COMPANY
1204 North Allen Street
Milwaukee, WI 53208

OUR ORDER NO. 47954
YOUR ORDER NO. 84289
DATE OF ORDER 6/14/--
SALSESPERSON R. B. Ross
WHEN SHIPPED 6/21/--
VIA Lane Express

SOLD TO:
ABC Company
P.O. Box 244
Milwaukee, WI 53201

Terms of Payment: 1/10, n/30          INVOICE DATE: 6/22/--

| QUANTITY | DESCRIPTION | UNIT PRICE | AMOUNT |
|---|---|---|---|
| 2 | AC-54 Panels 2' x 8' | 19.76 | 39.52 |
| 4 doz | B-8614 Bolts | .14 | 6.72 |
| 150 | C-5623 Screws | 12.53/C | 18.80 |
| 1 gross | L-9006 Washers | .95/doz | 11.40 |
| 40 | D-6311 Dividers, 14" x 12" | .75 | 30.00 |
| | | | 106.44 |

# Assignment 27

| Part A | | Part B | | |
|---|---|---|---|---|
| | | Date of Payment | Cash Discount | Amount of Payment |
| 1. Cash discount | 11. Past due | 21. June 8 | $ 2.19 | $ 435.72 |
| 3. Cash discount | 13. Net | 23. Sept. 9 | 25.90 | 2,564.05 |
| 5. Cash discount | 15. Cash discount | 25. May 10 | 240.00 | 7,760.00 |
| 7. Cash discount | 17. Net | 27. Nov. 21 | 16.50 | 533.50 |
| 9. Past due | 19. Net | 29. Aug. 2 | 108.51 | 5,316.99 |

# Assignment 28

## Part A

| Amount of Discount | Net Price |
|---|---|
| 1. $ 13.99 | $ 55.96 |
| 3. 9.375 | 28.13 |
| 5. 199.99 | 299.99 |

7. $53.99 (Net price)
9. $160.97 (Net price)

## Part B

| Amount of Trade Discount | Net Price |
|---|---|
| 11. $ 0.67 | $ 1.73 |
| 13. 1.62 | 5.98 |
| 15. 174.95 | 150.05 |

17. $9.90
19. $32.38

## Part C

| | | |
|---|---|---|
| 21. 14-2 Toggle bolts ....... | $ 49.02 | |
| 1¼″ Steel wire nails—shingle ........ | 382.00 | |
| 1″ Steel wire nails—roofing ........ | 352.20 | |
| Total .............. | $ 783.22 | |
| Net ..................... | | $334.83 |

| | | |
|---|---|---|
| 832 MC Micrometers ... | $ 476.00 | |
| 832 MD Micrometers ... | 595.00 | |
| Total .............. | $1,071.00 | |
| Net ..................... | | 481.95 |
| NET INVOICE DUE ............. | | $816.78 |

| Net Cost Factor | Net Price |
|---|---|
| 23. .765 | $ 1.53 |
| 25. .9025 | 4.24 |
| 27. .855 | 54.72 |
| 29. .48 | 480.00 |
| 31. .36 | 180.00 |

# Chapter 10
## Selling Goods

# Assignment 29

## Part A

| Amount of Markup | Selling Price |
|---|---|
| 1. $ 0.69 | $ 3.44 |
| 3. 69.60 | 162.40 |
| 5. 242.85 | 388.56 |

| Amount of Markup | Markup % |
|---|---|
| 7. $ 1.15 | 24 |
| 9. 165.00 | 100 |

| | |
|---|---|
| 11. $0.95 (Cost) | 17. $27.31 (Cost) |
| 13. $31.88 (Cost) | 19. $57.50 (Cost) |
| 15. $109.12 (Cost) | |

## Part B

| Amount of Markup | Cost |
|---|---|
| 21. $ 4.32 | $ 17.27 |
| 23. 16.20 | 27.00 |
| 25. 478.80 | 319.20 |

| Amount of Markup | Markup % |
|---|---|
| 27. $160.50 | 45.9 |
| 29. 8.37 | 56.4 |

| | |
|---|---|
| 31. $0.79 (SP) | 37. $439.98 (SP) |
| 33. $17.12 (SP) | 39. $3,125.00 (SP) |
| 35. $77.00 (SP) | |

# Assignment 30

## Part A

| | |
|---|---|
| 1. $6.35 | 7. $1.97 |
| 3. $24.76 | 9. $86.03 |
| 5. $12.00 | |

## Part B

| | |
|---|---|
| 11. $8.12 | 17. $7.86 |
| 13. $2.80 | 19. $152.18 |
| 15. $9.58 | |

## Part C

| | |
|---|---|
| 21. 3¢ | 23. 25¢ |

| 25. 65¢ | 31. $94.95 | Part D | |
|---|---|---|---|
| 27. 95¢ | 33. 21¢ | 37. NDMBC | 39. *03621* |
| 29. $6.99 | 35. 97¢ | | |

# Chapter 11
## Figuring Gross Pay for Payrolls

## Assignment 31

### Parts A and B

| | Overtime Rate | Overtime Hours | Regular Pay | Overtime Pay | Gross Pay |
|---|---|---|---|---|---|
| 1. | $6.30 | 14 | $168.00 | $88.20 | $256.20 |
| 3. | 8.475 | 5 | 226.00 | 42.38 | 268.38 |

### Part C

| | Time and a Half Rate | Double Time Rate | Regular Pay | Overtime Pay | Gross Pay |
|---|---|---|---|---|---|
| 5. | $8.25 | $11.00 | $209.00 | $16.50 | $225.50 |
| 7. | 7.50 | 10.00 | 180.00 | 55.00 | 235.00 |

### Part D

9. $289.48
11. $678.40

## Assignment 32

### Part A

| 1. | Monday | —$52.92 |
| | Tuesday | — 41.16 |
| | Wednesday | — 39.20 |
| | Thursday | — 36.00 |
| | Friday | — 47.04 |

3. $55.00
5. $53.70
7. $50.81

9. $45.50
11. $62.70

### Part B

13. $1,250.00
15. $1,148.72
17. $1,040.00

# Chapter 12
## Figuring Time Payment Plans and Short-Term Commercial Loans

## Assignment 33

### Part A

| | Total Time Payment Price | Finance Charge |
|---|---|---|
| 1. | $ 180.00 | $ 11.00 |
| 3. | 606.35 | 68.85 |
| 5. | 2,754.96 | 254.96 |

| | Total Cost of Loan | Finance Charge |
|---|---|---|
| 7. | $ 562.56 | $62.56 |
| 9. | 1,026.00 | 76.00 |

*Any digit.

## Part B

| Finance Charge | Monthly Payment |
|---|---|
| 11. $ 63.84 | $28.44* |
| 13. 26.40 | 38.64 |
| 15. 77.76 | 44.06* |
| 17. 416.25 | 94.90* |
| 19. 10.50 | 35.08* |

## Part C

| Finance Charge | Annual Percentage Rate |
|---|---|
| 21. $22.00 | 16% |
| 23. 48.00 | 12 |
| 25. 69.00 | 9.8 |
| 27. 29.76 | 10.5 |
| 29. 85.56 | 9 |

21. Due date — Oct.17
    Discount period — 66 days
    Bank discount — $5.50
    Proceeds — $494.50
23. Due date — Jan. 17
    Discount period — 40 days
    Bank discount — $6.67
    Proceeds — $993.33
25. Due date — Nov. 23
    Discount period — 75 days
    Bank discount — $5.42
    Proceeds — $394.58
27. Due date — May 13
    Discount period — 18 days
    Bank discount — $2.55
    Proceeds — $597.45
29. Due date — Mar. 28
    Discount period — 15 days
    Bank discount — $4.17
    Proceeds — $1,595.83

# Assignment 34

## Part A

| Due Date | Interest Charge | Maturity Value |
|---|---|---|
| 1. July 5 | $37.50 | $7,537.50 |
| 3. Sept. 18 | 4.69 | 504.69 |
| 5. June 28 | 5.42 | 405.42 |
| 7. Nov. 26 | 53.33 | 1,053.33 |
| 9. Mar. 29 | 94.44 | 5,094.44 |

## Part B

| Bank Discount | Proceeds |
|---|---|
| 11. $ 7.50 | $ 492.50 |
| 13. 14.17 | 835.83 |
| 15. 22.17 | 927.83 |
| 17. 20.83 | 4,979.17 |
| 19. 8.33 | 391.67 |

## Part C

31. Due date — Aug. 31
    Maturity value — $757.50
    Discount period — 30 days
    Bank discount — $3.79
    Proceeds — $753.71
33. Due date — Sept. 19
    Maturity value — $1,218.40
    Discount period — 66 days
    Bank discount — $15.64
    Proceeds — $1,202.76
35. Due date — Oct. 5
    Maturity value — $201.08
    Discount period — 25 days
    Bank discount — $1.05
    Proceeds — $200.03
37. Due date — May 18
    Maturity value — $808.00
    Discount period — 15 days
    Bank discount — $3.37
    Proceeds — $804.63

# Chapter 13
## Inventory Valuation, Cost of Goods Sold, and Depreciation

# Assignment 35

## Part A

1. $9,312.00

## Parts B, C, and D

| | |
|---|---|
| 3. $772.50 | 9. $1,530.00 |
| 5. $742.00 | 11. $1,465.00 |
| 7. $2,710.00 | 13. $1,625.00 |

**15.** $29,000.00  **19.** $17,500.00
**17.** $22,000.00

Part F

**21.** $94,000.00
**23.** $49,400.00
**25.** $75,120.00

# Assignment 36

Part A

| | Annual Depreciation | Accumulated Depreciation | Book Value End of Year |
|---|---|---|---|
| **1.** | $ 125.00 | $ 125.00 | $ 550.00 |
| **3.** | 206.25 | 618.75 | 1,031.25 |
| **5.** | 47.50 | 47.50 | 182.50 |
| **7.** | 1,037.50 | 3,112.50 | 1,687.50 |
| **9.** | 15.00 | 75.00 | 75.00 |

Part B

| | Annual Depreciation | Accumulated Depreciation | Book Value End of Year |
|---|---|---|---|
| **11.** | $840.000 | $ 840.00 | $1,260.00 |
| **13.** | 50.00 | 350.00 | 50.00 |
| **15.** | 281.28 | 6,200.00 | 600.00 |
| **17.** | 133.33 | 333.33 | 266.67 |
| **19.** | 650.00 | 4,550.00 | 650.00 |

Part C

| | Annual Depreciation | Accumulated Depreciation | Book Value End of Year |
|---|---|---|---|
| **21.** | $160.00 | $ 160.00 | $ 340.00 |
| **23.** | 165.00 | 660.00 | 215.00 |
| **25.** | 700.00 | 4,200.00 | 1,200.00 |
| **27.** | 40.00 | 300.00 | 100.00 |

Part D

| | Straight Line | Declining-Balance | Sum-of-the Years-Digits |
|---|---|---|---|
| **29.** | $1,200.00 | $2,600.00 | $2,000.00 |
| **31.** | 1,200.00 | 936.00 | 1,200.00 |
| **33.** | 1,200.00 | 337.00 | 400.00 |

# Chapter 14
## Binary and Hexadecimal Number Systems

# Assignment 37

Part A

**1.** 30          **5.** $1001101_2$
**3.** 198          **7.** $100111110_2$

Part B

**9.** 36
**11.** 425
**13.** $2C_{16}$
**15.** $3DF_{16}$
**17.** 1
    1
    1
    1
    ‾
    1
    0
    0
    1

**19.** 0  1
    0  0
    1  1
    1  0
    ‾  ‾
    0  1
    1  1
    1  0
    1  0

Part C

**21.** 1,482          **25.** $2961_{16}$
**23.** 321,031          **27.** $59C4D_{16}$

Part D

**29.** $1001000_2$          **37.** $2ED_{16}$
**31.** $10010_2$          **39.** $28C8_{16}$
**33.** $101011111_2$          **41.** $8E7_{16}$
**35.** $3B6_{16}$          **43.** $24B_{16}$

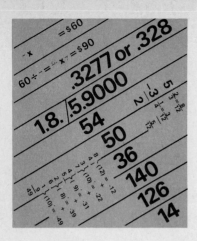

# INDEX

complex fraction:
    defined, 71
    reducing, 71-72
compound interest:
    calculating, 195-198
    defined, 181
compound interest tables, using, 196-198
Consumer Credit Protection Act (Truth-in-Lending), 245
consumer loans, 245
cost as the base for markup:
    finding the cost, 222-223
    finding the percent of markup, 222
    finding the selling price, 221-222
cost of goods sold:
    finding, 263-264
    inventory valuation and, 259-264
crossfooting, defined, 14
Customer-Bank Communication Terminal (CBCT), 170

D

daily balance, 174
daily rate, 196
date of origin, defined, 182
day rate, 234
decem, defined, 1
decimal:
    converting a, to its percent equivalent, 91-92
    defined, 1
    dividing a, by a decimal, 36-37
    dividing a, by a whole number, 37-38
    multiplying a, by a decimal or a whole number, 26
    multiplying a, by a proper fraction or by a mixed number, 64-65
    multiplying by a, with a fractional ending, 28
    subtracting a, from a whole number, 21-22
    subtracting a whole number from a, 22
decimal equivalent:
    defined, 75
    finding the, of a common fraction, 75-77
decimal equivalents and fractional equivalents, 75-78
decimal fractions:
    changing a, to a common fraction in its lowest terms, 48
    defined, 45
    reducing, 71-72
decimal mixed number:
    defined, 6
    multiplying by a, that has a decimal aliquot part, 83-84
decimal number:
    converting a, to its binary system equivalent, 277-278
    converting a, to its hexadecimal system equivalent, 278-279
decimal number system, 1-8
decimals:
    adding long columns of, 14
    adding of, horizontally, 14
    adding of, that have common fraction endings, 54
    adding of, vertically, 13
    addition of, 13-16

changing cents to, 78
comparing, 6-8
division of, 35-40
multiplication of, 25-30
reading and writing, 3-4
rounding off, to a given number of places, 27-28
subtraction of, 21-22
writing, from words, 4-5
decimal to hexadecimal, converting, 280-281
declining-balance method of figuring depreciation, 269-270
denomination, defined, 119
denominator:
    common, 51
    defined, 5
    least common, 51
deposits:
    checks and, 167-170
    making, 169
depreciation:
    calculating, 269-270
    defined, 259
depreciation methods:
    comparison of, 270
    declining-balance, 269-270
    straight-line, 269
    sum-of-the-years-digits, 270
differences, estimating, 159
digit, defined, 1
disclosure statement, 245
discount period, 252
discount rate, 252
discounted notes payable, finding the proceeds of, 252
discounted notes receivable, finding the proceeds of, 252-253
discounting:
    interest-bearing notes, 253-254
    non-interest bearing notes, 252-253
discounts:
    bank, 252
    cash, 207-210
    chain, 214
    equivalent single, 216
    trade, 213-216
dividend, defined, 35
dividing by ten and its multiples, 39-40
divisibility rules, 47
division:
    defined, 35
    review of, with whole numbers, 35-36
divisor, defined, 35
drawing account, defined, 241
due date and exact time:
    finding the, when the given time is in days, 182-183
    finding the, when the given time is in months, 183-184
due date, defined, 182

E

earnings record, employee's, 236
Electronic Funds Transfer System (EFTS), 169

308                                                                    Index

endorsement:
blank, 168
restrictive, 168
endorsing, 168
EOM (end-of-month) dating, defined, 208
equivalents:
aliquot parts and fractional, 81-84
decimal, 75
decimal and fractional, 75-78
fractional, 75
equivalent single discount of a series, finding the, 216
estimate, defined, 157
estimated inventory value:
gross profit (or markup) method, 261-262
retail method, 262-263
estimating:
products, 160-161
quotients, 161-162
sums and differences, 159-160
with rounded-off numbers, 157-162
extension, 30
extra dating, defined, 207
exact interest, 188-189
exact time:
defined, 181
finding the, between two dates, 182

F

face value of a note, 251
factor, defined, 25
factors, 25
Federal Insurance Contributions Act (FICA), 236
FICA taxes, 236
finance charge:
defined, 245
finding the amount of the, 245-246
first-in, first-out (FIFO) method of inventory valuation, 260
fiscal period, defined, 259
fraction:
defined, 45
dividing a, by a mixed number, 70-71
dividing a, by a whole number, 69-70
like terms, 51
lowest terms, 46
terms of the, 45
fractional equivalent:
defined, 75
finding the, of a decimal fraction, 77
finding the, of a decimal fraction with a fractional ending, 77-78
fractions:
addition of, 51-53
division of, 69-72
multiplication of, 63-66
subtracting, by borrowing, 58-59
subtracting, without borrowing, 57
subtraction of, 57-60
types of, 45-48

G

gram, 122
grand total, 14
greatest common divisor (G.C.D.), defined, 46
gross, defined, 140
gross profit (See markup)

H

hexadecimal and decimal conversion table, using a, 279-281
hexadecimal number, converting a, to its decimal system equivalent, 278
hexadecimal number system, 278-279
hexadecimal to decimal, converting, 280

I

improper fractions:
changing, into mixed numbers, 48
defined, 45
installments, defined, 245
interest:
banker's, 251
compound, 181
compounded annually, 195
compounded daily, 196
compounded monthly, 196
compounded quarterly, 196
compounded semiannually, 195
compounding, at different periods, 195-196
defined, 181
exact, 188-189
figuring, the time element in, 181-184
ordinary, 187-188
simple, 181
interest after date, 251
interest-bearing note, 251; discounting, 253-254
interest due at maturity, 251
interest to follow, 251
inventory:
merchandise, 259
perpetual, 259
physical, 259
inventory valuation and cost of goods sold, 259-264
inventory valuation, methods of:
first-in, first-out (FIFO), 260
last-in, first-out (LIFO), 260-261
specific identification, 260
weighted average cost, 261
inventory value, estimated, 261-263
invoices:
defined, 201
preparing and checking, 202-204
purchase orders and, 201-204